# STRANGER INTIMACY

# AMERICAN CROSSROADS

Edited by Earl Lewis, George Lipsitz, George Sánchez, Dana Takagi, Laura Briggs, and Nikhil Pal Singh

# STRANGER INTIMACY

CONTESTING RACE, SEXUALITY, AND THE LAW
IN THE NORTH AMERICAN WEST

Nayan Shah

UNIVERSITY OF CALIFORNIA PRESS

*Berkeley   Los Angeles   London*

University of California Press, one of the most distinguished
university presses in the United States, enriches lives around the
world by advancing scholarship in the humanities, social sciences,
and natural sciences. Its activities are supported by the UC Press
Foundation and by philanthropic contributions from individuals
and institutions. For more information, visit www.ucpress.edu.

University of California Press
Berkeley and Los Angeles, California

University of California Press, Ltd.
London, England

Library of Congress Cataloging-in-Publication Data

Shah, Nayan, 1966–
    Stranger intimacy : contesting race, sexuality, and the law in
the North American West / Nayan Shah.
        p.    cm. — (American crossroads ; 31)
    Includes bibliographical references and index.
    ISBN 978-0-520-27085-5 (cloth : alk. paper)
    ISBN 978-0-520-27087-9 (pbk. : alk. paper)
    1. Foreign workers—North America.    2. Migrant labor—
North America.    3. Sex and law—North America.
4. Citizenship—Social aspects—North America.    I. Title.
    HD6300.S53   2011
    304.8'7305409041—dc23

                                    2011030381

Manufactured in the United States of America

20   19   18   17   16   15   14   13
10   9   8   7   6   5   4   3

In keeping with a commitment to support environmentally
responsible and sustainable printing practices, UC Press
has printed this book on Rolland Enviro100, a 100% post-
consumer fiber paper that is FSC certified, deinked, processed
chlorine-free, and manufactured with renewable biogas energy.
It is acid-free and EcoLogo certified.

# CONTENTS

# ILLUSTRATIONS

## MAPS

# ACKNOWLEDGMENTS

A history worth sharing is often the most difficult to discover, fathom, and write. In the journey to write this book, I have tugged on obscure clues in many a courthouse and archive that have unraveled less visible threads that fan out in every direction. This book is very much of its own time, creating a bridge between the moment I live in and the era and places of the early twentieth century. It also emerged through the time in my life, as I drew on experience in my career as a historian and teacher and transformed my life and perspective when I moved to California. Over more than a decade, I have circulated throughout the coasts, mountains, farms, forests, deserts, cities, and suburban sprawl of western North America to discover the marvels and challenges of these places. In my time in Tucson, San Francisco, and most of all San Diego, I have made my way alongside intimates, friends, and neighbors and created a way of life that I cherish. In these many places where I lived for a time, dug into records, reflected, spoke, listened, and wrote many drafts, I wove together this book from many disparate threads.

The project began from the serendipity of a library shelf walk when Professor Bill Novak oriented me to the University of Chicago Law Library in 1994. A compendium of California jurisprudence published in 1928 yielded intriguing citations of Punjabi and Chinese defendants in appealed sodomy cases. When I returned to California in 1996, I began the first of many detective searches for court records in the California State Archive in Sacramento and in the courthouses in Marysville, Yuba City, and Stockton. Soon afterwards, the video documentarian Richard Fung and the art historian Bruce Russell led me to dozens of attorney general case files bearing the last names "Sing" and "Singh" in the British Columbia Archives in Victoria. I visited this archive, and many others across the continent and beyond over more than a decade to make sense of the shards of compelling evidence of the lives of migrants from British colonial India and their journeys through China, the Philippines, Panama, Cuba, Fiji, Mexico, Britain, and throughout Canada and the United States. It became clear to me that this book would follow South Asian migrants of the early twentieth century and illuminate their relationships with diverse peoples and their deeper and wider scales of association and contact.

Institutions have supported my work and I wish to acknowledge that material support. Research trips to visit archives, libraries, courthouses, and historical societies in British Columbia, Washington, Oregon, California, Arizona, New Mexico, Colorado, Utah, Texas, New York, Washington, DC, Maryland, Ontario, and Britain were supported by the Binghamton Foundation, the University of California San Diego Academic Senate, and the University of California San Diego Humanities Center. Fellowship support released me from full-time teaching duties and provided the time, opportunity, and convivial research environment to complete drafts of the book manuscript. I benefited tremendously from the generous support of the Rockefeller Foundation Humanities Fellowship project on Sex, Race and Globalization at the University of Arizona, the Freeman Foundation Distinguished Visiting Professorship in Asian American Studies at Wesleyan University, and the University of California Humanities Research Institute project on Gender and Sexual Dissidence, as well as sabbatical support by the University of California San Diego. My thanks to department chairs Eric Van Young, Danny Vickers, John Marino, and Pamela Radcliff, and Deans Georgios Anagnostopoulos, Michael Bernstein, and Seth Lerer for enabling me to modify my teaching schedule and take sabbatical leaves. I especially thank Seth Lerer for a timely grant from the Dean of Arts and Humanities Innovation Fund that helped defray reproduction and permissions costs of the photographs in the book.

My research would not have been possible without the assistance of intrepid archivists and librarians who worked tirelessly under the strain of diminished budgets and worsening conditions at municipal, provincial, state, federal, and colonial archives, at local historical societies, university archives, and county public library history rooms in the United States and Canada. I am most grateful to the countless clerks who work in county court houses retrieving records for those with immediate, urgent, and often dire court business. I appreciated every one of them who took time from pressing court business to help find, sort, and retrieve musty 1910s and 1920s register books and case records that had not been destroyed by fire, flooding, neglect, or periodic and cataclysmic record reduction programs. The assistance of the clerks and all of those who manage and store these records was invaluable to my research. The many superb librarians at the University of California, San Diego, and especially Elliot Kanter, have provided me with invaluable assistance in locating books, microfilm, and digital resources.

Early in my research, two pioneer scholars of early twentieth-century South Asian migration in North America, Karen Leonard and Joan Jensen, generously shared their research notes, printed and microfilm materials and their counsel. The legal scholar Leti Volpp and the historian Margot Canaday shared files from the U.S. National Archives from their own research forays. I have been assisted in processing archival materials and retrieving and organizing research by several dedicated undergraduate and graduate student assistants: Lauren Cole, Cutler Edwards, Samantha Huang, Miwon Kym, Ryan Reft, and Maki Smith.

My colleagues Pal Ahluwalia, Sunil Amrith, Lisa Armstrong, Anjali Arondekar, Vivek Renjen Bald, Alan Bérubé, Anne Blackburn, Tom Boellstorff, Laura Briggs, Susan Cahn, Margot Canaday, Hazel Carby, George Chauncey, Ernie Chavez, Patricia Chu, David Churchill, Nancy Cott, Susan Coutin, John D'Emilio, Michael Denning, Gina Dent, Sarah Deutsch, Ann DuCille, Mary Dudziak, Lisa Duggan, David Eng, Steven Epstein, Rod Ferguson, Estelle Freedman, Stuart Gaffney, Rosemary George, Farha Ghannam, Jonathan Goldberg, Gayatri Gopinath, Kevin Grant, Inderpal Grewal, David Guitérrez, Ramón A. Gutiérrez, Judith Halberstam, Catherine Hall, Janet Halley, Chad Heap, Lynne Huffer, Nan Hunter, Brent Gordon Ingram, Allan Isaac, Matthew Frye Jacobsen, Miranda Joseph, Moon Ho Jung, Priya Kamani, Indira Karamcheti, Jonathan Ned Katz, Kehaulani Kauanui, Elizabeth Kennedy, Aisha Khan, Regina Kunzel, Matt Lassiter, John Lewis, Erika Lee, Mary Liu, Eithne Luibhéid, Martin Manalansan, Bill Maurer, Dilip Menon, Leisa Meyer, Joanne Meyerowitz, Natalia Molina, Michael Moon, Scott Morgenson, Chantal Nadeau, Mary Odem, Peggy Pascoe, Mary Poovey, Claire Potter, Vijay Prashad, Jasbir Puar, Pamela Radcliff, Chandan Reddy, Ian Iqbal Rashid, Sandip Roy, Gayle Rubin, Bhaskar Sarkar, Sudipta Sen, David Serlin, Dara Silberstein, Jane Singh, Nikhil Pal Singh, Alexandra Minna Stern, Marita Sturken,

Ann Laura Stoler, Stefan Tanaka, Lisa Trivedi, Leti Volpp, Chris Waters, Meg Wesling, Robyn Wiegman, Ken Wissoker, Scott Wong, and Judy Wu offered spirited criticism, invaluable advice, and suggestions that helped me conceptualize and revise the book.

Faculty and students also gave generous feedback, asked perceptive questions, and made helpful suggestions when I presented portions of the project at Binghamton University, CUNY Graduate Center, Columbia University, Concordia University, Emory University, Hamilton College, Macalester College, New York University, Occidental College, Ohio State University, Smith College, Swarthmore College, Syracuse University, Trinity College, Wesleyan University, Williams College, the University of Arizona, the University of British Columbia, the University of California Berkeley, the University of California Davis, the University of California Irvine, UCLA, the University of California San Diego, the University of California Santa Barbara, the University of California Santa Cruz, the University of Illinois at Chicago, the University of Manitoba, the University of Maryland, the University of Michigan Ann Arbor, the University of Texas El Paso, the University of Washington Seattle, the University of Wisconsin Madison, the University of the Witwatersrand in Johannesburg, South Africa, and Yale University. I have also benefited from questions raised by the discussants, panelists, and audiences at presentations at the American Historical Association, the American Historical Association Pacific Branch, the American Studies Association, the Association of Asian American Studies, the Organization of American Historians, the South Asian Feminist Studies conferences at UC Santa Cruz and UC San Diego, the Western History Association, and the UCLA Queer Studies graduate conference.

In San Diego, I shared many chapter drafts with a convivial and invigorating writing group and benefited tremendously from their careful attention and suggestions. I thank Luis Alvarez, Jody Blanco, Yen Espiritu, Tak Fujitani, Fatima El Tayeb, Sara Johnson, Lisa Lowe, Curtis Marez, Stephanie Smallwood, Shelley Streeby, Danny Widener, and Lisa Yoneyama for their spirited commentary.

Niels Hooper has patiently stewarded this book at the University of California Press, and I am grateful for his enthusiasm and vision for the project. The incisive comments of the anonymous readers' reports and George Lipsitz's astute suggestions have been invaluable for strengthening and clarifying the book's arguments and evidence. I am honored to be in the American Crossroads series again. Many thanks to Eric Schmidt and Rose Vekony for coordinating production of the book and for the fine work of the staff at University of California Press. I particularly would like to thank the copyeditor Peter Dreyer for his attention to detail and editorial guidance and the cartographer Bill Nelson for the maps he created for the book.

Portions of Chapters 2, 3, and 5 appeared originally in different form as research articles under the titles "Between 'Oriental Depravity' and 'Natural Degenerates': Spatial Borderlands and the Making of Ordinary Americans," *American Quarterly* 57, no. 3 (September 2005): 703–25; "Policing Privacy, Migrants and the Limits of Freedom," *Social Text* 84–85, 23, nos. 3–4 (Fall–Winter 2005): 275–84; and "Contested Intimacies: Adjudicating 'Hindu Marriage' in U.S. Frontiers," in *Haunted By Empire: Geographies of Intimacy in North American History*, edited by Ann Laura Stoler (Durham, NC: Duke University Press, 2006), 116–39. I thank Duke University Press and the Johns Hopkins University Press, respectively, for permission to publish the work in revised form in this book.

The multiple generations of my blended family have both supported and indulged me in this endeavor. My parents inspired me with their own histories of migration, transience, and settlement in Maryland, and the remarkable stories of the many people who visited and stayed for a time at our home. My father introduced me, when I was a high school student, to the sociologist Haridas Mazumdar, who came to the United States in the 1920s and taught for decades at the University of Arkansas. I read his essay on early twentieth-century Indian immigration to the United States and the political struggles for citizenship and equality. That was the first time I understood that there was a hidden history of immigration prior to the more familiar one of the late 1950s to 1980s wave of South Asian students and extended families, of which I am a part.

Ken Foster has inspired me throughout the research, always at the ready to listen to my archival discoveries and quandaries, ask questions, offer imaginative ideas, take a pen to my writing, and even in a pinch to serve as a dedicated photocopier at archives. Many a long hike along the coast or in the mountains has turned into an energetic and creative conversation that has sent me back to my desk to write and revise. With Ken I have reconsidered every version and chapter of the book. His confidence and encouragement in my ability to handle difficult questions and intractable problems pulled me through. Ken's father Bud, an avid reader and storyteller, enjoyed our historical discussions and debates and always asked after the progress of the book. I am sad that he will not be able to read it, but I take comfort in knowing that I finished the book he wanted to read. This book exists because of Ken's love, advice, care, and unfailing certainty that this history had to be told and I needed to write it.

*San Diego, California*

# Introduction

During the first half of the twentieth century, the western regions of the United States and Canada offered an enticing vision of mobility and opportunity for those willing to migrate there. As the story is usually told, numerous families from settled communities both within and outside the United States and Canada took up that challenge and made the journey, essentially transplanting the settled society of two centuries of European colonization of the Americas from its eastern seaboard to its western expanses.

Yet if we look carefully into the historical record, we find that transient migrants of varied races and classes circulated, worked, and mingled across the North American West in the first third of the twentieth century. In 1924, on reclaimed marshland in the Sacramento River delta, a twenty-three-year-old Native American worker shared a bunkhouse with half a dozen South Asian and Afghani men on a Chinese-owned ranch. In 1916, a justice of the peace in Yuma, Arizona, married a young African American woman from Mississippi and a man from India. In 1912, in Gate, Washington, young white workers from Duluth, Minnesota, drank and brawled with their fellow millworkers on a Sunday afternoon near the railway depot. In a Japanese woman's green market in Vancouver, a South Asian man bought a pound of cherries for young white male newspaper vendors. A mother and her teenage children fleeing the Mexican Revolution cooked meals for the Mexican, South Asian, and black men who worked on a ranch in San Elizario, Texas.

*Stranger Intimacy* reassesses the contradictory demands, meanings, and opportunities of transience and settlement that fueled capitalist expansion, aggravated rule-of-law governance and goaded the fortunes of diverse and democratic societies. White urban and agrarian elites and settlers, in seeking to monopolize the advantages of mobility for themselves in the early twentieth century, cast transient male migrants as marginal and replaceable labor, disruptive to the social order and irritants to the political future of democratic nations. In British Columbia, California, and Washington, the political yearning for a republic of settled families over transient male laborers contradicted the patterns of interstate and international migration that accounted for 80 percent of population growth decade after decade during the first third of the twentieth century. This political vision obscured the economic reliance of the lucrative industries of timber processing, infrastructure and building construction, orchard cultivation, and cotton, rice, and wheat farming on low-wage, short-term migrant laborers.

The political tensions between the demand for transient workers and aspirations to settled family society in both Canada and the United States, however, justified local and federal laws to deny any political voice or social status to transient workers. From police campaigns to incarcerate vagrants to implementing racial restrictions on immigration, voting, and property ownership, governing bodies isolated transients from civic association and democratic promises of equality. Continuing this pattern of marginalization, in the second half of the twentieth century, policy makers and scholars have erased the history of transient migrants to promote national assimilation narratives that emphasize nuclear family settlement.

This book uncovers international migrants' practices of social navigation, community building, and participation in interethnic social worlds that undermine the containment efforts of nation-states and empires. As a way to understand the larger picture, it particularly follows the experiences of South Asian migrants in collaboration with domestic and international migrants and their struggles over social and intimate relations in the first decades of the twentieth century in the United States and Canada. Nearly 30,000 male migrants from British colonial India were among the hundreds of thousands of migrants from around the world who converged on small towns and new cities in western North America for seasonal work in agriculture and timber processing. Within North America, international migrants generated adaptive frameworks of gender and domesticity, creating forms of community that continually renegotiated social and legal boundaries that seemed designed to frustrate the liberty of mobility and association. County and municipal court records document the specificity of some of the ordinary episodes of stranger intimacy experienced by such migrants, chronicling often contentious everyday interethnic encounters that ended up in courtrooms before magistrates and judges.

The complexity of gender and sexual diversity in intensive migration societies is also visible in the local legal records of sexual crimes, domestic disputes, and social disorder. The records of contestation in the courts demonstrate, not only prosecutors' efforts to regulate migrants' behavior, but also migrants' refusal to be absented from public recognition, and offer alternative conceptions of intimate ties, legitimate domestic lives, and public status in both conflicts and collaborations. Their struggles over companionship, domesticity, and public life illuminated the ways in which they participated in political battles over tenancy and labor contracts, property transactions, immigration regulations, naturalized citizenship, and the organization of capital and community.

Within this context, it is worth noting that the historical scholarship on interracial marriage and same sex relations has rarely intersected. This book uniquely pairs the histories of several hundred interracial marriages of South Asian men and Mexican American or white women in the early twentieth century with original discovery research that documents more than a hundred cases of illicit sexual contact between South Asian, white, European immigrant, Chinese, and Native American males. The resulting combination illuminates how the state and elites distributed protection and resources in ways that exacerbated the vulnerability of transience for most migrants and enhanced promises of settlement for a select few.

At the turn of the twentieth century, the United States and Canada responded to this immense plurality of human mobility and the demands of industrial capitalism by developing a system of democratic government in which large swaths of their residents were proscribed from full participation. Both nation-states experimented with developing a "white" political democracy and forging racial apartheid by subordinating, segregating, and exploiting nonwhite "races." During the first half of the twentieth century, Canadian and U.S. politicians, officials, police, and judges curtailed and denied access to property and tenancy markets, naturalized citizenship, and marriage based on race. Local court disputes poignantly illuminate struggles for association and strikingly lay bare how deeply and personally the containment of democratic ideals impacted the social, economic, and political experiences of migrants. By the late twentieth century, North American policymakers were attributing the success of Canadian and U.S. pluralistic, democratic societies to a societal paradigm that sustained the rule of law, property rights, free expression, immigrant assimilation, diverse association, and family stability. White political and economic elites hailed the triumphant achievement of pluralism and liberalism and vigorously erased the history of exclusion and dispossession.

The South Asian transnational migrants who form the pivot of this book both followed and departed from the overwhelming waves of more than thirty million migrants who left colonial India from 1834 to 1930. More than 90 percent of South Asian migrants ventured across the Bay of Bengal to work in plantations in British imperial possessions, including four million to Malaya and the Straights Settlements, eight million to Sri Lanka, and fifteen million to Burma. Most of these migrants were Tamil, Bengali, and Bihari male laborers and families whose passage and recruitment were "assisted" by debts and obligations to regional merchants coordinating placement with British plantation owners. Another two million were recruited on indenture contracts to work on plantations in British and French possessions in the Caribbean and the Pacific and Indian Oceans.

Punjabi migrants composed a part of the approximately two million merchants, travelers, and soldiers who journeyed throughout Southeast Asia and across the Indian Ocean, following opportunities and networks in Hong Kong, Macao, Shanghai, Singapore, and Manila. A much smaller number, approximately 80,000 of these ambitious Punjabi, Sindhi, Gujarati, and Afghani merchants, former soldiers, and laborers filtered beyond coastal Southeast Asia to migrate in search of opportunities in Canada, Australia, Hawaii, the United States, Mexico, Panama, and Argentina. It was the migration of these "free" emigrants that ignited immigration controversies in Canada and the United States.[1]

South Asian migration and circulation in North America in the early twentieth century vividly illustrates the chasm between national citizenship and representative democracy and everyday struggles for dignity and the insistence on associating widely in society. This book's trajectory from the local encounter to national citizenship reevaluates the social, legal and political process that drove the state's presumption that social stability could be achieved through an invented normative family in the face of mass migration and its non-normative sexual relations and domestic life. Both the United States and Canada restricted the parameters of national membership to heteronormative standards of intimate social relations, rendering illegible and illegitimate the multiple forms of sociality and domesticity that had prevailed in western states and provinces before World War II.

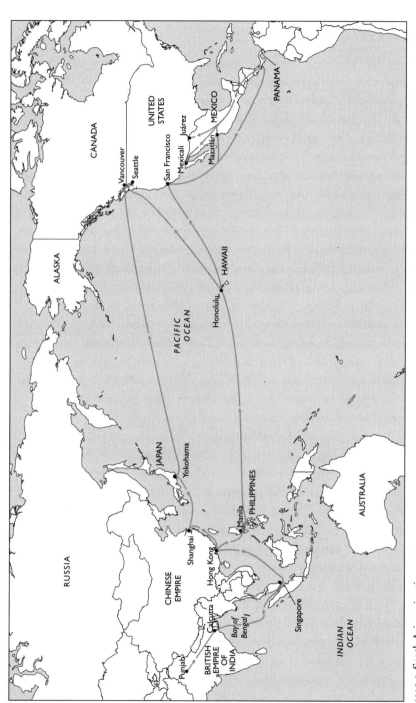

MAP 1. South Asian migration routes

## UNSETTLING HISTORY

This book challenges three conceptual stabilizations that haunt historians and constrict their ability to write about movement and change. These three stabilizations are (1) permanence over transience, (2) the nuclear family household, and (3) polarized sexuality. The first challenge is to tackle the overwhelming advantage of writing of permanence as opposed to transience. The availability and potency of state documentation of settlement and property relations undermine our ability to conceptualize mobility and transience as central concepts in historical analysis. Analyzing the web of unconventional association and ties alongside more conventional expectations throws into bold relief the focus of immigration history on signs of permanence and settling that are recorded and recognized by the state. Buying property, negotiating a lease or contract, marrying, recording childbirth and school attendance, undertaking business, applying for citizenship, and participating in political processes are all interpreted as acts of immigrant belonging. Settlement, putting down roots, claiming both present ties and a future stake in a new place are crucial to both the individual and collective histories of immigration and national history. Yet migrant history must also take the measure of elastic and shifting movement, impermanence, and the discontinuous array of work, affiliations, places, friends, and strangers. Transience and discontinuous ties to place make tracking migrancy in conventional linear time a distortion of migrants' actual experiences.

Focus on permanent settlement begets a reliance on the second conceptual stabilization—the persistence of the ahistorical assumption that the nuclear family is the necessary model for social vitality and political participation. The myth of the nuclear family serves as a conceptual crutch that renders any other form of kinship and household structures pathological, aberrant, and incompatible with cultural support and political privilege. It obscures the varied forms of household social organization, labor and financial strategies for maintaining multiple households, and the intricate affective and social lives of its members. It occludes all the necessary transits and circulation of people between households, workplaces, and leisure spaces. The fiction of the contained household draws attention away from the many permeable forms and structures of cohabitation that exceed even our understanding of multigenerational, extended, transnational households.

International migrants have shaped and struggled for the meanings and practices of liberty and belonging through a range of both local and transnational affiliations and alliances. Historians, sociologists, and anthropologists have interrogated the material life, social dynamics, and political discourses of Asian American bachelor society. These studies have revealed rich layers and webs of intimate ties that are expressed in transnational kin networks, interracial marriages, and various temporary intimate encounters, ranging from prostitution and taxi-dance romances to courtship and same-sex relations.[2]

Conventional accounts of stable, insular, and self-sufficient households are also unable to make sense of the social and intimate experiences of those who migrate and their continuing connection to those who remain behind. Migration creates unanticipated breaks and detours in spatial and temporal cycles and schedules, producing new ways of life. Life schedules are stretched and reimagined via new strategies of circular global migration that timed return visits to village homes strategically and concentrated child-rearing responsibilities on parents, wives, and siblings in joint-family households. Migration disorganized domestic and social life in places of both origin and transmigration. In the case of South Asian migrants who journeyed by rail and by boat from villages in Punjab and Bengal to the port of Calcutta and then on to Hong Kong, Singapore, and Shanghai, migrant men lived in all-male domestic settings in military barracks, dormitories, boardinghouses, and bunkhouses.[3] Kinship networks in the places of origin realigned to accommodate the migration of men and boys from extended families and villages and adjusted uneasily to the increasing dominance of women-centered communities in the towns and villages of origin and remigration.[4]

The third conceptual stabilization is the presumption that human erotic desires and activities can be neatly distinguished as either heterosexual or homosexual. Scholarship in the history of sexuality, gender studies, and queer studies denaturalizes bodies, gender, and erotic interest, unhinging the formula that binary gender roles exhaust the direction of erotic interest, categorizing human erotic desires as either heterosexual or homosexual. For four decades, scholarship that historicizes sexuality has been skeptical of universal essence or single patterns or fixed models of sexuality in human society. Scholars historicized the development of perspectives in contemporary European and North American society that predicate sexuality as the source of the individual self and as the main mechanism that converts the personal and subjective into either systematic identity or group pathology.[5] In contrast, this book examines how societies and communities organize erotic life and meanings and the swift and slow ways in which changes transpire. It pays careful attention to the contested politics of sexual ethics, gender status, and erotic interest in subcultures and dominant cultures alike. Whereas various twentieth-century theories of sexuality have treated individuals as either normal or pathological, historical study should be concerned with how the idiosyncratic, messy, and contradictory undermine and complicate the ways in which sexuality has been deployed as the key organizing principle of social life. Understanding sexuality as an analytic rather than as a fact draws attention to considerable variance of erotics, relations, and meanings in society, as well underlining the dynamics of power involved in stabilizing and constraining human variation. Queer theory questions the fixed distinction and polarization of gender as the basis of heterosexuality and diagnoses the expenditure of cultural and political labor to stabilize sex (male/female) into binary gender oppositions (masculine/feminine) that set the direction of sexual desire into valuing heterosexuality as normal and natural.[6]

My approach is to examine the meanings, practices, and organizing principles that emerge in the wake of sexual contestation and transgression. By assessing the dynamics linking power and social status in legal conflicts, I analyze the regulation of sex and gender, as well as the fluid meanings and practices of gender expression, erotic interest, and social relationships that emerge in multiple social, cultural, and temporal contexts. This approach interprets a wide range of associations and transient relationships, rather than simply tracking the development of sexual identities or sexual communities. And by challenging the assumption that people are endowed with singular and fixed sexual essences, I am able to analyze the impact of practices, expressions, and interests that are not static and fixed at any life stage but mobile over the life course and social space.

Unraveling the anachronistic stabilizations of settlement, nuclear family, and sexuality reveals how powerfully these assumptions have prioritized the settled heterosexual household as the privileged model of social organization and political participation. The liberty of broad and capacious associations among the poor, migrants, and foreigners came up against countervailing forces and visions of democratic society, forces and visions that organized individual political status almost exclusively through the participation of white adult men in self-sufficient, economically and emotionally contained family households. In liberal political philosophy, men gathered the capabilities of self-possessive individualism through their emotional, intimate, and ethical training in households. The public attributes of intimacy include the capacity to be the author of one's own life direction; to possess the ethics to manage a coupled relationship and domestic dependents; to engage with the demands of contract and the ownership of property; and to be a sovereign political subject able to negotiate freely with others in the political debate that sustains democracy. Enlightenment ideals emphasize how adult men in family households learned the ethics and practices that would enable them to participate in democratic debate, to claim the entitlements and resources of national citizenship, and to command privacy from state intrusion. However, women, servants, the poor, and racial minorities were judged by empowered men to be bereft of the capacity to exercise rationality and independence in their intimate ties. This assessment produced rampant justifications for inequality and the subordination of those deemed incapable of self-rule.[7]

## LEGAL ARCHIVES AND STRANGER INTIMACY

This book critically examines law as an archival repository, a form of knowledge and reasoning, and strategy of governance. Legal sources play a pivotal role in documenting sexual relations, transgression, and contestation. In the first part of the book, culled from policing and criminal prosecution of migrant men, legal sources illuminate the broader social strategies, economic relations, and political tensions that emerge in global migration and capitalism. As an archival source, legal cases provide a rich and untapped resource, which I analyze for competing understandings of honor, ethics, gender roles, friendship, and kinship within the rich web of social and economic dependencies necessary for survival.

The legal record is a challenging source with which to interpret the experiences of marginalized and aggrieved communities because of how the documentation scripts and judges the relevance of evidence, shapes procedural argument, and influences the outcome of justice. However, the collation of testimony, legal arguments, and court decisions also reveals contradictory and suppressed perspectives and narratives of everyday life. In rule-of-law governance, the legal judgments and prohibitions often subtly uncover the material conditions of encounters and networks that suture divergent social worlds. The traces and shards of dissident sociality and sexual practices that emerge from courthouse records reflect the web of local social and economic relations.

The interpretation of legal records underlies the book's first section, "Migration, Capitalism, and Stranger Intimacy," which focuses on expressive cultures and experimentation with sexuality and gender in the context of capitalism and mass migration. Chapter 1, "Passion, Violence, and Asserting Honor," explores the networks of global migrant circulation and the rise of commercial entertainment that created the settings for the swirl of intimate and violent cross-racial encounters in British Columbia, Washington, Oregon, and California in the first fifteen years of the twentieth century. The chapter examines how cultural understanding of male authority, honor, and social dependency came to be racialized and gendered to absolve and normalize violent white mobs and to denigrate and isolate interracial romance and stranger intimacy. Chapter 2, "Policing Strangers and Borderlands," analyzes legal records of vagrancy, public indecency, and sodomy to illustrate how insistently migrant laborers crafted alternative publics and communicated codes of male honor, privileges, and hierarchy as they strategically remapped spaces and sensibilities labeled as deviant. Chapter 3, "Rural Dependency and Intimate Tensions," examines the pivotal role of intimate ties and dependency for South Asian participation in tenant farming and labor contracting.

Together these three chapters systematically contrast different ways that social regulation and policing shaped the mobility of transient women and men, how migrant social experiences differed in urban centers and rural agriculture camps, and the varying strategies and options available to migrant laborers, labor contractors, tenant farmers, and landowners in creating, sustaining, and defending intimate dependencies. By mapping the social and sexual practices among working men, we can better understand the uneven process by which middle-class marriage and courtship and its norms of public intimacy emerged and ultimately dominated sites of industrial agriculture and settlement in western Canada and the United States in the early twentieth century. The regulation of interracial intimacy within the political economy also illuminates the legislative and political process that led to the passage of the Alien Land Laws in the 1910s and 1920s across the U.S. West. Property ownership and leasing prohibitions were part of a broader effort to regulate intimate lives, expelling South Asian men and other Asians from personal associations and legal recognitions, thereby limiting their participation and their potential for prosperity in western agricultural development. The combination of miscegenation laws and Alien Land Laws produced state-sponsored family forms and circumscribed participation in the economy.

The range of associations that emerge in the legal records also reveal the broad socioeconomic diversity of South Asian migrants, from short-term laborers to students, labor contractors to farm tenants, businessmen, and farm owners. The strategic ability to organize capital and navigate legal systems distributed benefits of opportunity and access, as well as shaped the potential to move from transient to settler. Male migrants brought different sets of resources, capabilities, and opportunities to mobilize legal advice and credit. Some South Asian migrants' skills in spoken English, English-language literacy, and familiarity with British bureaucratic systems aided them in seeking guidance from lawyers and county clerks.

Archival records in county courthouses, state and provincial archives, and federal archival repositories chart the successful operation of the rule of law and bureaucratic registration of economic activities and social commitments. City, county, parish, state, and provincial archives recorded property relations, labor contracts, marriage contracts, and civil and criminal proceedings. While the process of registration and documentation in the county courthouse recognizes independent individuals, it also certifies their interdependent relationships through state-sanctioned kinship, labor agreements, and property arrangements. This documentation demonstrates both state regulation of the capitalist political economy and its operation at microsocial levels to recognize and protect social alliances and relations through the force of the state.

The second section of the book, "Intimacy, Law, and Legitimacy," examines the legal reasoning that shaped criminal jurisprudence and concretized civil registration's role in ratifying legitimate intimacy as the cornerstone of the social and political order. Legal reasoning in this era grappled with competing and swiftly evolving social conventions, while attempting to stabilize the regulation of sexual practices and social ties in order to mold gender, sexual, and national norms. This section pairs chapter 4, "Legal Borderlands of Age and Gender," on transformations of sodomy jurisprudence, with chapter 5, "Intimate Ties and State Legitimacy," on marriage regulation. Together, these chapters examine the borders and boundaries imposed by laws and regulations on erotic, affective, and social relationships. The assertion of the state's monopoly in regulating legitimate intimate relationships developed in administrative licensing, registration, and judicial civil and criminal prosecution that corralled human relationships into race, ethnic, age, moral, and sexuality categories.

Both chapters scrutinize legal reasoning and interpretations of consent and "natural" sex and kinship ties. They demonstrate how the production of normative genders, sexualities, and national identities transposes erotic and social variations into a kaleidoscope of deviant intimacies from sodomy to polygamy. In the first three decades of the twentieth century, there was considerable judicial innovation in adjudicating marriage, divorce, cohabitation, rape, sodomy, and indecency. With diverse, large-scale international and domestic migration, interracial contact proliferated, shaping legal interpretations of sodomy, vagrancy, and age of consent. The concept of "legal borderlands" highlights the unsettled assessment of criminality, consent, and human nature that was occurring at the same time as legislatures and jurisprudence attempted to standardize human subjectivity and define "proper" intimacy. Among its many consequences, legal regulation prevented and prohibited male adolescent relations with foreigners and vagrants. These proscriptions both ultimately contributed to the wholesale criminalization of sodomy and homosexuality, regardless of consent, and simultaneously helped create and institutionalize normal American masculinity. Conversely, the legal concept of consent reordered gender and nationality in the state administration of the legitimacy of heterosexual marriage. These chapters establish how the identification and vilification of "deviant intimacies," "degenerates," and "perverts" produced normal sexual, gender, and national identities, and in the process standardized human subjectivity and generated a socially sanctioned definition of proper relationships.

The final section of the book, "Membership and Nation-States," examines the nation-state promotion of intimate personhood, conjugal marriage, and domestic dependency to organize exclusion from and inclusion into national entry and national membership. After addressing local encounters and legal regulation, the third section of the book shifts the terrain of analysis to membership in the liberal states of Canada and the United States. In the first decade of the twentieth century, Canada, as a dominion of the British Empire, and the United States, with an empire in the Pacific and the Caribbean, exerted authority and harnessed new administrative procedures to regulate human mobility. By retracing migrant journeys through British spheres of control in India, Hong Kong, Shanghai, and Singapore, and American spheres of control in the Philippines, Panama, and Hawaii, the book here focuses on the impact of the historical process of nationalizing and regulating migrant mobility that emerged as states deployed surveillance systems and developed bureaucratic policies. Also in this period, U.S. and Canadian national border control agencies distinguished Asian from European migrants in the development of distinctive regulations and exclusions. Chapter 6, "Regulating Intimacy and Immigration," compares the shifting routes of South Asian migration to illustrate the tensions between border-control technologies that nationalize, regulate, and constrain migration and informal systems of kinship and commerce that facilitate migration flows across oceans, frontiers, and empires. Alongside the nationalization of migration, the chapter examines how technologies such as passports, marriage certificates, and interviews furnished immigration inspectors with detailed information about kinship and resources. This broad information was then narrowly filtered into circumscribed nuclear family frameworks to regulate mobility and entry at the border.

Chapter 7, "Strangers to Citizenship," investigates how bureaucratic immigration and naturalization policies scrutinized intimate dependency, morality, and class in Canada and United States, creating knowledge that marked South Asian migrants as racially and morally suspect and deviant. In the 1910s and 1920s, immigration policies in both countries paid close attention to documentary proof of marriage and kinship, filtering legitimate human passage through national borders by sorting racial labels, gender roles, and moral and sexual judgments. In the 1930s and 1940s, the United States reluctantly recognized interracial marriages and interracial families within its boundaries and granted allowances to noncitizens with American-born children. These exceptions to administrative regulations enlarged and reinforced the individualizing of human subjects with different histories to fit conventional definitions of morality, respectability, and responsibility. A liberal humanitarianism began to ease the strict racial boundaries of immigration and citizenship in favor of promoting heterosexual families and laying the groundwork for family reunification policies irrespective of race in the post–World War II era.

## RACIALIZATION AND THE ELUSIVE CONTAINMENT OF MOBILITY

Racialization has always shaped understandings of social normalcy or pathology as it relates to sexuality, gender, and household formation. In Canada and the United States, racialization and presumptions of social organization tempered and shaped expectations of belonging and the distribution of the privileges of U.S. and Canadian national and imperial British citizenship. Scholars of Asian migration, for example, have struggled to unravel the powerful nineteenth- to mid-twentieth-century depiction of the migration history of transient male migration to North America as a pernicious threat to democratic politics, economic distributions, and social morality.[8]

The United States and Canada have had a persistent and continuous presence of racialized and non–normatively sexualized noncitizens, who are socially and economically entangled with national citizens in urban and rural locations across the continent. In the early twentieth century, law and administrative bureaucracy and the human sciences organized human variety through prolific taxonomies of race, ethnicity, nationality, and religious difference that implied different human capacities, talents, and moralities. These differences combined with assumptions of deviant and pathological sexualities and gender and were deployed to assign legitimate avenues of participation in civic life, as well as to justify exclusion.[9]

There is a proliferation of terms to designate racial and ethnic differences that circulated in culture, politics, and law alongside migration flows. From the mid nineteenth to the mid twentieth century, migrants from Asia to North America were racialized as to their places of geographical origin: as Orientals, Asiatics, and Mongolians, as well as a repertoire of ethnic/national/religious categories such as Chinese/Chinaman, Japanese, Korean, Filipino, Hindu, Mohammedan, Turk, and Afghan. Migrants from British colonial India faced a variety of classification strategies, from geographic, ethnic, and religious faith to the racial and imperial. In terms of broadly geographic terms with an underlying racial designation: East Indian or Asiatic; in terms of religion: Sikh, Hindu, Mohammedan, and even Buddhist were used. Migrants from British colonial India were categorized in Canada and the United States by the racial and ethnic term "Hindu," apparently short for their place of origin—Hindustan—as well as referencing an axiomatic racial category codified in the 1911 *Dictionary of Races* created and used by the U.S. Immigration Service.[10] In the taxonomy of "races" living in the United States in the early twentieth century, the category of "Hindu" was multivalent. It was both derisive slang and the descriptive racial identity of these predominately Punjabi migrants—whether Sikh, Muslim, or Hindu by religion. More often than not for Muslims, the category of Turk capaciously referred both to residents of the Ottoman Empire and to Muslims across Asia. Afghan simultaneously referred to region and the rule of the Afghani monarchy. Occasionally, the specificity of region, linguistic heritage, or diasporic community was referenced by terms such as Punjabi, Bengali, Afghan, Arabian, or Parsee. This variety of ethnic and religious classifications in the early twentieth century raises the question of whether the use of "South Asian," a geopolitical term developed in Cold War social science and area studies, simultaneously masks differences and presumes a collectivity that may not exist on the ground. In census and official immigration records, race varied from color-based designations of white, black, "tawny," and brown to designations that racialized imperial geography and national origin/ allegiance, such as Turk and Hindu.[11]

In both the United States and Canada, the complex maneuvers of racializing persons from British colonial India necessitated relational borrowing and boundary creation to fix these people between "Asiatic" and white in national and transnational projects of determining belonging and placement in the status hierarchy. The relational racialization insistently recruited the examples of "Oriental" or "Asiatic" (Chinese and Japanese) races and contrasted them with white/Caucasian and black/African in order to determine how racial boundaries included, straddled or excluded "Hindus." Other groups, such as Portuguese, Filipinos, and Mexicans, because of skin complexion, histories of ethnic plurality, and social and economic aspersions, were handled as "in-between races" in North America.[12] Specific racial schemas of political belonging determined how Canadians attempted to draw a racial boundary onto universal British imperial subject status, and how Americans deployed Asiatic exclusion from immigration and naturalized citizenship to designate the new arrivals from India.

In order to make racial boundaries hold, however, the race makers had to believe in racial essence and presume racial purity. They fixed the vector of racial mixture and contained racial identity even when confronted by social ties that mixed and blurred racial boundaries. Yet reexamination of cross-racial marriages and alliances reveals ways of expressing ethnic plurality rather than fixing ethnic polarity and subordinating one heritage to another.

In a similar fashion, the explanation that structural forces of migration and displacement lead to alternative domesticities and homosocial domesticity need not follow only one direction of causality. The momentum of migratory moves across oceans and through an archipelago of locales could just as well be motivated by a desire to escape from conventional domestic structures and seek alternative life routines, schedules, and environments. Male migrants' social lives could sustain an appetite for passionate engagement, sociality, and feeling otherwise from conventional expectations. Fleeting encounters need not always prompt an interest in recreating kinship and in fashioning familiar domestic life, but could result in seeking alternative socialities, experimental intimacy, cooperative economies, and coalitional politics. Buffeted by the urgency of material survival, experimental intimacy attempts to stave off isolation, alienation, and poverty. For many male migrants, both living within the couple form and in male-ensemble communities exceeded conventional security in kinship lineage and traditional domesticity. The compulsory sociality of work, leisure, and public space provided new opportunities and environments and required new survival strategies to fend off alienation and isolation.[13]

State policies of containment could not suppress how insistently diverse people shaped their own visions of liberty and sustained ties of companionship, partnership, association and intimacy. The liberty of association generated a range of social strategies and practices, feelings, and beliefs that shaped the ligaments of association either in advance of or in the wake of formal politics. This variety of everyday encounters, some fleeting and some lasting months or years, illustrates the forms of intimacy between strangers. By addressing an expansive range of erotic and affective ties in democratic life, this book offers a fresh understanding of how people associate in ways that both unsettle and shore up social norms.

In the charting of policing and daily acts of resistance, the book illuminates the social spaces, possibilities, and tensions that foster democratic association and produce radical alternatives to nation-state and class-privileged citizenship. In the first half of the twentieth century, international and domestic migrants developed both informal associations and formal alliances with anticolonial, radical labor and anarchist groups, new religious organizations, and civil liberties and noncitizen advocacy organizations. The contests between transient associations, radical organizations, and liberal nation-states deepens the historical understanding of how states diverted and suppressed radical impulses in the first decades of the twentieth century in favor of the project of nationalizing migrants and citizens and its containment of ties to national allegiance, monogamous marriage, and family life. By the mid twentieth century, the U.S. and Canadian nation-states required that immigrants live in ways that could be contained and tethered to legitimate forms of sociality, domesticity, livelihood, and political allegiance. The book underscores the inherent instability of fixed boundaries and the democratic possibilities of heterogeneous bodies and practices in social and spatial borderlands, even as criminal law, civil registration, and nation-based identities stratified intimate mobility.

# PART ONE

# Migration, Capitalism, and Stranger Intimacy

## CHAPTER I

# Passion, Violence, and Asserting Honor

South Asian migration to North America has been part of a broader international movement of peoples since the 1790s. Sailors, servants, peddlers, and merchants from Madras, Bombay, and Bengal appear periodically and fleetingly in memoirs, customs registers, census records, and newspaper accounts from ports on every North American coast from Salem, Massachusetts, to New Orleans, and from Victoria, British Columbia, to Mazatlán, Mexico. In the 1890s, charismatic Hindu and Buddhist spiritual teachers and anti-imperial crusaders arrived to speak at gatherings in Boston, New York, and Chicago, the most famous being Swami Vivekananda, who addressed the 1893 World Parliament of Religions in Chicago. On the cusp of a new century, turbaned Sikh royal artillerymen traveled across Canada by train from Montreal to Vancouver after participating in Queen Victoria's Diamond Jubilee in London in 1897. They encouraged other Punjabi soldiers in Hong Kong, Shanghai, and Singapore to seek labor and business opportunities in North America. In 1899, four Sikhs disembarked at San Francisco's Pacific Mail Docks, catching the attention of onlookers and a reporter, who appraised them as the "most picturesque group" of "fine-looking men." Bakkshlled (*sic*) Singh, who spoke English fluently, was singled out as "a marvel of physical beauty. He stands 6 foot 2 and is built in proportion." The four men planned to seek their fortunes in California before returning to their homes in Lahore.[1]

Such worldly, cosmopolitan, adaptable South Asian travelers thrived in settings across the globe. They were seen as dashing, resourceful, and hardworking. The military self-discipline and masculine prowess of Punjabi men was widely praised. Their demeanor, dress, beliefs, and habits were depicted as exotic and curious, but rarely as threatening.

These appealing romantic perceptions of cosmopolitan men shifted rapidly in the first decade of the twentieth century, when more than 9,000 South Asian migrants arrived in Vancouver and Victoria, British Columbia. Many crossed over the border to Washington and Oregon and later migrated directly to Seattle and San Francisco. Orchards and farms, railroad and road construction, and timber mills and salmon canneries employed South Asian male laborers for weeks, months, and even years at a time. Beginning in 1904, first several hundred and later a thousand or more South Asian men arrived annually on the docks in Vancouver, Seattle, and San Francisco. The newcomers faced concerns and fears similar to those generated in previous decades by the steady arrival of Chinese and Japanese laborers. In nineteenth- and early twentieth-century Canada and the United States, political debate and cultural narratives characterized migration from Asia as an "invasion," "subversion," and unwelcome "amalgamation" that threatened the establishment of European "civilization" in the Western territories and states. White Americans and Canadians feared labor competition, interracial marriage and sexual seduction, and disease and immorality believed to be introduced by Asian male workers.[2] Fears of Chinese men kidnapping white women and addicting them to opium and of Japanese and Filipino men courting and seducing naïve European immigrant and other white women had simmered in political debates, fiction, and newspaper reports in the late nineteenth and early twentieth centuries. The discursive frenzy around the need to protect white women and girls from various ethnic Asian men prompted miscegenation legislation throughout the West.[3] From 1907 to 1913, the inclusion of the formerly exoticized and attractive South Asian men in this frenzy became evident as mobs drove South Asian workers out of numerous towns and cities in the Pacific Northwest and Northern California. Alongside accusations of unfair labor competition with white workers, politicians and newspapers circulated stories about women and children who had been indecently harassed. The claim of defending honor dovetailed with broader assertions that the presence of South Asian men demoralized white working families.

Two encounters of interracial association graphically illustrate the tension between attraction and fear that percolated in rumors that were used to justify driving-out campaigns and riots in Pacific Northwest and Northern California towns. Darrah Singh was shot dead on the stairway of the Spokane Rooming

FIGURE 1. Two men smoking a hookah, Clatsop County, Oregon, ca. 1910s. Courtesy Clatsop County Historical Society. Neg 5887.

House in Vancouver on October 22, 1907. Police arrested his drinking partner, English-immigrant Edward Bowen, running down Cordova Street minutes after shots rang out. Six years later, on October 4, 1913, on the shoreline south of Richmond, California, dockworkers found Rosa Domingo's battered nude body anchored by weights at the end of a long wharf. Her Portuguese immigrant family accused Said Ali Khan, who lived nearby and had courted Rosa, of her murder. His disappearance set off a statewide manhunt.

Based on newspaper accounts, the murders of Darrah Singh and Rosa Domingo were interpreted as crimes of passion. They book-ended a volatile seven-year period of driving-out campaigns and rising political agitation for immigration restriction and the removal of South Asians in western North America. These specific and sensational cases served as morality tales distributed to white audiences of the perils of stranger intimacy and interracial contact that incited passion and deadly violence. Both the possibility and the fear of interracial associations became freighted with dangerous and harmful consequences, also articulated in labor polemics, political oratory, and legal appeals. The presence of South Asian migrant men and their contact with white Americans and European immigrants elicited fascination, attraction, interest, and anxiety. Indexing both personal harm and social danger, the murders seemed to presage the potential disintegration of society.

Mob violence targeted South Asian workers. The breakdown in law and social order unleashed monstrous behavior. White men destroyed bunkhouses, stole possessions, beat South Asian men, and drove them out of town. The mob's extremes of cruelty and humiliation could not readily be rationalized and required allegations of depravity that blamed victims and absolved the rioters. Mob violence was not judged on the basis of individual crimes even when there were arrests for disorderly conduct. These arrests were rarely prosecuted, and the prosecutorial and policing system, so disturbed by the breakdown of law and order, readily forgave and forgot the violent transgressions. Vigilantes slipped into a convenient anonymity, and the victims of violent attacks were forced to flee, confronted with an indifferent state. Finally, they were forgotten.

The political forces seeking to establish a political narrative that vigilante mob violence was infrequent, aberrant, and justified were formidable. By forgetting the wider conditions for violence, any economic and political critique that might implicate powerful economic interests narrowed considerably. Instead, a racialized and sexualized threat was identified. The restoration of the social order stoked a belief that passions could be curbed, and that the perpetrators of mob violence must be absolved and allowed to return to their everyday lives. Public fear, horror, and incomprehension were redirected at the alleged actions that incited violence and thereby justified the vengeance claims and the guiding system of gendered honor and racial subordination.[4]

## FEAR OF SOUTH ASIAN STRANGERS IN CANADA

Although the number of South Asian men migrating first to Canada and then to the United States was small, they attracted extraordinary interest and concern. The immigration of South Asian men to British Columbia averaged only a few dozen annually in the first years of the twentieth century and then grew to 2,124 in 1907 and 2,623 in 1908. The numbers are negligible compared both to average immigration annual numbers and the overall population of British Columbia. The Province's population doubled in the first decade of the twentieth century, from 178,657 in the 1901 census to 392,480 in 1911. Vancouver's population grew from 27,000 to over 100,000 in a decade.

Chinese and Japanese immigrants' numbers increased much more slowly, however, than those of Canadian settlers and American, British, Scandinavian, and Italian immigrants. Chinese immigrants numbered 14,885 in 1901 and increased by 40 percent to 19,568 in 1911. The number of Japanese immigrants nearly doubled, from 4,597 to 8,587, in the same period. In 1901, East Asians accounted for 10.9 percent of the overall population of British Columbia, but the proportion declined to around 7 percent in subsequent decades. The South Asian population was a much smaller share. The 1911 Canadian Census reported a population of 2,292 South Asians, which was 9.5 percent of the Asian population and little more than 0.5 percent of the overall population. The popular and ubiquitous nineteenth-century vision of British Columbia as a "white settler" society developed in advance of when the population of white Canadians and European immigrants surpassed the indigenous and Asian population in the 1891 census. In subsequent decades, the Canadian-, British-, and American-origin population rose exponentially and bolstered the championing of the notion of an exclusively "white settler" society, which would hold sway until the Asian immigrant population boomed at the end of the twentieth century.[5]

Small overall and proportional numbers did not dampen the intensity of curiosity, concern, and fear in Vancouver and Victoria newspapers' depictions of South Asian immigrants. In 1906, labor unions and labor councils in western Canada voted on resolutions urging the federal government to curtail immigration from India. Edward Stevenson of the Saskatchewan Executive Committee of the Trades and Labor Congress of Canada warned that the onslaught of "large numbers of Hindoos" precipitated a "moral and industrial menace in a predominating Anglo-Saxon community" and that South Asian labor competition would jeopardize the precarious improvement of Canadian "white working men['s]" living standards.[6] White labor unions' political vision of managed labor competition and social entitlements for white workers repeatedly clashed with white elite capitalist strategies of labor recruitment and exploitation.[7]

Transpacific shipping companies needed large numbers of passengers to sustain their routes, and they coordinated recruitment efforts with monopoly railroad companies and timber companies, as well as with industrial fisheries and canneries that required pools of temporary unskilled laborers for boom cycles. Over the decades, they had readily recruited Chinese, Japanese, and European immigrants. The corporations sought to minimize commitments to Asian workers. They hired temporary workers and expected that these workers would readily disperse when employment dwindled. By contrast, European immigrants and white workers from other parts of North America demanded to be treated as settlers and political stakeholders, insisting

FIGURE 2. "The arrival of the first Hindus in Vancouver," November 1905. Courtesy City of Vancouver Archives. Port P1551 N. 862.

on improved working conditions, wages, and a voice in local governance and municipal investments. Since the 1860s, white workers and white businessmen had exploited the vulnerability of Chinese and Japanese workers, and in the twentieth century, South Asian workers were likewise exploited.

Labor leaders in the Victoria Trades and Labor Council condemned South Asians' "peculiar religious convictions, loathsome habits and obnoxious manner of living" as insurmountable obstacles for South Asian migrants to "assimilate with white people or perform duties of desirable citizens" of Canada, and therefore justified their expulsion from Canada.[8] Edward Stevenson, of the Saskatchewan Trades and Labor Congress, and George Grey, president of the Victoria Labor Congress, spread rumors of suspected sodomy between male South Asian passengers and of "the worst forms" of venereal disease having been diagnosed by Canadian immigration public health inspectors. These allegations echoed concerns about the sexual immorality and disease spread by Chinese men and proliferating in labor camps and bunkhouses in Canada, South Africa, and Australia. Despite their warnings of white aversion to Asians, labor leaders feared that these despised immigrants would associate with white residents and

European immigrants and blend into the economic and social fabric. Canadian labor and political leaders particularly feared the growing presence of South Asians, who as British imperial citizens could demand broader forms of social and political recognition than Chinese and Japanese immigrants.[9]

Canadian labor leaders argued that halting future South Asian immigration would deter "imminent" and explosive protests and violence from the white Canadian "proletariat."[10] Their warnings recalled campaigns against Chinese immigrants in 1880s and 1890s in western Canada and the United States and the immigration exclusions enacted in North America and in the white settler British colonies of Australia, New Zealand, and South Africa.[11] By 1906, Canadian and U.S. labor leaders and anti-Asian politicians added the "hated Hindu" immigrant to the rhetoric of the inassimilable and dangerous "Asian." Their warnings presciently predicted the cascade of urban violence and vicious harassment that began with "anti-Hindu" riots in Bellingham, Washington, in September 1907 and subsequently spread throughout Pacific Northwest.

## MALE TRANSIENTS, SEXUAL THREATS, AND MOB VIOLENCE

Bellingham, a Washington boom town on the Northern Pacific rail line between Vancouver and Seattle, had a thriving lumber-processing industry, which drew laborers across the border from Canada and from throughout the United States. In the first decade of the twentieth century, many of the cities and small towns in coastal Washington and Oregon doubled, if not tripled, in size. Bellingham grew 220 percent, and, typical of these booming resource-extraction and processing towns, much of the workforce in the Pacific Northwest consisted of young single males. The local economy was at the mercy of commodity prices and demand in distant markets that could absorb the massive outpouring of processed raw materials. At the turn of the century, construction on the Midwestern prairie and the spectacular building boom in San Francisco after the 1906 earthquake and fire fueled demand for lumber boards and shingles manufactured in Bellingham. The sudden boom only reinforced anxieties about the precariousness of demand, the visible increase in worker competition, and the possibility of unemployment.[12]

On September 4, 1907, two nights after a Labor Day parade where fiery orators railed against South Asian workers taking jobs and working for lower wages during the spring and summer in Bellingham lumber mills, a gang of

MAP 2. The Canadian and U.S. Pacific Northwest transborder region

white men ambushed two South Asian men and chased them to the tidal flats of Bellingham Bay. One of the South Asian men escaped the crowd by leaping onto a passing streetcar. The mob captured the other man, beat him, stripped him of his turban and clothing and chased him into the water. When the police arrived, they found the naked and shivering South Asian man standing knee-deep in water, dodging rocks being thrown at him by two white "youths." Later that night the mob regrouped and stormed boardinghouses where South Asian workers lived. They broke down doors, pulled occupants from their beds, forced half-dressed men into the street, and set their possessions on fire. The mob, which eventually numbered 500, chased some of the South Asian men out of town. Newspaper accounts characterized the unanimity of the crowd and members of the police force, who "recognized the universal demand of the whites that the brown men be expelled." The police ended up "herding hundreds" of terrorized South Asians into the police station basement, where they were locked up, ostensibly for their own protection.[13]

Although the Bellingham city council "deplored" the lawless behavior of the white and European immigrant mob "in molesting innocent people," they defended the mob for their restraint, explaining that they were motivated by a "spirit of self preservation" over "personal hate or religious intolerance."[14] The violence was interpreted as a battle of white employers versus American and European immigrant white workers. Bellingham's businessmen saw the barely concealed hand of labor unions behind the riot and the driving out of 400 South Asian men. Even if carried out by "boys," the violent attacks had the "full approval" of "every branch of organized labor." Company agents and out-of-state investors interpreted the show of force and the scapegoating of Asian workers as "in all probability the first step in unionizing the mills," something that had been vigorously rebuffed for years.[15]

Notice of the class chasm was swiftly recast, however, as a salvo to protect white families from disreputable single men. The Bellingham city council investigation and report blamed the "Hindu manner of living" for being "demoralizing to family ties" and lowering the economic and "moral standard of white workman" and charged that in spite of their "peaceful and quiet manner," the "Hindu population" in Bellingham was "a menace to the citizenship and moral standing of this community."[16] This argument that Asian workers precipitated economic and moral catastrophe for white workmen and their families had been rehearsed for decades in the labor and political debate against Chinese and Japanese immigrants.[17]

A Bellingham newspaper, *American Reveille*, reported that on the Sunday afternoon prior to the violence, "dark-skinned men [had] congregated on the street corners, crowding women off the sidewalks," and that women and girls had allegedly been "insulted on street cars."[18] This justification for the violence was circulated widely in the international press. The *Montreal Daily Herald* and *San Francisco Chronicle* published the same correspondent's dispatch that combined economic competition with gender defamation in its pithy analysis of the racial crisis: "Every day, whites are being replaced in the mills by the Asiatic. The invaders have become bold and insolent, [with] many instances of women being pushed into the gutter, insulted on street cars."[19] The headlines revealed striking editorial differences, however, with the *Montreal Herald* sympathizing with the victims as "British subjects" and the *San Francisco Chronicle* vilifying the "Hated Hindoo."[20] The *London Times* expressed suspicions of the charges of insulting white women in the U.S. context, because the ubiquity of the sexualized insult had been deployed against black men to justify lynching in the American South. In London, the editors of *The Times* were well acquainted with the anti-lynching campaigns led by Ida B. Wells in the 1890s, when U.S. newspapers had racialized the victims of the mob to excuse the violence.[21]

News reports underlined fears of male strangers and the threat they posed to the public good—in particular, the worry that coarse, amoral "roving men" unattached to wives and children were a sexualized menace to working-class men, women, and children. Public thoroughfares were perceived as unsafe for women and children, and there were considerable efforts in the late nineteenth and early twentieth centuries in Canada and the U.S. West to sanitize these places of public circulation. The presence of South Asian men in public exacerbated fears of sexual contact, however, which were reframed as threats to women and as justification for the race riots in Bellingham, Washington, in 1907. The violence aimed at South Asians spread throughout the Pacific Northwest, with anti-Asian political meetings, clashes, and campaigns in Vancouver, Everett, Anacortes, Aberdeen, Grays Harbor, and Seattle. On September 8, 1907, fighting between South Asian and white workers broke out in an Aberdeen mill. A week later, on September 13 and 16, there were riots against South Asians on an Alaska-bound steamer and a raucous saloon fight between Swedes and South Asians. On Halloween night in Boring, Oregon, gunmen attacked a "Hindu" bunkhouse and Bhingwan Singh died of gunshot wounds. On November 2, 1907, white American and European workers in Everett, Washington, made good on labor leaders warnings with a "demonstration" march to "scare the Hindus" that turned into a driving-out campaign.[22]

South Asian workers fled Bellingham and crossed the border to find safety and work in Vancouver, where the presence of Asians on the downtown streets and in the workforce was significant. After the anti-Chinese riots in February 1887 in Vancouver, the Chinese population continued to grow, reaching nearly 7 percent of the population overall in 1901. In the first decade of the twentieth century, the Japanese population grew rapidly, and by 1907, Asians made up 10 percent of the total population of Vancouver. Although timber harvesting was largely the preserve of European immigrant and native white workers, lumber mills in the region hired Asians for rough, unskilled, and seasonal work. By 1901, Japanese formed 25 percent and Chinese 12 percent of the workforce in lumber mills. South Asian workers joined Japanese workers in the sawmills, while Chinese workers were concentrated in shingle mills, which heightened anxieties that "whites" had been "driven out" of all timber-processing jobs.[23] White unemployment fears were exacerbated by the large influx of European immigrants from eastern Canada, Britain, and the United States in the second half of the decade.

Imperial ambitions, capitalist interests in mobilizing resources, finance, and labor flows were in dynamic tension with political society intent on circumscribing the membership rights and privileges of national citizenship. The riots, protests, and driving-out campaigns in the boom-and-bust mill towns of the Pacific Northwest were intensely local disturbances connected by shared perceptions of racial threat and illustrated how Swedes, Greeks, and other immigrants registered their membership in a political constituency that named itself white. The British and American empires had every interest in enabling the flow of workers and capital to energize trade and intensify production and consumption. The free-trade empires sponsored, protected, subsidized, and cultivated national wealth and production through tariff systems, plantation systems, and colonization, but channeled capital to maximize the profit of investors and limit competition. They desired the rapid deployment of capital and the recruiting of new groups of mobile labor that could follow the labor-intensive and demanding industries that the capitalists had invested in.[24]

In Canada, particularly in British Columbia, the shared identity that emerged among settlers from Scotland, England, Ireland, Canada, and the United States coalesced around British origin.[25] A counterforce to the state support of capital development, populist democratic groups marshaled cartels and subsidies to circumscribe national membership. Their demands for controlling and constraining the influx of some racialized workers was a response to stabilizing economic dislocation, mitigating material deprivation, scarcity, and the distributions of wealth and property. The formation of white racial identity enforcing the boundaries of national membership was expressed in localities with a rapidly growing population of migrants converging not only from Canada and the United States but internationally. The significance of rallying around a national and racial identity demonstrated both the anxiety and the persuasiveness of enforcing national membership. The extralegal violence sharply blocked the mobility of South Asian laborers and limited their opportunities, because the threat of violent attacks made employers cower. However, it did little to broaden ownership and opportunities for most white workers, even when it did enable them to lay claim to being deserving of government assistance and employment.

In 1907, a sharp economic contraction, bank panic, and falling stock market resulted in significant economic disruption. Industrial production dropped sharply by 11 percent nationwide in the United States, imports dropped by 26 percent, and unemployment nearly tripled to 8 percent.[26] The 1907 depression caused a sharp decline in the demand for timber products in the Canadian Prairie provinces, and Vancouver workers faced the crush of insecurity, with large-scale layoffs in both the immediate area and the wider region. The recession in the region drew more transient and unemployed workers into the city, waiting to learn of opportunities elsewhere. Three days after the Bellingham Riot, a crowd of 10,000 people gathered for an anti-Asian parade organized by Vancouver's newly established chapter of the Asiatic Exclusion League (AEL). The San Francisco–based white labor political organization had established chapters in Seattle, Bellingham, and Vancouver during the summer. Arthur Fowler of the AEL's Seattle chapter traveled to Bellingham on September 6, 1907, to assess the impact of the riots and traveled onward to Vancouver to participate in the parade. At the parade, he delivered a rousing speech and urged Vancouver residents to follow the example of the Bellingham driving-out campaign as a solution to Vancouver's Asian problem. He urged the crowd to march on Chinatown, and that night, a mob did so and destroyed the businesses and lodging houses of hundreds of Chinese and Japanese residents.[27]

## DEFENDING MALE HONOR

In October 1907, a month after the Vancouver Riots, Edward Bowen, a twenty-one-year-old English laborer, who had arrived in British Columbia in

June of that same year to work on the railroad, was arrested for the murder of Darrah Singh. The day after being fired from his job as a night watchman for the general hospital, Bowen had met Singh in downtown Vancouver. That day, Bowen spent the proceeds of his last paycheck. He bought a hat and a pistol, which he showed off to fellow beer drinkers in the saloon at the New Fountain Hotel downtown. His friend Russ told Bowen that "it was a foolish thing to carry a weapon like that under the British flag." Bowen had paid up his room at the City Rooming House and had purchased a couple of meal tickets, but he was running out of money.[28] He was a bevy of contradictions. His claim of a physician father and "fairly well educated" speech were betrayed by a "cockney accent" and his Vancouver work as an unskilled laborer. Sociable and garrulous, Bowen met two turbaned South Asian men at the Fountain Saloon and invited them to "drink and to talk" about their lives in India and China.[29] They left for the Alexander Hotel, where a bartender named McDonald recalled the two turbaned South Asian men as unusually tall, "towering head and shoulders over the rest of us." He also noticed Bowen's enthusiasm for the men, who had served in the "King's Army in India." McDonald remarked that they were "two fine looking men" and that the three were "evidently" on good terms. The bartender noted that Darrah Singh, wearing a yellow turban and suit, had carefully inspected his money before paying the tab.[30]

Meeting in saloons was fairly typical for transient workingmen. The saloons, hotels, and boardinghouses on East Cordova Street were a borderlands zone, between the wharves, Chinatown, and the downtown business and retail district, where workers, transients, and respectable men passed through. As the historian Robert McDonald has described, transient and seasonal workers flooded the downtown streets for recreation and for practical exchanges as part of their daily lives, becoming part of "Vancouver's floating population." The lack of public squares and parks and the proximity to boardinghouses and saloons in the zone between the waterfront and Chinatown made it a hub for congregating and crowds. Downtown was especially busy in the evenings, with "thousands of people wandering about" in front of department stores "on Sunday nights with nowhere to go," because blue laws shut down the saloons and pool halls. The respectable classes and city officials, who lived their intimate lives in the privacy of spacious homes with gated yards in suburban residential areas, projected a vision of city streets as "neutral places where people filled time and occasionally did business." Vancouver's floating population made "public streets an integral part of their daily lives," however, and their presence made it "contested terrain."[31]

At one corner of a crowded saloon, Darrah Singh and his companion shared anecdotes about their time in the military in India and China with Edward Bowen, who spoke about his life in London and his journey across Canada. Their conversations inevitably turned to current prospects; Bowen perhaps explained his discouraging prospects with summer stints in railroad construction and a night watchman's job. Darrah Singh who had been working in the region for two years probably shared his dissatisfaction with sawmill opportunities in British Columbia and his plans to immigrate across the border to Washington. Perhaps they shared stories of their homes in Punjab and in London; or traded impressions of saloons and boardinghouses, the uncertainty of work, the frequency of layoffs, and the caprice of employers. Maybe they had opinions about the recent riots and clashes between white workers and Japanese and Chinese workers, about the wariness of the merchants and saloonkeepers, and the heightened police presence downtown.

Their friendly conversation and generosity in buying drinks among strangers took a turn after Darrah Singh invited Bowen to return to his room in the Spokane Rooming House, where Bowen expected to share a bottle with Singh and his companion. Bowen recalled that once there, Darrah Singh began to unwind his turban and take off his trousers and vest. Bowen sat on the bed, and the other man left the room, switching off the light. Thinking this was a joke, Bowen got up, switched the light back on, and sat back down on the bed. When he explained that he was planning on leaving, Darrah "put his arm around my back." Singh "was laughing," Bowen claimed. He placed one hand on Bowen's "privates" and stroked the back of Bowen's hand with the other. Bowen rose to leave, but Singh "caught hold" of his shoulder and "forced" him onto the bed. Incredulous and horrified, Bowen, then "realized what he was going to do" and "shot him."[32]

Darrah Singh had been a familiar and frequent guest for two years at the Spokane Rooming House on the corner of Cordova and Carroll Streets. The innkeeper, a man named Gilbert, described Singh as "very much of a gentleman in his ways and dress . . . better than the ordinary Hindoo." When Gilbert found Darrah Singh shot on the stairwell, he testified that Singh was wearing "shirt and trousers, or pajamas" and was "tidily dressed." He appeared to have his turban on, but Gilbert could not remember "whether it was a whole turban or not." His daughter Agnes Gilbert recalled that Darrah Singh's yellow turban had "untangled a little in the hallway when the body was moved."[33]

In the wake of the anti-Asian riots the month before, the district was heavily policed, and three officers came rapidly to the scene. Police Constable

McCuish was the first to respond to the shooting. McCuish found the Gilberts with the body. He turned the body over and "opened his vest" to "find the bullet wound in his chest . . . and blood oozing out." Five minutes later, Officer Gillis came up the stairs and they took the body into the room. Gillis recalled that Singh's "yellow turban was loose and fell off." Detective McLeod was walking down Cordova Street when five men told him about "some trouble"; "this boy had shot a Hindoo" who had accosted him. When McLeod arrested Bowen near the corner of Abbot and Cordova Streets, Bowen exclaimed that he had "shot the Hindoo because he tried to bugger" him.[34]

The identity of the man who had accompanied Darrah Singh to the saloon and boardinghouse remained unknown. However, another friend, Natha Singh of Seattle, testified at the trial and revealed Darrah Singh's plans to migrate to the United States. Natha Singh crisscrossed the Canadian and U.S. border frequently for work, and in 1906, he had befriended Darrah Singh when they worked together at a sawmill in Port Moody, the former Canadian Rail terminus and timber-processing town on the outskirts of Vancouver. A few days before the shooting, they had met again in Port Moody, and Natha had encouraged Darrah to move and work in Seattle, despite the recent driving-out campaigns and clashes in Bellingham and other Washington towns. Natha advised him of immigration procedures, including a mandatory health inspection, and had accompanied him to the U.S. immigration office in Vancouver earlier on the morning of his murder.

Natha Singh's testimony offered an alternative motive for Bowen's murder of Darrah Singh—robbery. At the U.S. immigration office, Darrah Singh had presented the U.S. authorities with $200 in cash to prove his financial worth. Darrah's wallet and the $200 could not be found after the murder. The deputy attorney general of British Columbia, Hugh Archibald Maclean, seized on the missing "Hindu purse" and argued that Bowen's motive in visiting Singh's rooming house had been armed robbery, which had turned fatal. Bowen's unemployment, drunkenness, and possession of a loaded gun motivated his greed when he spied the contents of Singh's wallet at the Alexander Hotel. Since neither the "Hindu's purse" nor the cash was found after the murder, Maclean speculated that Bowen had "probably thrown away the purse" in the attempt to flee. Without the motive of greed, Maclean was at a loss to understand Bowen's enthusiasm for socializing with Singh in the bars and returning to his room with him.[35]

Bowen's defense attorneys argued that the murder was not the result of "old time malice" or a "tipsy quarrel." They argued that Bowen had been forced into a vulnerable position with two physically larger and stronger men and insisted that a "man had the same right as a woman and was justified in taking life to protect his honor."[36] Bowen had expressed shock and claimed that he was "overcome with horror." Acting on impulse, Bowen's revulsion and fear had overcome his rationality, and he had resorted to deadly violence with the newly purchased pistol in his pocket.

The meeting in all-male saloons, which excluded women to prevent prostitution, and visiting at the boardinghouse demonstrated how readily associations across race and ethnic differences could develop and the extent of male camaraderie of meeting, drinking, and sharing stories and woes. These activities created the potential for homosocial alliances that could shore up male solidarities and trust. This homosocial environment satisfied social needs, but physical closeness and signs of sexual desire provoked vigilant anxiety. Attempts to thwart physical intimacy disrupted male camaraderie and redirected its expression as a potential threat to male honor. Racial difference amplified the threat and reinforced the distress of promiscuous association. Conventionally, male honor was invoked to undergird the protection of women in kinship relations—wife, sister, and daughter—who were threatened with unsolicited and unwelcome male attention and sexual interest. Male honor was invested in the protection of vulnerable female dependents from male competition. Bowen's defense hinged on the persuasiveness of the analogy of his vulnerability to that of a woman.

In their coverage of the case, local newspapers picked up on Bowen's defense of male honor under threat and vulnerability to immoral foreign men. The *Vancouver World* empathized with Bowen's youth and "inexperience" in confronting the "horrid situation" of assault by "a huge Hindoo, a man described by all as a very fine specimen," and described his use of deadly force as "common sense" and justified.[37] The historian Angus McLaren, who analyzed the case, speculates that Bowen and his counsel sought to use the "community's revulsion against homosexuality" as a ploy to justify robbery and murder. The prosecutors deftly dismissed evidence of the alleged sexual attack by underlining how honorable, circumspect, and respectable Darrah Singh's behavior had been at the bar, and his personal history at the boardinghouse. The jury agreed with the prosecution that a "man in protecting his honor was not justified in taking a life" and returned a verdict of manslaughter. Bowen was sentenced to ten years in prison.[38]

Despite Bowen's conviction, sexual suspicion of South Asian laborers persisted. It shifted the location of the perceived threat from white female victims to white male victims and crystallized how adult men could experience feminized vulnerability. Although the jury refused to condone murder, even in defense of a man's honor, the public culture recognized the dangerous moral and sexual affront, underscoring suspicions of interracial socializing.

## MALE HONOR, FEMALE PERIL

The defense of white honor became an umbrella justification for anti–South Asian violence in the Bellingham riots and in many subsequent driving-out campaigns in Oregon and California as South Asians continued to immigrate to the United States. In three events, white male mobs justified their violence with allegations of South Asian men behaving indecently and harassing white women and girls. In 1909, in the Northern California farming community of Live Oak in Sutter County, white residents formed a lynch mob and drove "Hindu" workers out of town after allegations of Hindus' "indecent exposure in the presence of women and children." District Attorney Lawrence Schillig called for an investigation into the riots, the driving-out campaign, and the victims' allegations of robbery. Although two white men were arrested, neither was charged with a crime, for "lack of evidence." At the conclusion of the investigation, Schillig reported to California's governor that the "Hindus" had promised to "obey the laws of decency," and the state would enforce prevailing landlords' regulations on crowding in workers' houses.[39]

In 1911, in Fair Oaks, eighteen miles east of Sacramento, three young white men, the sons of local farmers and fruit growers, led a raiding party on a "Hindu camp" of workers employed by the Fair Oaks Fruit Packing Company. The white men drove eleven South Asian men from the camp and later defended their actions as a necessary retaliation against the men, who had allegedly been annoying and harassing young girls in the surrounding neighborhood. The *San Francisco Examiner* reported that local citizens defended the young men, who were arrested and imprisoned in Sacramento awaiting trial. The following night, fourteen "young men of the neighborhood armed with guns and pistols, wagon spokes and other weapons" marched onto an old house that South Asian workers were renting and "drove" another group of "Hindus into the country." Their behavior chillingly mirrored that of a lynch mob, with the same strategies of violent, extralegal punishment for alleged harassment of white girls. South Asian men escaped lynching or torture but were warned of fatal consequences if they returned for work.[40] As the historian John Pettegrew has argued, the "lynch mob best illustrates homosocial power. In killing thousands of African American men for rumored sexual transgressions," lynch mobs asserted "white masculine authority" and simultaneously policed "access to women" and demolished attempts by African Americans to assert "economic and social power."[41]

To be sure, there was a difference between lynch mobs and driving-out mobs in the outcome of their rage. On the Pacific Coast, South Asians, like the Chinese before them, were numerous enough to be perceived as a threat, but not a sufficiently widespread presence to nullify the belief that they could be expelled and erased. Their presence was fleeting, a temporary nuisance that could be permanently eradicated, and the driving-out mobs underlined the transience. White mobs beat South Asian men, destroyed their possessions, and robbed them of cash and valuables, but did not feel the need to send symbolic messages in the shape of corpses. The driving-out mobs asserted male authority and policed contact, but they were seeking to eradicate their targets, not to impose deference and servitude by force. Unlike in the case of the Native Americans whose land, resources, and claim to place white settlers had usurped, the desire to humiliate and deter any return outstripped the desire to kill. A successful campaign to drive them out would, it was hoped, result in all of the targets' departure. The aim was to rally a broader white public to deport them from the nation and deliver a stern warning to any other Asian arrivals of fatal outcomes. The removal of the Asians was intended to punish and instruct landlords and business owners and curb their power to hire and lease to a denigrated racialized group. Once the suspect laborers were gone, the message tempered landowners' and businessmen's cavalier demonstrations of liberty to employ and serve anyone. The driving-out mob created boundaries of presence through rituals of propriety and punishment that defined the sense of control over place for white workingmen. Their disruptive power curbed the dominance of white businessmen, the white middle class, and local government.

The government's ritual of absolving and forgetting the lynch mob's unlawful violence underlined the fact that the social, economic, and political order had been shaken but not usurped. The spectacle of a brutalized body hanging from a tree served as warning to those who could not be eradicated and erased. Lynching's value within an arsenal of terror was most effective in subjugating populations of African Americans and Chicanos, whose political subordination and economic exploitation was necessary for the preservation of the social order.[42] The campaigns to drive out South Asians simultaneously addressed moral disorder and labor competition, both of which "demoralized" white family life and particularly white male breadwinners' ability to protect and sustain their dependents. Chasing South Asians out of the vicinity of towns and work camps was intended to erase their presence and their employment. Fears of the demoralization of public life became crystallized in accusations that South Asian men verbally harassed white women and girls. The white mob reinforced the representation of helpless, frightened women requiring white male protection to survive outside of domestic society, as well as the dangers and impossibility of women and girls negotiating independence in a male-dominated public world without chaperones and protections.

In March 1910, in St. Johns, a sawmill suburb of Portland, Oregon, a squabble between a white man and South Asian men in a saloon erupted into riots. The labor newspapers attributed the "cause of the saloon fight" to allegations that the "Hindu had made an insulting and suggestive gesture to a young white woman, and he had actually put his hands on her and frightened her into a hysterical condition."[43] Labor newspapers characterized the population of 300 to 400 "Hindus . . . who form half the visible population at all times" as particularly prone to sexually suggestive commentary. In the commentary of the notoriously anti-Asian magazine *The White Man*, South Asian men allegedly crowded sidewalks and the "entrances of stores and would stare at and frighten the women and children and pass insulting remarks in pigeon [sic] English at the young women. The Hindus are accustomed in their country to use any language they see fit to women, and they keep up the practice in the United States."[44]

The trial, however, also revealed an emerging white male practice of harassment and humiliation that targeted South Asian men and punished them for their insolent conduct. In the grand jury trial, a foreman of the Williamette Pulp and Paper Company, Gordon Dickey, testified that walking between saloons, he had encountered "three or four men bringing a Hindu from the waterfront. One of them he said was a cook at a St. Johns hotel [and] knocked the Hindu down." Dickey pretended to protect the "Hindu's welfare," picked up the "end of his turban" and continued to unwind it. Police found the man stripped of his turban and badly beaten. Based on incriminating testimony about Dickey holding a revolver to the head of a South Asian man while another robbed him, a grand jury convicted Dickey of leading the riot that had led to the assault, robbery, and driving out of forty-nine South Asians.[45]

The perceived threat of South Asian men insolently addressing and insulting white women in public connected with the practice and texture of the terrorist violence against these South Asian men. The turban became a focal point of abuse and harassment. The turban was both a sartorial distinction and a cultural difference that was so identified with "Hindus" that it became a corporeal difference, an appendage. The *pagri*, or turban, referred to a long plain cloth that is manually tied and worn as a head-covering by men across India. The cloth's color, fabric, and the style in which it is tied indicate region, caste, and economic status, but throughout India, it symbolized honor and respect within and between communities. For Sikh adult men, wearing a specific *pagri*, referred to as the *dastar*, had by the eighteenth and nineteenth centuries become the accepted uniform, publicly declaring piety and observance of Sikh faith by retaining their uncut hair and keeping it orderly. British colonial rule and particularly the British Army reinforced the *dastar* as a standard marker of Sikh identity, and in the late nineteenth century, Sikh reformers intent on maintaining exclusive rituals and social markers bolstered the *dastar*'s symbolic significance for Sikh males' distinctive identity.[46] The turban is a demonstration of piety and public declaration of devotion in Sikhism.

In public space, white Americans identified the turban as a racial and sexual difference that could became a focal point of abuse and harassment. The act of forcibly unwinding the turban or removing it from the head of a Sikh man became an act of ritualistic violence that was intended to humiliate, shame, and terrorize the man. The exposure of unshorn hair assailed the spiritual values and dignity of Sikh men, redoubling the humiliation. The stripping of turbans was a tactic developed in the field of intra-masculine homosocial competition. The assault tactic played up the fear of "public emasculation," provoking anxiety and the avoidance of shame before other men. Even as homosocial competition empowered men as a social group over women, it also ensured "a seemingly constant specter of failure and humiliation among individual men."[47] White male workers and elites justified the violent humiliation of South Asian men in this way with intertwined allegations of wage competition, public depravity, and the demoralizing of white American "family ties." The harassment was intended to curb South Asian males' presence in public space and to punish them for their insolence in making any claim to equality. This strategy of racial subordination bolstered by the threat of humiliation became a key white ritual of maintaining racial hierarchy in a male world.

This training in white male privilege and the strategies of abuse were transmitted to male youth in California's Central Valley. Three decades later in the 1940s, Allan Miller, a white anthropology graduate student from the University of California at Berkeley conducted research in Yuba and Sutter Counties and reported how effective and ritualized racial harassment had become as an everyday practice: "Sikhs stay in foreign quarters of Marysville because they are ridiculed if they frequent regular bars, theaters, and restaurants. Gangs of high school boys harass [them] and grab turbans."[48] White male homosocial solidarity consolidated around the ridicule of the turbaned South Asian man. This racial subordination through ridicule and humiliation confined South Asian men to a tightly circumscribed world and heightened their wariness of interactions with the white public.

White Americans and Canadians pejoratively called South Asian men "ragheads" and described turbans as dirty, uncivilized, outside of sartorial conventions of modernity. The turban was also coded as carrying filth, a marker of the unsanitary and the disordered as well as the exotic alien. On the other hand, Sikh men considered their *dastars* as the ideal means of keeping their unshorn hair clean and orderly and maintaining a dignified appearance. The colors of their turbans carried spiritual and social status significance, but in North America, the white and yellow-colored turbans were often described as "soiled" and "dirty" because they collected and made visible the blowing dirt and sand common to the Imperial and San Joaquin Valleys. Even sympathetic white men commented on how the "soiled" appearance of the turbans contributed to justifications of physical separation and the frequent rationale for why South Asians were "unwelcome" in public accommodations such as "the better class of restaurants, picture shows and soda fountains."[49] In photographs, the juxtaposition of the turban with the wrinkled suit produced a particularly jarring and vivid contradiction in social assimilation. The willingness to adapt to a Western suit but to retain the turban marked the turban as an icon of spiritual difference manifested physically, like the sari and the veil. The turban became a sign of immutable cultural difference and was interpreted as an unwillingness to assimilate to white Christian norms.[50]

The turban also betrayed anxieties about the gender identities of South Asian migrants. Concerns about the long, unshorn black hair that was wound and sealed from public view by the turban stimulated rumors of gender masquerade. An anti-Asian labor magazine circulated rumors that "many Hindu women are brought to this country disguised as men and are employed [in the railroad construction camps] as manual labor along with Hindu men."[51] The historian Gerald Halberg, in an appraisal of the Bellingham Riots, claims that the few women in the "Hindu colony" were indistinguishable because they "dressed like men in trousers and coats" and "slept in the same crowded apartments with men."[52] These accusations of South Asian women dressing like, working alongside, and sleeping in the same apartments with South Asian men betrayed anxieties that distinct gender roles and behavior were eroding and being undermined by South Asian migrant workers. In another story reported by a local labor newspaper in Sacramento, a number of "Hindus" were shopping in a department store when one of them was taken ill. When a physician examined "the Hindu" and diagnosed appendicitis, the "Hindu" was discovered to be a "woman" disguised as a man.[53] Although it is highly unlikely that women lived among the men, these anecdotal examples all underlined the gender masquerade and social duplicity of South Asians, as well as suggesting an inability to distinguish between working-class South Asian men and women by dress and comportment.

The masculine dress, comportment, and role of suspected South Asian women heightened anxieties about men's and women's equality and indistinct gender roles and behavior emerging in the United States during women's campaigns for suffrage. It threatened the naturalness of gender differentiation that justified gender inequality (feminine subordination to masculinity) and the organization of separate spheres of work and life. Gender-normative womanhood and manhood were fashioned and anxiously stabilized in reaction to widespread transient and international mobility, the racial stratification of society, and nationalist defense of privileged membership.[54]

Drawing racial and civilizational distinctions of dress, behavior, recreation, and livelihood shored up white supremacy and nationalism. At the same time, it naturalized subordination of racialized migrants' presumed incapacity for maintaining the "natural" gender binary and inequality. In the transient migrant world populated by masculine adult males, gender ambiguity and the diminishment of gender distinctions in dress, labor, and recreation underscored a world turned upside down. Loose-fitting shirts over trousers, bulky winter coats, and turbaned long hair were the uniform of South Asian workers. For white male observers, the contradictory dress strategies transposed verities of masculinity onto female bodies and femininity onto male bodies. As Clare Sears has vividly illustrated, the feminization of Chinese miners because of their robes and their long hair braided in queues in Gold Rush California troubled gendered norms and accelerated the terms of racial subordination in anti-Chinese politics. The threat of gender ambiguity in the feminization of South Asian men or masculinization of South Asian women was expressed in taunts and mockery of their dress and long hair bound under a turban. The practice of racial mockery was a strategy to assert heteronormative white masculinity, repudiate gender atypical comportment, and corral gender trouble in a racialized body. It drew attention away from dress reform, public behavior, and political challenges issued by white women. Gender and sexual transgression was policed and produced racialized borders, but it also redoubled the moral crisis and required the shoring up of dominant gender norms and distinctions.[55]

As reports of South Asian female masculinity multiplied, the racialization of gender reversal animated curiosity, anxiety, and eroticism in the slide between unbearded male youth and masculine women. What was the consequence if there were women among the men? What would it reveal or defy? The stakes of legible and differentiated gender were tremendous. An undifferentiated mass of male-dressed laborers defied the social prescriptions that purportedly removed women from manual labor outside the household. However, this ideal harbored an implicit racial contrast that championed white women's release from manual labor in contrast with nonwhite women's servitude. It fed the concern for unattached, unmarried women living in honor-compromised and immoral sexual relations with men. On the one hand, the fear of widespread and morally indifferent sexual impropriety and male loss of control over "loose women" continued to presume heterosexual alliance. On the other hand, there could be gendered camaraderie among masculinities and asexual and homosocial alliance. The possibility of masculinities that did not require a specific male embodiment made the idea of a gendered alliance between male-bodied persons and female-bodied persons disquieting and the purported naturalness of the gender divide illegible.[56]

But the victimization of South Asian women also fed a racializing caricature. The rumors of unmarried women living among men fostered an image of sexual immorality and a wholesale absence of respectable domestic culture, making it impossible to distinguish between the bunkhouse and the brothel in the South Asian migrant community. The policed urban vice district was not the sole playground of transient men but merged with their bunkhouses, rented lodgings, and work camps. It also fed accusations that South Asian men had coerced women to sexual servitude.

But it also revealed a more fundamental and distressing anxiety that there was no natural, self-evident differentiation of gender roles and capabilities. This concern resonated more widely than the peculiar customs of South Asian migrants and resonated with the anxieties of many men who saw the weakening of cultural distinctions of gender roles and capabilities that spearheaded the entry of women into higher education, professions, and the campaign for women's political equality at the ballot box and in serving in public office. If bodily gender difference was not the fundamental justification of political, social, and economic inequality, then little could curb the demands for gender equity. Rather than capture the full freight of commonsense-defying implications, the suspicions of women disguised as men in South Asian work camps, and the attendant implications of prostitution, promiscuity, and immorality, provided one more avenue to contain gender trouble in a racial problem and, fleetingly, displaced it from the struggle over gender equity in the rapidly changing white social order in North America.

In both the United States and Canada, the period from 1910 to 1914 witnessed heightened political tensions and surging controversy over the entry, political status, and economic privileges of Asian immigrants. Politicians, newspaper editors, and labor leaders alleged that Immigration Service employees on the Pacific Coast were bribed, exhibited favoritism, and freely allowed the entry of South Asian laborers, Japanese "picture brides," and Chinese merchant wives and children. Despite the zeal of immigration inspectors to create new restrictive criteria, intensive interrogations, interminable detention, and institutionalized deportation of Asian male laborers and Asian women, the fact that any Asian immigrants managed to enter the United States despite intensive scrutiny, rather than an absolute exclusion, angered the most vitriolic and vocal opponents of Asian immigration. Popular newspapers and anti-Asian labor organizations featured worries about the arrival of South Asians across the border with Canada and through the U.S. possession of the Philippines. Fears of high birthrates among Japanese picture brides and of Japanese immigrant families populating and dominating agriculture in California and Washington were featured in the campaigns for the passage of the Alien Land Law by the California Legislature in 1913 and similar laws in Washington, Arizona, and other western states.[57] At stake were the reproduction of Asian immigrant communities and the populating of the western United States with new migrants who were marked as undesirable, like the previously excluded Chinese immigrants. The "Asianization" of undesirable immigrants was a strategy of denying the entry of entire groups. However, in practice immigration regulations assiduously managed the entry of Chinese, Japanese, Korean, and South Asian immigrants by class and gender.

In Congress, California Representative Denver S. Church, who had been Fresno County district attorney from 1907 to 1913, led a vitriolic campaign for exclusion of the new Asian threat from India. A Democratic Party stalwart elected with the backing of the Asiatic Exclusion League, Church served in Congress from 1913 to 1919. Along with Congressman Ellison Smith of South Carolina, he introduced hearings and legislation to exclude South Asian laborers, labeled "Hindu." Congressman Church testified about the clannish, dishonest, and immoral behavior of Hindu laborers in Fresno as an illustration of their unsuitability for permanent settlement and assimilation to American society.[58] Successive bills in each house of Congress eventually resulted in the 1917 Immigration Act's "Asiatic Barred Zone" that extended the exclusion imposed on Chinese laborers to the entire continent of Asia and its adjacent islands.[59]

In 1913, amid legislative campaigns to restrict immigration and political pressure on federal immigration authorities, the uproar over South Asian immigration provoked labor councils in California to pass resolutions for total exclusion. In labor and popular cultural representation, "Hindus" were being painted even more vociferously as a vicious and immoral race. South Asians were caricatured as "rankly incompetent and have detestable personal habits." The South Asian was accused of "inferior workmanship" and called the "unbuilder of any community in which he may live."[60] Charging that the "presence of Hindus who flock on the streets and [in] the parks" degraded and debased "white families" who had to contend with their "obnoxious habits and ill smelling bodies," and that these South Asians were "single, [have a] roving disposition, do not make homes, [and] live [a] dog's life," the Stockton Labor Council advised the Immigration Service that their expulsion was the only remedy.[61] The labor magazine *The White Man* elaborated upon extreme representations of the sexual peril of South Asian migrants: "Both Mohammedans and Hindus are notoriously addicted to unspeakable vices that take hold of degenerate and decadent peoples," and they held "weird orgies" in their "settlements throughout the state."[62] This vitriolic and sensational commentary underlined the moral hazard and unsavory reputation of South Asian laborers.

## PASSION AND MURDER OF ROSA DOMINGO

The dire consequences of socializing between South Asian men and white women were telegraphed in the newspaper coverage of the sensational murder of Rosa Domingo, daughter of Manuel Domingo, a Portuguese resident of the small community of Stege in Contra Costa County on the eastern shores of San Francisco Bay. The newspaper coverage quickly focused on Said Ali Khan as the leading suspect in the case, and on his tempestuous courtship of Rosa Domingo for many months before the murder. Four days after Rosa Domingo went missing, her brother identified Said Ali Khan as an "ardent" suitor who was "very much in love with her" and had since March beseeched her to accept his proposal of marriage.[63] In the 1910s, Said Ali Khan, along with about eighty-five other South Asian men working for the California Cap Works and Metropolitan Match, found board in buildings among the factories in Stege. The town was connected by rail and road with Richmond and Oakland. Louis Navellier, a longtime resident, recalled South Asian workers climbing up the hill in a long line, coming back from work, with turbans wrapped around their heads, and that neighborhood children would run away in fright when they saw the men.[64] Said Ali Khan lived in a shack in Stege a half mile from the place where Domingo's body was found. Letters found in her South of Market room in San Francisco confirmed that she and Khan had been dating for months.[65]

Domingo and Khan were bound together in an urban commercial social world where unmarried men and women met and mingled. Unmarried young women worked in retail, manufacturing, and service positions, lived outside their homes in rooming and boardinghouses and engaged in contemporary rituals of dating and courtship. A consumer shift in the terms of courtship involved how men would "treat" women in the offering of gifts and paying for new urban amusements such as cinema, amusement parks, and arcades. Young women negotiated the exchange of entertainment and physical intimacy with men and developed moral and social distinctions to distinguish their sexual barter from the commerce of prostitution. Young women like Rosa Domingo could find work in pool halls, as waitresses in cafes, and in retail establishments.[66] She left her home and crossed San Francisco Bay and lived in a boardinghouse in the South of Market district. She and other young women were able to sustain new "patterns of living" because "capitalism allowed individuals to survive beyond the confines of family." While Rosa had frequent contact with her family and traveled back and forth regularly on the ferry, she developed an autonomous social and economic life and was able to join her wage-earning peers in manipulating social spaces to "invent new ways of meeting and sustaining group life."[67]

The urban entertainment venues of commercial culture were viewed by the elite, educated men who edited South Asian immigrant newspapers as traps to ensnare and challenge the moral principles of naïve single migrant laborers who had sprung from the ranks of farmers and soldiers. The elite South Asian writers criticized the commonplace socializing of migrant workers in North America as "Western Civilization curses," a combination of vicious urban commercial vice associated with saloons and "drink bills" that preyed upon the loneliness, isolation, and desperation of transient men with no social or domestic contact with women. The white American and European immigrant women who worked at and frequented coffeehouses, cafes, and pool halls tempted these men with the promise of attention and affection. The urban entertainment locations drew transient men's time and money, since they were far more hospitable spaces than the scarce shelter and deplorable accommodations in makeshift shacks and "lousy camp-bunk-houses" that they were forced to endure.[68] Elite South Asian men criticized the culture of North American courtship that Said Ali Khan navigated, where "love sick swains" made "certain swell cafes their rendezvous and commercialized love and musing," which they nostalgically and disingenuously contrasted with the alleged absence of red light districts in Asia and traditional customary rituals of marriage partnership and "strict social customs of monogamy."[69]

The letters between Khan and Domingo were publicized in newspaper reports that attempted to make sense of the mystery of the murder, emphasizing the commercial context of their courtship and how money had catalyzed the drama of their relationship. The availability of money, its promise, and its conversion into gifts demonstrated Said Ali Khan's financial capacity, trustworthiness, and ardent devotion. The promise and absence of money and gifts fueled Rosa Domingo's interest and her dissatisfaction with Khan. Khan's letters promised gifts and money as entreaties to seek forgiveness for quarrels. The police released a letter to the press where Khan begged her to see him. Khan wrote: " I must see you. I have $180 and my friend, I promise to see you, so don't disappoint me. You must come. Dress yourself up. I like to see you well dressed." Their meeting earlier in the morning had gone awry when he teased her by pretending that he had only a dollar. Khan explained: "I fooled you. I had $20. I bought a ring in Oakland for you. . . . Trust me and I will trust you." The price of the gifts and sharing Khan's wealth meant that Khan expected her to pledge fidelity to him. The honor and respect Khan expected from her and from his peers hinged on his reparations to win her forgiveness. He closed his letter with the assertion that he was "rich now. Good night honey bug."[70] Another letter that the police released was dated two weeks earlier and was riddled with hints of frequent quarrels. Said Ali Khan had unsuccessfully attempted to meet Rosa at her San Francisco home after a quarrel. Khan apologized for being drunk and quarrelsome, promising to "never fight you again." As a measure of his promise, he offered to buy " ten yards of silk for a dress" for her forgiveness and entreated her to come visit him at his home.[71] An *Oakland Tribune* reporter interviewed South Asian students at the University of California in Berkeley, who were astonished by the letters, which were expressive in idioms of romance and colloquial expressions, full of entreaties for forgiveness and casual offerings of money and gifts. The students unanimously doubted that a Muslim laborer from northern India would be capable of authoring these letters and believed that an American had ghostwritten them.[72]

In many ways Khan and Domingo's relationship was sustained by the interventions of their mutual friend Charles Riley, who confirmed their turbulent sexual relationship in his interview with the police, and much later admitted that he had indeed ghostwritten Khan's letters. Riley recalled that the couple had attended the Native Sons parade and celebrations in Oakland. After midnight, the couple arrived at Riley's home unexpectedly and asked to stay the night. Riley permitted them to sleep in the kitchen, but the next morning, as Riley was hitching his horse, Rosa stormed out of the house after a quarrel. She railed against Khan for departing and made him take back $17 that he had given her the night before.[73]

Khan's romantic history with Domingo and his disappearance made him the leading suspect in the crime, and police posted a $175 reward for his capture. Thousands of circulars were broadcast across the state and in Nevada, Oregon, and Arizona. The photograph and description emphasized that he was a sporting man wearing a double-breasted, square-cut, striped brown suit and "cheap tan shoes." He had a "smooth shaven, swarthy complexion, dark eyes," and occasionally wore a moustache. He "was 30 years old, 145 lbs and 5 foot 7 inches tall."[74] As the morality tale developed in the newspapers, the coverage highlighted the dangers of interracial courtship, with perilous implications for both new migrants and North American natives.

The South Asian male's assimilation to social and cultural norms provoked different levels of anxiety for observers and commentators in both the Vancouver case in 1907 and the Stege Case in 1913, and mirrored the anxiety expressed in the 1909 New York City case in which a Chinese dandy allegedly murdered a white society woman, as detailed by the historian Mary Lui.[75] Said Ali Khan was characterized as a dandy or sporting man, sharply dressed in urban American fashion, heightening the danger of partially assimilated, appealing South Asian men to white Americans. The white bartenders and boardinghouse keeper had also described Darrah Singh as well dressed, respectable, and a "fine specimen of a man." Yet Darrah Singh's distinctive clothing, turban, and beard set him apart. Said Ali Khan, on the other hand, was clean-shaven and wore a double-breasted suit and no headgear.

Khan's sporty fashionable attire was relatively new; he had arrived in the United States three years previously, after working as a police officer in Hong Kong. After disembarking in Seattle, he and his friend Zemair Khan, a "Mohemmadan" priest, whom the police questioned, had worked together in the Sacramento Delta as laborers on the Jersey Tract and Roberts Island. In early 1913, Said Ali Khan left agriculture and found work with other South Asian workers in a match factory in Stege. During the police interrogation, Zemair Khan expressed surprise at the transformation of Said Ali's dress, demeanor, and life, particularly at his double-breasted suit and clean-shaven visage in a photograph taken in a studio on the edge of Oakland's China-town.[76] Harwick, who had photographed Said Ali Khan and Rosa Domingo in September, recalled having seen Khan gazing for a half an hour, the day before Domingo's disappearance, at the poolroom across the street where she had previously worked.[77]

The urgency of locating Khan increased when a Richmond police detective, Charles Walker, discovered "coat buttons, [a] belt buckle," and other debris from her clothing in the stove ash box in Said Ali Khan's cabin. Following the discovery, police arrested his housemate Musa Khan, who denied, "ever seeing the girl" and knew "nothing of the crime" or the burned clothes. While holding Musa Khan in the Richmond jail as an accomplice, the police intercepted a let-ter addressed to Musa Khan from Said Ali Khan and publicized a translation of it in the press. In the letter, Said Ali revealed that he had no regrets about killing her, saying that his "heart was burning" from the money and gifts she took from him, and yet she had rebuffed his proposal of marriage.[78]

Said Ali Khan's movements by train followed a pattern of South Asian labor migration to intensive agriculture zones downstate. From northern California, he had fled to friends in Oxnard in Santa Barbara County, and from there barely escaped on a train to Yuma and then to Calexico on the U.S.–Mexico border. His resources were depleted, and it was impossible to find work in the Imperial Valley. After intercepting the letter, Contra Costa County Sheriff Richard Veale and Detective Ruiz boarded a train for Calexico and organized a manhunt for Said Ali Khan on the border. Police officers in the region were pressed into dozens of posses scouring the "Hindu camps in the hills" on the

U.S. side of the border. Sheriff Veale put a decoy letter at the post office in Calexico to lure Said Ali across the border, because they suspected he was hiding in the hills around Mexicali. At noon on Wednesday, October 15, Detective Ruiz arrested Said Ali as he tried to board a train in Calexico.[79]

In the aftermath of the arrest and before the journey north, Said Ali Khan at first confessed to Ruiz and Veale, claiming, "She would not go away with me after I had spent $250 on her.... This Rosa Domingo Riley fired my heart with love and revenge. She came to the cabin near midnight October 2nd. We talked a long time. She laughed at me. I got very mad and grabbed and threw her on the bed and floor. I put a knee on her throat and strangle[d] her." When she stopped breathing, he had wrapped her body in a blanket and thrown it off a wharf.[80] En route, he repudiated this confession made in the jail in El Centro. He insinuated that Charles Riley, a teamster and intermediary between him and "Rosa Domingo Riley," had written letters to Rosa, given him money to flee town, and accused him of murdering Rosa in a jealous rage. His letter also insinuated that perhaps Riley had married Rosa Domingo and was estranged from her. Despite the confusion, Sheriff Veale ordered Riley's arrest and held him for questioning.[81]

When they reached Richmond, the police dramatically took Khan for a view of Rosa's body in the morgue before her funeral, and then to her family's house, where her inconsolable father raged against Khan, "Let me at him. He killed my daughter, you beast." He attempted to spring upon Khan but was restrained by police officers. At the jail, his housemate Musa Khan was brought out of solitary confinement and sat with Said Ali Khan during his interrogation before District Attorney McKenzie and Sheriff Veale. After a conversation with Musa Khan, Said Ali confessed all the details of the murder, emphasizing that the night Domingo had come to stay with him, they had quarreled over money, and while she slept, he "quickly threw ... a long necktie" around her neck, pulled [it] tight and suffocated her to death." The next night, he had dragged her body to the pier and thrown it into the water. The next morning, he fled to Oxnard and eventually to Calexico. Khan explained that he had worked alone, and that Musa Khan had had no knowledge of the murder. His motivation was anger: "I killed her because she fooled me. She always wanted money, money, money and I have given her much."[82] With Khan's capture and publicity of his confession, the press intensified the racialization of the "crime of passion." The *Martinez Gazette* reported that the confession "required three hours for the clever young Mohammedan to give every detail of the story and it was a narrative that told of the philosophy of the east, his unholy love of the girl and his insatiable thirst for revenge when he found that he was a mere plaything in the hands of the wily young woman of whom he had become enamored."[83] His methods of murder and ability to evade the police were credited to his service as a member of the Hong Kong police force and eventually assistant warden of the Victoria jail. Just as surprising, he admitted to being a married man who supported his aging mother in India. The *Martinez Gazette* reporter characterized Khan as "remorseless," with surprisingly a "bright and cheerful disposition, joking with the other prisoners and jailers."[84]

The manhunt and confession had already played out in the local newspapers, so the developments at the trial two months later were of little surprise. The coverage set the scene and featured key arguments. At the trial, Said Ali Khan wore the same brown-and-white-striped suit that he had worn in the photograph taken with Rosa Domingo that had been broadcast statewide. Although other members of her family were likely present, the newspapers featured the anguish of her father, Manuel Domingo, who sat in the front row in the courtroom frequently sobbing and on one of two occasions arising and leaving the courtroom. Neither Charles Riley, who had ghostwritten letters for Said Ali Khan, nor Musa Khan was implicated as an accomplice.[85] District Attorney Taylor argued that Said Ali Khan had "killed Rosa Domingo because she took his money and refused to live with him," and that her murder had been "brutal, premeditated and remorseless."[86] The jury returned a verdict of first-degree murder, and Judge Lattice sentenced Said Ali Khan to life imprisonment in San Quentin.

When the jury returned the verdict, the *Martinez Daily Gazette* reported, "the Punjabi" was "calmly smoking a cigarette displaying no more emotion or concern than he had displayed during the progress of the trial." Before the jury rendered its verdict, Said Ali, "who speaks good English," said, "I loved the girl and I grew crazy in the head when she wanted all my money, I spent over $750 on her. I do not care what they do to me," though he feared death by hanging. The closing address to the jury by Assistant District Attorney Ormsby, the newspaper said, was a "masterful effort" in prosecuting the "crime of the century," emphasizing that the "fiendish act" had in the first place been "degrading the young girl"; the harm had already been done by interracial seduction and romance before his brutal "murdering of her in cold blood."[87]

Violence recoded interracial intimate social interactions with South Asian men as brutal, perilous, and irrational. The intimate publics populated by South Asian migrant workers were represented in the press as shot through with menace, sexual threat, and fatal ends. Fears of South Asian male predators and allegations of unwanted sexual contact justified white males' turban-stripping, beating, robbing, and physically driving them out of their homes, workplaces, and towns, harassment that was a variation on the threat of lynching. The coverage of the violent death of Rosa Domingo and her father's anguish also allowed authorities officially to "remember" her as white, when in life as the daughter of a Portuguese immigrant, she was part of a multiracial lower class of questionable racial composition, considered at best "off-white" socially and legally.[88] In her tragic death, she became more useful as a "white" woman undone by her weakness for a suave "Asiatic" man.

These episodes of violence emphasized the vulnerability not only of white women but of white males as well, and the violent consequences of interracial interaction. They also focused concerns about the necessity of upholding male honor. Narrating the circumstances and the results of the riots and driving-out campaigns followed a narrative arc where male honor was challenged, threatened, consolidated, and finally restored. The terms of sex and sexual partnership were emblematic of the threat to male honor, which was based on the negotiations between men over their possessions and dependents. The public display of intimate family life, the possession of wife and children, situated adult males' status among one another and informed the possibility of egalitarian relationships between men. The partnership of heterosexual marriage and the relationships between mother, father, and children were rendered as the elemental form of human association, the sole model of intergender relations, and the indivisible basis of all community. Yet despite the substantial institutional support for this, in actuality there existed a more complex array of sexual and social organization within society.

These interactions in equal parts stimulated fear but also fed the fascination with the exotic difference of South Asian masculinities. That fascination, exoticism, and dread may have circulated in a variety of different directions. There were persistent examples of interethnic attraction and desire in Edward Bowen's and the bartender's appraisal of South Asian men, in the desire of those men to interact and communicate with young men like Bowen, and in the kinds of comments and interest demonstrated between South Asian men and European immigrant and white American women. Rosa Domingo and Said Ali Khan's attraction, their tempestuous courtship, and occasional cohabitation were intelligible and cause for alarm retrospectively by neighbors, friends, Rosa's siblings, and local businessmen.

Who killed whom could be the vital difference. Comparing Bowen's murder of Darrah Singh with Khan's murder of Rosa Domingo seems improbable at first. In both sensational murders, the legal system maintained its authority as an arbiter of justice. In both instances, irrespective of race, the culprits were investigated, discovered, and brought to trial. Juries convicted and judges sentenced them. However, the trials illuminated a more capacious reality of the vibrant social dynamics of interracial relations in urban cultural environments and the widespread cultural and political anxiety about sexual immorality that attached to South Asian men in the wake of these murder trials.

The South Asians were characterized as appealing and attractive cosmopolitan men. In Vancouver, the prosecutors marshaled Darrah Singh's military service, courtly demeanor, his enviable physique, and his neat and tidy dress as counterpoint to the dishonorable behavior and conduct of Bowen. On the other hand, Bowen's defense and the press, which narrated the story, pursued implications that Singh was unable to control his passions and had grievously misinterpreted buying Bowen drinks and following him to his room as an invitation to physical intimacy. The homosocial communion of drinking together was built on trust that had boundaries and limits on physical contact. The key for Bowen's defense was interpreting the intentions of strategic forms of touch into the logic of sexual advance and the fear of forcible assault.

Male honor was more tangled in the murder trial of Said Ali Khan. Much to the astonishment of some of his friends, Khan had become adept in exercising the commercial qualities of courtship in U.S. society. He bought clothes and shoes and groomed himself in ways that fitted the image of the urban sporting man, and he expressed his masculine capacity through the variety of gifts, money, and promises in the commodified economy of gifting that had evolved. The value, size, and frequency of the gifts were a constant source of tension and fights, but also the avenue of reconciliation in their relationship. Rosa Domingo's conduct, revealed by his letters and eyewitness testimony, was depicted in local newspapers as that of an imprudent single woman whose loose sexual behavior and acquisitive materialism had landed her deep in a dangerous relationship. Rosa Domingo was also an independent woman who worked in the commercial culture and lived independently of her family, able to travel alone late at night and unconcerned about the image of her chastity. She freely and passionately expressed and pursued her romantic desires. She expected Khan, her father, and male friends to respect her judgment, wishes, and autonomy, until her death demonstrated the fatal consequences of female autonomy.

Khan's unbridled anger at his perceived humiliation by Rosa Domingo's acceptance of his gifts but refusal of his proposal for marriage outweighed any appreciation of her choices in relations and life. He interpreted her broad sexual latitude and social autonomy as license throughout their courtship and treated her as a person with whom he had to negotiate, persuade, and prove his ability and capacity to be an ardent paramour and a generous and attentive husband. Yet, in the end, her independence fueled the ferocity with which he flaunted any social curbs on his own behavior, from his reluctance to ask her father's permission to marry her to his own suppression of the fact of his concurrent marriage to a woman in India. Yet the consequences of Rosa Domingo's relationship with Said Ali Khan were not routed in the press, public eye, or courts through an appraisal of her conduct, but rather through an account of the brutality of her victimization, expressed most stingingly in the father's loss of his daughter, heard in his vengeful cry when he saw Said Ali Khan. The father's honor had been defied and denigrated, first in the absence of his approval of the romantic relationship with his daughter, but foremost in the brutal taking of her life and disposing of her body at the wharf.

Within the arenas of commercial leisure, interracial encounters thrived. These two murder cases detail the breakdown of rationality and self-control unleashed by passions and ending in murder. The defense of male honor, though providing an intelligible rationale, neither excuses nor fully explains the murders. The defense of white honor, which was used to justify white male vigilante protection of white women and children and the white vigilante violence of campaigns to drive out South Asian workers, curbed the autonomy of movement and association for all. The specter of dangerous foreign men required white male oversight. Their honor in defending white women and children became a communal and racial property that trumped actual property damage and physical violence. Beating, stripping, and destroying the possessions of South Asian men was understood as effectively securing the integrity of white families, their livelihood, and their community as against the liberty and security of nonwhite men, their landlords, and their employers. In vigilante violence, public harassment, and murder trials, journalists, attorneys and politicians refashioned white honor as a clarion call for white men in western North America to guard against the new racialized and sexualized threat of South Asian men.

## CHAPTER 2

# Policing Strangers and Borderlands

The majority of the male workers who circulated through the cities and towns of western Canada and the United States during the first two decades of the twentieth century did not migrate with their families. Neither, however, were they alone, isolated, alienated, or anonymous. Their presence challenged the ways in which people associated and public life was lived. In cities like Vancouver and Sacramento that were hinged by rail and roads to rural hinterlands where transient men worked temporarily on ranches and in orchards, lumber mills, and railroad construction, the mobility and sociability of male workers refashioned domestic arrangements, physical space, and commerce, bringing males from different places, cultures, and classes together in "spatial proximity" and "volatile contact." Encounters between men like Darrah Singh and Edward Bowen occurred in streets and alleys, inside and outside of saloons, theaters, pool halls, restaurants, and bars, and in navigating railroads, tramways, stage depots, and stables. In these spaces, male contact was energized by gestures, practices, and social possibilities. A flurry of feelings and social sensibilities swirled about the moments of contact.[1]

In transit zones with a concentration of mobile men, social subjects were created through recognition, interest, and desire. As an ever-changing assortment of men and boys moved through the city, their social behaviors flourished in ways that appeared anonymous in police and elite surveillance, but the frequency of encounters produced familiarity among the working men and boys. In these spaces of encounter, mobile men negotiated associations, created and recognized new ones, and explored and tested the boundaries of homosociality, masculinity, and public culture.[2]

In that sociability a stunning picture emerges of the character of daily life among men in western Canada and the United States. This rich texture of migrant sociability challenges conventional assumptions that men's public status depended on their possession of families. Who men were and how they related to each other was not stable or standardized. Men regarded and related to each other in plural, contingent, and situational ways. The public visibility and social life of migrant laborers challenged the exclusivity of normative male subjects and instead revealed the plurality of racial, class, and socially marginal masculinities that traversed daily life. The ensemble of plural masculinities shaped everyday encounters and negotiated respectability and morality that supported class, age, and race hierarchies. The social relations and erotic contacts revealed conflicting meanings of male prerogatives and of male honor. Unraveling the complexity of plural masculinities and their expressive and social terrain also underscored the overlapping, constantly mediated, and mutual constitution of social life, even as these male migrant worlds were considered to be underworlds or at best marginal to respectable society.[3]

Migrant men's social activities drew public attention when they erupted into fatal violence, property damage, and riots. Their daily social contact was often relegated to questions of maintaining public order and policing when addressed by official politics in Canadian and U.S. cities and towns. Social historians have creatively drawn from police and vice committee records at the turn of the century to understand the texture and meanings of that contact. Frequently, however, the categories and formal social codes developed out of police surveillance, as well as press and reformer surveillance, reinforce an impression of social disorder and a world outside of politics. Daily confrontations and evasive actions, as the historians Robin Kelley and Steven Hahn have noted, "coalesce outside organized politics into daily acts that have cumulative effect on power relations." The motivations for daily acts might be economic survival or expressions of pleasure, desire for companionship or loneliness, boredom or despair.[4] These subaltern counterpublics often give possibility to and express "dangerously and scandalously cultivated" intimacies arrayed in opposition to bourgeois social expectations and state regulation.[5] Even when migrant and transient men were excised out of equitable political and social status, they insistently participated in public life. Their insistent presence presented a rebuke to the promise of equality in democratic life and underscored a widening chasm between settlement and transience in securing public status in localities and nations.[6]

Together transient migrants forged relations of "stranger intimacy" that shaped more than random and quixotic rapport. Certainly migratory work and transportation crossroads produced environments of compulsory sociality, but it was the appetite for passionate engagement, the determination to smash alienation, and the desire for visceral solidarity that created both fleeting and enduring relationships. Stranger intimacy is an avenue for analyzing a "public world of belonging" in which the verbal and gestural cues, ethical codes, and cultural frames that transient men exchanged and elaborated generated a vibrant public culture for participating in and "witnessing intense and personal affect." As Michael Warner has eloquently argued, stranger intimacy created another model of "human closeness" that was distinct from family and institutional relationships that have the potential to recast the values and practices of association in making public life and a "counterpublic" that can bring democratic community into being. Intimacy among strangers points to how "strangerhood" is a crucial ingredient for public meeting. Even as conventional status may determine the basis of trust, civility, and conviviality for many, both participants and observers of migrant social worlds professed fluency in alternative habits and codes of erotic sociability. The widespread accessibility of these codes made this public world a counterpublic, which often defied and wrestled with public presumptions that contact and more significantly "affiliations" were tightly linked to kinship, marriage, religion, ethnicity, race, and economic interests as the pathways to "commonality." Rather, the practice of searching for commonality required myriad forms of communication and "constant imagining" to create community.[7]

Structural forces alone did not inevitably lead to alternative and homosocial encounters. Male migrants sought out and created appealing alternatives to and escapes from conventional and traditional domesticity and sociality. These experiments in social relations and intimacies were forged by challenges of migratory work and life. Through feeling and loving otherwise, migrant males' experimental intimacies were attempts to buffer the material challenges of survival and kept isolation, poverty, and death at bay.

## MIGRANTS AND ZONES OF TRANSIT

The potential of migrant sociability and stranger intimacy is visible in the rapid transnational movement in and through Vancouver at the turn of the century.

Arriving by way of the Burrad Inlet waterfront or the Canadian Northern and Canadian Pacific train depots, lumbermen and salmon-fleet workers headed to Vancouver's Gastown, to the east of the city's respectable shopping district, city hall, and courthouses. In Gastown, the streets were lined with saloons, hotels, lodging houses, provision shops, employment agencies, and cheap recreation facilities—movie houses, poolrooms, and shooting galleries. A few blocks south of Gastown were the gaming houses, opium dens, restaurants, and brothels of Chinatown, and further on, at the edge of False Creek, were the brothels of Shore Street. In Gastown and Chinatown, transient men found, "the saloon, the hotel, the street became home, the place where sociability occurred and information about employment was acquired."[8] Across North America, similar urban transit and transient districts developed into the Minneapolis "Gateway," San Francisco's South of Market, New York's Bowery, Chicago's North Clark Street, and Omaha's Skid Row.[9]

The transient male population shaped Vancouver's urban geography and public order, but gender proportions diverged dramatically between residents of Canadian, American, or British origin and European and Asian immigrants. Vancouver's population doubled in the 1890s, from 13,000 to 27,000 in 1901. Even in 1911, when the city's population tripled and surpassed 100,000, there were three males for every two females, and this imbalance was even greater among adults and among European and Asian immigrants generally. The population growth came from all quarters, but Canadian, U.S., and British-born residents of Vancouver made up the overwhelming majority of the population by 1911, topping off at 84 percent of the total population, compared to less than 50 percent of the population in 1891. Males constituted 53 percent of city residents born in Canada and the United States, and 63 percent of the British-born, but gender ratios were, however, sharply less equitable in Vancouver's Greek, Italian, Austro-Hungarian, and Chinese communities, which were from 73 to 97 percent male. Although these European and Asian immigrant communities constituted 14 percent of the total population, they formed the majority of the adult male workforce, indispensible to building, road and sewer construction, and the extraction and transportation of British Columbia's natural-resource wealth.[10]

The proliferation of single-family home neighborhoods south, east, and west of Gastown attracted working-class and middle-class families of British, Canadian, and American origin, who lived in newly constructed cottages and California-style bungalows, in fundamental contrast to the shacks,

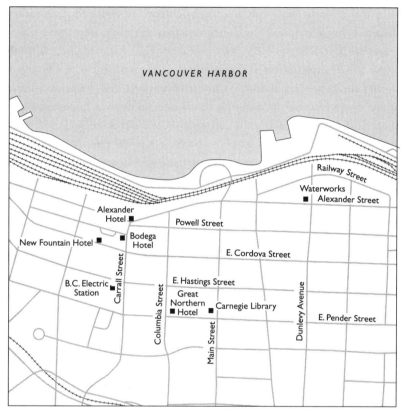

MAP 3. Central Vancouver Gastown and Chinatown

lodging houses, and cheap hotels concentrated in Gastown, Chinatown, and Vancouver's business core. Asians and non-British European men predominated in these districts and were separated spatially and socially from the homes of working-class and middle-class white families.[11] These geographic boundaries were reinforced by the behavior on the streets, the presence of transient men and female prostitutes who flouted sexual and moral propriety. Social and moral boundaries of acceptable and unacceptable behavior were established, as well as boundaries of public circulation for respectable women and men. The adjacent fashionable shopping districts, city hall, and courts on Gastown's western boundary were sharply policed, and the marking of Gastown and Chinatown by race, transience, and immorality served as a cultural and social barricade from respectable white family society.

In many North American cities, civic authorities tolerated prostitution, "despite periodic outbreaks of church-centered moralists" who urged that it be stamped out. Vancouver city government and the police had informally tolerated female prostitution in the locations where transient men converged. During the 1890s and 1900s, the nexus of brothels and street prostitutes shifted frequently from Gastown's southern boundary in Chinatown and Shore Street and then north of Gastown on Alexander Street and the Burrad Inlet waterfront. In 1913, pressure mounted from moral reformers and evangelical Christians for Vancouver police to cease tolerating segregated districts and actively close down brothels in the South Shore area and Chinatown. European women from France, Austria, and Germany, Chinese women, and black and white women from the United States were frequently arrested on charges of vagrancy, prostitution, and keeping a disorderly house. They were fined from $30 to $50 instead of serving thirty days in jail. The raids on brothels also claimed men, who were arrested and fined specifically for frequenting a disorderly or bawdy house or jailed for vagrancy and on drunk and disorderly charges more generally. The raids and arrests closed down brothels but also dispersed female prostitution to other parts of the city.[12]

Male migrant sociability stretched throughout these overlapping districts. Within blocks of Chinatown, Gastown, and Shore Street, the Canadian Great Northern Train Depot and the CPR freight yards drew adult men and male youth to loiter, meet, and converse. During the months of August and September 1910, undercover police detectives, informers, and casual workers paid close attention to encounters between white, black, and South Asian men. As the skies darkened in August 1910, a white laborer named Harry Pussey waited for a friend to arrive on the 10 P.M. train at the Canadian Northern Train Depot. His friend never arrived that night, but he began conversing with Sam Singh while he waited, and the two men developed a relationship over several weeks, meeting in the evenings near the train station.[13] On subsequent nights, they walked together in the evening, and Pussey tried unsuccessfully to lead Singh into the freight yard, on the advice of his confidant "Boots," "the coloured bootblack" at the station.[14] On Monday, August 31, 1910, Edward Brooks, another bootblack who shined shoes near the depot, caught a glance from Dahl Singh standing at an open door of a building in the alley and followed Singh's gestures to come to the doorway. Brooks entered the house and talked with Singh for fifteen to twenty minutes before turning back.[15] Four days later, on September 3, 1910, A. W. MacNeil, a private detective who

FIGURE 3. Sikh men crossing the street at the corner of Granville and West Hastings Streets in downtown Vancouver, 1908. Photo Philip Timms. Courtesy Vancouver Public Library, Special Collections. VPL 5236.

assisted Great Northern railroad watchmen, returned from the toilet behind the Carnegie Library at 10:30 P.M. Harri Singh greeted MacNeil, and they began to talk.[16]

These men were initially anonymous, but quickly became recognizable to one another in their frequent circulation and encounters in a geographically condensed environment. George Chauncey has critically analyzed the "supposed anonymity" of urban amusement and "vice" districts in Manhattan in the same period. Chauncey and other social historians have drawn upon police court records and vice committee reports to analyze the social and cultural terrain of male encounters. The purpose is to illuminate the ways in which "people manipulated the spatial and cultural complexity of the city to constitute" neighborhoods and community despite the interference of police and vice reformers.[17] Analysis of Vancouver police court dockets and prisoners' and attorney general's records provides a vivid picture of the cultural terrain on which men of different backgrounds communicated social and erotic interest. Glances, gestures, and movements conveyed interest and attention, curiosity and fascination, disinterest or disgust. Eye movements, hand gestures, and comportment while standing or walking provided a code shared by the men and apprehended by the police. The codes transmitted both recognition and misunderstanding. For instance, as Sam Singh approached Harry Pussey, he "rattled some change in his pocket" and followed Pussey, who glanced back frequently as he left the Depot and walked home. Pussey and Singh held each other's mutual interest, and Pussey did not appear distressed when Singh declared, "I just want to play" and invited Pussey to his shack. His affection for Pussey was underscored by a later declaration, "you are my dear."[18] Pussey interpreted Singh's expression of a desire to "play" with his memory of subsequent invitations in which Sam Singh had made cavalier displays of five- and two-dollar bills.[19] He responded to Singh's invitation to "play," which was interpreted by the prosecutor and defense attorneys as evidence of a coy but consenting male prostitute.

When the bootblack Edward Brooks described his conversation in the alley doorway and Dahl Singh's proposal to "use his private" for fifty cents, Brooks claimed that he "wouldn't stand for that," and he left the house. Brooks's apparent outrage was, however, belied by the fact that he lingered and continued conversing with Singh for an additional fifteen minutes after the offer was made. The prosecutor, a Mr. Kennedy, readily interpreted Singh's proposal to "use" Brooks as "he would a woman." The defense attorney, Russell, expressed astonishment that Brooks had lingered if he was truly offended and argued that the offer did not "amount to an attempt" to commit a crime against nature, adding that there was nothing criminal when a "man makes a suggestion, and the other man says he won't entertain it." Kennedy argued, however, that the proposal conspired against public order and the public good.[20]

How men communicated interest and manipulated space offers a window into understanding the ethics of association and sociality between strangers and anonymous men who, through recurring encounters, became familiar with each other. What behavior, claims, or offers are comprehended and expected, and which are a shocking surprise? The conversation between Edward Brooks and Dahl Singh over fifteen minutes meandered and ranged broadly over male banter and joking that regularly and crudely interspersed homoerotic joking, threats, and teasing about sexual service and rape of other men. Such joking is the staple of conversation in all-male environments such as military units, boarding schools, and jails. Drawing a fine line between teasing and proposition is difficult with an abundance of sexual communication and the interchangeability of women and men as either erotic interest or sexual abuse targets. In the police courts, the men remembered and testified, not to banter, but to unvarnished, direct demands. The result was that comments that might have been jokes, insults, or flirtation were amplified into serious proposals, worthy of criminal complaint and prosecution.

Police presence and the imperatives of policing to avoid public disorder were central to these encounters. In the 1910 incidents around the Great Northern Station, both Pussey and MacNeil, at strategic moments, enlisted the same plainclothes police detectives who circulated around the station to shadow subsequent encounters with the South Asian men.

The decision to enlist police assistance was entangled in a broad network of communication, surveillance, and participation among working men on the street, peddlers, merchants, private detectives, juvenile detention officers, and undercover police detectives. For instance, Harry Pussey's encounters with Sam Singh were observed by "Mush," a man identified as a police informer, who hung around the Depot. His regular communication with the police remade his status from vagrant to reliable informant. "Mush" introduced Pussey to Detectives Jewitt and O'Grady, who set up a sting operation and arranged for Pussey to follow Singh back to his shack on Monday night, September 5, 1910.[21]

Well before the arrest, arraignment, and court hearing, the detectives' trust of Mush and Pussey demonstrated that the police had already determined in advance who were the suspects and who were the innocent in seemingly reciprocal encounters. It also revealed how seemingly random encounters were staged by the surveillance of police detectives and informers, resulting in a surge of arrests that summer. In the preceding five years, Vancouver police had arrested five or fewer men in an entire year for male-victimed sexual crime. In 1910, that number more than tripled to fifteen arrests, with spikes in arrests for gross indecency and sodomy in August and September 1910. The following year, Vancouver police courts recorded only five arrests, before climbing back up in 1912. The spikes in arrests necessitated coordination between undercover police detectives, a network of informers, and willing testimony from propositioned men.[22]

Detectives Jewitt and O'Grady's suspicions were already aroused, and they participated in an impromptu sting initiated by a disappointed client, the private detective A. W. MacNeil, who at first accused Harri Singh of pimping and fraud. Harri Singh had provoked MacNeil's interest and fury when he had been misled by Singh's invitation to see "a girl," but found none available in the empty room in an alley building. MacNeil's heated fight with Singh led him to seek the assistance of Officers Jewitt and O'Grady that night. When MacNeil returned, he accosted Harri Singh in the alley again. This time he solicited an invitation to Singh's room in a shack off the alley building, prompting Singh to ask whether MacNeil would "like to have a good time." Even though he claimed later that he was baffled by Singh's "incomprehensible" elaboration, MacNeil not only expressed interest in Singh's ambiguous inquiry but offered his own proposition, "Do you want to fuck me?" MacNeil claimed that Singh nodded vigorously and affirmatively. For the private detective and the policemen he enlisted, Singh's presumed status as a vagrant enabled a seamless shift from pimping a female prostitute to the solicitation for male sodomy. When they retreated to Singh's shack, the presumptive threat of disorderly conduct broadened the police's purview of public surveillance. A light flashed inside the room, and Singh bolted the door and said, "No talking, no talking, men outside." MacNeil shoved Singh aside, however, and unbolted the door, and O'Grady and Jewitt barged in and arrested Singh for attempted sodomy.[23] MacNeil's, Mush's, and Pussey's roles as instruments of police surveillance and entrapment enabled them to avoid the fate of other adult men arrested and prosecuted for sexual crimes in similar circumstances, as when John McAllister, a night watchman, caught Frank Clark, a twenty-four-year-old auburn-haired, blue-eyed U.S.-born-logger, with a twenty-five-year-old black-haired Chinese cook called "Wong Chinaman" on May 31, 1906. Both men were convicted of sodomy and sentenced to three months' hard labor.[24]

In the wake of the arrests and the police surveillance, what remains striking is the observation of abundant contact between men across differences of race, language, age, and class and how alert they were to each other's movements, responsive to gestures and eager to converse, all of which signaled an interest in erotic association. This reinforces the writer Samuel Delany's observation that the vitality of queer public life and sexuality has thrived on the abundance of "contact" between widely dissimilar people, despite marginalization and policing, that reverberated in meetings in the highly mobile and transient districts of Gastown and Chinatown in Vancouver in the early twentieth century.[25] Delany's vision of democratic public life emphasizes the impromptu and random belonging that emerges in the proximity, communication, and contact of strangers. "Border intimacies" between "strangers and acquaintances" flooded migrant public spaces and produced uneasy sociability and vulnerability among men who "share their time, their meals, their room, their leisure, their grief, their knowledge, their confidences" within relationships that may yield intense relations outside of family, work, and "obligatory camaraderie."[26] City elites, prosecutors and police referred to men they arrested as isolated, without attachments, and "anti-social." However, these men insisted on promoting social encounters and enlisted diverse other men, demonstrating how socially enmeshed and dependent they were even in moments of discomfort, unease, and disputes.[27]

Public records in Vancouver of police and magistrate court files, British Columbia attorney general's records, court proceedings, dockets, and police arrest photo books create a multilayered optic to view the dynamics of a social milieu that was freighted with concerns about immoral and criminal behavior. Even when the proliferation of activity was puzzling to authorities, prosecutors sought to fine-tune the arrests that attracted police suspicion into criminal charges and prosecutions. Relatively few cases came before a full jury trial. Most arrests resulted in fines and limited jail terms administered by police courts. Chapter 4 will examine how laws that criminalized sexual relations between men developed and how rules of evidence and legal reasoning shaped how laws were applied. The narrative details in court hearings and statistical data compiled by the police could be interpreted as a public social world. We can turn and view the kaleidoscope in a particular light and witness dimensions of male transient social relations and how the social world they forged was crucial to the economy, government regulation, and urban culture.

## POLICING AND TARGETING TRANSIENT MEN

The late nineteenth and early twentieth centuries saw the rise of the municipal police force in North American cities, largely in order to protect the public from vice and social disorder. From 1906 to 1916, over 75 percent of all police arrests in Vancouver were for public drunkenness, drunk and disorderly conduct, and vagrancy. The overwhelming majority of the police arrests were concentrated in a sixteen-square-block region encompassing Gastown, Chinatown, and the downtown business district and targeted the stranger sociality of transient men. Disorderly conduct and vagrancy were particularly frequent, and suspects were detained on umbrella charges. Most were fined, served short jail terms, and were released. However, detained suspects could also be prosecuted for more precise and severe misdemeanors and felonies. Both "disorderly conduct" and vagrancy required the presence of the public. However, the former criminalized conduct as either disrupting activity of other members of the public or inciting other people to unlawful action, while the latter criminalized status.

Even as the population had grown, during the 1906 to 1916 period, the number of annual arrests for drunk and disorderly conduct averaged 1,000 annually, but it skyrocketed to from 3,000 to 4,000 annually in the 1911 to 1914 period, before dropping back to the 1,500 in 1915 and 1916, when the Great War draft and mobilization was under way. Monthly arrests for drunk and disorderly conduct began increasing sharply in the summer of 1910 and through to the fall 1914. Monthly arrest numbers began to average 300–400—some of which could be accounted for by police actions in public speech disturbances and soaring unemployment in 1913. Vagrancy remained relatively steady at a few hundred cases per year. Vagrancy arrest cycles for the entire period demonstrated a sharp jump in arrests in the winter months of November to February, when numbers could total more than one hundred a month, from a steady monthly rate of sixty or fewer from March to October. In the winter months, as transient men entered the city from lumber camps and fishing vessels, vagrancy arrests could often double the summer arrest numbers. Rates of conviction in magistrates' courts and fines for drunk and disorderly conduct consistently exceeded 90 percent, except in 1911 and after 1913, when they dipped to 80 percent. Vagrancy arrests led to jail time or fines 60 to 70 percent of the time.[28]

In the late nineteenth and early twentieth centuries, vagrancy laws became a general umbrella under which migrants and delinquents could be policed, disciplined, and criminalized. The demands of capitalist development created mobile populations, but politicians and moral reformers condemned the social dynamics of unsteady work and temporary housing that were generated in the wake of human mobility. A vagrant was a transient, lacking reliable work, home, or family. In Canada, vagrants were characterized as "lewd or dissolute persons" who were prone to habits of immorality—intoxication, prostitution, gambling, sodomy, or cross-dressing. In California, the shift from an explicit condemnation of prostitution to a broad policing of sex occurred when the vagrancy law was simplified in 1903 to criminalizing an "idle, lewd, or dissolute person."[29]

Police surveillance for potential vagrancy also produced scrutiny about the activities and movements of migrants and created the atmosphere to pursue suspicions of interracial social contact and potentially more specific felony charges. Vagrancy policing spatially mapped spaces of presumed safety and danger and recast social contact in terms of morality and immorality. General vagrancy policing, as in the Vancouver police raids, honed surveillance and specific arrests for running or participating in opium dens, gambling dens, and bawdy houses. At most, each month, there were a couple of arrests for sodomy, gross indecency, or indecent assault. Arrests for male-directed sex crimes were more likely than rape and seduction cases to lead to court trials and convictions. Police walking the streets on their neighborhood beats observed and regulated public activity. The periodic waves of arrests for bawdy houses, prostitution, gaming houses, and opium dens reflected, not so much a rise in immoral activity, as a periodic public and political "outburst of concern about moral issues" that reflected fears, insecurities, and moral crusades. As Eric Monkonnen has effectively argued, the sharply increased numbers of arrests for particular moral-order offenses are best described as "arrest waves" rather than crime waves.[30]

At night and in the early mornings, police in the Chinatown and Gastown districts paid attention to potential vagrants and drunk and disorderly suspects. At 2 A.M. on December 12, 1908, the undercover detectives N. McDonald and David Scott observed Nar Singh, a man they had "recognized" at night earlier in the week. Standing outside the Great Northern Hotel on Pender Street, Nar Singh accosted a drunken white man, and they then parted. McDonald crossed the street, approached Singh and engaged in conversation.[31] McDonald remembered that Nar Singh motioned with his hand and asked him, "You like to come with me?" Singh caught McDonald by the sleeve and "waded across a vacant lot" to an alley behind the Chinese Hospital and between False Creek and Pender Street lined with the Mainland Transfer Company's horse stables and workers' shacks. Singh brought McDonald into the stables and behind a wagon and then took off his coat and vest and put them on the back of the wagon.[32]

After a deliberately complicated journey, the pantomimed interaction between the two men behind the wagon suggested the negotiation of a range of sexual options. Singh moved to unbutton McDonald's clothes, but the latter brushed his hands away. Singh then took down his braces and pants and went down on his knees with his back to McDonald; he tried to reach back with his hands to catch hold of McDonald's pants. Sensing McDonald's inaction, Singh got off his hands and knees and turned around facing McDonald. Singh then held the fly of McDonald's pants and unbuttoned the top two buttons. When McDonald put his hand over Singh's hand, Singh motioned to his mouth. McDonald testified later that he rebuffed Singh's offers. With the pantomiming of oral sex and McDonald's ambivalence, both Singh and

McDonald appeared familiar with a highly developed lexicon of sexual roles, acts, and codes.

Officer Scott had waited at the corner of Pender and Columbia for about ten minutes, when he saw McDonald and Singh come out of the stables. They all met at the Chinese Hospital. Scott and McDonald exchanged places, and Scott followed Singh to his room at the rear of 112 Pender Street East. McDonald followed the two into a bunkroom with "five or six Hindus lying on beds," but turned outside and let Scott follow Singh in the room.[33] The shacks and sheds tucked into the alleys and among the stables and outhouses were typical substandard housing for many transient men. Men crammed together into rooms either divided into small cubicles covered with wire mesh or filled with bare wooden bunks, with thin pieces of canvas strung from posts and beams. These bunkhouses had outhouses, or shared bathrooms if there was indoor plumbing.[34]

Nar Singh did not register concern that Scott had replaced McDonald. The room was dark, the lamp had burned down, and Singh removed his boots and coat. When Singh approached Scott, he placed one hand on Scott's face and over his chin and his other on Scott's pants fly. Detective McDonald then swung the door open, Singh jumped up to the bunk, and the two detectives arrested Singh for attempted gross indecency.

Detective Scott stressed his judgment that Singh was sober and therefore fully conscious of his behavior. At the arrest Singh, "walked as straight as anybody and asked us to please let him go."[35] On February 8, 1909, Singh appeared before Police Magistrate A. Williams in the Vancouver Police Court on a charge of gross indecency. The immigration official W. C. Hopkinson was sworn in as the interpreter. Hopkinson had a knowledge of Hindi and Punjabi from service in the British colonial government in India and had developed a reputation for hostile surveillance of the Punjabi community in Vancouver and investigations on the U.S. Pacific Coast. The defense attorney, McTaggart, objected to Hopkinson's role as interpreter and requested two additional South Asian translators in order to ensure accurate translation.[36] The police magistrate committed Singh to trial, and on August 5, 1909, Singh was found guilty of gross indecency.[37]

Following British criminal codes, the Canadian federal criminal code defined gross indecency as a crime "in public or private" by "every male person" who "procures" or "importunes" any person for sexual conduct. Oral sex was never explicitly mentioned in the criminal code, but it was readily understood by the police, prosecutors, and judges. Although men guilty of the offense could receive a punishment of up to five years' imprisonment and "whipping," usually the term of imprisonment was substantially less.[38]

In 1916 and 1917, gross-indecency arrests snared laborers, cooks, unemployed men, and soldiers. When the race of the men involved was not white, arrest dockets noted that they were "Greek," "Chinese," or "Hindu." Some men were imprisoned for six months. One received a suspended sentence on a bond of $500, and another was committed to an asylum.[39] Several "Hindu laborers" were arrested in 1916 and 1917 for the offense. In September 1917, a South Asian man named Burdah and a Chinese man named Long Sung were convicted of gross indecency and imprisoned for six months. The year before, on March 9, 1916, two "Hindu laborers," Gunga Singh and Love Singh, were arrested for assault, and at their trial charged with gross indecency, on the testimony of R. A. McDonald, a twenty-seven-year-old army private in the 158th Battalion. In that case, the tangle of accusations and countercharges of violent robbery and sexual assault were, however, dismissed for insufficient evidence of sexual misconduct.[40]

## SUFFERING HONOR, YOUTH, AND THE TRANSIT FROM ADORATION TO VIOLENCE

Although most cases of sodomy, gross indecency, and indecent assault involved adult men, Vancouver city detectives, prosecutors, and onlookers paid particular attention to European immigrant and white Canadian youths, particularly boys who hawked newspapers. Middle-class reformers viewed them as a nexus of social perils and vulnerable to the dangers of the streets. Shopkeepers resented their presence and their activity. In order to survive and succeed, these male youths negotiated relationships and the use of space with the peddlers, saloon owners, shopkeepers, police, and clients.[41] As a number of literary scholars and cultural historians have noted, newsboys were also a nexus of adult male erotic interest and desire. They are lionized in Horatio Alger stories for their quick-witted, intrepid ability to navigate the dangers and opportunities of the streets and their pluck and ingenuity in selling their papers. Horatio Alger's own biography reveals a record of pederastic suspicion that shaped his personal life, and, as Michael Moon has argued persuasively, homoerotic intergenerational affection also shaped his fiction and the popularity of his tales on valorizing the market, mentorship, and masculinity.[42]

FIGURE 4. Street car, pedestrians, and newspaper boys on Carrall Street from south side of West Hastings, Vancouver, 1908. Photo Philip Timms. Courtesy Vancouver Public Library, Special Collections. VPL 6986.

Immediately after the outbreak of World War I, Vancouver police detectives diligently secured the assistance of teenage boys, particularly street-corner newspaper vendors, to coordinate efforts to entrap South Asian men in situations of solicited companionship and sex. Street-level communication between newspaper vendors and working men frequently found its way into police court hearings as solicitation of sexual conduct. In 1916, the interactions between adolescent newspaper vendors, their friends, police detectives, and South Asian men in Vancouver yielded complicated visions of affect, honor, and public worlds. A young Italian immigrant hawker of *The Province* and *The World* newspapers called Nicky Ferrar, or Nico Ferrari, met Jagat Singh and Kehar Singh over a couple of weeks. Jagat Singh invited the youth to his house to "make good friends," and another afternoon, Jagat offered him "good money" to come with him. On Friday evening, February 11, 1916, he encountered both Jagat and Kehar on Carrall and Hastings Streets. Over the next hour, the youth hawked papers and talked to various men and boys around a circuit of several blocks down Carrall Street, up Cordova, and down Columbia and up Alexander Streets. Jagat and Kehar trailed behind, occasionally engaging him in conversation. Outside the Vancouver Mission, Jagat Singh showed him fifty cents, and Kehar Singh showed him two dollars.[43]

At 8:45 P.M., Ferrar and his friends congregated at the tram stop, and a juvenile curfew officer named Capon, who knew Ferrar well, because he had been apprehended for curfew violations and petty theft and had served brief sentences in the Juvenile Detention Hall, admonished them to get to their homes before curfew. Electric streetcars fanned out to the suburban single-family-home districts to the east, west, and south of the city's downtown core. Vancouver remained small enough that wage earners could reach work in the heart of the city from the suburbs by foot and by streetcar within thirty minutes. Many of the newsboys lived in mixed working- and middle-class family neighborhoods east and south of downtown Vancouver.[44]

When Ferrar's friends and fellow newsboys took trams home at 9 P.M. that night, Capon suggested to Ferrar that he stay behind and seek out Jagat and Kehar Singh. Five minutes later, Ferrar found Kehar leading a drunk Jagat Singh to the "public toilet facing the Bijou Theater" and engaged them in conversation in the alley. He testified that the men had "demanded he drop his pants for the money." As they negotiated over money, Jagat Singh invited Ferrar to his room. Detectives Crewe and Imlah then arrested the men on the street.[45]

The public visibility of the tram stop and street allowed the encounters between the South Asian men and white youths to be witnessed broadly. The streets and alleys were mobile, unbounded "theaters" that dramatized social meetings and enhanced the expression of fascination, curiosity, and persuasion, as well as "conflict, repression and resistance." In the theater of public space, postures of aggression, respectability, pleasure and suffering combined to create the ensemble of plural masculinities in daily public life. The witnessing and participation in skirmishes explored the limits and possibilities of testing social and erotic boundaries in working male-centered public space. Officer Imlah claimed that a number of teamsters, engineers, and male bystanders had observed the "Hindus with the boy and passed remarks about it. People on the street noticed it."[46]

The massing and interactions of different travelers at the tram stops and in the train stations heightened the dramaturgical staging of public space. The encounters at tram stops, on the streets, and in the streetcars possessed the quality of both collective activity and witnessed isolated drama.[47] The intimacy, affect, or negotiation between males commanded the attention that might follow heterosexual courtship rituals of dating and the outdoor strolls of married couples in the respectable commercial district nearby. In Gastown and Chinatown, clumps of men walked together, conversed with each other, with vendors, and with newsboys, observed arguments, and participated in fistfights. Working-men's encounters were far more various and publicly visible than those of married men and their wives and children in respectable residential neighborhoods.

Public drunkenness became a key ingredient for police and white onlookers' suspicions about the motivation for the encounters between South Asian men such as Jagat and Kehar Singh and white newspaper boys like Nicky Ferrar. Later in the courtroom, defense attorneys and prosecutors questioned witnesses about the state of inebriation they had observed. For both the defense and prosecution, visible drunkenness dramatized an underlying assumption that the men faced the conflict of desire versus will, that alcohol consumption blurred a man's capacity to check his desire. Drunkenness frequently featured as an explanation of uninhibited action and loss of self-control. However, it continued to summon a notion of persistent homoerotic desire beneath the homosocial that was in sober moments effectively rerouted or suppressed. When prosecutors and witnesses denied that the men appeared drunk, they angled more to the consumption of alcohol as loosening self- and social control and promoting deviance and possibly perversion. In the testimony offered in the courts, the police, bystanders, and male youths fluently communicated a keen knowledge of social codes of working-class male encounters that heightened an interpretation of erotic interest that overwhelmed any other social interest in camaraderie or affection. These publicly accessible codes and judgment fostered both zealous policing and active participation in the social system.

Another encounter between male newspaper vendors and a South Asian man illustrates the complexity of how that intense and personal affect was observed and the tensions riven in the "public world." Early one evening in July 1916, a plainclothes police officer named Campbell intercepted two sixteen-year-old newspaper vendors, Paul Martin and Frankie Donaldson, who were talking to and followed by a drunken Jawalla Singh. Jawalla told Campbell that he loved "that boy, Paul Martin [pseud.]," and Campbell suggested that Singh "go ahead and buy him something."[48] Nicky Ferrar, who was throwing stones at a sign outside of the Bodega Bar, rounded the corner, discovered Paul and Frankie and the two adults, and joined them. The youths all followed

Singh into a Japanese grocery store on Powell Street, where he bought Paul a pound of cherries.

The interaction between working-class and immigrant men and male youths on the streets was not considered "intimate," but rather a satisfying of "needs" and "urges." Yet the declarations of friendship, care, and affect by transient and illiterate migrants, who left little other record of their desires and emotions, reveal an emotionally complex world. For instance, how does Jawalla's declaration of "love" translate? Was it erotic desire or a statement of abiding affection and care? Ideas of love have varied cultural and social meanings. How are we to understand what Jawalla Singh meant by his declaration and his gift if we look toward the cultural resources in Punjab? From the thirteenth to the nineteenth centuries, lyric poetry about adult male observation of the beauty of male youths circulated among literary elites and in oral recitation in marketplaces in Central Asia, Iran, and northern India.[49] Afsaneh Najmabadi and C. M. Naim have explored the poets' homoerotic fascination with and longing for male youth, the offers of gifts, and the metaphors of unrequited affection as strong elements in a public culture that metaphorized romantic friendship and erotic attachments between adult men and male youth as idealizations of beauty and longing and as publicly expressed pathways of both spiritual seeking and social and communitarian life.[50]

The expression of "love" in premodern Persian and Urdu poetry threatened and disrupted social conventions, since "to love was to assert one's individuality and reject any and all social defined identities." In poetic meanings, "love" is associated with physical illness, social malady, and social disapprobation irrespective of the object of sexual desire. In Urdu literature, love between two males did not receive "particular or exclusive social disapproval," since all expressions of love were socially disruptive and transgressive.[51] Yet the social purpose was emphasizing how the attraction created a "test of faith," and Sufi philosophy and Ghazal poetry emphasized how confronting desire and lust was necessary to train "the spiritual eye on God alone." Sufism rescripted codes of honor and heroic masculinity by embracing a new heroic endeavor through the spiritual conquest of the desiring self. The theme of the "crushed heart of the poet at the hands of the cruel and beautiful" young man or woman enhanced the "courage" and framed the suffering honor of the poet's public reputation. Ghazals expressed "suffering" as the "ultimate pedagogic experience" that combined tests of personal and social honor and paved the road to transcendence. These transcendent goals became eclipsed, however, by expressions of "public suffering" caused by thwarted and unrequited affection for boys or for women that "became an end" in itself.[52]

Jawalla Singh's public declaration of "love" for Paul Martin to another adult male, Campbell, expressed his adoration, longing, and unrequited affection. These meanings were socially reinforced by Campbell's supportive suggestion that Singh offer a gift to Martin. Drawing on a tradition that Jawalla Singh was familiar with, the public declaration of "love" followed a culturally specific aesthetic purpose, which he also could recognize as socially disruptive, transgressive, and a source of personal suffering. The public suffering occasioned by worship of a male youth and the latter's apparent indifference fed the adult's willingness to give gifts, protection, and aid.[53] Campbell's ability to respond to this pattern of affection, romantic pursuit, and gift giving depended on a familiarity with these social patterns expressed in North American hobo cultures and immigrant Greek and Italian cultures. The intergenerational expressions of middle-class adult men's "interest" in, affectionate desire for, and mentorship of male youths also appeared in nineteenth- and twentieth-century Anglo-American popular literature. Male youths were familiar with and fluent enough in these expressions to respond to and manipulate them, and also to express their own interest in and fascination with the adult men.[54] The offering of gifts, aid, and protection may have had a sexual and erotic purpose, but it may also have been a response to shared economic and social vulnerability and an interest in dependency to survive.

The Japanese women who ran the grocery store where Jawalla Singh bought the cherries directed him to the New Zealand Boarding House, where Jawalla rented a room and Paul Martin and Nicky Ferrar accompanied him up to it. Frankie Donaldson, who stayed behind on the street, directed Campbell to the boardinghouse when he returned with another police constable. There, Campbell climbed on the shoulders of a colleague to look over the open transom, a tactic typical of sodomy arrests, where the eyewitness report of a police officer—whether obtained by looking over a transom or through a keyhole—was the key to conviction. This characteristic voyeurism, with its plausible framing of anal intercourse, made sodomy a staged, witnessed, and profoundly public act.[55]

Singh's defense attorney accused Nicky Ferrar and Paul Martin of receiving payment from the police for entrapment, which they denied, but they both readily admitted that they had done what the police officer told them to do. The defense attorney raised suspicions about the teenagers' characters, and their complicity and interest in participating in police entrapment. Five months earlier, Nicky Ferrar had made a similar accusation against Jagat and Kehar Singh. Nicky's success and the money he reaped from the police were well known among the other boys on the street. Paul Martin had learned that Nicky and other teenagers had received $14 from the police detectives for their work in previous cases.[56] John Hawley had frequently been in juvenile court for truancy and loitering on the streets past curfew. These infractions had earned him short sentences at Mr. Collier's Juvenile Detention Home. Nicky Ferrar had frequently faced juvenile court hearings and had been sentenced six or seven times to Collier's for staying out late, loitering, and stealing. During the Jawalla Singh case, Ferrar was in police custody and accused of stealing $180. Ferrar's older brother had been in jail for burglary and other charges.[57]

In the magistrate's court, defense attorneys and even magistrates expressed concern about the frequency of street-level surveillance by plainclothes police detectives, coordination of male youths as police informers, and the pantomime of male prostitution in Vancouver. Paul Martin and Nicky Ferrar's frequent appearances in the juvenile justice system had made them acutely familiar with undercover police, truant officers, prosecutors, and judges. The two knew each other well, having met on the streets and during temporary stays in Collier's home for boys. They navigated relations with police and migrant males on the streets by negotiating out a complex strategy of enticement, solicitation, payment, threats, blackmail, and potentially prostitution. They were both vulnerable to street violence, had witnessed it, and had also participated in schemes to defraud men. They were put in positions beyond their own interests or control, but sidestepped their vulnerability to violence by pitting police officers and migrant men against each other. Both the policeman and the migrant men found them fascinating, alluring, and useful, and they attempted to extract compensation from both. Their savvy understanding of the lure they presented and their own physical vulnerability both to the police and to migrant men became recast by police, truant officers, and prosecutors as cautionary tales of how male youths become enrolled in a life of street hustling and prostitution.

Ferrar's and Martin's willingness to participate in a sting operation with undercover police detectives and extensive experience on the streets undercut their presentation of themselves as innocent victims. To allay suspicions of their own behavior and intent, the teenage boys had an important purpose in depicting their interactions with Singh as a radical shift from his dream-struck and romantic demeanor on the streets. Instead, they testified that Singh had been aggressive, demanding, and violent once they entered the rented room. Ferrar claimed that Singh had demanded that they take their clothes off and threatened to kill them if they did not assent to sex. Singh's pants were open and he could see "his privates," Martin declared.[58] The testimony emphasized the male youths' naïveté and passivity in contrast to Singh's allegedly unbridled aggression, and contrasted markedly with Singh's appearance of gentle affection on the street. The boys' testimony underscored their roles as unsuspecting "victims" of psychotic threats, not "accomplices" in the sexual crime. Judge Gregory was skeptical, however, of Ferrar's testimony and his repeated involvement in police entrapment in exchange for dropping theft charges. He handed Singh a suspended sentence and ordered him to report to the police regularly or forfeit a $500 bond.[59]

## SURVEILLANCE AND THE BORDERLANDS OF SACRAMENTO'S LOWER TOWN

Police surveillance of boardinghouses, brothels, pubs, and gambling houses in Sacramento, California, had increased sharply in 1918 under federal and public pressure to "clean up" the town in preparation for the construction of a military base. The ostensible concerns about the impact of female prostitution, venereal disease infection, and immoral gambling on male servicemen drew more police officers into the downtown district and intensified their scrutiny of the interactions of foreign migrants and male youths. In such an atmosphere of intensified moral policing, boardinghouses and an array of other sites became "semipublic" spaces.

Two police officers patrolling downtown Sacramento on Friday night, February 10, 1918, observed Stanley Kurnick, a "nineteen year old boy of Austrian descent," in the company of Jamil Singh, a forty-year-old "Hindu"; both were ranch hands who had found temporary work in the surrounding Sacramento and San Joaquin Valleys. Conversing on the street corner, Kurnick complained of hunger and living on the streets. Jamil gave him seventy-five cents for a meal, then later offered to share his room at the Colusa Rooming House. Later that night, the police followed a lead from a street informer to the boardinghouse. Officer Parker "looked through the keyhole and saw a boy

FIGURE 5. Men sitting on wooden sidewalk in San Francisco, 1910. Courtesy Bancroft Library, University of California, Berkeley. BANC PIC 1905. 02717.

lying face downward on the bed with his clothes partly off" and the "Hindu," also with his clothes partly off, lying on top of the boy, "going through the motions" of a man "having sexual intercourse." The officers broke open the door and arrested both men.[60] Officer Parker's characteristic voyeurism and improbable strategy of looking through the keyhole made the alleged anal intercourse a theatrically framed and public act. Sodomy was of such implicit public interest that at the trial neither the prosecution nor the defense attorneys compelled the police officers to explain their interest, justify their search without a warrant, or disclose their source of information. The protection of public morality was sufficient justification for police intervention in the "private" rooms of boardinghouses.

The precipitous slide to sexual immorality was swift in the suspicions of white onlookers and the police. The week of Jamil Singh's arrest, police surveillance also led to another arrest when Tara Singh befriended eighteen-year-old Hector McInnes, a Native American, originally from Truckee in the Sierra Nevada mountains, on a street in downtown Sacramento, giving McInnes fifty cents for a meal and to rent a room at a lodging house on L Street run by a Japanese, Koro Shigo. Tara followed McInnes and was assigned to an adjoining room. In the early morning hours, two police officers, Malone and Weisler, arrived at Shigo's boardinghouse to pursue anonymous leads "on the streets" that there "was a boy up there, with a Hindu." The officers found McInnes naked in bed alone and the doors between the adjoining rooms locked.[61] Under pressure from the police, McInnes later testified in court that Tara had come into his room at nine o'clock that night. McInnes, who had taken off his pants, but left his shirt on, and was ready to go to sleep, claimed that Tara had climbed into the bed, begun to "feel around" his body, and then lain on top of McInnes, attempting to penetrate him. Despite Tara Singh's denial that he had seen McInnes that night, he was arraigned for attempted sodomy.[62] Notwithstanding the circumstantial evidence of a South Asian man and a Native American youth being in adjoining rented rooms, Judge Henderson doubted the credibility of McInnes's statement and concluded that "the difficulty of these cases lies in the character of the boys who allow themselves to be used," making "their testimony not worthy of belief." Unlike the swift trial and sentencing of Jamil Singh, the prosecution of Tara Singh dragged on for months, and the case was ultimately dismissed in June 1918.[63]

In both of these cases, in the recording of testimony from arrest, arraignment hearing, trial, sentencing hearing, and appeals, the police, prosecutors, and judges transmitted their prejudices in revealing interpretations. The judges' decisions at the various levels of court proceedings were a conduit of circulating knowledge of the particular dangers of vagrant migrants and predictions of nefarious interracial sexual encounters between migrant males and youth. During a week of sodomy arrests, Judge Henderson, an uncommonly blunt police court judge, remarked that "Sodom and Gomorrah, Long Beach, California, and other places famous in history as being the scene where was practiced the fornicating of man by man must have spewed some of their descendants upon the city of Sacramento, in the form of several Hindus who have found their sexual gratification in the anus[es] of boys."[64] Judge Henderson's opinion was strongly influenced by the *Sacramento Bee*'s exposé of sex between men in Long Beach restrooms, parks, and homes that had led to more than fifty arrests in November 1914.[65] Henderson characterized Jamil Singh and Tara Singh as two of "the many Hindus that frequent the lower part of town, most of whom are Sodomites." Henderson was disturbed that McInnes had made himself a sort of "punk," or male prostitute, "for denizens of the lower end of town, of the Hindu race."[66] McInnes's Native American origins perhaps defined him more readily as a male street hustler. Unlike the

European immigrant Stanley Kurnick, McInnes did not receive prosecutorial defenses of his age or culpability.

Judge Henderson's vision of "Hindu Sodomites," delinquent European immigrant youths, and Native American "punks" translated the practices and identities of migrant men into an economy of male prostitution. His concerns focused on the spatial borderlands of semipublic spaces populated by nomadic subjects. Henderson's language reterritorialized Sacramento's "lower end of town" as a public site of sexual perversity that required police surveillance, incarceration of its "immoral inhabitants," and protection for the middle-class and respectable families who might unwittingly travel into this vice district. Lower town Sacramento provided cultures of leisure, entertainment, and rest for transitory migrants. Its restaurants, saloons, bars, brothels, boarding-houses, hotels, streets, and alleys provided services for migrant men looking for work between harvests and planting cycles in the adjacent hinterlands.

In the court record and the testimony, gestures of financial assistance and offers of sharing accommodations between migrant males were recoded in the courtroom prosecution as illicit transactions that were flagged by police and prosecution as vagrancy, sodomy, and male prostitution. Yet in the cracks of this testimony, we can also read a different story. Reinterpreting fragments from Jamil Singh's testimony at the sentencing hearing reveals an alternate rendering of intimacy and nomadic ethics in migrant social worlds. In the interstices of his responses, which were supposed to confirm his predisposition to criminality, Jamil Singh narrated a moral economy of duty that included sending regular remittances to support his wife, widowed mother, and son in India; an absence of "social opportunities" or "education" for advancement in India; avoidance of gambling and drugs, and infrequent use of liquor, though he acknowledged that he had been drunk on the night of the arrest. "I have always been industrious; I have always associated with Hindus," he declared.[67] He expressed incredulity that he was being convicted of a crime. Perhaps he believed that his reputation among his peers and performance of his duty shielded him from scrutiny. Perhaps he believed that his generosity in feeding and housing another worker was a reasonable exchange for physical intimacy. He may have believed that Kurnick had invited and agreed to physical intimacy, and that the police and courts were unreasonable in interfering. Maybe Singh could not fathom that his interactions with Kurnick were criminal. Did those actions that the authorities definitively labeled "unnatural sex" compute as "sexual" or "an assault" in the way that an attempt at physical intimacy with a female would certainly have done? Singh's incredulity may have been a desperate attempt to defend himself and to entreat the judge's mercy, but it also contains within its narration shards of alternative ways of expressing his own reputation for responsibility and generosity to his family, his people, and to the working strangers whom he encountered.

When Judge Glenn sentenced Jamil Singh to seven years in San Quentin State Prison, Singh interrupted and claimed that he had not received "justice." He denied committing any crime and accused Kurnick of trying to "rob him." Judge Glenn ignored the outburst, but in his decision stated: "In pronouncing this sentence, the Court desires to say that the defendant here is probably not any worse than the young man. I am inclined to think, notwithstanding his testimony, that he was equally guilty. Of course, he is a young man, eighteen years of age, and probably of low mentality; but nevertheless they are both equally guilty and in the Court's opinion, I think the crime was consummated."[68]

Where Jamil Singh may have seen a moral social universe, at the arraignment hearing of Tara Singh, Judge Henderson remarked that both cases were evidence of a "mass of deviants" that had descended into Sacramento and created a district of immorality where they could satisfy "immoral" and "degenerate" urges. Henderson complained to his colleagues of the general reputation of "Hindus" and their "extremely low moral condition" and disrespect for the law. He expressed outrage that District Attorney Farrell had been approached by South Asian men who insinuated that they would offer bribes to drop the two separate cases against Jamil Singh and Tara Singh. Henderson vociferously denied the presumption that Sacramento public officials were "venal" and could be bribed to allow the "cases to die," and he hailed Farrell's integrity in having "paid no attention to these advances" and treated their occurrence as a joke.[69] For Henderson, police, and prosecutors, the spatial concentration of male prostitution produced a sexual public for its surveillance and created boundaries of what social status and which actions the umbrella of privacy could protect. Irrespective of the efforts of migrant males to remove their intimate activities from public view, the very transience of migrant life cast all their activities outside the boundaries of domestic privacy. The norms of public morality offered valued public status and the shield of domestic privacy to married couples, but thwarted a similar pursuit of privacy for migrant males.[70]

## PUBLIC VISIBILITY AND REPUTATION

The churning of migrants through Vancouver and Seattle was directly related to the cycles of timber harvesting in locales spread like spiderwebs across the Pacific Northwest. In the nineteenth and early twentieth centuries, western North America was not only a site of convergence for global streams of workers but also drew massive capital investment from eastern Canada, the United States, and Europe. Capital investment to build the railroads, roads, and harbors necessary for agriculture and the extraction of natural resources produced the material contours of the social geography of migrants' lives and livelihoods. Railroads both brought workers and raw materials together and were sites of social contact. In the Pacific Northwest, men and boys found work in the instant towns that emerged along the main line and spurs of the Northern Pacific Railroad Line, which ran across the northern tier of the United States from Minneapolis–Saint Paul through North Dakota and Montana across the Cascade mountains and joined the line built in the late 1880s that hugged the coast of Puget Sound. The line ran from Blaine at the border with British Columbia, down through Bellingham, Seattle, Tacoma, and Lacey to Centralia and Portland, Oregon. In 1890, the Northern Pacific Railroad extended tracks south from Lacey to Centralia, and a train depot was built in Gate City, which became a thriving railroad center and mill town in the early twentieth century. Young European immigrant men eager for work in the lumberyards of Washington State came from Minnesota and Dakota towns in the early twentieth century.[71] Asian immigrants traveled up and down the railroads of the Pacific Northwest coast looking for work in sawmills and cordage factories. In 1912, South Asian workers who had worked in Portland, Seattle, and Vancouver found work at the Gate City Lumber Company.

The circuit from train depot to bunkhouse was the social terrain that brought Clarence Murray, whose family had migrated from rural Minnesota, and Jago and Bram Singh, who came from India, together in Gate, Washington. On a Sunday afternoon in March 1912, Clarence Murray and his cousins Ed Murray and John McGuire got off the 2:30 passenger train at the depot at Gate. Clarence, nearly eighteen years old, worked at the Gate City Lumber mill for a couple of weeks. Standing at the rail depot, Clarence recognized two co-workers, twenty-three-year-old Jago Singh and thirty-two-year-old Bram Singh, among a group of "Hindu" men standing near the tracks. The two men invited Clarence and his cousins to their rooms to smoke and drink.[72]

FIGURE 6. South Asian
immigrants at the Canadian
Pacific Railway Station, Frank,
Alberta, ca. 1903. Courtesy
Library and Archives Canada.
Credit M. T. Good / Mabel
Tinkiss Good Collection.
PA-125114.

Since Gate had a local prohibition ordinance in effect, the men's retreat from the train depot to the bunkhouse was necessary to find a semi-private space to drink. The workingmen in Gate lived in hotels that had been converted to bunkhouses on either side of the railroad tracks, on the outskirts of the township of Gate, about a mile from the center of town. The long narrow buildings were partitioned into small rooms, six feet by six feet, where two men often bunked together. In one of the hotels, one side of the building housed "Hindus" and the other side "white" men.[73] Although such rooms did not, of course, provide the privacy of a middle-class home, they served temporarily as domestic spaces and offered respite from the intrusive attention outdoors at the depot.

That Sunday afternoon, the South Asian and white men were in a revolving circuit of drinking, socializing, fighting, and reconciling, with different men coming in and out of the bunkhouse. Clarence Murray, his cousin Edward Murray and a friend, Clif Chamberlain, went into Bram's room on one side of the tracks. The white men were all from established families in Gate. The communal sharing of alcohol and the social encouragement of intoxication made the encounters between dissimilar males adhesive. The sharing of liquor enhanced social relations, freed submerged desires, and also made interactions between men fractious and violent. Their party broke up when a glass of whiskey broke and Bram chased Clarence out of the room, swearing that he had dropped the glass. Another of Clarence's cousins, Jack McGuire, came upon the fight outside the "Hindu Camp" at about 3 P.M. Bram Singh was threatening to "lick" Clarence but Jago Singh and Don Singh held him back. In anger, Bram Singh ran off and began picking up rocks on the railroad track and throwing them aimlessly. Jago Singh reassured Clarence of his friendship and invited Jack and the others to their rooms for another drink, saying, "the other fellow couldn't do anything to him." They drank a quart of whiskey over about half an hour; then Jack, Ed and Clif prepared to leave, but Clarence decided to stay behind with the South Asian men. At 4 P.M., Dwight Murray, Clarence's older brother, saw Clarence outside the "Hindu Camp" and spoke with him. "The boy will be all right with me; I am his friend," Jago Singh assured Dwight, and so Dwight left Clarence with them. Dwight remembered that Clarence was "pretty well intoxicated but not drunk."[74]

The men who gathered that afternoon over drinks and conversation saw themselves as social, convivial, passionate, liable to tease and fight, all in the process of "making friends." The intimacy between these strangers was enabled by the curiosity of working alongside one another and living nearby, allowing their social worlds to overlap. The men lived apart in "Hindu," Japanese, and white "camps" or bunkhouses by the depots, and the white single-family houses a half mile away from the tracks materially defined racial difference and spatial boundaries. The combination of liquor, desire, and violence would, however, rock the social gathering hours later.

In the court case that followed, the moral and ethical drama was between South Asian men. Rohmdlla and Aramo, two South Asian men who worked at the Gate City Lumber Company and boarded at the hotel, criticized Jago and Bram Singh's behavior that afternoon and alerted Clarence Murray's relatives to return to the hotel. Rohmdlla and Aramo observed a drunk Clarence Murray "crying" at about 4 or 5 P.M. Aramo claimed that Jago had pushed Clarence "by force," and that Bram had held his hand over Clarence's mouth to stifle any cries. At the court hearing, Aramo, intent to prove his morality and code of homosocial camaraderie, appealed to Bram Singh and Jago Singh "not to commit this crime . . . I say it make us too unpopular in this country."[75]

Three hours afterwards, both Aramo and Rohmdlla went to look for Dwight Murray after 8 P.M. in the evening. As Dwight followed the men to the bunkhouse, he met his cousins Ed Murray and Jack McGuire, who joined them in retrieving Clarence from the "Hindu camp." Each of Clarence's kin described discovering Clarence unconscious, partially undressed, and exhibiting telltale signs of sexual assault: "His pants were down, his shirt was pulled up, rolled up pretty nearly to the shoulder blades," and his clothes and body were "oily" and "all doped up with some kind of oil or grease" that seemed to "smell like Vaseline." In the same room, they found Don Singh laying on the bed asleep "with his pants open." While they were getting Clarence together to take him home, Bram Singh stormed in and allegedly yelled, "What the God Dam[n] business you fellows got in here. . . . Get to hell out of here and go home." They carried Clarence out, and he was vomiting on the way to the Company bunkhouse. Clarence remembered drinking with Jago and Bram, but he had lost consciousness and only could recall the trip back to the company bunkhouse at night.[76] In the trial, the defense attorney brought no witnesses, and the jury swiftly returned a verdict of guilty of sodomy against Jago, Bram, and Don Singh.

## REDEEMING REPUTATIONS

P. L. Verma, who had served as a translator for part of the trial, orchestrated a campaign for clemency for Don Singh. In addition to raising questions about court procedure and unreliable eyewitness accounts of Don Singh's presence at the scene of the assault, Verma offered the Parole Board an explanation of the sexuality and morality of "Hindoo" men. Verma attempted to reframe the prosecution of Don Singh, which relied upon guilt by association and proximity to the passed-out victim, to redeem Don's reputation. Verma characterized sodomy as a "great and unnatural sin among Hindoos" and it was unlikely that "a good Hindoo citizen is addicted of that habit." He quickly set aside the disturbing affronts to white masculinity by the revelations of South Asian men sexually penetrating a white male to focus on the status and behavior of the one married man in their company. Verma defined a "good Hindoo citizen" as a religious observant, married man. Marriage was a deterrent to the "addictive habit" of sodomy: "Don Sing[h] is married and married men do not like things like that, they are never addicted to such unnatural habits. They have to look far into the future. They are tied down by the weight of marriage."[77]

Verma presented exemplary "Hindoo" married men as possessing sexual self-restraint and monogamous morality, much like the images of respectable white American manhood. The practice of sodomy was coded as a habitual practice that could be addicting for the unmarried man whose unregulated behavior was ruled by irrational passion. Verma produced a moral code for married male migrants, for whom future responsibilities at home loomed large, that contained injunctions to avoid the entanglements, distractions, and costs of transitory sexual encounters. The imperative against sodomy was less about steadfast heterosexual preference than about the need for containment within and for marriage and the legitimate progeny that it would produce.

Verma skillfully marshaled compassion for Don Singh and his predicament and invoked a sympathetic hearing for Don's wife, including a letter from her to bolster the appeal for his parole, in which she wrote, "Life to me is not worth living, I have no body to support me."[78] The pitiful wife was an archetype; her letter was translated for the parole board, but she was never named except as Don Singh's wife, his dependent. However, the success of the appeal to pity and compassion necessitated that she appear to be a worthy and helpless dependent. Verma created a scene of what the historian Karen Halttunen has called "spectatorial sympathy," which produced a "tableau of pitiful suffering," with a helpless woman's body bearing the "burden of the sympathetic gaze."[79] According to scholars of nineteenth-century Anglo-American sentimentality, such a powerful scene could arouse a sympathetic response and "call to action."[80] In his letter, Verma emphasizes the wife's "miserable condition" and her "cries for help," because she is without means of male support and will become destitute. Don Singh's "misfortune . . . has fallen on her head. She will . . . starve to death unheeded, if no steps are taken for granting Don Singh his liberty." She feared that his case was "hopeless" and his imprisonment could last twenty years.[81] Her letter articulated both despair and powerlessness, inviting the assistance of the empowered, both Verma's advocacy, and the parole authorities' sympathetic judgment. As Amit Rai has noted, the "rule of sympathy" both marked and created "racial, gender and class inequalities" by emphasizing the pitiful status of the victim as it paradoxically "bridged" these inequalities through the compassionate subject's "identification" with misery, fear, and despair.[82]

Verma's campaign for Don Singh was enhanced by the sympathetic portrait of the pitiable wife as well as by the rehabilitation of Don's public reputation. Verma enlisted testimonials from Don's white employers and landlords in Portland, who praised him as an "honest, well-behaving gentleman" and a "trustworthy," "reliable and industrious" worker with a gentle, unassuming disposition.[83] Twenty men, who had signed their names in either Punjabi or English, endorsed a petition of the "Hindoos of Portland" for Don Singh, drafted by Verma. The petition characterized Don Singh as "always a law-abiding citizen," "from a good family," and possessing "temperate habits."[84]

These qualities of honesty, temperance, and industriousness were certainly values that the warden and parole board would uphold as evidence of Don Singh's character. However, the petition of his friends also revealed Sikh communitarian values that may for them have demonstrated a different vision of his humanitarianism. His friends considered Don Singh to be a devout man, who worshipped regularly and was considered a "missionary" for the charitable work he did. His generosity was legendary in his community in Portland, and he was known to help others financially in times of distress. The support of the community of South Asian laborers and Singh's employers in Portland created a credible portrait of a civic-minded and responsible immigrant in the United States and became crucial to Don Singh's appeal. The other two men who were convicted, Bram Singh and Jago Singh, had no such local support in Gate, Portland, or elsewhere.

The final and perhaps most crucial element in making Don Singh a subject for compassion was the assessment prison authorities made of his advocate, Verma. Certainly, Verma's English education and resourcefulness in soliciting and collecting testimonials, creating petitions, and meeting with the prison warden, Reed, made such an appeal strategically plausible. As Ann Stoler has argued, the interplay of compassionate and reasoned administration placed a high value on assessing "good character" by the observation of an individual's "comportment," "tastes," and "cultivating the right sentiments."[85] In addition to his formal dress and respectfully articulate communication, Verma demonstrated his sentiments of justice and equity. In the florid conclusion of his appeal, Verma invoked the ideals of "American Justice . . . Equality and Brotherhood" to win the intercession of the warden, whom he personally thanked for his "kind and philanthropic [sic] words that you love our nationality just as you love your own. Your words that Hindoos are treated by you as brothers still ring in my ears."[86] The rhetorical invocation of American justice and cross-national brotherhood to dislodge racial antipathy appears to have assured the warden of Verma's integrity and shared values. If Verma could be trusted, then perhaps the warden and parole board could identify with the plight of Don Singh and his wife.

The moral empathy generated by Don Singh's good character and the pitiful condition of his incredulous wife in India may have loosened the suspicions of the warden and parole board about the trial testimony. Their decision was not based on Don Singh's character or Verma's sentiments, however, but on other legal criteria that Verma presented that disputed Don Singh's purported role in the crime. The board reflected on the conspicuous absence of eyewitness testimony that placed Don Singh in the bunkhouse room when the two other South Asian men were explicitly identified. Don Singh's participation in the crime had been implied because police had discovered him sleeping in the same room in which the unconscious "white victim" was found. The sympathetic treatment that Don Singh received from the prison warden and the parole board did not disrupt the judicial certainty that Clarence Murray had been sodomized, nor did it temper the conviction of Jago Singh and Bram Singh. In 1913, the Prison Board determined that there was grave doubt that Don Singh had been present at the commission of the crime, and on October 14, Washington State Governor Ernest Lister commuted Don Singh's five-year sentence, of which he had served eighteen months.[87]

Verma had succeeded in winning Don Singh's parole by casting the abstract category of "Hindu marriage" as producing moral and respectable manhood and then offering the canvas of Don Singh's public character as exemplary. Verma analogized the Hindu married man as the serial copy of the white (Christian) married man. He characterized such an individual as steadfastly faithful, circumspect, and responsible: a "good family man." The sympathetic judgment for Don Singh also protected the reputation of South Asian married men generally. His status as a married man offered Don Singh an alibi of respectable sexuality and morality. The power of "sympathy and morality," as Amit Rai has shown, both created and targeted the "heterosexual family" for compassionate assistance. It distinguished him from the two unmarried men, whose convictions were not in doubt.[88] In rallying to support Don Singh, South Asian men in Portland distinguished reputable, moral men from disreputable men by ignoring the other two convicted men and disparaged the honesty of the South Asian eyewitnesses for falsely implicating Don Singh. Verma was able to present a unified reputation for Don Singh by emphasizing his personal commitment to his wife and his charity among his peers.[89]

Verma's successful campaign enabled Don Singh to recover the property of a public self—his reputation. Singh's reputation was tied with the responsibilities of his overseas marriage and its demands of moral rectitude. His reputation's rehabilitation enabled the review of his conviction and his freedom from imprisonment. The public status of a married man, however, was contingent and uncertain in Singh's experience as a migrant laborer whose wife lived in India. In his file at the Washington State Penitentiary, there is a 1930 FBI report that catalogues a litany of public drunkenness and disorderly conduct convictions in Washington, Oregon, and California during the 1910s and 1920s. The spellings of the name of the man are different, but the FBI has catalogued them all as the same Don Singh who received clemency for a sodomy conviction in 1913.

In analyzing the Newport, Rhode Island, naval scandal in 1919, the historians George Chauncey and Margot Canaday have demonstrated that it was a common tactical move in this period to shore up reputation status in order to shield one from suspicion of sexual interaction.[90] The efforts by Verma to defend Don Singh and reclaim his married man's honor from lurid allegations and circumstances did not blunt the broader suspicions of South Asian unmarried men, and in particular Jago Singh's and Bram Singh's convictions. The campaign for Don Singh's clemency dissented against the overwhelming representation of South Asian immorality, but its horizons were limited. It did not directly contest hierarchies and in fact reinforced the public status hierarchies of married men over unmarried migrants. For Don Singh, the ensemble of his marriage, his suffering wife, and testimonials as to his spiritual devotion, piety, and charitable service provided a shield against suspicions of improper behavior. Verma's intercession to rehabilitate the reputation of Don Singh placed "Hindu" married men alongside Christian American men by challenging blanket suspicions of the immoral "Hindu sodomite." However, it could not completely dislodge police aspersions of interracial association with probable immorality and perversion.

## REGULATING SPATIAL BORDERLANDS

In Vancouver, Sacramento, and Gate during the 1910s, the police, immigration authorities and bystanders observed and acted upon the interracial encounters in the spatial borderlands where transient male workers converged. The geographical spaces between the business district, transportation hubs, and respectable residential districts generated locations of unconventional meeting, communication, and relationships. As Gloria Anzaldúa recognized, these mandate strategies of social survival in the borderlands by "the squint-eyed, the perverse, the queer, the troublesome, the mongrel, the mulatto, the half breed, the half dead; in short those who cross over, pass over or go through the confines of the 'normal.'"[91] This process of traversing the boundaries and confines of the normal embraces the heterogeneity of borderland bodies and practices, which flourish in spaces that range far beyond sovereign national boundaries. The borderlands historian Emma Perez challenges the exclusions of racialized sexualities and the dominant historical narratives by encouraging the mining and reinterpreting of the borderlands legal archive for lost and silenced heterogeneities. By casting a queer and critical borderlands perspective on the state's records, Perez advocates reassembling alternative histories embedded in the legal archive.[92]

The documented testimony in police court records reveal the texture and spaces of inter-ethnic social life, ranging from casual conversations begun in streets and alleys to bars, tram stations, and railroad depots. Public encounters and visibility enabled the street politics of public life. Men swiftly moved socializing from the streets to rented rooms, bunkhouses, and workers' shacks. These spaces were the settings for casual, fortuitous, and dangerous encounters between men and boys of different ethnicities and ages.

Through these encounters between strangers, South Asian migrants forged intimate possibilities around plural masculinities to engage in public life. They negotiated and assessed honor, reputation, authority, and strength in developing relationships between men. However it was social practices that gave the relationships substance. Men engaged in practices of gift-giving, visiting, mentorship, and sharing interests. Their forms of exchange encompassed buying drinks and their visits to bunkhouses and rooms, sharing observations and opinions, and transacting business deals. However, the exchange of money between working males became flagged as illicit transactions of hustling and prostitution. The jostling and confrontation of plural masculinities generated expressions of affection, friendship, care, and camaraderie in tension with feelings of distrust, duplicity, hostility, manipulation, and force. Males on the ground judged the ethics, conscience, and intentions of their peers. Court cases were rife with mens' and boys' assessments of trust, injustice, improper sex, violence, and fraud, with claims of robbery, extortion, duplicity, and entrapment, as well as companionship and sexual advances welcomed or rebuffed.

The variety of social dependencies reinforced the fragility of male autonomy and the necessity of interdependence for survival.

Most of the arrests and trials analyzed in this chapter were "attempts" at sodomy or gross indecency that were flagged for prosecution through white male interpretations of the exchange of money and gifts, as well as gestures, requests, and demands. These few dozen court cases of improper sex involving South Asian men occurred across a decade at the same time in Vancouver and Sacramento. At any given point in time, some 2,000 to 3,000 South Asian men were living, working, or passing through Vancouver. Many of the most publicly prominent men of the community were cosmopolitan, courteous, dapper, and fluent in English. They were involved in business and participated in political debate. The vast majority were laborers who were trustworthy, employed men who rented rooms, bought meals and supplies, socialized at pubs, and formed real estate partnerships to invest in land and business in the surrounding region. Most of the court cases in Vancouver and Sacramento occurred in the 1910s, as the South Asian population in Vancouver and Sacramento began to decrease after the period of unencumbered immigration to Canada from 1904 to 1908, and to the United States from 1906 to 1913. In Vancouver, there were an average of ten sodomy and gross indecency arrests a year. Yet every year, thousands of native-born white, European immigrant, Chinese, and Japanese men were arrested, jailed, and fined for drunk and disorderly conduct, vagrancy, or frequenting gaming houses and brothels.

As rare as they were, court hearings in cases of alleged sodomy and gross indecency offer greater detail and texture of the world of everyday leisure and its myriad forms of familiarity and interracial contact that shaped both mutual exchange and violent conflict. Nestled among the cases of improper sexual contact were other mutual erotic relationships that did not achieve the notice and notoriety that accompanied the arrests. Deepening police and public suspicion of interracial male association suppressed and made illicit forms of social contact. It hastened pressure to make social and physical distance strategies of survival and hardened racial boundaries and age boundaries in circumscribing the mobility of contact. These homosocial spaces, in turn, came to be contested sites of state surveillance, intrusion, and exclusion to maintain proper "morality" and "manhood" and suppress illicit and threatening intimate ties across racial divides. The surveillance required that the prosecutors and judges interpret white male activities as either sexual masquerade or male prostitution, which, in turn, heightened public suspicion that the interactions between foreign men and white laboring men were disreputable. South Asian men, targets of police surveillance and entrapment, had little recourse to defend themselves against charges of sodomy and immorality, except to try to prove their individual moral rectitude and proper marriage in India, at best an uncertain legal and cultural argument. The politics of reputation are enmeshed in providing evidence of ethical and respectable manhood.

## CHAPTER 3

# Rural Dependency and Intimate Tensions

In the first decade of the twentieth century, South Asian migrants sought work opportunities in timber mills in the Pacific Northwest and farms and orchards in California. In the 1910s and 1920s, the majority of South Asians worked in farming. From the 1910s to 1930s, South Asian migrants concentrated in three California agricultural regions, the Sacramento Valley from Butte and Glenn Counties to Sacramento County, the San Joaquin Valley from San Joaquin County to Fresno and Tulare Counties, and the Imperial Valley on the border with Mexico. Like many of the Japanese, Chinese, Filipino, and Mexican migrants alongside whom they worked, South Asians faced tremendous obstacles in prospering in the cash-crop economy and climbing the agricultural ladder to become labor contractors, sharecroppers, or tenant farmers. Many migrants faced uneven and restricted access to distribution networks, capital markets, and the courts that governed property and contractual agreements. They were vulnerable to exploitation and the vagaries of both informal and legal labor, tenancy, and lending arrangements. Since farmers contracted with labor recruiters, migrant laborers often worked at unofficial wage rates outside of the contract between the employer/farmer and labor contractor.

Their survival as farm laborers, tenants, and farmers depended on the rich density of interethnic contact that knitted friendships into temporary or lasting relations across linguistic, cultural, and age differences. The structure of the agricultural economy encouraged border intimacies between "strangers and acquaintances" that spilled over into work, leisure, and domestic life. These border intimacies were situational ties forged by transient workers

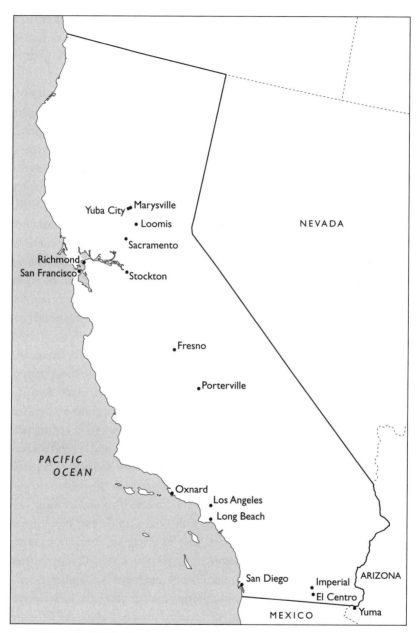

MAP 4. The state of California

and farmers to pool resources and labor and develop relationships of trust to ensure economic survival and social conviviality. Border intimacies thrived in labor-intensive, migrant-drawing, and capital-organizing small-scale tenancy and sharecropping agricultural production.

Success in harvests, wages, and profits depended not only on the vagaries of weather, markets, and infrastructure but also on the intricate and dependent human relations between migrant workers, labor contractors, sharecroppers, farm owners, food distributors, railroad companies, equipment dealers, and bankers. Agricultural production involved a range of explicit and implied contracts for work, labor recruitment and management, sharecropping, tenancy, improvement liens, and property ownership. These contracts in labor, profit sharing, and property were associations that were nourished and sustained by mutual trust and expressive male honor similar to the basis for consensual social, intimate, and erotic relations. Material survival relationships infused the social and erotic, just as affect and trust made contractual economic ties possible. These economic partnerships over labor and land tenancy reveal disputes over sexual intimacy that unravel the inner workings of agricultural production as well as the material features of border intimacies.

In the shadow of an American agrarian ideal of the independent farmer and his nuclear family, California's agricultural system in the early twentieth century fostered interdependent relationships. Sustaining an autonomous domestic household was not feasible for either most international migrants or domestic migrants whose livelihoods depended on agricultural labor. A variety of intimate dependencies and border intimacies were forged alongside and beyond the idealized domestic households of married couples and their children. The public status of the conventional family was counterpoised with the public status of the shifting ensemble of male migrant workers, foremen, labor contractors, and tenants and their strategies of domestic and social alliances that enabled survival. Prior to the 1930s, there were high male-to-female sex ratios and a greater predominance of non-family households in agricultural rural California from Sutter and Yuba to San Joaquin, Fresno, Tulare, and Imperial Counties.[1]

The shifting dynamic of economic power reversed prevailing racial hierarchies in employment and confounded social relationships. Like the Japanese, southern European, and Middle Eastern immigrants who prospered on American farms in the early twentieth century, South Asian contractors, tenant farmers, and landowners hired white American men, women, and children to labor in the fields.[2] Nearly a decade before the exodus during the Great Depression's Dust Bowl, itinerant white families migrated from Kansas, Missouri, and Oklahoma and other Great Plains and midwestern states looking for labor opportunities on California farms.[3] Migrants from across the Mediterranean from Spain, Italy, Balkans, Greece, Lebanon, Turkey, and Armenia converged on the rich farmlands of California, as did Native American, Chicano, and Mexican migrants.

In rural California, domestic and international migrants created social conventions and boundaries that governed cohabitation, social relations, and sexual intimacy. Interethnic relationships tested those social boundaries and also twisted racial and economic hierarchies that alternatively invested some mixed class and race relationships with mutual recognition and equal status and recast the status and hierarchy of others. The complexity of direct economic relationships of co-worker, contractor-worker, and landlord-tenant produced both familiarity and tensions. Workers' bunkhouses, temporary encampments, and ranch houses merged domestic space with work space, and that proximity and interconnectedness of work, both domestic and social, created the particular context of intimate and sexual relationships.[4]

The freedom of contract, based on trust and mutual agreement of all parties, necessitated that persons could freely choose their associates and would be neither obliged nor coerced. Judgments about the capacity to trust and to be trustworthy shaped property transactions, debt transactions, and labor contracts. The judgments were formed and tested in social arenas. And as much as classic economic theory highlights these relationships of trust as the cornerstone of independence, they surely illuminated webs of social and economic dependence. How men and women determined which new associates were trustworthy and how they could judge honorable behavior emerged through the vagaries and challenges of daily life.

However, the capacity to associate freely socially and economically was often constrained. The political climate frequently shoved out unprivileged persons by feeding social aspersions on the trustworthiness and ethics of particular groups of people. The partnerships, friendships, and cohabitations recast, reinforced, and even reversed prevailing economic and social hierarchies. The accusation of betrayed trust and of adult men forcing their will on females, male youths, and children disrupted the emergence of sporadic social tolerance for a variety of forms of social intimacy and domestic arrangements.[5]

Border intimacies thrived in the spatial overlaps, social mingling, conviviality, and cooperation demanded by small-scale agricultural production. Both observers and participants recognized and sometimes flagged social, cultural, and class distinctions, but only retrospectively after the revelation of abuse did these distinctions become barricades. Legislative enactment and enforcement of laws that purposefully aroused suspicion about all interracial associations and partnerships had the effect of narrowing and winnowing intraracial contacts and the promotion of exclusive racial cartels as necessary for security and survival. Both anti-competitive laws and hardened social customs placed both contracts and associations in the realm beyond legal protection and social probity. By the end of the 1920s, there was a tightening of legitimate social, erotic, and economic interactions and cooperation.

## PARTNERSHIP, SEDUCTION, AND FORGING ALLIANCES

In the early twentieth century, the North American West saw rapid capitalization and intense economic development. Speculative and state-subsidized investments in rail transportation, water, electricity, and communication infrastructure had created uneven economic opportunities, fostering both large-scale corporate agriculture and sharecropping. These investments in California, Arizona, Oregon, Washington, and British Columbia made the large-scale production of cotton, lettuce, fruits, and nuts for national and international markets viable and drew migrants from across the continent and the globe. Like other Asian migrant workers, South Asians worked on road, irrigation, and railroad construction as well. South Asian men had left the sawmills of the Pacific Northwest for the irrigated farms, orchards, and vineyards of California, Arizona, and New Mexico. South Asian migrants concentrated in fruit orchards and rice cultivation in California's Central and San Joaquin Valleys and cotton and lettuce production in the Imperial Valley of California, the Salt River Valley of Arizona, and the southern Rio Grande Valley of New Mexico in the first third of the twentieth century. Some South Asian men were able to work their way from seasonal labor to tenants and eventual owners of farmland, particularly in the San Joaquin and Imperial Valleys of California, the Salt River Valley of Arizona, and the southern Rio Grande Valley of New Mexico. By 1902, the extension of railroad lines from El Paso to Tucson, their connection to lines in California and the Midwest, and the expansion of refrigerator car service expanded the transportation and distribution options for the marketing of perishable fruits and vegetables and enhanced the productive uses of irrigated farmland in California, Arizona, New Mexico, and Texas.[6]

FIGURE 7. Men working in the fields, San Joaquin Valley, 1909. Courtesy Bancroft Library, University of California, Berkeley. BANC PIC 1905. 02718.

World War I fueled food demand, and grain and farm produce prices soared. During the boom in agricultural product prices in the 1910s, hundreds of South Asian migrants were able to climb the "agricultural ladder" and rise from transient laborer to sharecropping tenant, and eventually several hundred bought property in partnership. South Asian activists fighting for India's freedom from Britain were savvy to the success of South Asian farmers in the United States. In the 1917 issue of *Hindustan Ghadr*, a San Francisco–based Indian freedom publication, Ram Chandra advised "shrewd and courageous" South Asians in California to take to the ranches and provide the "grain and other provisions" necessary for the war effort worldwide. Chandra saw this as a time when South Asian cultivators could reap tremendous personal profit and aid in the effort for Indian independence by growing "produce industriously and intelligently," by demonstrating loyalty and service to the American nation, and by accumulation that would "come in usefully [sic] for attaining the freedom of India."[7] The revolutionary activists did not guide migrants to California agriculture; they did, however, hope to channel the success into support for the independence of India from Britain. Ram Chandra offered prescriptive advice that was actually descriptive of trends on the ground. A confluence of timing, favorable markets, basic English-language abilities and familiarity with legal contracts and banking were all factors that assisted some South Asian migrants to organize capital and become successful cultivators in the early twentieth century.[8]

The ability to organize capital demanded all kinds of associations and ties. Ethnic solidarity could neither explain the variety of interethnic relationships that made the rapid circulation of partnerships for agricultural cultivation possible nor account for the rapid cycling of success and failure. Partnerships involved several men, a combination of international and domestic migrants who were necessary to cobble together capital and labor resources for tenancy, sharecropping, and property-purchase agreements. These partnerships were constantly shifting, evolving, and renegotiated. Sharecropping, tenancy, and subtenancy arrangements flourished on verbal agreements and handshakes. Occasionally, these arrangements were formalized and registered in county courthouses. Formal contracts and informal agreements specified arrangements of bundling funds, dividing up responsibilities for labor recruitment, cultivation, and harvest. The purchase or lease of equipment, capital improvements, and property purchases necessitated informal credit from proximate peers, including successful tenant farmers and labor contractors, and formalized contractual loans from established farmers, equipment dealers, and banks. These relationships developed out of familiarity and reputation sustained in local environments. People who worked together found ways of expressing trust and placing their financial and social well-being in the hands of others, whom they might have known only for weeks or months. The process of developing trust about financial exchanges underscored a process of social intimacy. Inevitably, social encounters, erotic relationships, and marriages leavened these friendships and partnerships in the rapid circulation of new migrants and rapid boom-and-bust cycles of commercial agriculture in the previously marginally cultivated land tracts in the southwestern United States.

Beginning in 1916, a number of Punjabi farmers and tenants began to marry Mexican American women, and a few married white women. Mexican Americans were able to marry South Asian men, circumventing anti-miscegenation laws, because county clerks recognized similarities in complexion as indices of the "same race." In California, Arizona, and Texas alone, more than 250 documented marriages led to mixed-race families. These marriage alliances also secured farming property and business partnerships between Mexican American and white male kin and South Asian men.[9] Courtship and the encounter of potential spouses were mediated by the shape and structure of economic ties. Yet the focus on married couples underscored an expectation of permanence and settlement. Among the ties of legitimate marriage were many other economic and social ties that produced both durable and transitory relationships. Understanding the dynamics of affective sutures that sustained material partnerships is crucial to understanding the local political economy and the vitality of border intimacies in the early twentieth century.

An economic partnership and friendship between a white native of Independence, Kansas, S. H. Hays, and Bachin Singh, a Punjabi immigrant, at first intensified and then split apart over the courtship of Hays's seventeen-year-old daughter. In February 1917, Hays rented a wood-framed house for his wife and three daughters on cotton fields that Bachin Singh was cultivating along the highway between El Centro and Imperial. Bachin Singh had already had several profitable seasons leasing irrigated plots, and he offered Hays a third of a share of the harvest in return for Hays's coordination and hiring of laborers to harvest the crop. During a trip in June 1917 to consider extending their business partnership to lease a fifty-five-acre property west of Imperial, Singh expressed interest in courting Hays's seventeen-year-old daughter, Bunie. Hays demurred and told Bachin that his wife and he would not permit their daughter to "take any company" until she turned eighteen.

Hays was fiercely protective of his daughters' well-being, and he believed that he and Singh shared an understanding of the codes of male honor governing courtship, parental permission, and the protection of young women's reputations for chastity. Redirecting Singh's interest, he encouraged him to visit with his older daughter, Ruthie Palmer, who was estranged from her husband and visiting her family from her home in Kansas City. In early August, the first night Ruthie arrived, Bachin Singh visited the family and took Ruthie on a walk.[10] However, Bachin's interest in Bunie persisted, and he begged Hays and his wife to reconsider Bunie's age threshold for courtship. Although his wife was reluctant to make any "agreement" with Bachin about Bunie, Hays was impressed with the "awful nice" courteous man who respectfully requested the "privilege to come and see the girl," adding that few men acted as respectable suitors anymore.[11] Hays believed that they shared the same values and expectations of honorable male behavior and courtship rituals. In response to Hays's threat to kill any man "who runs over my girls," he received Singh's promise to "not mistreat the girl" or harm her reputation. He vociferously distinguished his conduct from that of other Punjabi men. Hays's memory of the conversation served as foreshadowing of his sense of betrayal by Bachin's conduct and telegraphed a prevailing reputation of dishonorable behavior of some South Asian men in the Imperial Valley.[12]

MAP 5. Imperial Valley, California, and its borders

During the summer months of July and August, Bunie Hays recognized Bachin Singh's interest in her while she worked with her sisters "chopping cotton." Bachin later told her that he "loved" her when she was "chopping cotton," but he was too "shy and scared to . . . come down in the field to talk." With her parents' permission, Bachin Singh began courting seventeen-year-old Bunie, with her older sister Ruthie as a chaperone, in late August. Bachin took Bunie out walking, "for fresh air to the hay pile," rode in Bachin's automobile twice or three times a week, taking trips to the nearby town of Imperial, and courted at night on the veranda. After several weeks, Bachin "fell out" with Ruthie, and he "gave all his time to Bunie" until early October.[13]

Bunie testified that Bachin Singh had promised every time he visited that he would marry her the following month. One night about midnight, after the rest of the family had gone to bed, Hays checked the irrigation flows, while Bunie and Bachin continued to visit on the veranda on the east side of the house. Testing his suspicions of their courtship, Hays snuck past the haystack and outhouse and crept onto the porch unnoticed. There Hays caught "them in a position that didn't suit" him. Hays was stunned to find Bunie leaning back in a chair with Bachin "between her legs . . . trying to do harm to the girl . . . . having intercourse with the girl."[14] When Bachin saw Hays climb the porch, he "jumped back" and sat in a chair across from Bunie. Bunie leaped up and ran into the house. Hays followed and berated her, "Is that the way we raised you to do?" He threatened to whip her and "she dropped her head and began to cry." When Hays got his gun and threatened to kill Bachin, his ailing wife deterred him from doing anything "to get into trouble." She advised her husband to prosecute him.[15] Bunie explained that she had been seduced by the promise of marriage and given in to Bachin's entreaties, having sexual intercourse with him several times on her parents' porch and in his automobile.[16]

Dishonoring Bunie's chastity and reputation betrayed Hays's trust and threatened the two men's friendship. Hays confronted Bachin Singh and accused him of "act[ing] like a rascal," to which Bachin responded, "We were only loving." Hays replied "that is a devil of a way to love . . . you promised me when I let you come to see the girl you wouldn't mistreat her." Bachin dared Hays to request a doctor examine "the girl," but then had second thoughts about his dare and promised to tell Hays the "truth" of their relationship if he didn't "prosecute" him and "hurt" Bunie. He assured Hays that his intentions continued to be to "marry the girl." Hays was relieved by Bachin's promise to marry Bunie and believed that his pledge "settle[d] it between" the two men.[17]

As Hays recounted this reconciliation, Singh expressed concern that Hays would feel "cold" toward him and declared that he felt ashamed of the way he had betrayed Hays's trust that he would conduct himself honorably with Bunie. Hays accepted the apology and declared that they should resume "treat[ing] you good as if you were a brother of mine." To underscore this feeling of brotherhood and integrating himself into the Hays family, Bachin promised that after their marriage, he would cease farming in Imperial and move back to Kansas with the family.[18] The sentimentality over brotherhood, however, became pitched toward Singh's family responsibilities in India. In the weeks that followed, Bachin revealed that his brother had sent several letters urging him to return to India. Hays responded, "If I had a brother that far away and hadn't seen him for as long as you have been away, I would want

to go home and I said I don't blame you for it." Bachin insisted that the timing of marriage plans with Bunie was contingent on the urgency of a return
visit to India.[19] Bachin became increasingly distant during the harvest season,
however, and visited Bunie infrequently. Both as an act of sentimental and
economic interest, Hays had gathered his own family from different parts of
the United States to pitch in with his share contract with Bachin. First his
older daughter and then, in September, his son and daughter-in-law arrived
from Duluth, Minnesota. His son became involved in Bunie's courtship by
hand-delivering letters from an increasingly anxious Bunie to Bachin Singh.[20]

In the fall, when the cotton harvest finished, Bachin and Hays renegotiated
another year of their share contract. With the U.S. entry into World War I,
farm prices and demand accelerated. The war and the commodity boom put
both Singh's departure plans for India and Hay's plans for Kansas on hold.
Marriage plans also receded. In a desperate attempt to force Bachin Singh to
honor his marriage pledge, on February 15, 1918, Bunie Hays filed suit against
Bachin Singh for seduction.[21] Seduction cases were a tool adapted to working-
class legal culture and could be mobilized to regulate a young woman's social
and sexual activity by her parents and redeem the reputation and welfare of
a pregnant woman through marriage to her male lover.[22] The seduction complaint had two elements: first, for having sexual intercourse under promise
of marriage, and, second, for damaging the status and body of a chaste, vir-
ginal woman, who was considered the property of her father.[23] The Imperial
Superior Court did not hear the case until May 1918. Dr. F. W. Peterson's testimony made the resolution of the case more urgent, however, when he disclosed that Bunie was nearly six months pregnant.[24] The revelation of her
pregnancy and her premarital sexual relationship with Bachin made Bunie
vulnerable to charges of indiscriminate promiscuity. Her attorney had to protect her reputation as faithful to one man and chaste except for her relationship with Bachin Singh under the false promise of marriage. Bachin Singh's
defense attorney insinuated that Bunie was incapable of accurately naming
the presumptive father, since she had had many sexual liaisons with laborers hired by her father who worked alongside her during the cotton harvest.
She categorically denied that she developed social familiarity with "Mexicans
and any Negroes" and said that she had not conversed with any of the other
"Hindu" field workers, who she disparagingly commented had " rags on their
heads," drawing a distinction about assimilation and class between these men
and the clean-shaven, turbanless Bachin Singh.[25]

Singh and Hays had intertwined financial commitments. The Hays family had been preparing to return to their former home in Independence, Kansas, but they were waiting for the harvested cotton to be sold and for the outcome of the seduction suit. Singh's defense attorney accused Hays of extortion, claiming that Hays had offered to settle the case out of court for $1,000, rather than forcing Singh to marry, which was the typical resolution of seduction suits. Hays was dissatisfied with his cotton-picking contract with Singh and claimed onerous challenges in hiring workers and maintaining a decent profit margin on the crop sublease agreement. These challenges led Hays to rely upon his daughters, son, and nephews, in addition to Mexican and black migrant male laborers. Hays expected that Singh would forgive his debt of $110 and share the proceeds from the cotton sale. The complexity of these financial ties and constraints did not, however, sway the jury as strongly as a $5 check to a local dry goods store that Bachin Singh had written as a gift for Bunie. The gift, along with the testimony of Bunie and her father, served as proof of their romantic relationship and disproved the defense's position that the Hays family had concocted the sexual accusation in order to renegotiate more favorable terms for the subcropping contract.[26] The border intimacies of the Singh and Hays entanglements were rife with economic negotiations and intensified by pleasure, anger, betrayal, and an insistence on reconciliation. Marriage was supposed to be the resolution of the seduction charge, yet as the court case proceeded, both sides nursed animosity because of the charges of blackmail and betrayal.

## BUNKHOUSE COHABITATION AND TROUBLED MASCULINITY

The subleasing and labor-contracting arrangements between Singh and Hays were typical of the intensive cultivation of rice, grapes, stone fruit, citrus, cotton, and lettuce, which demanded a flexible workforce. Ranch owners negotiated with labor contractors or with their tenants to prune, plant, or harvest. Labor contractors recruited individual local tenant farmers, workers, and networks of families and relatives to furnish workers for a specific job at a local orchard, farm, or ranch. Itinerant work gangs of men, boys, and families with children marketed their labor on a contract basis and pooled resources for rent, food, and travel expenses. On ranches, itinerant work gangs, individual laborers, and families often found temporary housing in bunkhouses, tents, barns, and freestanding houses.[27]

FIGURE 8. North Pacific
Lumber Company Sikh
sawmill workers pose for
the camera, ca. 1900s.
Photo Philip Timms.
Courtesy Vancouver Public
Library, Special Collections.
VPL 7641.

Work gangs formed based on a combination of kinship ties, shared village
and caste affiliations, and shared circumstances of travel and work. And the
constant "traveling, eating, sleeping, working and socializing together created
deep ties of friendship, trust, and respect" that rivaled the depth of biological
kinship relationships. As a measure of their endurance and significance, work-
gang friendships were recast with kin-like terms (brother, cousin, uncle, etc.)
affirming the intimacy of the relationship.[28]

Tightly knit work gangs often shared ethnic, regional, religious, and linguistic ties, but the recruitment and management of workers did not retain
an exclusive ethnic homogeneity. Chinese, Japanese, and South Asian labor
contractors managed Korean, Chinese, Filipino, Mexican, South Asian, and
Afghani workers. Just as often, contractors and foremen supervised work
teams of a range of ethnic and religious backgrounds. In the 1920s and 1930s,
the California Division of Immigration and Housing periodically inspected
labor camps for the safety and sanitary conditions of latrines, bunkhouses,

and kitchens and collected periodic information about the number, ethnicity, and gender of the residents. In most instances, South Asian camp operators and foremen recruited a wide range of Filipinos, Mexicans, Japanese, white Americans, Chinese, Russians, and Koreans, as well as Hindus and Afghans. Workers often shared housing, kitchens, and dining quarters, and families with children were often separated from male workers' bunkhouses.[29]

Joining the streams of international migrants and white and black migrants from the East and Midwest in the 1910s and 1920s, Native American men in the Sierras migrated for seasonal work in the Sacramento and San Joaquin Valleys and lived in towns and cities between jobs. In March 1924, John Willis, a twenty-three-year-old Native American, worked more than two months on the Tom Foon Ranch on Sherman Island and shared a community bunkhouse with "a number of Mohammedans, either Hindus or Afghans." The community bunkhouse could accommodate ten to twelve men in its primitive architecture. A four-foot-by-eight-foot wooden plank bed, divided into body-length "cleats," or partitions, ran along the walls. Each of the workers laid out his bedroll and blankets to make his individual bunk, though the shelf was broad enough to "permit of two men lying in the bunk, especially if lying sidewise." These conditions were typical of the temporary bunkhouses on ranches, farms, and orchards.[30] At the very beginning of March 1924, a new arrival, Aijmad Khan, came from the Imperial Valley and joined the other ranch hands in the bunkhouse. After of couple of rainy nights, Aijmad complained of leaks over his bunk and declared that he would move into John Willis's bunk. At three o'clock in the morning of March 4, Aijmad Khan moved into Willis's bunk. Sleeping on his side facing the wall, Willis alleged that in the middle of the night, Khan opened his underwear and attempted to "stuck [his penis] into" Willis's rectum.[31] With the assistance of the foreman, Willis filed a complaint in Georgiana Township two days later.

In the police court hearing, Willis expressed incredulity at Khan's behavior and stressed his dismay at the inversion of gender roles. Willis described pushing Khan out of the bunk and yelling, "'What do you think I am [?], [that] ladies stay in this place?'" Willis was bewildered by the gender inversion and outraged at being taken for a passive, sexually available object of Khan's lust. Willis's reaction indexed both horror at being misidentified as a woman and incredulity that any woman would likely be caught sleeping in a bunkhouse. The affront to Willis's masculinity was redoubled in Willis's declaration that Aijmad was "not a man to do this kind of business." Apparently,

Khan's conventionally masculine appearance and behavior confused Willis about Khan's desire and conduct and incited anxiety about his own masculine appearance and status. That night Willis beat Khan handily and threatened him with further punishment in the morning. Willis recalled that the other South Asian and Afghani men gathered around and shamed Aijmad Khan. Aijmad put his clothes on and ran out of the bunkhouse and did not return.

In his plea for the judge's empathy, Willis claimed that his courage to fight the humiliation of attempted sexual assault derived from his Christian faith, saying, "No body help[ed] me but God. That is the only one to help me." Justice Bunnell sympathized with Willis's appeal to transcendent justice and admired his intelligence, "clean-living" morality, and ability to communicate in English fluently, though "not perfectly." Justice Bunnell contrasted John Willis's honesty and his "clean cut, athletic build" with his characterization of Aijmad Khan as a forty-year-old "Hindu or Afghan" man "of degenerate appearance."[32] Bunnell disparaged the disappearance and cowardice of Willis's "Afghani and Hindu" co-workers who were reluctant to testify against a man of their own "nationality or his race." Sacramento Police located two of the men who shared the bunkhouse, Neby Bux and Abdullah, who testified that they had been awoken by the yelling and the fight; however, neither corroborated Willis's charge of sexual assault. Bunnell held Aijmad Khan for a $1,000 cash bail. In June 1924, the case was dismissed for inconclusive evidence.[33]

Temporary cohabitation in bunkhouses made workers vulnerable to domestic and sleeping arrangements outside of their own choice and familiarity. Their financial vulnerability made them reliant on strangers and new acquaintances for help, care, and congenial coexistence. These associations were frequently troubled by clashes in habits, behavior, and expectations. The tension between Khan and Willis erupted in the middle of the night and shattered the general equanimity of the bunkhouse and the workers who had gathered at the ranch over weeks and months. Especially in moments of distress, migrant workers relied on mutual respect and mutual defense if wronged. The rough justice of the bunkhouse that Willis described had shown unanimity in the anger at and shaming of Khan, but when Willis sought the intervention of the police and courts, the camaraderie collapsed into ethnic allegiance and protection of "one of their own" in the courtroom. Whatever solidarity existed between the other Afghan and Sikh workers and Willis surely fell apart when Willis enlisted the ranch foreman, district attorney, and police to hunt down

FIGURE 9. Punjabi man and
youth photographed at Carroll
Studio, Marysville, California.
Courtesy University of British
Columbia Library, Rare Books
and Special Collections. Jermeja
Singh Hundel Family Fonds,
BC1953–8.

and subpoena the men and compel them to testify against Khan in an adver-
sarial police interrogation and the courtroom.

From the perspective of the reluctant Afghan and Sikh witnesses, Willis
had repudiated the rough justice of the bunkhouse in favor of courthouse
justice. His efforts appeared perplexing to his comrades. After all, Willis had
thrashed and driven away Khan. The violent and public performance had made
Willis's masculine prowess and reputation even more secure. The bunkhouse
residents, by shaming and driving Khan out, had reinstated the boundaries
of acceptable behavior and affirmed Willis's honor over Khan's disreputable
actions. However, Willis's dissatisfaction with the punishment and his isolation as a Native American laborer drove him to involve his supervisor and the
police. In the process, his need for justice from the legal system made his bunkhouse comrades wary. They were suspicious of police power and feared that
they might be harassed or humiliated for a mistaken comment; the district

attorney's and judge's treatment of Neby Bux and Abdullah in the police court confirmed these suspicions.

Border intimacies were fragile. The shared trust of the bunkhouse was shattered for Willis by the assault and, as a consequence of his peers' judgment, lost for Khan on that rainy night. Whatever efforts the Sikh and Afghan men made to restore order in the bunkhouse by casting out the perpetrator of abuse, however, were considered by Willis and outsiders to be insufficient, further eroding the trust and respect necessary to make the interdependency in the bunkhouse viable.

Sustaining a system of justice within the confines of a bunkhouse was also a matter of survival. Workers' needs for remunerative work and the constant shifting of hours and locations by labor contractors also mitigated their interest in taking time to participate during precious work hours in the display of justice and punishment in the courthouse. For the transient agricultural workers, the courts and police could only circumscribe their opportunities. The agricultural production system had made labor contractors the linchpin for jobs and material survival.

## INTIMATE DEPENDENCIES, MALE HOUSEHOLDS, AND IMPROPER DOMESTICITIES

Border intimacies could be brokered differently as farmers, large and small, relied on labor contractors to directly hire, house, and supervise laborers. By delegating the supervision, payment, transportation, and housing of workers to the labor contractor, the employer bypassed both direct control and responsibility for workers.

Labor contractors emerged from the ranks of migrant work gangs of Chinese, Japanese, Filipino, Mexican, Portuguese, and South Asian workers. An ability to speak English and knowledge of local wage rates, potential employers, and work conditions created the conditions for taking a leadership role in a work gang. Contractors or "bosses" often negotiated contracts, bargained for wage rates, set hours and duties, and served as paymaster. Successful labor contractors would disassociate themselves from a particular work gang and hire short-term pick-up crews.

Labor contractors recruited and managed workers. These contractors negotiated labor need and wages directly with farmers and sharecroppers who needed workers for planting, pruning, and harvesting. Contractors were often experienced with the planting and harvesting cycles in regions, perhaps had begun their agricultural careers as migrant laborers but had skills in organizing and managing workers and communicating with farmers. They saved enough money to recruit, transport, and house workers and developed relationships with farm and orchard owners and sharecropping tenants. In California, these contractors were Chinese, Japanese, Portuguese, or Armenian, and in the 1910s and 1920s, in certain localities, South Asian men became labor contractors. The South Asian contractors often got their start in recruiting and managing other South Asian workers, but several became successful and recruited other Asian, Mexican, and white laborers.[34]

Two hundred and fifty miles south and west of the Sacramento Valley, in the foothills of the southern Sierra Nevada range, Hamit Khan, a forty-year-old contractor, organized work gangs to harvest and tend grapes and fruits trees around Strathmore in Tulare County. Khan had come to the United States in 1908, worked in Oxnard, and moved to the Strathmore district in Tulare County in 1921. Over the decades, he had accumulated enough capital and experience to be a highly successful labor contractor, one who uncharacteristically did not rely on ethnic ties to succeed. During the peak of the fruit-harvesting season in the mid-1920s, he boasted that he employed nearly eighty-five men, women and children, "all white persons."[35] Hamit Khan's survival as a labor contractor employing white American and European immigrant harvest workers in Tulare County is all the more remarkable given the animosity of white workers against South Asian competitors. In August 1921, twenty white workers harassed and "deported a Hindu Worker" from the Francis Ranch fifteen miles north of Visalia, the county seat of Tulare County. The night before, they had warned the owner to fire "Hindu grape pickers while white men [were] out of work." Francis complied and let go his "Hindu" workforce, but one man had the misfortune to arrive the following day ignorant of that news.[36]

In August 1925, Hamit Khan developed a relationship of cohabitation and bed sharing for nearly a year with one of his employees, Elzy Luna, a boy aged fourteen years and eight months when they began to live together. Luna's heritage was Basque, and his family had lived in the United States for a couple of generations. His father, John Luna, and his family had worked frequently during harvests for Khan, and John had permitted his son Elzy to work the harvest as a timekeeper and live with Khan for the better part of a year. The position paid $2.50 per day and room and board and continued during the school year.

Khan rented a four-room house near the harvest and housed four teenagers for a two-week period. With his parent's permission, Elzy moved in with Khan, and three other local youths, fourteen-year-old Lester Newell, his nine-year-old brother Ronald Newell, and sixteen-year-old Merlin Hunting, who was nicknamed "Half Dead" because of his somnolent behavior. Once school began in mid-September, the other boys returned home, but Elzy insisted that he would rather stay with Hamit Khan. Mr. Luna remembered granting his permission and telling Khan, "If Elzy like[s] you and you like Elzy, all right." During the school year, Elzy alone moved with Hamit Khan to a big brown house on a forty-acre ranch where Khan was raising and harvesting grapes under a share arrangement. Although Elzy's wages fluctuated with the agricultural cycle and school attendance at Strathmore Union High School, Khan continued to pay him well. Elzy had responsibility for keeping workers' timecards, tallying boxes of picked fruit, and writing Khan's checks, as well as working in the orchards. He lived with Khan until he quit working as a timekeeper in the first week of August 1926. During the eleven months of cohabitation, Elzy visited his family every Sunday and frequently stayed home overnight. His twin Elmsley occasionally came to visit Hamit and Elzy. Two months after Elzy moved out, Hamit Khan hired him to work at Crossroads Store, a grocery, and small restaurant that Khan had bought in Strathmore. Aware that Elzy "wanted a saxophone very bad," Hamit Khan offered him either $20 a month or a saxophone in exchange for working at his store after school.[37]

Shortly afterwards, in October 1926, the township's constable, Churchill, investigated the relationship between Luna and Khan. Churchill's investigation of Khan was triggered by an October 1 raid on the Porterville ranch of Arjan Singh, which resulted in his arrest for sodomy with a seventeen-year-old white youth, Alexander Quinn.[38] The raid on Arjan Singh's ranch brought to the surface rumors among high school students and youths who worked part-time during the harvest season. Pursuing a lead, Churchill interviewed Luna at the Crossroads Store and then demanded that Luna accompany him to Khan's home to search for a Vaseline jar and other evidence.

Bunking together and even bed sharing were not unusual for farm laborers, yet it is intriguing that the eleven-month companionship between a white teenager and an adult South Asian man did not arouse greater suspicion at the time on the part of the parents, neighbors, and their employers. A year before the investigation, his housemates had teased and educated Elzy about the sexual nature of his relationship. Although Elzy and Hamit lived together for eleven months, they lived alone for all but the first two weeks. The prosecution focused on those first two weeks and enlisted the testimony of his housemates.[39] The sleeping arrangements in the Fisher ranch house separated the five males into two beds in adjoining bedrooms. Although Hamit disputed that he shared a bed, both Lester and Elzy testified that they shared a bed with Hamit, who slept in the middle. Elzy described that on the first night, after "an hour and half . . . Hamit turned over my way, I was laying on my stomach, and he put his arm around my back and tried to pull me over my side. I didn't know what the act was to be, and finally I moved over there and he began playing with my penis." Then, Elzy testified, Hamit "must have put Vaseline . . . on the opening of my bowels, and I didn't know what this was at first, and afterwards he put his penis in the opening of the bowels . . . he remained till he seemed satisfied, and then he took it out." The sexual activity, Elzy claimed, "happened practically every night."[40] Lester claimed that he felt the bed shake at night and heard the opening of a jar, but did not see anything in the darkness.[41]

That first night Elzy did not resist, he claimed, because he did not know what "the act" was until he learned from Lester and Merlin the next morning. According to the court testimony, Lester and Merlin educated Elzy about the sexual nature of the act the very first morning that they all bunked together, but apparently none of the three found it alarming enough to bring it to the attention of their parents. Lester continued to share the same bed as Elzy and Hamit but did not have any physical encounter with Hamit. Lester, Merlin, and Ron continued to live and work with Hamit for two weeks. They apparently did not dissuade Elzy from working for, living with, and sharing a bed with Khan for an additional ten months.

Perhaps the lack of alarm could be credited to the fact that Elzy considered that the arrangement benefited him in materially substantive ways. When questioned by the prosecuting attorney, "Now Elzy why did you allow Hamit Khan to do these things to you?" Elzy responded that Hamit had "bribed" him with higher pay and the living and board arrangements, which included entertainment. Elzy testified to the novelty and appeal of going to "shows," eating meals in town, and driving Hamit's car—all of which he thought a "very good time."[42] The endurance and public status of the relationship was highly unusual on many levels. First, it was surprising that a teenager whose parents lived nearby spent nearly a year sharing a house with a labor contractor. Although Elzy regularly visited with his parents and his family throughout the year, his residence was with Hamit. Second, there was the fact that Hamit had given Elzy a great deal of responsibility over his business and relied upon his accounting skills and honesty to keep it profitable. Elzy's wages, in part, provided support for the rest of the family, as well as affording him a life outside the home. Third, Elzy and Hamit had a highly visible public presence in the cafes and theaters in the small towns of Porterville and Strathmore. Elzy maintained that he had lived and worked for Khan for eleven months because Khan was a persuasive man and "could talk nearly anybody into anything." Hamit Khan's public confidence and ease with Elzy, evident in the regular wages, responsibilities, and frequent public outings, appeared to assuage any serious suspicions of an inappropriate relationship between the two for fourteen months.

Despite this persuasiveness and garrulousness, Elzy maintained that Hamit Khan never spoke of their sex or their intimacy. For Elzy, the "bribes" were implied, but never explicit. He claimed that there was never any conversation around the bed-sharing and sexual relations; Khan "never said a single word" about the sexual act. Furthermore, there was never an explicit offer or condition regarding the exchange of restaurant meals and vaudeville shows in town for sex or for a promise of silence.[43] In Khan's testimony, however, Elzy's erotic interests and sexual practices were not a completely taboo subject. Heterosexual courtship and masturbation were an active topic in their everyday conversation. Khan recounted frequent occasions when Elzy had asked to borrow his car to "see my girl," or go to a party, but Khan demurred, insisting that Elzy get permission from his parents. When Hamit relented when Elzy asked to "take his sister out," he discovered that Elzy had lied and gone for a "joy ride" with his girlfriend, as he had originally planned.[44] In addition to the requests to use the car on dates with high school girls, Elzy's sexual behavior drew competing interest from the opposing attorneys. The defense tried to make a case that Elzy was sexually overindulgent, unrestrained, and obsessed with his own pleasure. Under questioning from his defense attorney, Hamit Khan testified that he had caught Elzy masturbating in the morning on seven or eight occasions. He expressed embarrassment in divulging details in public court, but he insisted that he frequently had to rouse Elzy out of bed in the morning by pulling the "blanket away from him," discovering that he was "playing with himself" and consequently running late for school. Hamit also insisted that he had caught Elzy "playing with his penis, at night . . . more than once." He said that the practice made Elzy indolent; he "thought that is not good for young boys," and he had warned Elzy that the behavior would make him "crazy pretty soon."[45] When Khan appealed the verdict, the California

Attorney General's office turned the accusation of Elzy Luna's habitual masturbation into an indictment of Khan's character: "The fact that a full grown normal man would stand by and permit a fourteen year old boy to indulge in such a pernicious practice is most improbable."[46] The prosecution used Khan's testimony about Luna's habits to insinuate that Khan was neither normal nor moral in permitting masturbation.

The prosecution emphasized that Elzy was "innocent" of sexual knowledge, and that Khan had manipulated and overpowered him. The testimony of Elzy's housemates shed further light on Elzy's consciousness and conduct. Elzy's "innocence" had been shattered after the first night, and Elzy himself characterized the relationship as "bribery." His physical intimacy with Hamit made possible the courtship that Elzy had planned of the high school girl. The logic of Elzy's claims held that he was "bribed," that his frequent passive sex with Hamit gained him access to restaurants, shows, and, most important, the car with which to pursue his own romantic and sexual liaisons.

The broad availability and the increasing affordability of automobiles, particularly Fords and Dodges, in the 1910s and 1920s democratized the ownership of mechanized mobility. Successful labor contractors and tenant farmers like Khan had accumulated enough capital and credit to take advantage of the proliferating installment loan programs offered by local dealerships and manufacturers. During the 1920s, installment credit led to a boom in automobile and farm equipment purchases in the rural agricultural United States.[47] Cars became increasingly significant in both economic and social life in rural America, revolutionizing courtship rituals and sexual trysts.[48]

This freedom to use the car became a source of tension and discord between Elzy and Hamit. Troubles in their relationship began to appear in late spring of 1926. On May 17, 1926, Elzy had driven Hamit's Dodge coupe and "wrecked" it in an accident with a white schoolgirl driving a Chevrolet. Hamit did not blame Elzy, though he recalled his magnanimousness on the stand: "I do feel like nothing against his dad—I don't feel like nothing against the boy, because he got to learn . . . I told Elzy, . . . you white boy, I said, I feel like always treat [you right]." He had not held Elzy or his father accountable for repairs to the Dodge coupe.[49] However, Khan was furious several weeks later, when his work gang was picking plums on the Terry Ranch, and Elzy drove away in his car without permission or explanation, leaving Khan and his pickers stranded at the ranch.[50] Elzy testified that they were often at cross-purposes with regards to the use of Khan's car: "Sometime I wanted to go to a party or something and he wanted to go to town on business and he wouldn't let me go, he would want to go hire men and I would want to go to a party or something like that, he would take the car and go."[51] Elzy's breezy explanation of their disputes reveals a telling intimacy and familiarity. Elzy believed that he had a claim on his employer's car. His understanding of their cohabitation and sexual relationship evidently seemed to him to make his role different from that of other employees. During the summer of 1926, the relationship between Elzy and Hamit deteriorated swiftly. After months of Hamit treating Elzy to dinners at restaurants and vaudeville shows, they had now become increasingly quarrelsome, and Hamit frequently publicly disparaged Elzy as a "bum" and not "worth a darn."

Elzy Luna's unusual intergenerational relationship with Hamit Khan during his high school years was exposed in the criminal prosecution. The court trial and confession of his relationship with Hamit Khan temporarily put Elzy out of synch with the path of normal manhood. However, retrospectively, it was an aberration. Hamit Khan was convicted and sentenced to seven years' imprisonment, and his appeal was turned down. In the immediate aftermath of the trial, the prosecutors had narrated an untypical high school student story of Elzy's naïveté and material desire, enabling Hamit Khan to commit serial sexual abuse and obtain Elzy's acquiescence with bribes of access to entertainment, car, and an income independent of his parents. Did the narrative of Khan's abuse invite social sympathy for Elzy or public humiliation when he returned to his parents' home and the trial aired public knowledge of his relationship to Khan? The complexities of his past social associations and erotic relationship may have persisted during the 1930s, when Elzy Luna played the saxophone in a "three-piece band throughout the southern San Joaquin Valley." He continued with a robust social and erotic life and only "settled down" more than a decade after the trial. In 1937, at twenty-five, Elzy Luna married twenty-year-old Virginia Carter. Together they raised two daughters and ran a small business, and he died at the age of ninety-two in 2003, a year after her death. During his mature adulthood, he exercised leadership in the very same community in which he had experienced a tempestuous adolescence and public exposure of sexual abuse, serving as a member of the local school board and president of the Strathmore Chamber of Commerce.[52]

Hamit Khan appealed his conviction, which the Appellate Court upheld. The impact of Khan's extended trial and appeal ran parallel to the swifter conviction of Arjan Singh, who pleaded guilty in the lower court. In another case, in 1918, Joella Singh, an illiterate farmer who had arrived in the United States in 1908, had been convicted in Visalia Superior Court of sodomizing a white male youth, Kenneth Baird, whom he had hired to work on his leased ranch in Exeter, twenty miles north of Porterville.[53] During the sentencing hearing, the judge characterized Singh as having "no accomplishments" and "indulging in sodomitical practices," and sentenced him to seven years in San Quentin. Six months earlier, he had been prosecuted on a similar charge under the alias of Joe Cabin in Porterville, but was allowed to plead guilty to simple assault and sentenced to five months in jail.[54]

In these cases on the edge of the southern Sierra Range, consent to an economic relationship between South Asian male employers and young white employees became recast as sexually abusive. The age of Elzy Luna, Kenneth Baird, and Alexander Quinn underscored their innocence and vulnerability. It also revealed how these South Asian defendants understood the exercise of male privilege. Unlike Arjan Singh and Joella Singh, who admitted to charges of attempted sex with male youths, Hamit Khan contested the accusation and presented himself as a generous employer concerned about the welfare and morals of the male youth placed in his charge by his parents. Khan argued that he had supported Elzy and provided him with opportunities, and that Elzy had abused that trust by his reckless use of his car. He insisted that Luna had produced a sexual accusation out of spite and denied that their relationship was sexual or abusive. Yet Khan had power over Luna's livelihood, living arrangements, and schedule. In his testimony in court, he sought to reverse the meaning of the economic power relationship by demonstrating that he could neither discipline nor control the youth. Khan framed his intimate relationship with Elzy as one of avuncular responsibility, which his parents and neighbors had also believed for the eleven months they lived together. Yet the shows, meals, car use, and saxophone purchase also corroborated the idea that Khan acted to satisfy Elzy's desires. The border intimacies of shared work, leisure, and domestic life illuminated the centrality of material exchange and abused trust in Khan and Luna's relationship.

## SEXUAL ACCUSATION AND PROPERTY CASCADE

Like Hamit Khan, Carter Singh had been successful in leasing land or operating share contracts with landowners and partners. By parlaying earlier successes in labor contracting and tenant farming into partnerships, Singh had come to own small plots of land in Tierra Buena on the edge of Yuba Township in Sutter County. He was among the several hundred farmers who were successful and able to establish some degree of permanence up and down the spine of California. His first land purchase in February 1913 was a ten-acre plot he acquired with another South Asian farmer, Mayo Singh. In 1916 he expanded his holdings with seven acres of property sold by his neighbors Charles and Sarah Wilbur.[55] On that property, he built a house, invested in grape cultivation, and in the fall of 1922 built an evaporator to dry trays of grapes into raisins.

The evaporator required substantial investment in capital, close supervision, and new training in work processes. As he had with land, cultivation, and equipment costs, Singh adeptly used small loans and business partnerships to capitalize his investment and reap the benefits of a lucrative new line of business, which he extended to grapes harvested by his neighbors. In the 1910s, simple techniques were promoted for home, farm, and large-scale food processing. The fruit was put on wire frames and carried through a drier that exposed it to hot air from a heater below. The cost of building the drying kiln, which was fifty feet long, twenty-two feet wide, and eight feet tall, was relatively modest.[56] Singh drew from the extensive land grant university and government advice to small farmers and their promotion of evaporators to process crops that would otherwise quickly deteriorate on long rail journeys east. To dry the grapes that fall, Singh had built his own evaporator, a small building with a furnace that would heat it to 150–165 degrees. Singh and his employee Vasquez would pile grapes onto trays, align several trays on carts, and then push the carts into the evaporator to dry and cure the grapes into raisins.[57] The evaporator ran day and night, and every couple of hours they would change trays, putting in trays of green grapes to replace trays of cured raisins. A neighbor and longtime resident of Sutter County, Charles Wilbur, visited Carter Singh's ranch nearly every day the evaporator was running from November to December 10. Wilbur came out of curiosity to learn about the evaporation process and its effectiveness in drying Thompson seedless grapes, which he also raised. He estimated that the "very intense" heat of the evaporator was 150 to 165 degrees.[58]

Manfred Watson and his family had crisscrossed the nation in search of general farm work and opportunity, traveling from Oregon back to Illinois and Missouri and then spending a short time in Modoc County, on the eastern slopes of the Cascade Range at the northern edge of California, before traveling down to Sutter County to look for work. Carter Singh had recruited a number of workers, Chinese, South Asian, Mexican, and white, to harvest his grapes and to prepare them for drying. When Singh approached Watson in Sutter City for help in fixing a wagon wheel on October 16, 1922, the Watson family were looking for work and a place to live. Singh offered Manfred work, and the Watson family moved into a tent on his ranch. At the time, the main house was occupied by "Hindus and Chinamen," laborers who were harvesting grapes on the land. After several weeks, Manfred, his wife, Aura, and their four children moved into the house, and Carter Singh slept in a shack on the side of the house.[59]

On Friday afternoon, December 13, 1922, Manfred Watson appeared before W. E. Tucker, the justice of the peace in Yuba Township and lodged a complaint against his employer Carter Singh for committing the "crime against nature" on his nine-year-old son Lloyd Watson on December 4, 1922. On January 3, 1923, Tucker held a preliminary examination of the charge and ordered bail set for $2,000.[60] J. E. Elbert of Marysville served as Singh's attorney, and District Attorney Arthur Coats prosecuted the case.

When he was not in school, Lloyd Lester, aged nine, one of a pair of twins, explored the ranch with Carter Singh and his father, often going out in the vineyards, helping feed the horses, and watching the activity around the noisy evaporator. Lloyd often went around to Singh's shack, which was attached to the main house, sometimes when Singh was cooking, and Singh often offered him food.[61] At the court hearing, Aura Watson, Lloyd's mother, testified about how she learned of Lloyd's condition and assault. She had not observed anything unusual on the day of the alleged assault. She habitually arose at 5 A.M., and at about half past five, she needed to "get the fire built and breakfast started." Lloyd got up before any of the other children arose and went out to the toilet. On Wednesday, December 6, Lloyd complained to his mother of diarrhea, "all the time of running off of the bowels, he couldn't hold passages." When Aura questioned him further that evening and asked, "Did you get hurt?" and Lloyd responded that some boys at school had kicked him. Then two days later, he "came home from school and looked awfully pale and crying and went to the toilet." Aura followed him and asked him what was the matter; Lloyd then cried and told his mother that "Carter Singh did this, that Carter Singh corn-holed him."[62]

Lloyd Watson testified that on the morning of December 4, 1922, at 6 A.M., he had been on his way to the outhouse when Carter Singh called him over to the evaporator, 100 yards away. Lloyd testified that Singh took him into the "evaporator room and began to take down my breeches." He started to pull away, but Singh held him face down on a bed in the evaporator. Lloyd claimed that Carter "put his thing in my corn-hole . . . . his prick in my backside."[63] Carter stayed in him for five or ten minutes, and then he buttoned up his breeches and ran away. Lloyd did not yell out at the time, and he claimed that it didn't hurt until two or three days later.

Lloyd's father and mother took him to the offices of Dr. Everett Edwin Gray, a physician in Marysville. The medical exam did not confirm a sexual assault and raised more questions about Lloyd's pain and discomfort and the story he had told his mother. Dr. Gray discovered no other "trouble" at the time aside from pinworms in the rectum, which, he explained in court, was a common intestinal condition for children and caused a lot of irritation around the rectum. He found no evidence of sexual assault, but when Aura Watson told him that the "man was diseased," he prescribed medicine for gonorrhea and acute conjunctivitis as a precaution against future infection, in addition to a rectal injection to treat the pinworms.[64]

The heat intensity of the evaporator became the focal point for the prosecution and the defense. The defense attorney, Elbert, attempted to develop a case that the assault was implausible and that Lloyd's father fostered "ill feeling" against Carter Singh and was intent on damaging him. Elbert brought F. A. Vasquez and his wife Catalina to the stand to testify that they lived with their children in the garage on Carter Singh's ranch, about twenty-five feet from the evaporator. Mr. Vasquez testified that on the mornings of the 4th to the 6th between the hours of 4 A.M. and 9 A.M., he was working at the evaporator, which had been running practically continuously for several weeks. Neither he nor his wife saw Lloyd Watson or any other child near the evaporator on those mornings. Vasquez said that the evaporator's heat level was so high that it would have been impossible to stay there for any more than a few fleeting minutes.[65]

Wilbur agreed that it was "extremely improbable for anyone to be in the evaporator for 10 minutes." When Carter Singh took the stand, he explained that he had built the evaporator in November and ran the furnace continuously from mid-November until about December 15. He was incredulous at the idea of putting a bed in the evaporator while it was running, saying, "No sir, you think a man wants to die[?]" and explaining that it "burns the raisins dry and . . . [it] burns a man dry too."[66] When questioned by the defense attorney as to whether Carter had ever taken Lloyd Watson into the evaporating plant, he was appalled, "My God, no." Carter insisted that he kept children away from the evaporator because of the dangerous heat. When asked if he had put "his penis in Lloyd Watson's behind," he replied emphatically, "My God, no."[67]

When Manfred Watson took the stand, Elbert prompted him to talk about wage disputes and threats he had made to Carter Singh. In the days before Watson filed the criminal complaint, Elbert alleged that Manfred and Carter had argued over back wages, Manfred insisting that he was owed $195 and Carter maintaining that it was only $22.50. In front of three South Asian laborers, Manfred threatened Carter, "I will fix you, and I will put you in jail if you don't pay me $195." Elbert further questioned Manfred about his attempts to directly "extort money" and peppered him with questions, challenging him to admit that he had offered to "drop the case" and leave California if Carter Singh paid him $10,000.[68] When Judge Mahon ruled that those accusations were inadmissible, Elbert chose not to bring to the stand more than a half-dozen South Asian and white men as eyewitnesses to Singh and Watson's disputes.[69] Elbert feared that South Asian men accusing a white man would have no credibility with an all-white-male jury, and his defense was predicated on Manfred Watson's desperate extortion of Carter Singh and use of his son's accusations to secure financial gain.

Lloyd Watson's testimony made it clear that he had experienced trauma, but the source was disputable. Was it from pinworms and diarrhea? Was it bullies tormenting him at school or sexual abuse at the hands of another youth or adult? If an adult, was his assailant Carter Singh or someone else? Could an assault plausibly have happened in the extreme temperatures of a running evaporator? Could it have been somewhere else on the ranch? What was the connection between the accusation of sexual assault and the financial dispute between his father and his employer? Nine-year-old Lloyd's ability to narrate what happened, after initial reticence, and to use explicit colloquial language such as "corn-hole" revealed an astonishing and disturbing awareness of male homosexual relations. When questioned by the defense attorney, Lloyd explained that he had learned the meaning of "corn-hole" from an older boy in Missouri at the age of three. He did not elaborate on what that "learning" entailed, but that story suggests at the very least teasing if not explicit emotional or physical trauma at a very young age. Lloyd denied being coached by his father to make the accusation, and the prosecutor focused on his mother and not his father as the parent who shepherded Lloyd through the investigation and trial.[70]

After the superior court jury convicted Carter Singh, he appealed the case to the California Supreme Court. In the meantime, his criminal trial unleashed a wave of civil suits and revealed the intricate economic ties in which white and South Asian farmers, supply companies, banks, individual mortgage holders, and lawyers in Sutter County were involved. The Shasta Lumber Company of Marysville had supplied Carter Singh lumber and materials to build the evaporating plant and placed a lien on his property for $423.53, expecting payment when he auctioned the raisins.[71] On the eve of Singh's preliminary criminal hearing on January 2, 1923, Shasta filed a civil suit and claimed 394 twenty-five-pound boxes of raisins held at C.B. Harter's warehouse. The court ordered Sheriff Manford to hold a public auction to recover the debt. At the auction, the raisin crates were sold to Shasta Lumber Company, which resold the inventory for a handsome profit and erased any potential losses from Singh's debt.[72] Carter's business partners scrambled to get back money owed to them. Former district attorney Lawrence Schillig, who had assisted Singh with filing property purchase agreements and invested in the farm operations, won a court order to recover $470.13 with interest. Kesen Singh, who had a written agreement for a loan made in September won a court order to recover $418.50 in addition to court costs and interest. Yet the court orders did not necessarily have priority in the eventual settlement of Singh's estate.[73]

The criminal case and the initial flurry of civil suits brought Josephine Conwell, who held the mortgage on his property, into the fray. Her attorney maneuvered the case so that she would be the first to be paid out in the settlement. Conwell was the widow of a general merchandise storekeeper and lived with her elderly mother in Tierra Buena.[74] Nearly a year after Singh's arrest, on November 10, 1923, Sheriff Manford held an auction of Singh's real property. Conwell was the highest bidder for the property at the auction, and she took the property at a distress sale price, paying $3,449.46 for seventeen acres of cultivated land, buildings, and equipment. Despite the court's ruling in favor of the creditors Lawrence Schillig and Kesen Singh, Conwell's claims took precedence, with the proceeds from the sale paying off $3,080.84 of the mortgage balance and $300 in attorney's fees to Conwell. So for an additional $400 on top of her mortgage loan, she secured the property for herself, paid her legal costs, and ensured that no other creditors would receive proceeds from the property auction. Even the valid claim of David Canning of the Rideout Bank, Marysville, who was due $813.50, remained unpaid. The judge had already invalidated the claims of most of Carter Singh's friends and neighbors, such as Charles Wilbur, John Mohammed, and another South Asian man, named Butta, who claimed to have lent Carter Singh $4,000 for his legal defense, in favor of the banks, companies and the holder of his mortgage.[75] Those who held legal documentation of debt, mortgages, and liens, hired highly respected attorneys, and mobilized additional cash to corner the court auctions, succeeded in paying off earlier investments and seizing the very property they had leveraged to more profit. Carter Singh had demonstrated creativity and resourcefulness in organizing capital, managing debt, and capitalizing production, but his investments and those of his peers were lost in court judgments and auction to the highly capitalized and protected white business and commercial investors.

### PERVERSE SOCIALITY AND ALIEN COMPOUNDED

The primacy of capitalist financiers and the precedence that mortgage and corporate creditors took over individuals already revealed the uneven terrain that vulnerable small working farmers faced. However, the legislature and courts sought to tilt inequity further and unequivocally in favor of a racial cartel and use the courts to justify the leeching of capital from nonwhite working farmers. Carter Singh lost his property in civil proceedings on the eve of the enforcement of the California Alien Land Law on South Asians after the U.S. Supreme Court repudiated the white racial qualification for naturalized citizenship for South Asian men. Irrespective of their actual citizenship status, all immigrant South Asians in the United States became "aliens ineligible for naturalized citizenship."

Hamit Khan's continued success as a labor contractor and tenant farmer in the mid-1920s was all the more remarkable, since at the time, California district attorneys were enforcing the stringent provisions of the Alien Land Law and scrutinizing the land contracts of South Asian and Japanese tenant farmers and squeezing them off the land. Immediately after the 1923 Supreme Court decision rescinding naturalized citizenship for South Asians, federal prosecutors and California district attorneys coordinated efforts to denaturalize South Asian men and also to remove land that they had acquired in contradiction to the Alien Land Law.[76] Prosecutors and judges in California, following the lead of the U.S. Supreme Court, expanded the racial reach of the category of "alien ineligible for citizenship" and mobilized the racial marker that excluded Asians from full participation in the land market and contractual protections afforded to "free white persons."[77] With access to national citizenship restricted on the basis of "race," the Alien Land Law gave a racially defined economic cartel a monopoly on purchasing and leasing agricultural land and participating in land leasing and sharecropping partnerships. In Western agricultural development, the ability to use, lease, mortgage, and draw equity off of land was central to the ability to organize capital. By sharply circumscribing participation in the capitalizing land economy, whites enforced a racial cartel and sharply policed the border intimacies between business partners, tenants, and landowners that had led to prosperity for some Asian farmers.

In 1924, district attorneys in Fresno, Los Angeles, and Imperial Counties began to prosecute South Asian and Japanese farmers who had contracted to share in the profits of the harvest. In Fresno County, District Attorney Ernest Clark announced to the public that "Japanese and Hindus can be employed on ranches, but the wage must be reasonable, neither exceptionally large nor exceptionally small; bonus contracts in which the alien gets a small wage and then draws a bonus at the end of the year are barred; ineligible aliens can have no interest in the soil whatsoever, except in their capacity as laborers working for a reasonable wage." The D.A.'s "ultimatum" was expected to immediately remove Japanese and South Asians from their dominant position in vegetable truck farming.[78] The legislature and the state attorneys were defending a strategy to turn all Asians into wage laborers and undermine their ability to accumulate and organize capital in the agricultural business.[79] Hundreds of South Asians farmers were anxious to renew leases, fearful that the government would invalidate even their sharecropping arrangements; many wrote to the British consul for guidance and assistance. Leases in the Thousand Isles region of the Sacramento Valley for vegetable and corn farms and more than 60,000 acres of leased land in Imperial County for cotton cultivation were relinquished. Some farmers migrated to Arizona, New Mexico, and Texas.

In the 1920s, several southwestern states, as well as midwestern and southern states, passed alien land legislation modeled on California's or held electoral referendums that justified the use of state powers to wrest property ownership and transaction rights from Asians. In some states and localities, these laws were less rigidly enforced, but periodically police and local and state attorney generals placed Asian land claims under intensive scrutiny and threatened tenancy and land possession arrangements.

Violent enforcement of Arizona's Alien Land Law in 1934 and 1935 in the Salt River Valley in rural Maricopa County drew national and international attention. Several hundred Japanese and several dozen South Asian farmers had continued to farm successfully in the Salt River Valley for more than a decade after the passage of the Alien Land Law. However, in 1933, the Arizona Legislature amended the Alien Land Law to define attempts to transfer property to "aliens ineligible to citizenship" as conspiracy, with penalties of up to two years' imprisonment and $5,000 in fines.[80] The legislative campaign to criminalize land transfers between noncitizen parents and children or between citizen and noncitizen business partners galvanized militant white protesters to harass farmers who they believed were circumventing the Arizona Alien Land Law. The accusations ignited a firestorm of white political violence and demonstrations to oust Asian farmers from the valley. Japanese and South Asian farmers were subjected to anonymous threats, vicious property damage, and other illegal violence, and legal machinery was mobilized by the district attorney's prosecution of Asian farmers and their non-Asian partners and associates. The Japanese and South Asian farmers sought aid from the Japanese and British consuls. Nationwide news coverage and diplomatic protests forced the federal government to intervene and quell the violence. Although South Asian farmers and their attorneys repeatedly called attention to the vigilante activities, sheriffs and district attorneys prosecuted Asian farmers and white partners for conspiracy to evade the Alien Land Law and feigned inability to curtail anonymous and "random" attacks on persons and property. British officials, skittish of public controversy, protested privately and reluctantly in defense of their British Indian subjects, in contrast to the public and frequent protests lodged by Japanese diplomats on behalf of the much larger number of Japanese farmers under duress.[81]

The Alien Land Law was a legal tool to squelch economic competition. The British consul in Los Angeles investigating the Salt River Valley disturbances argued that the root cause of the white agitation was intense competition among Salt River Valley producers of lettuce shipped in refrigerated trains for sale in winter markets in the Midwest. The economic contest pitted a few "big American growers" who held two-thirds of the land against a large number of "small independent growers" who through partnerships, lease, and sharecropping arrangements included "150 Japanese families and 26 British Indian families." The British consul pointed to the nefarious designs of the large corporate "American" growers, who found that the competition of independent growers seriously undercut their ability to "fix monopoly prices." Using the 1933 passage in Arizona of the criminal conspiracy amendment to the Alien Land Law as

FIGURE 10. South Asian workers standing with white men and children in rural British Columbia, ca. 1900s. Courtesy Royal BC Museum, BC Archives. Image B-06052.

legal justification, corporate growers had incited a "small group of white grow-ers to set up a violent anti-alien agitation" as a key part of an overall business strategy to force out large numbers of independent growers and to undermine price competition. The British consul argued that it was "economic interest pure and simple," masquerading as racial antipathy, that drove the violence and the enforcement of racially discriminatory laws. A confluence of factors and odd alliances fueled the crisis. The British consul alleged that the leader of the agitation, Fred Kruse, was both a German immigrant and had "Communist tendencies," and had roused white American men to drive out Japanese and "Hindu" farmers. Large capitalists and anti-immigrant white American farm-ers had thus joined forces with a German immigrant and suspected com-munist. An upcoming November 1934 election had pressured the Maricopa County district attorney and sheriff, both candidates for reelection, to prove their support of legal protections for white farmers by aggressively prosecut-ing Asian farmers and their business partners. Many Japanese, South Asian, and white men who leased land were arrested for conspiracy, but only one was formally indicted. The British consul supported the status quo racial property ownership cartel by offering that "Hindu" farmers were "not breaking the law, since they were sharecroppers not property owners." For the consul, then, the rule of law, no matter how discriminatory, bolstered the claims of South Asian farmers, leaving aside the unfairness of a system of racial and economic exploitation that made Asians acutely vulnerable to harassment, legal jeopardy, and economic insecurity.[82]

The deepest ramification of the enforcement of the Alien Land Law, however, was that it intensified the environment of intimidation and acute vulnerability to prevent everyday interracial association and intimacy. The white politically enfranchised citizen class used the blunt instrument of law and the power of the state to convert provisional "free white persons," in this case, British subjects from India, into vulnerable noncitizens, who were no longer economically "free" because they were no longer "white." Simultaneously, state power was being mobilized in other parts of the United States to deny economic access to Chinese and Japanese immigrants, as well as their U.S.-born children, and constrained African Americans and Mexican Americans in systems of debt peonage and chain-gang prison labor. The state government intervened to single out Asian immigrants who were deemed "racially ineligible for naturalized citizenship"—a special pariah caste—severing their social and intimate ties and undermining their economic and political value. Racial identity had become a legal disability to contract. Alien Land Laws intervened to force land and labor agreements over property, tenancy, and share arrangements underground, bereft of judicial protection, creating new juridical inequities for the very immigrants who were managing to succeed in organizing capital and creating livelihoods. By undermining economic partnerships, this made all associations by Asian immigrants acutely vulnerable and suspect.

The structure of laws and policing for Asian immigrants dismantled the public value and equity of their social associations arising from intimate ties of friendship, partnership, sex, and marriage. Partnerships and contracts like marriage licenses and birth records were the legal recording and state recognition of association and kinship.

Alongside the tumult and vulnerability of informal ties between workers, contractors, and property owners, Alien Land Laws made illegitimate and suspect, not only contracts between partners, but also attempts to transfer property between parents and children when one parent was an alien ineligible for citizenship.

The governing and managing of migrants reveal, not only the demands of an economic system and the political and legal orchestration that enabled it, but also the shaping of social relations of work, cohabitation, and association on a local scale. Migrants on the verge of settled and landed existence were forced to the borders of legal life and forced to seek transience over permanence.

South Asian migrants who worked as laborers, who organized workers, leased farmland, and owned property did so within webs of dependency. The presence of noncitizen workers, contractors, farmers, and landowners was crucial to a thriving commercial agricultural economy, but they were also the most acutely vulnerable and intensively regulated in their behavior, ties, and livelihood. Much critical attention on how migrants were regulated by government and companies has focused on national gatekeeping and transnational labor recruitment, but state intervention to suspect and exact economic punishment in intimate association and partnership made migrancy and the floating life the most viable option.[83]

## ALIEN LAND LAWS AND ECONOMIC STRATEGY

Just as growers used criminal conspiracy law to quell competition from independent growers who were not white, Alien Land Laws deployed eligibility for naturalization to cement a racial divide, denying Asian immigrants the right to participate equitably in the land purchase and lease market and the prevailing sharecropping system. This racial cartel in the agricultural property and contract market paralleled early twentieth-century legal developments in California and other western states to racialize Asians and restrict legitimacy to intraracial intimate ties by cordoning off "immoral" sex in male-to-male relations and interracial heterosexual relations.[84]

The general process of defining marriage through racial boundaries and sexualizing and delegitimizing male-to-male intimacy outside of marriage produced a subsidy for heterosexuality. Policing who could own, lease, and participate in contractual relationships over land produced an anti-competitive cartel. It restricted who could use land as a key source of capital. It also cast a racial definition through national citizenship by restricting access to the land market to immigrants who could prove whiteness. This racial cartel in market participation paralleled the racial bounding of marriage and inheritance rights. Policing what sex, marital ties, and progeny had the legitimacy of state recognition and the authority of market rights produced a simultaneous subsidy of whiteness with heterosexuality. In this melding of household status, racial purity, and transactional rights to property and contract, the concept of normativity was deployed as an anti-democratic tactic to restrain the viability of the border intimacies forged by heterogeneous association. The state narrowed access to markets and to the courts. It diverted economic security, legal protections, and capital accumulation to "white" people who could monopolize racial standing and aggrandize profit with impunity.

Alien Land Laws were part of a broader effort to regulate intimate lives, expelling South Asian, Chinese, Japanese, Korean, and any other suspect "Asians" from personal associations and legal recognition that were crucial for western agricultural development and protections of the individual from large corporate interests. It drove the presumption that state stability could be achieved through subsidies to "permanent" and "white" families, even as the labor of nonwhite and transient migrants made the gains of economic possibility viable. The policing and prosecution of how people lived, sexually and domestically, readily exposed inequitable distributions of land and labor and the political and legal system that subsidized and normalized those distributions. The policing and prosecutorial attention to social associations of migrant men and the spatial borderlands of migrant agricultural production amassed an unruly and contradictory mass of new social knowledge for the state.

# PART TWO

# Intimacy, Law, and Legitimacy

## CHAPTER 4

# Legal Borderlands of Age and Gender

The intensive policing and prosecution of interracial social and erotic relationships between males from urban Vancouver, British Columbia, to rural Tulare County, California, produced legal dilemmas and destabilized certainties about what counted as consensual relationships. The prosecution of cases of sodomy and gross indecency engaged legal reasoning and legal rules to address both male culpability and vulnerability that hinged on the interpretation of age, gender polarity, and coercion.

In the early twentieth century, new legislation tightening definitions of proscribed sexual acts, partners, and disorderly public activity created a surge of arrests. Misdemeanor arrests for vagrancy and public indecency swept up large numbers of men, but those cases were disposed of rapidly through fines and jail time imposed by police courts. However, the increased laws and scrutiny over felony sexual crimes drew questions about legislative scope, evidence rules, and the targets of punitive sentences. South Asian laborers and tenant farmers rallied support for one another, mounted united defense strategies against questionable arrests, and gathered resources to hire attorneys. With the assistance of sympathetic and well-paid attorneys, the defendants in felony cases mounted appeals of trial court decisions that many suspected were prejudiced by all-white juries, evidence gathered by local police officers, and overzealous prosecutors.

New legislation and jurisprudence focused on narrowing and specifying what constituted sodomy, buggery, or "the crime against nature" and inventing new categories of proscribed sex acts, such as oral copulation and gross indecency.

Judges also paid close attention to the issue of whether male sexual partners were to be held asymmetrically or mutually culpable, adopting age standards from statutory-rape, criminal-accomplice, and legal-majority-status legislation. Finally, court decisions sought to distinguish between random eccentric criminal acts and the supposed criminal propensity of a class of individuals. Legal reasoning reinforced perceptions of sexual acts between men as sexual deviance and threats to sexual normalcy and normal national masculinity.

These dilemmas erupted over the shadowy terrain of the sexual subjectivity and vulnerability of male youth. In the early twentieth century, courts in California and British Columbia repeatedly confronted the issue of how to adjudicate the innocence or culpability of male adolescents in sodomy cases. Attorneys and judges grappled with how to understand adolescent male actions as a legal problem and crafted different analogies and age standards to draw a boundary between male adolescents and adult males. Here the concept of "legal borderlands" highlights the unsettled terrain of adjudicating consent and sexual nature in jurisprudence, even as legislatures were attempting to standardize human subjectivity and proper intimacy.[1] In line with jurisprudence's aim to develop abstract legal rules that could be applied universally, legal reasoning about sodomy negotiated and stabilized age boundaries, with the consequence of reinforcing polarized gender roles and expectations in order to protect male bodies from feminization. Legal reasoning insistently affirmed the unnaturalness of sodomy and the perversity and social damage of sexual relationships for pleasure not procreation. However, in seeking to explain the victimization and passivity of feminized male bodies, it stumbled not only in accounting for gender pliability and sexual diversity but in determining responsibility for sexual relations.

Although aiming at universal application, appellate courts relied upon racial, class, and national differences in developing verdicts and explanations for rampant sexual perversity and amoral criminality. Racialization and foreignness emerged repeatedly in providing the counterpoint to normal masculinity, white racial identity, and American and Canadian nationality.

In this book, this chapter on sodomy jurisprudence and the following one on marriage legitimacy shift attention away from how court records illuminated spatial borderlands to how legal knowledge resolves social dilemmas. Judges, attorneys, legislators, and legal scholars scrutinized dilemmas about sexual relationships to reconfigure legal rules, reasoning, and interpretation. Reconfigurations of legal knowledge stabilized the regulation of sexual practices and social ties by attaching gender norms to racial and national identities. Legal reasoning applied to relations of sex, domesticity, and kinship highlighted assumptions about intimate ties, behaviors, and morality that underscored both property relations and democratic associations. But it also revealed the power and consequences of bureaucratic civil licensing and registration of marriage and vital statistics that led to resources, market distributions, and state-sponsored entitlements. Yet the inventive uses of legal reasoning did not always produce stability and certainty. The term "legal borderlands" refers to the unsettled state of jurisprudence in assessing criminality, consent, and human nature, highlighting relationships, ties, and social conventions that exceeded, evaded, and could not be contained in the attempts to standardize intimate ties and human subjects through law.[2]

## SODOMY, STATUTORY PROTECTIONS, AND THE PROBLEM OF CONSENT

In the mid to late nineteenth century, sodomy arrests increased rapidly both in cities and in mining, farming, and ranching regions in western North America. Historians have attributed the sharp increase in sodomy prosecutions in New York and Toronto to the campaigns of child-protection and anti-vice associations in patrolling social and sexual contact. Their direct activities are less apparent in smaller towns and rural areas in the West, but the discursive worry about boys in sexual danger may have had repercussions for both police and residents.[3]

In 1850, California adopted an "infamous crime against nature" law, and five years later, the state criminalized "assault to commit sodomy," but left wide latitude for judicial interpretation of what activities, partners, and rules of evidence would result in criminal conviction. Sentencing ranged from one year to life in prison. Sodomy featured prominently as "against nature," but the criminal category could embrace all kinds of actors, and the scope of the acts was ambiguous. Sex acts between females and males could be punished under sodomy statutes and occasionally were, but historians have noted that since the 1880s in the United States, prosecutors were more likely to put forward sodomy complaints of cases involving an adult male and a male adolescent or male child.[4] Cases of two adult males or a male and female were prosecuted less frequently. The definition of sodomy narrowed to male-to-male anal penetration. There was greater police and prosecutorial concern about punishing adult male sexual conduct that involved male youth. But in the early twentieth century, there was also greater ambiguity and uncertainty about how to interpret male volition, consent, and violation.

In 1897, the California Supreme Court followed other U.S. state courts and limited prosecution of the "crime against nature" to anal penetration. In 1903, however, widening the scope of police scrutiny of sexual activity, the California legislature created the category of "lewd vagrancy," intended broadly to cover any behavior that the police might suspect to be prostitution or hustling. Further, the legislature criminalized any act that "outrages public decency."[5]

In the first three decades of the twentieth century, California legislators also passed a series of specific statutes to protect children. Rather than simply strengthening statutory rape and sodomy protections, the legislature criminalized adult acts, influences, and associations with minors that could be considered lewd or immoral. Among these offenses were performing a lewd act on a child under fourteen (1901); sending a minor to an immoral place (1905); performing degrading, lewd, and immoral acts in front of a child (1907); and contributing to the delinquency of minors (1915). These protections culminated in and were reinforced by 1929 legislation that criminalized loitering near schoolyards and child molestation. This regulatory regime to protect children did not specify "lewd acts" or "immoral practices" and "places," leaving considerable latitude to police, prosecutors, juries, and judges. In general, the legislature emphasized the dangers of adult strangers and offered judges and attorneys guidance in protecting children from adult association and acts.

The most intensive, confusing, and confounding legal borderlands involved the precise age and gender definitions of who constituted a "minor." The sources of guidance were often vague and conflicting in statutes. Judges and district attorneys acted in advance of the legislature to formulate legal rules about whom to try and whom to protect in charges of the "crime against nature."

In the last decades of the nineteenth century and the first decades of the twentieth, American and Canadian societies were undergoing a cataclysmic shift in social consciousness and legal protections for girls and their sexual relations with adult men. In the United States, state legislatures rapidly revised and raised age-of-consent standards and created statutory rape protections for girls. These protections were unevenly enforced, often resulting in greater scrutiny and interrogation of girls and young women, yet the concern about female vulnerability and the necessity for legal intervention had emerged as a state strategy for ensuring social well-being. Against the backdrop of prolific popular cultural and political representations of child prostitution, female abduction, child marriage, and white slavery, Progressive-era voluntary organizations and municipal government developed a web of social regulatory programs, ranging from juvenile courts to homes for unwed mothers, to protect and discipline female youth.[6] In order to create protections for young females, nineteenth-century women's organizations and social reformers lobbied to raise the age of female consent from prepuberty to the mid teens, and also to create statutory rape protections. In the late nineteenth century, in tandem with trends nationwide, the California legislature had increased the age of consent for sexual intercourse for females from ten in 1872 to fourteen in 1883 and sixteen in 1897. The legislature was deadlocked in lifting the age to eighteen until 1913, the year after women first voted in the state.[7]

Nationwide, women's movements had focused on protecting female adolescents from all males. Laws governing the age of consent provided a threshold for sexual activity by females, but the question was unsettled for male youth. In an era when cultural and legal borders of age and legitimate sexual participation for females were fixed by statute, there was great uncertainty about how to judge the vulnerability of male youth. Cultural and political understandings of adolescence were shifting radically. At what age did males have the capacity to consent? Did their ability to consent differ depending on whether their sexual partners were female or male? What statutory protections were available to boys as opposed to girls? What special legal status did male youth have? These questions raised an unsettling legal problem when conceptualizing a male legal subject who could consent to sodomy.

Judges, prosecutors, and defense attorneys employed three kinds of age thresholds to decide sodomy cases. The first age standard borrowed from statutory rape statutes that protected female victims (ranging from fourteen to eighteen). The second age standard relied on the criminal legal threshold of who constituted a criminal accomplice (fourteen). And the third age standard leaned on legal adulthood, or the age of majority (twenty-one). All attempted to set the boundary between childhood and adulthood. State legislatures steadily raised the age for permissible male-female sexual intercourse and marriage, and the ages of criminal accomplice and legal adulthood remained stable. Prosecutors, defense attorneys, and judges applied these age standards with considerable latitude, particularly as they readily shifted between understanding sodomy as a statutory crime, gendered violence, unnatural act, or bad choice. These three liberal legal understandings of age were rarely drawn into open conflict, but they often shadowed more express disagreement about the status of "consent," "innocence," or "corruption." The overlapping engagement of legal analogies and age standards generated considerable uncertainty about where and how to fix the boundary of childhood and adulthood. It also revealed ambiguity about the gendered bodies of male youths and anxiety about the malleability of adult males.

A 1912 California State Supreme Court decision in the appeal of *People v. Dong Pok Yip* became the ruling precedent for applying statutory protections for male youth. Subsequently, California Appeals Court judges drew on the decision for guidance on questions of age and consent.[8] The case involved a Chinese man, Dong Pok Yip, who had befriended nine-year-old Albert Hondeville at the Antioch wharf and taught him to fish. Later in the afternoon, Rodrigues, a Portuguese American bookkeeper with offices overlooking the wharf, observed the two "walking hand-in-hand." Suspicious, Rodrigues followed them behind the oil tanks to a brush of willows, where he described them as "stooping . . . with the boy in front and the Chinaman" behind him with his "hands on the sides of the boy's waist." Although he could not testify to penetration of Albert, Rodrigues claimed to have seen the back of the boy's overalls hanging down, and that the "Chinaman's" trousers were unbuttoned in front.[9]

At the trial, the eyewitness Rodrigues explained that Dong Pok Yip had been "trying to use the boy as a female."[10] This claim gendered the incident into a "crime against nature" by transforming the boy into a passive object that could be sexually acted upon and penetrated. By treating the boy as a feminized victim, attorneys and judges could analogize the sexual-victim status of underage females to the legal understanding of male youth. In the appeal to the California State Supreme Court, State Attorney General U.S. Webb elaborated on the analogy of statutory assault. Webb argued that the boy had been "overpowered," and that the circumstances were similar to those where a "schoolteacher takes indecent liberties with a female pupil" or a man lays "hold of" a woman and kisses "her against her will."[11] Supreme Court justices agreed and ruled that "consent" must be distinguished from "submission," despite the perception that the "boy was ignorantly indifferent and passive in the hands of the defendant." They argued that a "child of tender years or retarded mental development . . . in the hands of a strong man might easily be overawed into submitting without actually consenting."[12]

The jurisprudence of statutory protections for sodomy borrowed from the more-developed case law and statutes on rape. For a woman to prove that she had been raped, she had to demonstrate that she had put up the "utmost resistance." Rape convictions rested on judgments about the "consent" of the female. Laws on rape required that females explain how and and by whom they had been violated, and this was central to the criminal prosecution of their assailants.[13]

Statutory rape was supposed to shield girls from interrogation about their sexual history, conduct, and comportment. In practice, underage girls were often called upon to explain their conduct, behavior, dress, and history in order to prove their innocence. The way the statutory rape statutes were applied reinforced the presumption that male aggression and female passivity were "natural." Defense attorneys, social workers, and judges pressed underage females to explain whether a particular sex act and sexual partner had been invited, and to show that their general behavior had been moral, making them deserving of protection. Evidence of rape—forcible, coerced sex—did not challenge the belief that sexual intercourse between males and females was the only "natural" sex act and defined "normal" sexual relations.[14] Underwriting the new age standards that defined consensual sex between males and females was a conventional understanding of gender that naturalized male aggression in contrast with female vulnerability. Girls could be forced, persuaded, or duped into sexual relations with male adults, and the law had to intervene to protect them until they became capable of consent.

Statutory protections for girls had to be applied in cases where it appeared that male youths had solicited sex from adult men. This was a particular challenge in the Sacramento and Porterville cases discussed earlier, where the question of whether male youths were accomplices to criminal behavior initiated by adult men became central. As the juvenile justice system developed, minors who were considered "accomplices" could be tried on lesser charges and undergo rehabilitation and reform. In 1911, California statutes specified that a person above the age of fourteen could be charged as a criminal accomplice. This applied to prostitution. Even when girls were under statutory protections, prosecutors, defense attorneys, and judges parsed their behavior for signs of solicitation, encouragement, and consent to sex with adult males. In sodomy arrests, prosecutors and defense attorneys focused on male youths as potential accomplices to sexual crimes.

Courts repeatedly affirmed statutory protections for a "child of tender years" under the age of fourteen, but that left considerable latitude in assessing the culpability of male youth between the age of accomplice and the age of majority.[15] At what age threshold did a person achieve moral and mental development? Adolescence was a sharply contested, unsettled category that emerged from social reform and social science knowledge at the turn of the century, when sexual concerns infused social views of children, Jeffrey Moran argues. The publication of Stanley Hall's study of adolescence in 1904 marked a paradigm shift from conceptualizing teenagers and youth as "incomplete adults" to an understanding of adolescence as a distinctive intermediate phase of human development that was required to be recognized, studied, and regulated. Scientists' and social reformers' interest in this phase of human life became linked to concerns about this period's social and cultural transformations. Changing social mores, the rise of commercialized entertainment in both large cities and towns, shifting patterns of work outside the household for youths and young adults, both male and female, and the tremendous internal migration and immigration of the late nineteenth and early twentieth centuries fostered perceptions of the collapse of traditional family and social structures. Social reformers and commentators expressed fears that the widespread social and economic dislocations and social mobility created the conditions for sexual corruption and immorality. Youths were vulnerable to the perils of premature sexual activity that would not only have devastating health and social consequences for individuals but also spell ruin for society. The perceived vulnerability and needs of adolescents fueled the development of municipal juvenile courts, truant officers, social workers, psychologists, and counseling programs in the early twentieth century. These programs were charged with protecting vulnerable boys and girls from the sexual and moral dangers posed by urban vice and European and Asian immigrant males. The courts became a key arena for sorting out youth problems and rehabilitating delinquents.[16]

Above this age threshold of fourteen, defense and prosecution attorneys struggled over what made male youths accomplices to illicit sexual acts. The exchange of money or gifts for a sexual act constituted the most decisive material evidence of consent. In the early twentieth century, male street hustling was identified as a social problem for urban adolescent delinquents. Physicians, psychologists, sociologists, social workers, and sexologists interpreted encounters and transactions between men and male youths as part of an ensemble of criminal and sexual activity, on a sliding scale from petty theft, truancy, loitering, intoxication, drug addiction, and socializing with female prostitutes. Money changing hands between adult men and male youths was readily interpreted in cases in Vancouver and Sacramento during the 1910s as evidence of solicitation to commit lewd, indecent acts.[17]

However, if money did not change hands, judges reckoned with other signs of solicitation and encouragement. The question of how far to interpret consent of a male adolescent emerged in a police entrapment case in 1918 in Vancouver, where fifteen-year-old Travis lived with and worked for his father at a paper mill. At his father's urging, Travis told police detectives that Delip Singh, who delivered sawdust to the mill, had invited him to take a ride with him. Suspicious of Singh's intentions, the police suggested to Travis that he accept the invitation, and they would keep watch. On Saturday, July 20, Travis and Singh made an appointment to meet at the corner of Dunlevy and Union Streets at 8 P.M. Singh suggested a drive on Marine Drive, but Travis took him to his father's stables on Dunlevy. According to Travis's court testimony, Singh closed and latched the stable door behind them, and they walked to an empty stall in the back. While Travis watered the horses, Singh asked him if he wanted to earn some money. Singh gave the boy fifteen cents, spread a blanket on the floor, unbuttoned his trousers, and put his arm around Travis from behind. At that moment, two police detectives, who had been keeping watch in the loft upstairs, rushed in and seized Singh. A zealous officer testified that he had felt Singh's "privates" and asserted that the man had had an "erection." In his defense, Singh asserted that he had accompanied Travis to the stables to inspect a horse and while there had been seized by a call of nature, when the police appeared. Judge Cayley ruled that Singh's activities "showed preparation and intent to commit the offence of buggery." He dismissed Singh's explanation that he had been seized by a call of nature and called Singh's accusation that the police had unbuttoned his pants a "blatant lie."

However, Judge Cayley also had to consider whether Travis's testimony alone was sufficient to prove the charge against Delip Singh. The direction of solicitation mattered when Cayley determined whether Travis had consented to the activities that led to the scene in the stables. Cayley sidestepped the question of police entrapment by responding to the defense's case that Travis's request for Singh at Mrs. Amer Chand's store earlier that evening and his participation with the police entrapment was evidence of his "consent," with an interpretation of statutory sodomy. Judge Cayley contrasted "attempted buggery" with a hypothetical case of statutory rape upon a girl over the age of fourteen. "Whether the girl consented was a vital factor" in such a case,

Cayley argued. Significantly, it was "no factor" in whether the boy "consented or not." Cayley shared a prevailing understanding that a girl could "possess adult sexuality," could consent to sexual activity with an older man, and that her actions could be deciphered to provide a defense to a man accused of rape. On the other hand, Travis's invitation to Singh, creating the conditions for their encounter, and his knowledge of sexual activity did not "trigger" a similar "broad suspicion."[18]

As Stephen Robertson has demonstrated in a study of sex crimes against children in New York, differences based on gender determined how a victim's age affected the outcome. The appearance of physical maturity and sexual knowledge could sharply undermine the credibility of a girl's rape accusation, whereas maturity, knowledge, and action did not impact the credibility of boys' accounts of sexual assault. Even when older boys seemed active, the men were convicted in the same proportions as with younger boys, which differed starkly from the conviction outcomes for men accused of sexual assault of both young and older girls. Robertson argues that this "fracturing and distinction of female childhood" invested every act, word, and appearance of a girl with suspicion of false accusation and fabrication, whereas "childhood" operated as a safeguard for male children in spite of their words, acts, and appearance. To be sure, the effectiveness of statutory protections for boys was buttressed by an understanding of "sexual nature" that precluded that a boy would consent to sodomy and judged the "failure of his efforts to resist" an adult man as owing to "disparity of strength and circumstances." However, girls faced persistent public scrutiny of their sexual nature and availability to men. Unless the accused was nonwhite, adult white men persistently reinterpreted signs of assault on a white female as indicative of duplicity and possible entrapment.[19] When Cayley invoked the statutory protections for girls, these created a more powerful shield for Travis than they did for females. In dismissing the possibility that Travis might have consented to sex as "unnatural," the judge diverted attention from Travis's motivations. The statutory shield protected him from being charged as an "accomplice" in a sexual crime.[20]

At the appeal of Singh's conviction, the attorney for the defense, Harper, charged that that the police had "set a trap for this man" and encouraged criminal behavior. Furthermore, Harper questioned whether Singh's actions constituted an "attempt" at crime, since there had been no attempt at penetration. In the appeal, Harper was trying to persuade the judges to interpret the evidence of the case in line with the lesser charge of "soliciting." Chief

Justice MacDonald, writing for the court, focused on Travis's testimony, and determined that the sequence of events constituted both preparation and an attempt. MacDonald emphasized Singh's alleged use of force. Travis had testified that after Singh unbuttoned his pants, he "grabbed hold" of him to "lay" him down on the rug, causing the boy to say, "Ouch!" For MacDonald, this was "evidence enough" that there had been an "attempt" at sodomy.[21]

The credibility of a male youth, however, depended on the circumstances and the social status of the adult defendant of the alleged crime. In September 1913, a San Francisco case involving circumstances that transpired in a middle-class home had a very different result upon appeal. In the San Francisco Superior Court, Samuel Robbins, a fifty-six-year-old white bookkeeper was convicted by the reluctant testimony of sixteen-year-old Sidney, who claimed that Robbins had attempted to penetrate him while in a locked bathroom in his house, but was interrupted by the housekeeper, Mrs. Nute, trying to open the door. In the appeal to the California Supreme Court, however, the majority of justices argued that Mrs. Nute's testimony, though casting suspicious light on the defendant, did not sufficiently corroborate Sidney's accusation.[22] In overturning Robbins's conviction, the judges gave no credence to Sidney's explanation of trauma and his narration of the assault. The decision implicitly characterized Sidney as an unreliable accomplice and the producer of a false accusation. The judges decided not to heed Mrs. Nute's testimony, because she was a "prying" servant woman who had not actually witnessed the crime.

Social familiarity and shared middle-class status bolstered the defense of Robbins, a friend of the family, who frequently visited the home and was invited in while the parents were absent. After an afternoon playing dominoes and tennis, Robbins had suggested they wash up and led Sidney to the bathroom. Upon entering the bathroom, Robbins had locked the door, pulled down the shades of the "frosted" windows, and let the water run. Sidney testified that Robbins then sexually assaulted him, but the attempt was cut short when Mrs. Nute was heard at the door.

The judges accepted the defense's interpretation that it was "natural" that after a game of tennis the man and boy had washed their hands together in the bathroom and locked the door after themselves as a "simple precaution . . . to prevent" any interruption.[23] Such homosocial behavior between white men and white boys could be perceived as natural, moral, and pedagogically appropriate. Instead, the Supreme Court justices worried about Samuel Robbins's reputation, fearing that "friendship of a middle aged man for the lad" could be misinterpreted as criminal intent or activity. They argued that "in these days of the 'big brother movement' thousands of men throughout the country are systematically cultivating the friendship of boys, to the end that the influence of mature thought and association with men may aid in the development of the best qualities of the children."[24] The defense of the Big Brother movement, even though the mentorship program was irrelevant to the facts of the case, took on particular significance for the justices. Since the founding of the Big Brother movement, a volunteer program of mentoring by adults to prevent juvenile delinquency, developed by a New York city court clerk, it had expanded rapidly, with Jewish and Catholic chapters in cities across the country in the 1910s and 1920s. Justices were quick to repudiate any hint of impropriety in an unrelated middle-class adult stranger's volunteering to mentor a working-class or poor youth. Adult male mentorship was promoted as crucial in taming delinquent youth and thus reducing the case load in juvenile courts.[25] The fact that Robbins and Sidney had been playing tennis also fitted the Big Brother scenario—middle-class reformers encouraged physical fitness, sports, and camping to redirect energies that might otherwise lead to criminal and immoral behavior.[26] Ironically, the same activities produced a homosocial environment and possibilities for intimate relations between males. The judges' decision, however, revealed the anxiety that men of middle-class privilege would be considered suspect in their association with boys and young men. The judges maintained that middle-class white men could impart moral development and should, therefore, not "be convicted of degrading crimes upon mere suspicion plus the story of an accomplice."[27]

The difference between "natural" intergenerational male friendship and "unnatural" sexual predation thus depended upon the reputation of the adult. The defense attorney's use of "natural" homosociality and male modesty reinforced Robbins's credibility as a respectable man. The judges rejected the inference that Robbins might have taken advantage of that familiarity and instead let Sidney bear the trauma of sexual predation bereft of state protection. Branding Sidney an unreliable accomplice was all the more startling because Sidney had no history of juvenile delinquency or deceit. Robbins's defense succeeded because his white racial identity and respectable middle-class status overrode suspicions of sexual assault even when the victim also belonged to the white middle class.

In contrast, the social associations of Asian migrant men with "American," or provisionally "American," youths were perceived as inherently dangerous and catalyzed suspicions of immorality and contributing to delinquency. In the Southern California town of Imperial, a white bystander informed police of a South Asian man taking "boys" to his room to drink, prompting a police search of the Pioneer Rooming House and the arrest of Bugga Singh on the night of January 12, 1919, for contributing to the delinquency of minors. Standing outside the Portuguese Restaurant, known as a haunt of "Hindoo boys and coloured fellows," Bugga Singh had chatted with two office clerks, eighteen-year-old Ulysses Hudson and nineteen-year-old Edgar Ellis, and invited them to his rooms to share a bottle of whiskey. Although Ulysses found the invitation "unusual," he felt comfortable chatting with Singh and his friend Edgar. Singh took out a bottle from his pocket and handed it around, and the boys took four drinks apiece.[28]

Contributing to the delinquency of a minor was part of a broad array of protections that guarded against associations between adult men and male youths that could contribute to immoral purposes. In October 1926, Police Chief A. W. Reynolds raided a ranch four miles northeast of Porterville, California, and arrested Arjan Singh, forty-eight-year-old ranch hand, for attempting the "crime against nature" on a seventeen-year-old white "local boy," Alexander Quinn. The police charged Arjan Singh with a "statutory crime" and held Quinn on the charge of vagrancy, pending a hearing in juvenile court. Police suspicion of Arjan Singh's ranch in Porterville, California, had been ongoing for a couple of years prior to the sodomy arrest. Singh had been convicted of liquor possession and at the time was reputed for "making his house attractive to depraved boys by having liquor on hand."[29] The Tulare County prosecutor removed any semblance of the class-privileged privacy by pointedly defining the farmhand's rented house as a disreputable and illicit resort and condemning Singh's "disgusting Oriental depravity" in hosting pernicious socializing between "low down whites and Hindus of the same type." This reputation for contributing to the delinquency of minors through providing liquor and allegedly engaging in sodomy made Singh's conviction a victory for the prosecutors, who aimed to remove a "menace to society," which would be a "blessing to the community."[30]

Vagrancy sweeps and following leads to migrant workers' spaces and homes were a routine practice of police surveillance in the towns of California's Central Valley. In Marysville in February 1928, two police officers on routine patrol after midnight noticed a Ford coupe parked in a secluded spot, about a block away from residences. Officer McAuliffe's suspicions were aroused when he saw a dark man asleep leaning against the passenger window who "looked like a Mexican." When the officers pulled the man out, they discovered a "young man [who] was lying in the seat with his head under the wheel, his pants . . . down to his knees, his union suit underwear split . . . open, his coat . . . turned up and his rectum . . . exposed."[31] What had begun as police curiosity on a routine patrol was thus amplified by racial suspicion. Apparently, the presence of a dark man in a parked car at night was enough cause for suspicion. Although Officer McAuliffe had initially mistaken Rola Singh for a "Mexican," the officer treated his initial confusion over racial identity as irrelevant. The police suspected both "Mexican" and "Hindu" men, who were typically migrant laborers, unlikely to own automobiles, and likely vagrants. Racial suspicion quickly turned into a more serious police investigation when they discovered a white male partially undressed and unconscious in Singh's company. The police officers grabbed hold of the man, whose name was Harvey Carstenbrook, rousing him from a deep sleep, and he started to swing punches and fight them as they jerked him out of the car. The police officers arrested both men and hauled them to the police station for observation. Later that day after two medical inspections, Rola Singh was charged with the "crime against nature."

During the trial and appeal, the perception of youth protected Carstenbrook, who had accosted Rola Singh on the sidewalk near the stage depot and offered him a ride in his car. Carstenbrook explained that he had parked the car on a secluded street near Washington Square because he was too drunk to drive and that they both passed out until they were roused by the police officers.[32] Carstenbrook's loss of memory and insistence that nothing illicit had transpired between the men did not dissuade the police from enlisting a local physician to conduct invasive exams of his body and to take samples of hair from his anus and Singh's penis for further testing. Throughout the trial, the attorneys referred to him as the "Carstenbrook boy," and the judge presumed statutory protections precisely because of Carstenbrook's unconsciousness and lack of memory of how his pants had come undone when the police found him. Instead, the prosecution and judge admitted testimony of the examining physician to determine whether Singh had assaulted Carstenbrook. Carstenbrook's "boy" status shielded him from any further scrutiny and interrogation as a potential accomplice, and he was released from jail without charges, while Rola Singh was convicted and sentenced to seven years' imprisonment in San Quentin.

In the appeal, the defense attorney argued that "had Carstenbrook's person been subjected to such an assault, it is reasonable to say [he] would have experienced therefore some uncomfortable or unusual injury, and would have been eager to testify to such injury. There is no reason why he should be inclined to protect a strange Hindu, with whom he had no previous acquaintance. On the contrary, had he even suspected such an assault, he would have felt himself humiliated and outraged."[33] One could well argue that Carstenbrook would have suffered more humiliation by any public acknowledgment of sexual relations with Rola Singh. However, the appellate judges were not swayed, precisely because the medical testimony substantiated police suspicions and outweighed the denials of Singh and Carstenbrook.

The question of consensual sexual relations between two men was off the table, because the prosecutor and trial judge wrongly intimated that Carstenbrook was not quite twenty-one, "the age of majority." His identity, however, was shrouded during the proceedings. There were several puzzling elements that emerged in the trial testimony. Neither the prosecutor nor the defense attorney drew attention to Carstenbrook's ownership of the car and his solicitation of Singh outside the stage depot. Even when the defense attorney charged the prosecutor with coaxing Carstenbrook to skip the trial and remain absent during the afternoon when he was scheduled to testify as a defense witness, there was no additional speculation about the prosecutor's purpose or the conspicuous absence of testimony from a parent or guardian. Probate, newspaper notices, and voting records, however, revealed that Harvey Carstenbrook belonged to a local family that owned land and municipal business contracts dating back to the late nineteenth century. Harvey's father had died the year before and named him, as his eldest adult son, the executor of his estate, to be divided among his five children. The same sources indicate that Harvey Carstenbrook was identified as a twenty-eight-year-old lineman for the Pacific Gas and Electric Company, who had parked his vehicle nearly a mile away from his own residence in downtown Marysville.[34] Even if Carstenbrook's true age had been revealed in the trial, it would not have sidetracked the prosecution of Rola Singh. But it would have complicated Harvey's position vis-à-vis the legal system. The judges, prosecutors, and defense attorney all protected the "Carstenbrook boy" (as he was referred to in the court proceedings), because his "boy" status was crucial to the narratives that feminized the victim in sodomy jurisprudence.

The case of Rola Singh and Harvey Carstenbrook illustrates several conjoined processes. First, the case demonstrates how thoroughly racialization shaped the initial police scrutiny, interracial relationships served to justify intensive investigation, and criminal suspicion shifted seamlessly between Asian and Mexican men in California in the early twentieth century. Second, in order to assert white male victimization and exclude consensual sexual relations, prosecutors and judges were eager to resolve the crisis in judging the actions of a white male youth by manipulating the male youth's age and insisting on his unconsciousness. The prosecution in the case exaggerated the aggression of Asian male migrants and the victimization of white males, promoting the prosecution of Asian men. The application of statutory age standards to sodomy cases drew a circle of protection around white male youths and, in excess of the protection provided to underage girls, could foreclose scrutiny of the conduct and possible consent of the penetrated male.

## DISTINGUISHING NORMALITY FROM DEGENERACY

However, the possibility of consensual sex between two adult males or the acknowledgment of consent by a penetrated adult male unleashed disturbing questions for male judges and prosecutors. The lawyers appeared uneasy about compelling an adult male to verbally demonstrate that he had employed "utmost resistance," defend his conduct, and detail the violation of his body, as they would have done of any adult woman seeking remedies for heterosexual rape. These expectations disproportionately burdened lower-class and nonwhite females, even those under statutory protection.[35]

James Kerr, a prominent legal scholar who edited the compendium of the *Codes of California* in 1921, railed against judicial decisions that left open the possibility of consensual sodomy as a "travesty of justice." He feared that "a degenerate person or a person of depraved and low character and mind, by consent to the beastly act, could nullify the will of the legislature."[36] Kerr insisted that society must be defended from the "degenerate" and perverse individual whose consent to anal penetration inverted masculinity and thereby undermined the political and legislative criminalization of sodomy as "unnatural." The ferocity of Kerr's response indexed the severity of the perceived threat. Consensual sodomy produced an "alternative mode of being" and destabilized the polarization of gender, misdirected "natural" sexual desire, and unseated heterosexuality as the only "true identity."[37]

Kerr's demand that all male-to-male sexual relations be treated as illegitimate was imperative to fortify the vision of "normal" male sexuality. Statutory protections for male youth were not enough. Kerr argued for the statutory criminality of all acts of sodomy to guide male sexual activity into marital union and procreation with adult females. Although Kerr deferred the question of consensual sex between males by nullifying its legitimacy, judges and prosecutors could not ignore its widespread existence. Like sociologists, psychologists, and social workers of the era, they instead identified and distributed acts, behaviors, and persons into the categories of normal, degenerate, and delinquent.[38]

For decades, police discovery and prosecution of oral sexual activity had complicated and disrupted sodomy prosecutions. It also heightened the judicial curiosity of ascertaining male consent to sex with males. Although judicial precedents in the Anglo-American legal world limited sodomy to the specific act of anal penetration, male oral copulation was nonetheless condemned as degenerate indecency in political debate and popular culture. The specific criminalization of oral copulation was first enacted in English-language law in Pennsylvania in 1879. Six years after the Pennsylvania law, the British Parliament enacted the Labouchère amendment to prostitution legislation that identified oral sex between men as "gross indecency" and a misdemeanor crime, punishable by up to two years' imprisonment. Canadian laws followed British common law practices, but their implementation lagged. In 1859, when Canada systematized its criminal and civil codes with the implementation of the Consolidated Statutes, the law criminalized "buggery" as an offense punishable by death. A decade later, the maximum sentence was reduced to fourteen years in prison. In 1892, as part of a broader update of criminal law, Canada implemented its own statute for gross indecency. In the wake of the 1895 publicity of the prosecution of Oscar Wilde, a number of U.S. and British imperial possessions copied gross indecency laws.[39]

In California, the development of specific legislation against oral sex lagged considerably. For years the police had used "vag lewd" as a broad umbrella for misdemeanor arrests for more specific later prosecution, and prosecutors analogized oral sex to anal intercourse. The California Supreme Court limited the prosecution of sodomy to anal penetration. The California legislature did not act until motivated by a 1914 Long Beach case in which two undercover police officers infiltrated a variety of clubs and arrested thirty-one men for engaging in oral sex, but charged them with the misdemeanor of lewd vagrancy. The courts expressed concern with the frequent police recourse to the misdemeanor "vagrancy" charge to punish oral-genital contact. In 1915, the California legislature added to the penal code's list of serious felonies "fellatio" and "cunnilingus." After the California Supreme Court challenged the use of non-English-language criminal charges, the legislature in 1921 specifically criminalized "oral copulation."[40]

A striking example of how categories of degeneracy and normality converged and were reassembled appears in a 1928 Stockton case, when police arrested thirty-one-year-old Jack Lynch and seventy-year-old Keshn Singh for engaging in "sex perversion," specifically with Singh's penis in Lynch's mouth. The prosecution designated Keshn Singh as the accomplice, who had paid Lynch fifty cents and "upon whom Lynch practiced his vulgar employment."[41] At the trial, Assistant District Attorney H. C. Stanley deployed the categories of degeneracy, normalcy, and amorality apropos of the "ordinary American" in order to identify the internal and external threats to American identity. At the sentencing hearing, Stanley, doubting that intoxication had impaired Singh's judgment, instead believed his actions evidenced intrinsic foreign amorality that was incompatible with American ethical behavior, despite Singh's having lived in the United States for twenty-three years. Stanley argued that Singh showed no remorse about the "wrong" of his action and he "does not seem to be a person that regards such a practice as the ordinary American would." Stanley advocated Singh's incarceration as a preventive measure to stop him from "prostituting other men by furnishing himself as a subject to be acted upon, whether for or without compensation." Judge George Buck agreed and sentenced Singh to four years in San Quentin. As an amoral foreigner, Singh was cast as incapable of ever becoming an "ordinary American."[42]

On the other hand, Jack Lynch, a white man born in Wisconsin, appeared to be an "ordinary American." But he also possessed all the characteristics of a vagrant: he was unmarried at age thirty-one, a transient laborer who had journeyed from the upper Midwest to California in 1924 and worked erratically in lumber camps and restaurants throughout the state. He had amassed a long criminal record in four years in California, including vagrancy arrests and petty theft conviction. Under arrest in Stockton, he had allegedly admitted to the arresting officers that he frequently practiced oral sex on men in Modesto and Stockton.

The prosecutor concluded that Lynch was a "natural degenerate," and that his record of vagrancy and habitual sex perversion made him unlikely to "be cured" of his "vulgar" practices, which were "the incidental characteristic of the vagrant, who can never be regarded as a fit subject for society."[43] The case, a rare prosecution of two adult males, paired the amoral alien man with the white native-born degenerate vagrant. Neither man was considered a victim of the crime; rather, policing their behavior served ultimately to isolate degenerate and amoral subjects from American society and incarcerate unfit subjects of society.

The interracial association had incited police suspicion, however, and the conversion of immoral acts into sexual identities framed the legal prosecution. The categories of degenerate and pervert fortified an understanding of the normal. Some white middle-class men such as Samuel Robbins could sidestep the indictment of sodomy through their ability to preserve their reputations as moral subjects and normal men. Many more working-class men drew suspicion because of their transient way of life and were considered innately degenerate, inveterately criminal, or amoral foreigners. In the Lynch and Singh "sex perversion" case, police and prosecutors deployed whiteness strategically. In scrutinizing social contacts between so-called Americans and foreign nomadic males, the fundamental goal was to isolate "natural degeneracy" and prevent amoral foreigners from contaminating American society.

## REHABILITATING DELINQUENTS

The internal threat of the degenerate vagrant and the external threat of the amoral foreigner most perniciously converged in the potential corruption of male youth. During the 1910s and 1920s, California courts were interpreting the degree of male vulnerability and victimhood based on perceptions of age, consciousness, and the ability to narrate sexual transgression. The vulnerable and innocent male victim was characterized as someone who was acted upon without his will or knowledge. A child under the age of fourteen occupied this category, as did an unconscious male of an indeterminate youthfulness. Harvey Carstenbrook's silence and protestations that he had no consciousness of sexual assault demonstrated how the age boundaries could be flexed to accommodate unconscious males. Above the age of an accomplice and below the age of legal adulthood, male youths were in a more precarious position in the courtroom. Male youths of approximately the same age could be treated differently based on the men with whom they associated. In practice in the lower courts, judges, attorneys, and juries interpreted the conscious choice of teenage males such as Alexander and Sidney to socialize and participate with adult men based on the double-edged sword of statutory protections. Age and knowledge provided differential shields in the courtroom for male and female youth. The presumption of the normality of heterosexual sex, however, reinforced acute vulnerability for girls in courtroom interrogation. The older, more physically mature and sexually knowledgeable a girl seemed, the more suspicions of her consent were sharpened. Young males were more uniformly shielded, irrespective of maturity and knowledge.[44]

The parallel prosecution of some of these male youths for vagrancy and on other misdemeanor charges in juvenile courts demonstrates how legal proceedings served to rechannel the conduct of adolescent males and rehabilitate them into respectable sociality and sexuality. South Asian men convicted of sodomy were not immune from the potential of rehabilitation, particularly in jurisdictions with a strong system of convict labor and work parole, such as Washington State. Distributing incarcerated men to work programs throughout the state reduced incarceration expenses, provided cheap and constrained labor for capitalist development throughout the state, and enlisted businessmen in creating a pool of disciplined, immobilized, docile laborers. Some men had worked in the state for nearly a decade before being forced into the incarcerated labor system of rehabilitation. Channan Singh arrived at the Bellingham train station from Canada in August 1906, a year before the city was rocked by a violent "anti-Hindu" driving-out campaign, and found temporary work in lumber camps and timber mills across the state.[45] On one of his sojourns in Seattle, on June 24, 1914, he was convicted of attempted sodomy on a sixteen-year-old boy. Singh was drinking in downtown bars and went to his hotel room, where, he explained, "by and by a boy came in and I gave him fifty cents." A policeman followed into his room and arrested Singh for sodomy. In his defense, Singh blamed the male youth and immoral environment in which transient men were forced to live. Before his arrival in the United States, Singh explained, he had never consumed liquor, nor frequented "saloons and houses of ill repute," and generally associated with his "fellow workmen."[46]

After serving in Washington State Penitentiary in Walla Walla for thirteen months, he was released on work parole in July 1915 to the care of a grocery store owner, R. W. McCoy. McCoy kept Channan Singh working at his grocery store for the first couple of months and arranged for a more "steady job" at the Elliott Bay Lumber Company when seasonal work was available. In each of his monthly letters, McCoy praised Singh's "excellent conduct" and explained how imprisonment and closely observed work parole had "made a man out of him." Singh abstained from liquor and it was "impossible to even get him to go into a saloon." McCoy expressed a particular confidence in his trustworthiness by adding, "As you know a Hindu would not break his solemn word when given." Steady work and temperance could restore the morality of a South Asian man. After six months of positive reports Superintendent Henry Drum signed Channan Singh's final release from parole in January 1916.[47] The influences of steady work, disciplined habits, and avoidance of commercial vice were the key elements of the rehabilitation process in Washington State.

Work parole as an avenue to release convicts with good conduct prison records continued in the 1920s. In a similar case, in the lumber mill town of Cosmopolis on Washington's southern coast, Kisken Singh was convicted of attempted sodomy of a white male youth in January 1926. Police described Singh as "crazy with drink," and even with no memory of his actions, he pled guilty to "assaulted a boy." After serving a year in prison, he was released on work parole.[48] The work-parole system provided a profitable supplement to the convict labor system. Both systems reduced the state's incarceration expenses and created a pool of constrained labor for road construction and infrastructure development that enhanced private industry's capacity for resource extraction and exploiting capitalist opportunities in timber and agricultural development. Work parole provided inexpensive, constrained laborers who were accountable to their private sponsors. They could be paid considerably less than their fellow workers and their behavior was vigilantly supervised by their citizen business sponsors. The seemingly altruistic system was a public-private partnership for rehabilitating men into reliable, restrained, and disciplined wage workers under the moral supervision of their employers.[49]

In these early-twentieth-century court cases, the variability of the ethnic and racial identities of the male youths (European immigrant, Native American, and native-born white) demonstrates the broadening of subjects for the project of social rehabilitation into "normal" moral American men. While the racial boundaries for the social rehabilitation of male youths were malleable, the court cases underscored and justified the insurmountable racial boundary that perpetually defined Asian men as foreigners to the American nation. The amoral Asian could never be an "ordinary American" and was already defined as an unfit subject for American society and at the outer limits of the continuum between the "natural man" and the "natural degenerate." The "foreigner" and the "degenerate" were not legal categories, but were culturally and politically potent contextual categories that served both to identify and to explain moral peril.

Racial ascriptions of external threats such as "Oriental depravity" and "Hindu sodomites" had the taxonomic function of harnessing suspicion and identifying and amplifying targets for both the official police and the informal policing of community residents. They did not produce a categorical certainty, but if not all foreigners were immoral and degenerate, a culturally manufactured "tendency to immorality" nonetheless reinforced racialized suspicions. In sentencing hearings and judicial decisions, the interpretation of criminal behavior shifted the focus from the criminal act to criminal identities. And the very categories of fixing individual behavior into broad social categories were undergoing transformation. Categories of ethnicity and race had been employed descriptively, but they were now being harnessed to new categories such as degeneracy and normality. By the mid twentieth century, the broad categories of "normal" and "degenerate" would become interchangeable with the binary opposition of heterosexual and homosexual.[50]

The putative threat posed by the social practices of "amoral" alien migrants, domestic transients, and male adolescents thus simultaneously unsettled and shored up the constitution of normal American masculinity. The policing of degeneracy and anxious fixing of categories of unnatural sex and social conduct illuminated how liberal governance produced authoritative rule and social subjects to reproduce a society of normal and ordinary Americans. The conjunction of external danger (amoral foreign migrant), internal danger (degenerate vagrant), and the identification of subjects for flexible rehabilitation (delinquent youth) became the ensemble of social figures that required policing and prosecution.

Defining American and Canadian national identities with normalcy entailed policing male adolescent relationships with both external and internal nomadic subjects—foreigners and vagrants—who were fashioned as the embodiment of immorality and degeneracy. Prosecutors and judges in the early twentieth century created racialized and sexualized typologies of masculinity to police the relationships of roaming male youth and foreign migrants. Their immediate purpose was to identify the dangers posed to male youth, but the effect was to ensure a future for normative masculinity in both the United States and Canada.[51] Normative masculinity was preserved from the threats of other interloper masculinities, cast as foreign and degenerate. Yet the age and gender ambiguities posed by male youths confounded the jurists, forcing them to consider whether sodomy was an act of violation or invitation, to judge whether a youth was innocent, criminal, or delinquent.

The intensifying prosecution of sodomy, public indecency, and vagrancy in the early twentieth century gave way to a greater legal coherence of social figures that required governance. Judith Grbich has encouraged scholarly investigation into "the ways in which legal reasoning transforms the embodied imaginings" of particular lives into that "which passes for the 'normative.'"[52] The process of transforming "embodied imaginings" into normative subjects also produced a wide array of liberal life forms, both valorized and denigrated, that were shaped by legal, political, and cultural logics into a regulative field. In early twentieth-century political and legal liberalism, the most valued and valorized life forms were the normal man and normal woman, "fit subjects of society," who were seen to constitute national sexuality. The healthy, fit, reproductive capacities of normal men and women were affirmed as simultaneously "natural" and "civilized" by legal regulations that both shaped consensual and contractual monogamous marriage and curtailed putatively unnatural habits and vice.

Liberal governance and the policing of liminal social spaces also produced life forms that defined the boundaries of and threats to American and Canadian normalcy—the vagrant, the degenerate, and the delinquent—all of whom inhabited the expansive repertoire of the "abnormal" in law and social life. These new social subjects of liberal rule generated a paradoxical process of fortifying "the authority of normality and the deviancy of the abnormal."[53] The policing of internal and external nomadic subjects revealed the ambiguity and insecurity of cross-racial intimacy.

Court cases and jurisprudence contributed to the sociological and aesthetic knowledge needed to identify and regulate aliens, vagrants, and degenerates.[54] The state's imperative to prosecute sodomy forged a seemingly unassailable defense of normality and masculinity and produced an immense legal archive, which records its success at maintaining security. Through the process of abstracting legal rules and interpretation from particular court cases, the legal archive can be harnessed to reinforce authoritative and normalized legal subjects. But the very same repository can also be reinterpreted to expose rifts and crevices where competing narratives have slipped. These residual traces in the case records contradict and confound the normalizing of legal subjects.

The presumed propensity of vagrants and racialized foreigners to sodomy anticipated the consolidation of the dangerous figure of the "male homosexual pervert" as the dominant threat to the development of normal masculinity and sexuality. In the 1910s and 1920s, prior to the cataclysmic economic and social disruptions of the Great Depression, this convergence produced the perception that linked degeneracy with transience. As Margot Canaday has argued, correlating national identity with sexual normalcy was a new and uneven development of the twentieth century.[55] The categories of deviance and normality and the new definitions of sexual identity shaped the policing of male adolescents' relationships with both external and internal nomadic subjects—the foreigners and transients who were the targets of vagrancy and sodomy prosecution. Policing and judicial reasoning converted these social dangers into the categories of delinquents, vagrants, and degenerates. Reconfigurations of legal knowledge stabilized the regulation of sexual practices and social ties by buttressing gender norms onto racial and national identities and intensifying the criminalization of sodomy and homosexuality wholesale.

The judicial process revealed the unsettled meanings and embodiments of masculinity, adolescence, and normative sexual behavior. Case by case, the legal archive underlined racialized sexualities that endangered the state as well as national masculinity. Even as the prosecutors, judges, and legal commentators strove in each individual case to put borders around normal masculinity, the dilemma of judging consent to illicit sex or disreputable association repeatedly subverted any hope of fixed borders. Judges and prosecutors recognized that no matter how vigilantly they attempted to curtail specific sexual acts, partners, or practices, they could not corral the boundaries of normative masculinity or contain the attributes of national identity.

## CHAPTER 5

# Intimate Ties and State Legitimacy

The institution of marriage has been a linchpin for debates about morality, kinship, belonging, and citizenship. Through conquest, territorial expansion, and encouraging labor migration, empire-states and nation-states have confronted diverse intimacies and struggled to establish the legitimacy of intimate ties. The administration of legitimacy occurred in legislation, in judicial trials, and in registration and licensing procedures. In liberal rule-of-law states, judicial trials, in particular, are a flashpoint of controversy and debate over government legitimacy. Judges and attorneys attempt to fit the particular circumstances of individual cases into the categories of monogamous marriage, concubinage, bigamy, polygamy, and sodomy. In European and European-settler nations and colonies, within the hierarchy of legitimate and illegitimate relationships, Christian monogamous marriage often stands alone as the norm against an array of allegedly deviant intimacies that ranged from polygamy to sodomy. Liberal states have insisted on the universality of marriage. Despite widespread social and cultural differences, treaties have mutually recognized heterogeneous intimate ties sanctioned by empire-states and nation-states. In the capitalist political economy, marriage has become perhaps even more central as the translatable alliance of social standing for the legitimate distribution of land, labor, wealth, and status.

U.S. and Canadian women's historians and legal historians have demonstrated that the incorporation of land and people through conquest, slavery, and migration forced governments to confront variable situations of intimacy and kinship. Recent scholarship has amplified how the histories of conquest, colonialism, migration, and capitalist extraction made the U.S. West a frenetic site for social experimentation and regulation.[1] State and provincial governments in western North America created laboratories for legitimizing intimate ties and kinship, and "factories" for manufacturing gender roles and race definitions.[2]

In governing multicultural societies, U.S. and Canadian courts and administrations developed knowledge of customs, religions, and institutions, and classified social relations and people by ethnicity, race, and religious identity. Judges and attorneys sifted through local customs to understand how a particular marriage was religiously sanctified or legitimated by community acceptance. In the process, a steady stream of questions arose in adjudicating marriage relationships. Was the social bond and duty maintained by the couple's sharing of a household or by the vows they exchanged? Was it possible that the marriage could be dissolved by divorce, by the distance or length of time the couple were apart, or by abandonment?

The legislative regulation and judicial administration of marriage widened considerably in the late nineteenth and twentieth centuries with proliferating new standards of marriage age, race, and the contractual obligations of marriage licensing. How did South Asian male migrants and their female partners negotiate the power of the courts in regulating marriage? Some couples sidestepped racial restrictions of marriage licensing by applying in more favorable jurisdictions. Spouses, kin, and communities handled problems that arose from cohabitation, plural marriage, and abandonment outside the courts. However intractable disputes or failed arrangements necessitated that spouses and kin avail themselves of the courts and fit their problems into the legal categories of divorce, bigamy, and inheritance rights. The legal judgments over marriage legitimacy balanced ever-changing systems of race taxonomies, the judge's appreciation of traditional custom, and the exercise of humanitarian sympathy.

In court cases, the evaluation of a person's capacity for respectable legitimate marriage influenced the distribution and organization of land, labor, wealth, and status. The transmission of property, citizenship status, and immigrant entry was configured under the logic of marriage, respectable family formation, and the clear designation of dependents and heirs. The local adjudication of disputes over marriage and property reveals how the flexible interplay of sympathy and taxonomy shape the micropolitics of justice.

The complexity of these issues is apparent in the distribution of an estate in Las Cruces, New Mexico, in 1933. The estate case appeared straightforward;

two women, Soledad Garcia Jubala of New Mexico and Nami Singh of Punjab, each claimed to be the wife of a deceased man, Julio Jubala, and the heir to his estate. However, the simple dispute unleashed examples of diverse marriages and how they were lived and interpreted across three decades. A court dispute spawned inquiry into the life history of a migrant, the variety of his intimate ties, and the court's determination to judge legitimacy among a contentious sea of community standards, religious practices, and state sanctions. The inquiry confronted different understandings of marriage age, fidelity, and the requirements for cohabitation and consummation, and entertained debates over how to interpret abandonment or the validity of divorce. The debates produced by the marriages of Julio Jubala and his alleged spouses on two continents generated a rich legal field on how liberal secular government honored the particularities of diverse marriage customs, as well as creating rules, standards, and boundaries that corralled diverse marriages into an observable and manageable universal system.

Diversity in religious customs has frequently been at odds with the standardization of state legitimacy of marriage. In the United States, state legislators, federal bureaucrats, missionaries, and social critics created and defined the standard of Christian monogamous marriage and shored it up against an array of putatively deviant unions. As Nancy Cott has argued, assertions of differences of race and civilization buttressed the superiority of the marriage norm: the "marital non-conformists most hounded and punished by the federal government were deemed 'racially' different from the white majority. They were Indians, freed slaves, polygamous Mormons (metaphorically nonwhite) and Asians. Prohibiting divergent marriages has been as important in public policy as sustaining the chosen model."[3] Christian monogamous marriage occupied the normative heart of the continuum, and veering away on either side were an array of sexual-relations "horrors" and "female degradation." Knowledge of non-normative intimate ties circulated culturally among evangelical Protestant Christians in North America, and in what the historian Joan Jacobs Brumberg has so dramatically called "characteristic atrocities" of Asia and Africa, including "concubinage and polygamy; bride sale; . . . consecrated prostitution and sacrifice; . . . [and] child marriage," as well as sodomy, in all its possible non-procreative forms.[4]

My purpose is to understand the government management of intimate ties as a *process* that simultaneously shores up the norm and scrutinizes deviant unions. Despite the prevailing administrative, political, and cultural ratification of Christian monogamous marriage as the underlying norm of legitimate unions, government agents and judges confronted a diversity of intimate ties in localities. In the judicial and administrative handling, some ties were made either legible, visible, and legitimate or illegible, invisible, and illegitimate to the state. At the same time, other possible ties emerged that had local sanction through kinship and community support. Stray details within the court transcript and other legal documents undermined the certainty of judicial decisions and attorneys' briefs.

## RACIALIZING MARRIAGE PROHIBITIONS

Canadian and U.S. immigration laws made it nearly impossible for South Asian women to immigrate. Nonetheless, in the early twentieth century, a handful of South Asian women negotiated immigration barriers and migrated to Canada and the United States to join their husbands.[5] Unlike the handful of highly visible South Asian women in Vancouver who were married to economic and community leaders, the five Punjabi families in Northern California in Yuba City, Loomis, and Orangevale were relatively isolated and less able to create women's networks among themselves.[6] In British Columbia and the Pacific Northwest, a number of South Asian men married white and European immigrant women. However, anthropologists and historians have estimated that the overwhelming majority of South Asian men married Mexican immigrant and Mexican American women in Southern California, Arizona, and Texas from the late 1910s through the 1950s. There were also several instances of marriages with African American women in California and in the Southeast, Northeast, and Great Lakes regions.[7]

In the late 1910s, the labor market and marriage networks followed similar paths connecting South Asian male migrants who came to the Imperial Valley from the Northwest and Northern California and Mexican women and children who had fled the turmoil of the Mexican revolution and arrived in El Paso, Texas. From there they migrated and worked in the booming cotton fields of newly irrigated borderlands near El Paso, southern New Mexico, and Imperial County, California. The channels of migration were carved by the Southern Pacific passenger railway routes, which brought Punjabi and Japanese men from coastal California across the desert Southwest and into contact with Mexican men and women.[8] White and African American rural migrants from Oklahoma, Texas, Arkansas, and Missouri joined them, migrating by railroad

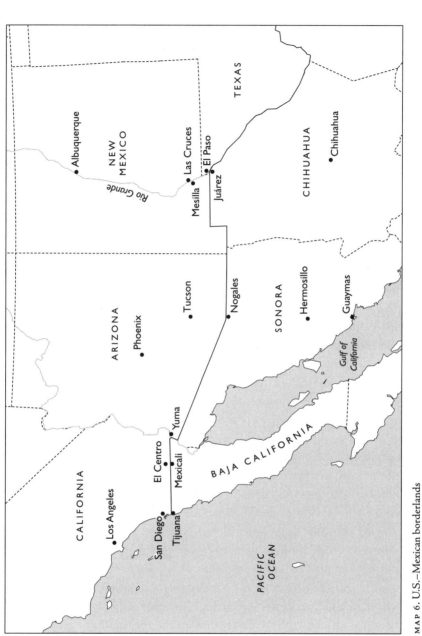

MAP 6. U.S.–Mexican borderlands

to harvest cotton. The spread of cotton culture to the San Joaquin Valley in California in 1919 accelerated the interstate movement, with diverse workers coming seasonally to harvest the cotton, while others remained permanently.[9]

Karen Leonard has examined patterns of South Asian men marrying Mexican sisters, cousins, mothers, and daughters in El Paso and in the San Joaquin Valley and Imperial County, California. The convergence of migration routes, associations developed through agricultural land-leasing partnerships, and recruited labor crews on newly irrigated commercial farms sustained these marriages. In Imperial County, the migration patterns and marriage networks of the Alvarez family converged with South Asian men's partnerships and friendships. The Alvarez family had fled the turmoil of the Mexican revolution. Doña Petra Alvarez, three of her daughters, Antonia, Anna Anita, and Ester, and her son Jesús arrived by train in El Paso in 1916. Learning of work opportunities in California, they quickly made their way by train to Imperial County, where the family settled and picked cotton on the Edwards ranch in Holtville for two South Asian tenant partners, Sher Singh and Gopal Singh. Within months, twenty-one-year-old Antonia had married thirty-six-year-old Sher Singh and eighteen-year-old Anna Anita had married thirty-seven-year-old Gopal Singh. The intensity of same-gender ties among both South Asian men and Mexican and Mexican American women tended to promote rapid serial marriages, often with significant age differences between men and women.[10] An older widowed daughter of Doña Petra's, Valentina, followed her family to El Centro with her four daughters. Valentina married Rullia Singh in October 1917. A month later, Alejandrina, her fourteen-year-old (stated on the marriage certificate to be eighteen) daughter had married a South Asian friend of Rullia's, a man who went by the American name of Albert Joe. The youngest Alvarez sister, Ester, married Harnam Singh Sidhu in Arizona in 1919.[11] As Karen Leonard has observed, strong women's networks developed from Mexican kinship ties and were "reinforced and expanded by marriages to Punjabi [men], settlement in particular localities and childbearing accompanied by compadrazgo [co-parenthood, godfather status] ties." The significance of *compadrazgo* relationships adapted Catholic baptism rituals and the naming of godparents to intensify and multiply kinship ties between adults in these mixed-heritage marriages between Mexican Catholic women and Punjabi men, predominantly Sikhs, but some of them Hindus or Muslims. The shared socializing and economic responsibilities of co-parenting and jointly raising children sutured and sustained business alliances between men and combined them with cultural, kinship and spiritual ties sustained by Mexican and Mexican American women to create novel, dense, deeply familiar joint-family ties that interwove into a "Mexican-Punjabi" community. [12]

Prohibitions on interracial marriage, which were unevenly legislated and varied by territory and state, stymied legitimate unions for Asian migrants. Miscegenation laws were neither universal nor systematic. As Peggy Pascoe has argued, anti-miscegenation laws "in the West, not the South, reached their most elaborate, even labyrinthine development, covering the broadest list of racial categories."[13] As Pascoe has demonstrated, miscegenation law was a "kind of legal factory for defining, producing and reproducing racial categories." The recognition of different races and legislative amendments state by state in the Western states produced the multiracial pattern of white supremacy adapted by Georgia and Virginia in the 1920s. Miscegenation law was a "national" and "multiracial . . . project of white supremacy rooted in white purity" that "placed non-Whites in structurally similar subordination to Whites," as if all social groups not identified as "White" presented the "same threat to whiteness."[14]

In Canada, there were no laws that specifically prohibited marriages between different races, but as Constance Blackstone has argued, there were laws in western Canada that prohibited white women from working for Chinese or Japanese men. Yet even without explicit prohibition, marriages between South Asian men and white and European immigrant women were infrequent. Politicians and moral reformers anticipated that social prejudices would hamper the frequency of interracial marriages.[15] In the first three decades of South Asian migrant settlement in British Columbia, there were a dozen marriages registered between white women and one black woman and South Asian men. The majority of women had migrated to British Columbia as children or young women. Their parents and their birthplace origins illustrate a diversity of British and North American origins, from Omaha, Nebraska, to Houston, Texas; from Hawaii to the Philippines; and from Niagara, Ontario, to Scotland, England, and Wales. Some of these marriages had the support of the bride's parents and were consecrated in ceremonies in Protestant churches. For instance, in Victoria in 1913 and 1914, Baptist and Presbyterian ministers married several white brides—Margaret Banloo and Alice Markle, both aged twenty-two, and Maude Alice Crowley, aged twenty-four—to South Asian men. The South Asian men, some of whom were widowers, worked as ranchers, farmers, and mill workers in or near Victoria and Vancouver.[16]

In rare instances, white women married South Asian men in a newly established Sikh temple (*gurudhwara*). The first Sikh wedding ceremony in Vancouver was between Bhai Munsha Singh and Annie Wright at a *gurudhwara* there on April 4, 1909, seven months after they had registered their marriage at the Vancouver courthouse. Teja Singh, a Sikh scholar educated at Cambridge University in Britain and Columbia University in New York, performed the wedding ceremony in the afternoon, and both the bride and groom were renamed in the presence of an assembly of devout Sikhs. Bhai Munsha Singh was given the new name of Gayan Singh and Annie Wright was renamed Labb Kor. Vancouver Sikhs invited Teja Singh, who lectured extensively on Sikhism in North America, to help educate the general public, who were hostile and ignorant of Sikh values and spiritual practices. Teja Singh took the opportunity of the wedding ceremony to relate the meaning of Sikh marriage vows closely to Protestant cultural norms. He explained that "marriage was a divine union of two souls and not a mere carnal bond," and that the duties of both spouses were faithfulness, loyalty, and being "strictly monogamous" in "thoughts and action." They were to achieve "peace and harmony" by "sacrificing . . . personal tastes and inclinations to each other." Teja Singh also had the couple vow to "live by the Sikh religion" and perform all the birth, marriage and death ceremonies" of their children according to "Sikh rites." Teja Singh's work in Vancouver extended far beyond officiating rituals at the *gurudhwara* and presenting public lectures; he established two key community institutions by drafting the by-laws and legally registering the *gurudhwara's* administrative organization, the Khalsa Diwan Society, and a closely linked real estate and investment company, the Guru Nanak Mining and Trust Company. Both institutions became critical to the development of Sikh community and to its public presence in British Columbia. [17]

Despite the lack of barriers in British Columbia, marriages were more frequent in the agriculturally intensive border regions of the southern United States with Mexico. Migration streams, work relations, and social experience of race shaped marriage patterns. In the Pacific Northwest, even though there were no miscegenation laws that prohibited interracial marriages in British Columbia or Washington State, there were few licensed marriages of South Asian men with white women. Legal acceptance did not mean that county clerks readily issued marriage licenses—they might curtly refuse to provide one, without offering any explanation to the humiliated couple. Hostility of relatives, neighbors, and ministers also dampened pursuit of the legal legitimacy of marriage. The small numbers of registered marriages paralleled work and social relations in the Pacific Northwest that reduced social opportunities and limited contact between men and women. In towns like Bellingham, Astoria, Linnton, and Gate in the Pacific Northwest, and even in cities like Vancouver, Portland, Seattle, and Sacramento, labor camps and boardinghouses socialized working men across racial lines, but also isolated them into a homosocial public world. South Asian men had contact with other transient and immigrant workers and laborers, contractors and employers, and shopkeepers. South Asian laborers were unlikely to meet and become familiar with white American and European immigrant women, except for the very few they encountered in retail and service positions. Encounters were guarded. The hostility of white society was expressed in driving-out violence, most vehement and frequent in Vancouver, Washington State, and Northern California, and interaction was limited to highly regulated and scripted suspicion. Fear of labor competition and rumors of insolence and disrespect toward white women crystallized racialized perceptions of South Asians as a sexual threat, corresponding to white fears of black, Japanese, and southern European men. In the Pacific Northwest, the rare romances and marriages that did occur were isolated, and therefore they did not create new heterosocial social networks enabling other meetings, romances, and marriages between South Asian men and European immigrant, white Canadian, or white American women.

In the middle of the nineteenth century, miscegenation laws that first prohibited white-black marriages and white-Indian marriages in the U.S. southeastern states were amended in western states to prohibit white-Asian marriages. The first laws in the United States that specifically prohibited marriages between white and Chinese spouses emerged in Nevada in 1861, Idaho in 1864, and Oregon in 1867. The race category of "Mongolian" enlarged the scope of prohibited groups to include Japanese and Korean in Arizona in 1865, in California in 1880, and in Utah in 1888.[18]

The multiplication of race and national prohibitions contributed, as Peggy Pascoe has observed, to "adding the race and gender pair of white women / Asian men to the project of protecting white womanhood," and Chinese, Japanese, Filipino, and South Asian men all figured in "miscegenation dramas" that "circulated in newspaper accounts of Asian men and white women attempting to marry." As Pascoe has eloquently argued:

No doubt these dramas captivated readers partly for the enticing lure of the forbidden, the new and exotic possibilities they pitted against traditional morality. But no matter how many readers may have fantasized about choosing interracial romance over legal propriety, there was no mistaking the moral of these stories—or their political effects. By reinforcing the impression that the function of miscegenation laws was to preserve the purity of white womanhood, miscegenation dramas closed off avenues of change. By showing young white women that their protection depended on the loyalty to their race, and by encouraging officials to pass and enforce miscegenation laws, miscegenation dramas served white supremacy by racializing and sexualizing Asian American men in relation to white women.[19]

Although the legal scholars Hrishi Karthikeyan and Gabriel Chin explain that the state's predisposition to segregate blacks and the visible Asian population was the best predicator of coverage by anti-miscegenation laws, demographics and racially discriminatory laws and policies were frequently disconnected.[20]

By the 1910s and 1920s, the greatest concentration of South Asians was in California, but their numbers and visibility in the Sacramento, San Joaquin, and Imperial Valleys did not lead the California legislature to target "Hindu" or "Asian Indian" specifically in miscegenation prohibitions, even when they racialized Filipinos as "Malay" in 1928. Legislators intent on preserving white racial purity and supremacy confidently presumed that prohibitions against "Mongolian" races would curtail marriages between South Asian men and white women. Two southern states, Virginia in 1924 and Georgia in 1927, specifically prohibited marriages of "Asiatic Indians" and white persons. Arizona, the only western state to do so, added "Hindu" to its marriage prohibitions in 1931. The specificity of ethnic and racial identities did not, however, completely determine whether marriages were licensed and legitimate.[21]

Racialization of Asian immigrants was neither automatic nor coherent in the United States. Deenesh Sohoni challenges the assumption that members of different Asian ethnic groups were originally grouped together based on their perceived racial characteristics. Analyzing how racialization operated in federal naturalization rulings and state miscegenation laws, Sohoni argues that racialization concepts distributed people from Asia into at least three racial categories—"yellow–Mongolians, brown–Malays, and white Caucasian–Asian Indians."[22] In the 1920s, however, law and administration consolidated a unified racial category of "Asian" or "Asiatic" and emphasized a presumed and shared incapacity for social and political assimilation to North

American societies. Proscribing social integration for people denied naturalized citizenship based on a circular and self-perpetuating category of racial
difference constructed "Asians" as a distinct, inassimilable race through immigration and naturalization laws and anti-miscegenation legislation.[23]

Despite the potent fear that none of them could be socially integrated
into U.S. society, Asian immigrants forged personal and domestic ties with
other migrants they encountered and persisted in seeking legitimacy in their
ethnic and local communities, as well as the legitimacy of local, state, and
federal jurisdictions when necessary and plausible. Karen Leonard has tabulated 230 marriages of South Asian men to white, Mexican, and black women
in Imperial County from 1916 to 1946, with half of the marriage licenses
obtained in Southern California and the other half in Arizona, Nevada,
and Texas. Marriage licensing became a powerful and invisible tool for judging a couple's fitness for marriage. Marriage reformers effectively undercut
the popularity of common law and community-sanctioned marriages by
demanding stringent regulations for licenses. By 1900, reformers had "turned
marriage licenses into the sole gateway to legal marriage" and made local
officials "the society's first line of defense against unwanted marriages." By
the 1920s, they turned "marriage license clerks into the gatekeepers of white
supremacy"—6,070 marriage-license issuers spread across the United States,
"a virtual army of bureaucrats perfectly positioned to enforce state miscegenation laws."[24]

The routine, ordinary, and invisible power of marriage licensing produced
a ritual practice underscoring the state and the law's role in the public affirmation of marriage. "The process of licensing applied to every couple who wished
to marry, stewarded couples through the public ritual of obeying the law and
provided the state with the perfect opportunity to emphasize the contrast
between couples who could—and could not—claim the privilege of marriage," Pascoe writes. Moreover, it afforded a "routine means" of enforcing race
prohibitions "well outside the glare of publicity that surrounded sensational
miscegenation dramas in the public press." Even in states where interracial
marriages were legal, local officials could discourage them and thereby "foster the social invisibility of interracial sex and marriage by, in effect, erasing
interracial couples from national marriage statistics, reinforcing the common
impression that, with or without laws to prevent them, interracial marriages
were extreme rarities." The "denial of license operated as a kind of public shaming ritual performed by state and local officials."[25]

In California, Arizona, and Texas, county clerks did use the category of "Mongolian" to prohibit some marriages, but they frequently relied upon assessments of "color" and complexion rather than "race" to approve licenses between South Asian grooms and Mexican brides. In many western localities, these marriage prohibitions were irregularly enforced and creatively bypassed by individuals, clerks, and judges to suit local conditions.[26] Although most couples were married in Imperial County, the county clerk sometimes posed difficulties, which led brides and grooms to apply for licenses elsewhere. San Diego County and Yuma County were the closest alternative and frequent destination for marriage licenses. For instance, although Bagh Singh Chotia and Grace Stove met and lived in Imperial County, they traveled to Yuma, Arizona, to marry in 1917.[27] In July 1927, when California legislation mandated a three-day waiting period between application for a marriage license and issuance, there was a decline in marriages in California and increases in Nevada and Arizona, particularly Yuma. This flow of out-of-state marriages with South Asian men, however, contributed in 1931 to the Arizona legislature adding the categories of "Hindu" and "Malay" to their prohibitions to marrying whites, thereby curtailing the frequency of marriages with South Asian and Filipino grooms in Yuma and elsewhere in Arizona.[28]

Dozens of marriages between Mexican and Mexican American women and South Asian men also took place in the vicinity of El Paso, Texas, especially at Canutillo and San Elizario in the El Paso river valley, where Sikhs farmed cotton, as well as in Las Cruces, New Mexico, where there were no waiting-period restrictions and no race prohibitions against marriage. In December 1918, in the El Paso County Courthouse, sixteen-year-old Felicita Soto, born in Austin, married thirty-year-old Harnam Singh Dhillon. Their courtship and marriage was sutured by labor partnerships and kinship networks in southwestern Texas, which, in turn, stimulated and sustained their migration to Imperial County, California, by 1920, where they raised the first of four children.[29] Adapting to changing laws and the varying racial classification by county court clerks, South Asian men and Mexican women met and received marriage licenses in different locations in the Southwest, from El Centro and Yuma to El Paso, and families were sustained by a network of information about work opportunities and community support shared by both South Asian men and Mexican and Mexican American women.

The state and social regulation made Asian and Mexican immigrants into perpetual nomadic subjects. Despite and perhaps because of their nomadic

subjectivity, they became adept at evading state-imposed restrictions on property ownership, marriage, and other forms of belonging. By pursuing marriages
in states without white-Asian marriage prohibitions, or working with county
clerks who observed similarities that accorded with commonsense understandings of color difference, or orchestrating marriages offshore, they were able to
undercut or evade the racial taxonomies of state-licensed marriage. However,
the state's role in legitimatizing or repudiating intimate ties was not limited to
the issue of marriage and birth certificates. It could also intervene when questions of citizenship status at the borders or inheritance arose.[30]

## LEGITIMATE HEIRS AND MARRIAGE CUSTOMS

A court case in the Rio Grande Valley town of Mesilla, New Mexico, raises
compelling questions about the state's interpretation of marriage in terms
of ethnic, religious, and race differences. On the night of December 27, 1932,
forty-five-year-old Julio Jubala was instantly killed when the truck he was driving was struck by a northbound freight train at the Mesilla Park crossing.[31] At
the probate hearing in April 1933, two women claimed to have been his wife,
one in Mesilla, Soledad Garcia Jubala, whom he had married in 1929, and the
second in India, Nami Singh, who claimed that they had been married in 1898.
Because of the claim of a first marriage in India, a fairly routine probate case
after a tragic death became a civil suit that played out over two continents and
over three years in the New Mexico court system.[32]

As the attorneys tried to probe and justify the competing claims of the two
women, the legitimacy or illegitimacy of the marriage in India came under
dispute. Especially in the early twentieth century, U.S. courts were sometimes
confronted with adjudicating the legitimacy of marriages consecrated in
India. Although accounts of marriage customs in British India such as dowry,
child brides and grooms, *zenanas* (harems), and *sati* (widow immolation)
circulated widely in the print culture of American evangelical Protestants
in the late nineteenth century, it was not until the migration of male laborers from Punjab in the early twentieth century that the legitimacy of marriages consecrated in India became a political or legal issue in localities in
North America.

After verifying the identity of the deceased, Julio Jubala of New Mexico,
as the same man as the Jawala Singh whom Nami Singh married in Punjab
in 1898, who had left India in 1907, Nami Singh's attorneys introduced

immigration documents and testimony from family and friends to show that
Julio/Jawala had arrived in Mesilla, New Mexico, in 1910 after stops in Hong
Kong, the Philippines, and Mexico. Nami's attorneys introduced testimony
that verified that the marriage had been properly consecrated and recognized
in British India. The New Mexico District Court enlisted the U.S. consul in
Karachi in British India to depose witnesses in Punjab. The consul summoned
Nami Singh, her father, Jawala's father, and a Brahmin priest. They testified
that the parents had arranged the marriage; Nami had been twelve and Jawala
eleven when they married in a Hindu ceremony in her home village on June
3, 1898. Nami declared that the bride and groom "had not seen each before
the day of the ceremony," which was typical of arranged marriages. After the
ceremony, she had lived in Jawala's father's house for six years. Jawala's father
explained that "at the time of the marriage of my son to Nami, neither party
were of puberty age," and three years later, after reaching puberty, they assumed
the "relations of man and wife"—a euphemism for having publicly sanctioned
sexual relations. Subsequently, they lived together for approximately three
more years before Jawala Singh left for the United States.[33]

International treaties obliged the United States to recognize legitimate
unions in Britain and its empire. The details of a properly arranged match, pre-
adolescent age of the bride and groom, and the timing of sexual consummation were the narrative of legitimacy produced by Nami's attorneys. However,
these very same details were deployed by Soledad's attorneys as indicators of a
morally "repugnant" and thereby illegitimate system of marital unions.

Long-distance migration and the protracted separation of spouses and families across the Pacific created a different sense of time, marital duty, and the
significance of kin networks in forging bonds of communication for Jawala's
family in India. The distance and the length of time away were "perfectly normal procedure," according to Nami's father, who claimed that at the time that
"many Sikhs were leaving the Punjab for America to seek employment."[34]
Although Jawala Singh had not written much to his family, his father received
"news of his whereabouts and activities" from a network of "friends, neighbors,
and acquaintances" who had also migrated to the United States.[35] Villagers
in Punjab kept tabs, principally by telegram and mail, on their relatives scattered in California and the U.S. Southwest. The same network had delivered
news of Jawala's death by telegram within days, and had, within weeks, sent
reports of the estimated value of his estate and information regarding local

attorneys.[36] From the perspective of Nami's family, Julio/Jawala had abandoned neither her nor them.

Marriage customs in India were not, however, timeless. In the late nineteenth century, a "Hindu marriage" between religiously observant Sikhs followed Hindu Brahmin tradition and was consecrated by a Hindu Brahmin priest, and the marriage between Jawala Singh and Nami had been consecrated in 1898. Nonetheless, in turn-of-the-century Punjab, although slowly and unevenly, relatively "fluid pluralist traditions were being replaced by more uniform and exclusive Sikh, Muslim and Hindu paradigms."[37] Hindu and Sikh religious reform movements had gained momentum in the late nineteenth century and the process of standardizing and differentiating sectarian marriage ceremonies had the backing of the British colonial state, even though the necessity of creating distinctions appeared to have more salience for religious leaders and urban elites than for many villagers. In pursuit of a purified and bounded Sikh identity, Sikh reformers championed new marriage laws that created state recognition for differentiating Sikh and Hindu rituals and ceremonies and vesting legitimating authority with the appropriate respective institutions. As Doris Jakobsh and Prem Chowdhry have demonstrated, this reform of Sikh marriage rituals also consolidated the authority of male religious leaders over communal traditions of women's popular rites and boisterous traditions in marriages and key life-cycle events.[38] These permutations of social transformation in marriage ceremonies and legitimacy in British colonial India were well beyond the concern and expertise of the New Mexico judiciary. Whatever critical commentary the American judges had about the customs and practices of marriage, they were obliged by international treaties to recognize a legitimate marriage consecrated in British India.

The distance and decades of separation created waves of silence and insight throughout the Sikh diaspora. Migrants kept some details of their intimate and social lives secret, while revealing others to kin at home, as well as to friends and kin who had also migrated. These fluctuating crests and eddies of silence and partial knowledge were most striking in who possessed knowledge about each union and where they lived. Julio/Jawala's friends and relatives from Punjab who worked in the Rio Grande Valley testified that they were aware of his dual marriages. For instance, when an El Paso friend, Bood Singh, quizzed him about having two wives, Julio responded, "[T]here will be no trouble. I have a wife in both countries."[39]

Julio was even intent on persuading Bood to do the same and marry a "beautiful girl" locally in addition to Bood's wife in India. Bood argued that it was against the law to marry unless you divorced your first wife in India. Julio said, "[Nobody knows] I am married. Here you can marry here too; nobody tell it to the courts."[40] However, Jawala was careful to keep the knowledge of his marriage in India secret in his home in New Mexico. His cousin Delip Singh, who had attended Nami and Jawala's marriage ceremony, became reacquainted with Jawala in 1929 when they met at an El Paso horse corral.[41] After Delip learned of Soledad, Jawala begged him to keep his marriage to Nami secret, saying, "[D]on't tell it so my Mexican wife will know it."[42]

If Jawala's practice of plural marriage was controversial among his friends and relatives in the United States, it is unclear whether the disputes between Jawala and his friends arose from a moral value of monogamous marriage in the Sikh and Hindu traditions or economic fears. The fear of losing land through the dissolution of marriages in community property states such as New Mexico and California haunted many Punjabi men in the early twentieth century. For some, the handful of divorces from marriages with Mexican American women that had resulted in the loss of land and savings served as a cautionary tale of the danger of marriages to women in the United States.[43]

These promises of silence were kept; in Punjab, no one admitted to knowing of Soledad, and in New Mexico, no one but Punjabi village kin and friends in the United States knew about Nami. Yet with Jawala's untimely death, all the secrets exploded. His neighbor Udam Singh corresponded with his uncle who lived in the same village as Jawala's father, Nathu Singh, about his death, his wife, and the value of his estate. Nathu Singh sent telegrams to his nephew Delip Singh in El Paso and Bhooja Singh in Yuba City to investigate the death.[44] Bhooja Singh, Jawala's paternal uncle, was a pivotal and controversial character in the trial. He lived in Sacramento County, but was in close touch with Jawala and traveled frequently to New Mexico. Bhooja was instrumental in alerting Nami Singh of her husband's death and securing an attorney in El Paso to represent her; according to Jawala's friends, Bhooja had pressured them to oppose the marriage with Soledad Garcia in 1929. Soledad testified that Bhooja had proposed marriage to her shortly after Julio's death. She rebuffed him, but he was approaching her through a tradition of remarriage, *karewa*, common in Punjab where a brother, paternal cousin, or paternal uncle of the deceased claims the widow as his wife. As Prem Chowdhry has analyzed, this tradition was popular in agricultural communities to retain property within the husband's patriarchal family, as well as to ensure support of the widow by a man's heirs, especially since widow remarriage was generally problematic. However, it undermined a woman's independent ownership of property and was practiced with little regard for the express wishes of the widow.[45]

## DIVORCE

The overwhelming evidence of Nami's legitimate marriage provoked Soledad's attorneys to argue that Julio must have divorced Nami prior to his marriages in the United States. In questioning Nami's family, they discovered however, that divorce was not a legitimate option in Sikh and Hindu communities in British India.[46] Both fathers were adamant that marriage under "Hindu religious rites" did not recognize "divorce granted to either party."[47]

Soledad's attorneys, nevertheless, insisted that Jawala had petitioned for divorce sometime during his travels in Hong Kong, the Philippines, and Mexico. There was no documentation of divorce between Jawala and Nami in New Mexico records, however, and divorce was not permissible in Mexico until 1915.

Neither could one argue that Jawala was unfamiliar with divorce proceedings, since a record search by the court revealed that he had been legally married in 1917 to a Maria Fierro and subsequently divorced her in 1929.[48] This marriage was a footnote to the estate case, but it exemplifies a submerged history of marital disputes in interracial marriages that surfaced to public view through divorce suits. Divorce petitions required evidence of "irreconcilable differences" and ascribed "fault" to one or both of the spouses. Frequently, both spouses accused each other of violence and mental anguish to justify the extraordinary circumstances of dissolving a marriage. Maria and Julio Jubala's marriage was rocked by allegations of domestic violence. In 1926, Maria had filed a complaint in civil court that Julio had "choke[d], beat[en] and bruise[d] her," causing her to have "black and blue spots and swollen places on her head and neck," and she testified in 1929 during her divorce proceedings that he had become increasingly violent and abusive.[49] Julio described his difficulties with Maria to his friend Udam charging, "that woman is fighting always, so I am going to divorce."[50]

Divorce was far more frequent among these marriages between South Asian men and the Mexican, white, and black women they married in the Southwest than the U.S. national average. In the county with the largest number of marriages, Imperial County, California, Karen Leonard has tabulated that there were fifty-nine divorce petitions from 1919 to 1969 involving first-generation husbands from India, stemming from the marriage disputes of forty-five couples. Over a decade of Maria and Julio's marriage, there were several petitions for divorce filed at the Dona Ana County Courthouse in Las Cruces.

Maria had been born in the U.S. territory of New Mexico, and Mexican American heritage like hers figured in only 20 percent of divorce suits. The vast majority—nearly three-quarters—of the wives who appeared as defendants in such divorce petitions were first-generation Mexican immigrants. Over 39 percent of these divorce petitions were contested, more than triple the national average of 12 percent. Wives on average filed three-quarters of American divorce petitions, but in Imperial County, with the largest proportion of South Asian men who married in the United States, the men filed 60 percent of divorce petitions.[51]

It was Maria who filed the divorce petition. After a particularly vicious fight on September 17, 1928, she accused Julio of "violently" putting her out of their home and calling her "vile and indecent names." She claimed that he had struck her "in the face and head, jerked her and beat her, tore her dress and used profane and abusive language." According to her testimony, Julio "cussed her up," struck her in the face, and "dragged her by the hair." She left him and went to live with her father in the adjacent community of Tortugas. Neither Julio nor his legal representative appeared in court during the divorce hearings to contest Maria's allegations of violence and beatings, which Maria believed were a consequence their inability to have children. In court, she claimed that Julio had told her that he despised her because she was "too old" and unable to "get any children." Although she had started other divorce cases before, she had withdrawn them after Julio made entreaties and promised a better marriage.[52] In the end, Maria's case against Julio was uncontested. Neither he nor his lawyer appeared at the court hearing, and the judge validated the negotiated settlement without his presence.

Court records from Oregon to New Mexico are littered with divorce petitions involving South Asian men. Even the fiercest accusations of physical and mental abuse did not necessarily, however, result in a divorce decree. For instance, a rough-and-tumble marriage and accusations of mutual neglect and violence played out in the courtroom in Astoria, Oregon. Soba Singh and Pauline, his Belgian American bride, met in Oregon and crossed the border to Vancouver, Washington, to marry on March 15, 1920. They lived in Astoria, where Soba worked for the Hammond Lumber Company, which employed a number of South Asian men. The couple lived in a rented house that Soba claimed that he had furnished. He said he had tried to make their married life "congenial," but the financing of household consumption resulted in fierce disputes. In a pattern similar to that found among men in Imperial County, it was the husband, Soba, who seven months after their marriage filed a complaint for divorce, after Pauline fled Astoria for her mother's home in Portland. Soba accused Pauline of unprovoked "cruel and inhuman treatment," saying that in "fits of pique and temper," she had pulled his hair, struck him, and cursed him with "vile language." Soba Singh was mortified when Pauline exclaimed in public that she had "married him just for his money" and "did not love or care for him," a sentiment allegedly expressed in the food she cooked for him and her refusal to dine with him. He accused Pauline of denying him the "many delicacies and choice viand[s]" that she bought with his money and instead feeding him "poor and cheaper" foods. She allegedly ridiculed him for "not being a white man," and refused "to eat at the same time or table" with him, claiming that "her white skin" precluded her from eating with "a black man." Soba represented himself as a "considerate," responsible, "kind" husband despite this abuse.[53]

In her counterpetition, Pauline Singh claimed that she had "tried to be a dutiful and true wife," but that Soba Singh was a jealous, neglectful, and violent husband who was a "ginger [sic] addict." She admitted that she had pulled her husband's hair to force him to apologize "for having called her a son-of-a-b." However, she countered that his physical and verbal abuse far outweighed her actions. Several times, Soba had falsely accused her in "vile language" of infidelity. In the heat of argument, he would brandish a revolver, "grab her by the throat," and demand that she confess to adultery. She had fled to her mother in Portland, fearing that "her life was in danger." She demanded $35 per month in alimony, arguing that despite his alleged "ginger addiction," he was a "strong, able-bodied man and in regular employment." Two years later, despite the accusations of violence, humiliation, and neglect recorded in public, hostilities subsided and the two reconciled. The judge dismissed the suit, after receiving assurances that the couple had "amicably settled their differences."[54]

It was even more difficult to pursue divorce when there were young children and the spouses' cohabitation was necessary for economic survival, particularly in the duties involved in agricultural cultivation and labor coordination. When Nellie Khan petitioned for divorce from Walayat Khan in 1925 Sacramento, they had three children, born since their 1919 marriage in Los Angeles. The family migrated frequently following harvests and farm-laborer opportunities from Brawley in the Imperial Valley to Willows in the Sacramento Valley. In April 1925, near Walnut Creek, Sacramento County, Nellie reported, her husband had "beat, slapped, kicked, and bruised" her and "their infant child," which she held in her arms, and thrown her out of the house. His "cruel, brutal, insulting and vicious" treatment led her to fear for her life and the safety of her children. As the wife of a labor contractor and migrant worker, Nellie Khan was acutely familiar with the contracting system's demands for unpaid labor and the variable income it provided. She had used this knowledge both to demonstrate her fidelity toward her husband, following "him from place to place" in California and working "in the fields for many hours each day," caring for the family, and "cook[ing] for a large number of men," and to support her demands for alimony and circumvent her husband's ability to hide assets and the proceeds of informal contracts. In addition to requesting that the court order Walayat to pay half his monthly income in alimony payments of $100 and grant her complete care and custody of three minor children, she suggested the means for the court to locate community property. Her attorneys made a motion to put a restraining order on Manual Patrick, a Walnut Creek farmer, in his payment of $500 to Walayat Khan. The success of the motion led to a swift reconciliation, perhaps aided by her attorney's pessimistic counsel that the court would be unable to enforce alimony payments, and that irrespective of the decree, Nellie and her children would be exceedingly vulnerable in a divorce. By April 17, 1925, the two had settled their differences and were living together again, resulting in the dismissal of the divorce suit.[55]

Jaget Singh and his Jamaican-born wife Alice, the daughter of South Asian and African parents, had married in Guantánamo, Cuba, in May 1918, and subsequently immigrated to the United States, like many others who had disembarked at ports from Baltimore to Jacksonville, Tampa, and New Orleans since 1900, including Chinese, Japanese, and Syrian migrants.[56] Jaget and Alice joined his brother Mehar in California, where they found work in the farm-laborer circuit and lived for most of their married life. Their separation in November 1924 was precipitated by a fight in their Stockton boardinghouse, where, Alice alleged, Jaget had jumped on her, beaten her, and cursed her until Stockton police officers intervened.[57] Alice had just lost her daughter, who had been born in Jamaica in 1915.[58] She feared that her husband would appropriate their savings and personal property, convert the property into cash, and take the money to India to build a house and purchase land. When Jaget Singh failed to appear in court in Stockton to contest Alice's claims, she was awarded the divorce by default.

Divorce cases often emerged after several petitions. The interwoven ties of multiple marriages of women from the same family and men's business partnerships sometimes precipitated tension between couples, sometimes enabled reconciliations. In 1918 in El Paso, Matilde Sandoval married Kehar Singh Gill, and they promptly moved to Imperial County. Although Sandoval's mother and sister had also married Sikhs, Matilde's marriage to Kehar did not last. Within a year, he filed for divorce in El Centro, claiming that Matilde had humiliated him in front of a South Asian friend and refused to keep house and cook for him. Her behavior outside of the house was even more disturbing to his values and expectations of a wife. Her shopping trips in town included purchases of dresses and makeup, which she wore to dances without him. Kehar viewed Matilde's desire for autonomy to participate in a public culture of socializing, beauty, and business, and her belief that male dancing partners did not equate to infidelity, as a threat to the marriage and defiance of his exclusive authority over her public social circulation among men. In the heat of arguments about morals and behavior, Matilde had threatened to leave Kehar, and she fled to visit her mother in New Mexico. At the urging of her mother and sister, she returned, however, and they reconciled in 1919. Marriage tensions persisted, despite the efforts of Matilde's relatives and their husbands' business and social ties with Kehar. In 1922, Kehar filed for divorce again, and this time they officially divorced. The contested suits indicate that couples fought fiercely for the values of their marriages and the survival of their partnerships, whether to hold poverty at bay, for the sake of their dependents, or to preserve kinship or community ties.[59]

## THE EMPIRE OF MONOGAMOUS MARRIAGE

There was no debate over the legality of the marriage of Julio Jubala / Jawala Singh to Soledad Garcia. A marriage certificate was produced that revealed that six weeks after his divorce from Maria Fierro, the forty-two-year-old Julio had married Soledad, who was barely aged sixteen and nearly four months pregnant, in March 1929. She married with the permission of her father, Domingo Garcia, who worked on Julio's farms.[60] Julio and Soledad had three daughters in quick succession; the first, Alicia, was born five months after their marriage. Esther and Julia soon followed. When Julio died, Soledad was pregnant with their first son, who was named Manuel.

Curiously, Nami Singh's attorneys did not raise moral suspicions about the context of Soledad's marriage. Neither they nor the judge commented on her youth, her father's economic relationship with the groom, the generational differences in their ages, or the advanced state of her pregnancy on their wedding day. Apparently as an issue of the law, Soledad's father's permission and the proper legal documentation allayed any doubts about the morality of the marriage and offered it irreproachable legitimacy. These issues appear as stray details in the court transcript and were never raised in the court record by the historical actors at the time. Documentation from marriage, birth records, and other civil suits reveals details that heighten the ambiguity of Soledad and Julio/Jawala's marriage, especially in relation to the claims made about the legitimacy of Jawala's marriage to Nami.

The principle of sanctioning the first monogamous marriage and the prohibition on bigamy influenced District Court Judge James B. McGhee's decision in 1934. McGhee wrote that "the testimony is overwhelming that the claimant, Nami Singh, was lawfully married to the deceased in India."[61] The precedence of Nami's marriage, no evidence of divorce, and the principle of marital monogamy guided his decision. Since Nami had married Jawala/Julio first, she was entitled to inherit. Judge McGhee knew that his ruling would "deprive the Dona Ana county widow, who married the deceased a few years since, [of] her share of the property, and that it invalidates her marriage."[62] In following the rule of law on the precedence of marriage and abiding by the governing principle of monogamy, the district court had put the estate's property in jeopardy, and thereby put the Mesilla widow and her children at the mercy of government financial support. Under the Alien Land Law, however, Nami Singh's status as an "Asiatic alien" prohibited her ownership of the estate's 125 acres.[63]

Soledad's attorneys made an aggressive appeal to the New Mexico Supreme Court on grounds of the immorality and illegitimacy of Hindu marriage. They argued that New Mexico was not "bound by a law or custom that is repugnant to its established public policy; and the Hindu child marriage [performed in India by a Brahmin priest] . . . is repugnant to the established public policy of the State of New Mexico."[64] The effect of Judge McGhee's decision would make Soledad Jubala "nothing more than a concubine and that would in the same breath bastardize the four innocent children"; the decision would take away five-eighths of Jubala's estate and "give it to a woman who contributed nothing to its accumulation."[65]

Soledad's attorneys inveighed against what they subsequently called "infant marriage" and its affront to New Mexico's age-of-consent laws passed from 1915 to 1929, which required parental consent for marriages of males under the age of eighteen and females under the age of fifteen. They insisted that the New Mexico Supreme Court must stand in solidarity with the British imperial government's crusade to eliminate the "custom of child marriages" in India and its "evil effects." They speculated that if the New Mexico Supreme Court upheld the judgment, the floodgates would open to deviant marriages, and New Mexico would be forced to recognize "polygamous marriage," "incestuous marriage," and "infant marriages of 7 year olds" if they were valid elsewhere. They argued that the sanctioning of "Hindu" marriages disrupted the "standards of morals in every Christian nation."[66]

In July 1936, the New Mexico Supreme Court reversed the lower court decision and found in favor of Soledad Garcia Jubala. Speaking for the court, Judge Blair argued that there was "insufficient evidence to overcome presumption that alleged marriage have been dissolved when deceased married in U.S."[67] The court accepted Soledad's attorneys' position that in order to marry in the United States, Jawala had to have divorced somewhere. They raised doubts as to the validity of Nami's marriage or whether it had been truly consummated, insinuating that marriage rituals between prepubescent individuals were nullified by the presumed inability to consent or have sexual intercourse. Judge Blair denied any "unequivocal proof" that "the marriage in India, if it ever existed, was a bar to legal marriage in New Mexico."[68]

Blair accused Nami Singh of making "no effort to communicate" with the deceased in twenty years and said that she had "asserted no claim or right of wife during his lifetime, but her interest, or that of others ostensibly in her behalf, became apparent only when the opportunity arose after his death to claim a community interest in an estate she had no part in earning. In the meantime he had married [the] appellant and reared a family of four children."[69] Blair linked the right to "community interest in an estate" to participation in the earnings of the estate or in the rearing of children as evidence of a woman's unrewarded labor.[70] In their unsuccessful appeal for a rehearing, Nami's attorneys claimed that Julio/Jawala had owned all his property prior to his marriage to Soledad, "Soledad brought him nothing . . . and helped him acquire nothing."[71] Of course, both sides ignored the real property value of

Julio/Jawala's marriage to and divorce from Maria Fierro, through which he had capitalized his position in Mesilla.

The State Supreme Court's reversal in July 1936 made Soledad Jubala the "legal widow" of Julio Jubala and the recipient of his estate of 125 acres, valued at $21,000.[72] She did not remain a widow for long. Three weeks after the conclusion of the suit, at the age of twenty-one, she married twenty-three-year-old Enrique Tellez of San Miguel, New Mexico.[73]

In both the lower and Supreme Court rulings, the judges had to delegitimize one union in order to recognize another, since bigamy was impossible to countenance. Soledad's attorneys contended that the specter of Hindu "infant marriage" practices would disrupt the standards of the "Christian nation" of the United States. The category of "Hindu marriage" drew analogies to an array of deviant marriages and resurrected heated political debates on nonmonogamous and family-brokered marriages.

In nineteenth-century political, moral, and legal debates, U.S. politicians and social critics characterized Mormon polygamy as an "Asiatic custom" and "Mohammedan barbarism" that enshrined a principle of female servitude.[74] In the early twentieth century, arranged marriages were a flashpoint of anxiety in U.S. immigration policy. Newspapers, missionary journals, and public policy debates emphasized the "coerced will" of Japanese picture brides and eastern European Jewish child brides. These marriages were also labeled as Asian "uncivilized customs" that undercut American sexual modernity, liberalism, and the superiority of Protestant Christian values.[75] The idea of "Hindu marriage" also enlisted the idea of "Asiatic" difference to define marriages arranged by parents between their children as coercive, nonconsensual, and potentially open to polygamy. In the nineteenth and early twentieth centuries, the U.S. nation-state had intervened to prohibit and punish plural marriage as a Native American, Mormon, Muslim, and Chinese religious practice and social custom and enjoined marriage laws on the state level to categorically deny government legitimacy to polygamy. This prohibition was also inscribed into immigration and naturalization laws, and as a condition of immigration entry to the United States and naturalization to U.S. citizenship, immigrants had to offer oaths to neither condone nor practice polygamy.[76] Comparatively, polygamy was also the object of contentious state regulation in the British Empire's management of intimate ties in India and of South Asian indentured and voluntary migrants in its African and Caribbean colonies.[77]

In the probate case of Julio Jubala, the New Mexico Supreme Court had resoundingly determined that the U.S. registered marriage was legitimate and deepened a commitment to a core norm of Christian monogamous marriage. Yet from the perspective of Nami Singh and her kin and community in Punjab, the U.S. system was disquieting. In prioritizing licensed Christian monogamous marriage, the New Mexico Supreme Court countenanced the abandonment of women in "deviant marriages." From the perspective of her family, Jawala had not abandoned Nami. However, the New Mexico Supreme Court decision made her an abandoned wife. Had the marriage failed? Or did the courts implicitly have to presume and condone that Julio/Jawala had abandoned his wife for the convenience of the state's monogamous marriage imperative? Otherwise, Jawala/Julio's two marriages in Mesilla would be perceived as serial concubinage. Although never explicitly stated in any of the testimony, it would be conceivable that concubinage was precisely how Jawala/Julio's relationship to Soledad was perceived in his community in Punjab during the trial. The Sikh/Hindu customs of the Punjabi village would not accept that a secular marriage license or even a Christian ceremony in the United States could trump a marriage bond solemnized by a Brahmin priest and witnessed by their families and communities. Nami's attorneys' first settlement offer in probate was to split the estate between the legitimate wife, Nami, and his four children by Soledad. This offer appeared to be a tacit acceptance of Soledad as a "concubine" who had no rightful claim to inherit. However, her children with Jawala might be potential heirs, despite their "illegitimacy" in the eyes of the community in Punjab. From their perspective, Soledad could have been a temporary concubine, a "necessary" provider of comfort and care to a man working far from his home village. Such a concubine could also potentially produce heirs who might be recognized in both the succession of property and lineage. Migrant men having wives and children on either side of the ocean was fairly common in both European and Asian migrations to the Americas in the late nineteenth century. From the perspective of both home and host societies, it was usually when the migrant man died and his property was disposed of that the implications of plural families had to be confronted legally and socially.[78]

Even as South Asian men, along with southern and eastern European and Middle Eastern men were burdened with a reputation for multiple wives, the charge of bigamy could also be made against their spouses. In 1918, in Imperial County, a seventeen-year-old white woman was charged with bigamy. Eva

McKee Singh married a white man as a strategy of escape from her first marriage to Bhagat Singh in her hometown of Muskogee, Oklahoma, on September 11, 1918, with the permission of her father. The Southern Pacific Railway connection between Oklahoma and Imperial County facilitated transit for work and marriage between the two localities. After her marriage to Bhagat Singh, she traveled with him to Imperial County, but she became dissatisfied with her "mode of life," and within a month, she "deserted him and married a white man," George G. Fariss. Eva Singh pled guilty to the charge of bigamy. Probation Officer Swanson interviewed the "wayward girl" Eva and concurred with her "excuse" that the second marriage would "free her from the Hindu." Swanson recommended that Judge Thomas W. Leahe, of Muskogee, "a friend of the girl's father," take custody of Eva and "take her home to her own people." The Imperial County judge agreed to the "solution," effectively putting an end to both marriages, and gave her a suspended three-year sentence. This case was easier and necessary to prosecute because of the physical proximity of Eva's two spouses. It also effectively repudiated Eva's capacity to engage in any marriage and ironically returned responsibility for her volition in intimate relations to her father, who had given his permission for her unhappy marriage to Bhagat Singh.[79]

The prosecution of bigamy could take several decades to reach its target, as demonstrated in several divorce cases in British Columbia. Judges would order the annulment of a second marriage when the bride learned of a previous marriage in Canada. For instance, in March 1940, a British Columbia judge annulled the marriage between Adele Lorrain Gujar and Harry Gujar Singh after Adele discovered that her newly wed husband had never divorced another white woman, Helen Taylor, whom he had married in 1918 in Revelstoke, British Columbia, and from whom he had subsequently separated.[80]

Julio Jubala's death precluded his prosecution for bigamy. Determining inheritance frequently emerged in probate courts when immigrant men died in North America, however, and when there were no permanent local repercussions, the courts reluctantly recognized bigamy. In San Joaquin County, when Dalip Bir Singh, a farm worker, died in 1945, the probate court liquidated his personal property and investigated his heirs in India for the distribution of $1,400 in cash. As a young man in Punjab, Dalip Bir Singh had married two women, Jiwi Kaur and Harnam Kaur. His dual marriages were recognized in his village, and the women shared a household with his male kin. The second marriage was probably an instance where Dalip remarried a widow of a male family member in order to keep property within the patriarchal family. The lower court recognized the first wife and turned over the full inheritance to her. The attorneys for both women appealed, arguing that since the distribution was in cash and not California real estate, and the women lived abroad, there was no harm in recognizing a marriage custom that was legitimate abroad. The superior court agreed, recognized both women as heirs, and distributed the inheritance equally.[81] Similarly, when a Chinese merchant died in British Columbia on a business trip in 1923, the estate was divided between two women whom he had legitimately married and lived with in China. The Canadian government reluctantly agreed to honor Chinese law and recognize both women in the distribution of the estate.[82] In both of these instances, since both claimants were outside the country, the distribution of cash between two wives did not undermine monogamous marriage in Canada or the United States.

The Julio Jubala inheritance dispute could be interpreted as an example of the courts supporting local heirs to ensure that the decision would not make the disinherited a local public welfare problem. Yet in the case of the estate of an Imperial County Sikh farmer who thrived in the 1920s and 1930s and whose fortune three widows contested after he died intestate in 1949, the result did not favor either of the American wives. The Imperial County superior court discounted the claims of two Mexican American women who asserted that they had been married to the deceased and were thus entitled to inherit his estate. Both women stated that they were raising children. "Finally a widow and children in India sent a claim, and a local Punjabi agent appeared to argue on their behalf. After lengthy correspondence and a detailed examination of the mail of the widow in India, the estate was awarded to her."[83] The state's purpose contradicted the approach taken by the New Mexico Supreme Court, which scrutinized and rejected the legitimacy of Indian marriage out of hand. Confronted with two women and children at home, the Imperial County court opted rather to send the money to the woman and her children abroad. This action avoided having to select either Mexican American woman as the rightful spouse and deal with the problem of bigamy in Imperial County.

Canadian provinces and U.S. states tolerated marriage customs that were recognized by the British in India and by the government of China, even when they contradicted the rules of marriage in North America. These examples of diverse marriages that were recognized and tolerated by the U.S. and Canadian jurisdictions reveal a quality of the secular state's authority rather than an endorsement of religion. As Talal Asad argues, "from the point of view of secularism, religion" can be confined "to private belief and worship or engaging in public talk," but does not make "demands on life." The boundaries of "legitimate" religious activity become increasingly limited by the very registration and adjudication practices of the modern nation-state, which aims to "regulate all aspects of individual life—even the most intimate," such as birth, death, or marriage.[84] Tensions arise when spiritual movements and secular states contest the definition and legitimacy of life activities.

Even when religious groups attempt to militate against secular power, they are locked within the parameters set by the secular state. In the 1850s, after Mexican law made marriage an entirely civil contract and required civil registration for legal marriage, religious ceremonies lost legal standing and also popularity. In an effort to combat the secularization of Mexico and the irrelevance of Catholic sacraments of marriage to Mexico's official registration of marriage, the U.S. National Catholic Welfare Council in the 1920s and 1930s, stepped up campaigns to "rectify" civil marriages for immigrants from Mexico who lived, worked, and raised families in the southwestern United States. In the El Paso region during the Depression, Catholic lay leaders and social workers developed contacts with Mexican immigrant women through the charitable distribution of flour and clothing. The National Catholic Social Welfare representative would convince the couple of the necessity of "rectification" and conferring the Church's legitimacy on the marriage. Parish priests would follow up in order to "marry in Catholic sacrament those Mexican Catholic and non-Catholic couples who have never been married" or who had "resorted to a civil ceremony." In 1934, among the cases of couples to be interviewed and "rectified" were "Juan Singh (Hindu)" and Trinidad Reyes, who lived in San Elizario, Texas, and had been married by a justice of the peace in El Paso, Texas, on July 22, 1924.[85] Yet even as the Catholic Church created new rituals to consecrate marriages that had already been registered, the U.S. government recognized secular marriage licenses issued by Mexican courts as proof of civil marriage for purposes of immigration, naturalization, inheritance, and social welfare benefits. The U.S. and Mexican states clearly asserted authority over the regulation of marriage, kinship, and reproduction. The state could both benignly authorize monogamy as a "Christian value" as well as ignore the Catholic marriage ceremony or "rectification" ritual because it was irrelevant for its purpose of recognition for national membership and social welfare distributions. The Catholic Church, on the other hand, campaigned to bring baptized Catholic women into the life-cycle rituals of their families by rectifying marriages and encouraging the enlistment of Church authority in the sacraments recognizing legitimate birth (baptism), adulthood (confirmation), marriage, and death (extreme unction). It accepted the space that the secular liberal society had carved out for the role of "religion" in society through law and registration.[86]

Janet Jakobsen argues that, paradoxically, "sexual regulation is such a passion" in U.S. politics because it is "constitutive of secular American freedom." Following the meanings of freedom through the framework of the Enlightenment, the Protestant Reformation, and the self-discipline of market capitalism, Jakobsen argues that sexual freedom is intertwined with the market, property relations, and the regulatory frame of marriage. In all of these cases of contested religious sanctification and civil certification of marriage, "the free individual is the individual whose sexual activity is regulated in marriage—a relation earnestly enforced by the reformer."[87] In the United States, even as Christian values are endorsed in the secular institution of marriage, the secular state enlists and selects what attributes of religion it is willing to endorse and certify as it consolidates "sexual imagination of marriage into the center of national life."[88]

## INTIMACY AND PROPERTY IN PUBLIC LIFE

In the New Mexico court case concerning the estate of Julio Jubala / Jawala Singh, "Hindu marriage" emerged as an "uncivilized" custom, of ambiguous morality, that compelled children to enter into marital union, and therefore could not be treated as a reliable social contract in the United States. In relation to the status and rights of women, the customs of societies from East to West Asia were equated with "Asiatic barbarism." In particular, parentally arranged marriages were perceived, not as contractual relationships between consenting adults, but rather as transactions for purposes of status and economic consolidation.[89]

Intimate publics are forged through the materiality of bourgeois property relations and through the theatricality of the intimate conjugal couple. Robyn Wiegman probes the "property logic of liberal personhood" by which the modern state "recognizes and confers personhood on the basis of contractual relations" and accords the capacity to be a "responsible agent" to the state, to other citizens, and to noncitizen dependents.[90] This process of mediating between private life and state recognition orders and organizes socialized affect, kinship, and economic relationships.[91]

Amy Dru Stanley has emphasized the significance of contractual economics in securing rights and state and social recognition of personhood in both labor and marriage contracts in the post-emancipation United States.[92] Despite evidence of a variety of intimate ties, "marriage" is presumed to be a "universal descriptor of conjugal relations" that reworks the proper connection between "man and woman, kinship and family and encapsulated the conflicts and contradictions of European colonial and settler society."[93] The property logic underscores the development of ethical humanity and the establishment of individual male autonomy.

Julio Jubala / Jawala Singh was able through successful engagement with contract, marriage, and property-management relations to navigate the social and legal landscape of Dona Ana County effectively for twenty years until his death in 1932. He was never charged with bigamy or made subject to proceedings under New Mexico's Alien Land Law. As a successful farmer, he was able to seek assistance from the county clerk, lawyers, and bankers to obtain and retain property. He managed two marriages simultaneously, as he boasted to his Punjabi friends in El Paso. The New Mexico Supreme Court upheld the idea that Julio Jubala had a de facto divorce from Nami Singh, assuming that his marriage in India had been dissolved, even though there was no documentation to support this.

From the very beginning, the suit in New Mexico was about the ownership of land and the legitimate claims of inheritance. As the case moved from probate hearing to civil suit in the district court in Las Cruces to the New Mexico Supreme Court hearing in Santa Fe, a spiral of claims and questions about the ownership of the land emerged. Julio Jubala succeeded as a farmer in Mesilla because he was able to manipulate New Mexico laws regulating property. Marriage to Mexican American women appears to have been the strategy Julio used to hold and accumulate farmland and circumvent the restrictions of the state's Alien Land Law, modeled on the California law passed in 1913, which was approved by the New Mexico electorate in 1921 as a constitutional amendment prohibiting an "alien, ineligible to citizenship under the laws of the United States" from owning or leasing land in New Mexico.[94] Chinese immigrants were explicitly denied naturalized citizenship, being neither "white persons" nor "persons of African nativity." The U.S. Supreme Court furthermore handed down decisions in 1922 and 1923 that denied "white person" status to Japanese and "Hindus" respectively. In the same period, federal courts conferred "white" status and therefore the ability to be naturalized and become property holders on Syrians, Lebanese, Sephardic Jews, Turks, and Persians.[95]

The courts' role in divorce proceedings was to determine the unsustainability of the marriage, as well as to devise a plan for the distribution of property, custody and care of minor children, and the payment of alimony. In community-property states such as California, Arizona, and New Mexico, husband and wife formed a legal partnership, agreeing that all goods accumulated would be divided equally when death or divorce ended the partnership. However, the husband had greater authority to control the partnership's property and could sell property without the permission of the wife, while she could not do likewise. Maria Fierro experienced this liability firsthand when she unsuccessfully sought an injunction against Julio Jubala's selling of a piece of property in 1923 while they were still married.[96]

Community property law and Julio's familiarity with local officials enabled him to continue to acquire land even after the Alien Land Law applied to "Hindus." Julio Jubala's attorney had manipulated the divorce settlement to Maria Fierro in 1929 in order to retain ownership of 125 acres of land; instead, he ceded her all their personal property, made her a cash settlement, and promised to build her an adobe home. Maria was concerned with domestic security in the aftermath of the divorce. Julio cornered the capital-producing property for his future economic viability. J. F. Nevares, the Dona Ana county clerk, who admitted to handling "business" for Julio, including administering real estate transactions and certifying marriage and naturalization petitions, refused to comment on how Julio dodged the enforcement of the Alien Land Law.[97]

A little more than a week after Julio's death, Soledad approached the Probate Judge Luis Martinez to appoint Nevares as the administrator of the Jubala estate in probate. Nevares managed the farms, paid the wages, and inventoried assets. Julio had been running a thriving business, growing hay, cotton, alfalfa, and cantaloupes on 125 acres. He employed half a dozen men seasonally and rented some of his land to the Stanley Fruit Company. In addition to farm equipment—tractors, hay compressors, plows, and corn crushers—Julio had eight mules, eight mares, four horse mules, and fifty chickens among his livestock. Under Nevares's management, the estate harvested thirty-five bales of cotton (valued at $1,050) and sixty tons of hay (valued at $540). Julio was a savvy businessman; before his death, he had engineered a contract for the state highway between Las Cruces and Organ, New Mexico, to be built on his property, for which he would receive payments totaling $6,000. In addition to the value of harvests, equipment, future payments, and bank deposits, the personal property of Julio's estate alone was valued at $10,700. The appraisers,

Pablo Salcido (a blacksmith who worked for Julio) and Domingo Garcia, Soledad's father, valued the three tracts of real estate at $7,200.[98]

Race and citizenship requirements for property ownership in New Mexico and the United States threw another wrinkle into the lawful inheritance of the estate. Soledad's attorneys argued that New Mexico's Alien Land constitutional amendment made it impossible for Nami Singh to inherit Julio/Jawala's real property. Nami's attorneys countered that treaty rights between the United States and Great Britain enabled Nami Singh to own land temporarily as a British citizen. According to a commercial diplomatic treaty between the two empire-states, which included imperial possessions in India, both British and U.S. citizens could inherit real estate in the other state's jurisdiction as long as that property was disposed of within three years.[99]

Citizenship and the possession of land were contentious issues in New Mexico. In the early twentieth century, New Mexico land had been leveraged away from Mexican American families through taxation burdens and intermarriage with Anglos.[100] Among a handful of successful Asian immigrants, Julio Jubala acquired land before and during his marriage with the Mexican American Maria Fierro and retained it through the subsequent divorce. Soledad's attorneys and the Supreme Court judges framed Soledad Garcia Jubala as the local woman, whose claim to the land might be drawn away by the claims of the foreign woman, Nami Singh. It was a twist to the more familiar story of how marriage to white men by Native American and Mexican American women had led to the "leaking out" of land from indigenous communities in the Midwest and southwestern territories.[101] During Julio's marriage with Maria, the property had been consolidated, but after his death, it "leaked" back to a Mexican American family through his widow's inheritance. Soledad's own citizenship status by virtue of U.S. birth was jeopardized by her marriage to Julio Jubala, an immigrant racially ineligible for naturalization. Within weeks of winning the suit, through her marriage to Mexican American Enrique Telles, Soledad regained her citizenship status and the land on which her father had labored.[102] Elsewhere along the border in the 1930s, in Southern California and Arizona, federal authorities and state district attorneys denied Mexican immigrant women naturalization after they had married South Asian men, and in several instances in California, they actively forced women to cede land title and leases under Alien Land Law provisions.[103]

The ability to be mobile, to own property, and to claim national membership were constrained by the evaluation of the intimate ties. Legal judgments about

marriage and inheritance drew cultural justifications from moral and civilizational differences, but enforced these distinctions on a terrain of uneven and
incommensurate racial taxonomies that bisected laws of marriage, landownership, and citizenship. Judges and attorneys played out taxonomies and sympathy in the process of adjudicating disputes. At the New Mexico Supreme Court,
Soledad's attorney's appeals to sympathy for a "Dona Ana County widow,"
whose marriage has been delegitimized by the court and whose status had been
summarily transformed from "widow" to "concubine," persuaded the judges to
doubt the legitimacy of the "Hindu child marriage." Unlike the district court's
imperative to solve the local problem when presented with evidence of Nami
Singh and Jawala Singh's marriage in India, the New Mexico Supreme Court
wrestled with the precedent produced by the discursive formation of "Hindu
marriage" and its analogous legal impact on a host of deviant marriage traditions—the fearful cascade to "infant marriage," polygamy, and incest. Moral
sympathy for Soledad's plight and the concerns about unwittingly validating
"repugnant" foreign customs shaped the New Mexico Supreme Court's scrutiny
of whether Nami Singh's marriage had ever been "consummated" or "dissolved"
to make her claim irrelevant to Julio Jubala's estate. Justice Blair's decision cast
dubious light on Nami Singh's motives and the legitimacy of her relationship
with Julio/Jawala. She and her "Hindu marriage" became Julio/Jawala's "past,"
with no relevance to the future distribution of his legacy and property.

It was through the juridical and administrative practices of governance from
the local to the national scales, that racial and sexual classifications developed
their shapes. As Ann Stoler has argued, the imperatives of "taxonomic states"
were charged with "defining and interpreting what constituted racial membership, citizenship, political subversion and the scope of the state's jurisdiction
over morality." Overall consistency of details and universal applicability of
these taxonomies and hierarchies was less significant than the "sorting codes"
and "technologies" that shaped the "circuits of knowledge."[104] The legal case in
Mesilla first did the work of performing and offering particular detail that
intensified knowledge of the array of racialized immoral and degenerate sexual
activities and relationships. The Mesilla case confirmed suspicions about the
cavalier disregard of U.S. prohibitions against polygamy among Asian and
Middle Eastern migrants. Even where polygamy was tightly regulated or prohibited, the histories of transoceanic migration produced unsettling anxieties
about the moral and social dangers of widespread concubinage as a counterfeit
of legitimate marriage.

The adjudication in court of marriage, divorce, and estate claims did double duty as well by consolidating and subtly diversifying the norm into a multicultural array underpinned by a shared value of monogamy. The court judgment in the Mesilla estate case deployed Christian marriage as an eternal social commitment and duty in a sea of transitory sexualities and encounters and the legal container for legitimate sexual activity. Civil registrations of marriage and divorce orders in localities in Canada and United States endorsed a secular version of monogamous marriage as the norm of legitimacy. At times, the container of illegitimate ties explicitly or implicitly engaged bigamy and adultery. The standard of monogamous marriage encompassed tolerance zones. By time, place, and circumstance, certain customs and practices could be grudgingly accepted or cast beyond the boundaries of the norm. Concubinage might be tolerated in the "frontier" of state expansion and outposts of empire, but as societies became settled and property inheritance imperatives increased, the state exerted pressure for informal relationships to be "regularized" and "formalized" into marriage. Similarly, both concubinage and female prostitution were understood as "necessary evils" of empire, settler colonialism, and mass labor migration, tolerated as practices that would purportedly forestall male-to-male sexual relations.[105]

In the Mesilla case, the international and imperial circuitry of customs and practices embraced British imperial administrators, Anglo-American missionaries, and U.S. attorneys. "Hindu marriage" oscillated from "uncivilized," because of practices of concubinage and pubescent brides, to "civilized" enough, as analogous to the monogamous marriage standard in North America. In the Mesilla case, a Hindu marriage abroad became the reservoir of intolerable contradictions to the fidelity of a local registered marriage that had produced four heirs. The particular context shaped how "Hindu marriage" was contingently viewed within and outside the norms of American society. Legitimating or delegitimating intimate ties, moreover, was a diagonal process that unfolded through a similar sliding scale of norms and deviance in British colonial India and elsewhere in the British, French, Dutch, and U.S. empires, where South Asian migrant laborers added to the mix of "races" necessary to sustain intensive capitalist cultivation and resource extraction.

Marriage has been both unstable and yet central to the production of citizenship and peculiarly entangled in the formation of racialized property-owning citizenship in the western United States. Nevertheless, how the norm of marriage was refracted through religion, ethnicity, and race is an important historical problem. Charting the comparative use of "sorting codes" in the governing strategies of the state, which shifted from taxonomy to sympathy, alerts historians to the variable dynamics of race and morality that compound and confound any easy hierarchy of sexual deviance. Legislatively and judicially, the state approached the variety of sexual and intimate relationships by recognizing both particular practices within a conduit of sympathy and irreconcilable differences that had to be disallowed.

Notwithstanding the narrow interpretive parameters of judicial and prison records, an investigation of government management of sex, race, and morality reveals hints of the histories that are lost and fragmented yet embedded within the history of the state. The Julio Jubala estate case carries suggestive detail about the telegrams and letters that were part of the communication network between Punjabi villages and U.S. towns. The meanings of the social institutions of marriage and kinship in Punjab were incommensurate with the emerging norm of legitimate marriage in the United States and British colonized India. For people from villages in Punjab, marriage had durability, duration, and ties that were far more expansive than the courts entertained. While the judges saw unwarranted influence in the actions of Jubala's uncle, father, and cousins, these men imagined family expansively as a broad umbrella of kin, rather than limited to a spousal pair and the progeny of the marriage union. In Punjabi villages, social and material well-being had broadened to deploy male kin across continents to mobilize resources for the collective use of dependents clustered in natal households. The adhesive of kinship adapted to migratory dispersal and intensified protections among migrant men whose ties to kinship systems, villages, and caste operated against the authority of the state. Such adaptive networks held women closely enveloped in the natal household system and distrusted women at the peripheries whose independence from that particular kinship system could be marshaled by their fathers, siblings, community leaders, and the agents of the state. The outcome of the inheritance of Julio Jubala simultaneously strengthened the worldviews of both the injustice of meddling family and the injustice of a prejudiced state.

International migration complicated the interstate negotiation of regulating and legitimating marriage and kinship. Nation-states, empire-states, and colonized states attempted to decipher, judge, and recognize marriage, kinship, and adoption ties within a general framework of monogamous and consensual marriage and blood and contractual kinship. The challenge often came when state agents either anticipated or were confronted by conflicts of intimate ties that migrants had forged in the disparate, transnational localities in which they lived. Marriage, its variability, maintenance, and dissolution, became the key grounds of state intervention. Conflicts over inheritance and sexual behavior outside of marriage revealed the tensions and the commitments by which international migrants managed and understood kinship, cohabitation, responsibility, and affection, often at variance with ascribed community norms and state definitions. At the turn of the century, the United States and the British Empire intensified marriage certification and legitimating kinship precisely because of their value in making intimate personhood the access point of political membership. In the process of judging legitimacy, courts and bureaucrats assembled an array of racial labels, assumed gender roles, and moral and sexual judgments to frame the human subjects who had to pass through both national borders and the distribution of migrants as disposable transients or valuable settlers.

However, for the liberal state, the stakes of judging intimate ties had tremendous consequences for crafting human society. It was not just a matter of governing "Hindu marriage" as either a site of deviancy or of reform. Nor was it only how "Hindu marriage" was placed among a continuum of unions that were categorically non-normative. Through their "deviance," these non-normative unions normalized and centralized Christian monogamous marriage as the only legitimate intimate union. The dynamics of compassion and judgment of intimacy demonstrate how the categories profoundly shaped the human subject. The evaluative process of assessing innermost character, judging the pathways of sexual and domestic relations, and defining the capacity to be a property-owning citizen provided what appeared to the administrators to be both a broad canvas and restrictive criteria of being human. Through this processing of intimacy, the state was elaborating a vision of society and polity and its legitimate participants.

# PART THREE

# Membership and Nation-States

## CHAPTER 6

# Regulating Intimacy and Immigration

After working in Vancouver in lumberyards and investing in real estate since 1907, Hakim Singh Hundel returned to Punjab in 1910 to tend to his family after the deaths of his wife and father. Hakim's widowed mother survived to care for his four sons, aged four to sixteen. After several months in Punjab, Hakim Singh sold his property and gathered his sons and mother to return with him to Canada. The family traveled by rail to Calcutta, then took a ship to Hong Kong, where Canadian regulations and steamship company policies forced them to separate. Hakim's documented Canadian domicile permitted only his own return to Vancouver, and the steamship company refused to sell passage to Vancouver to his mother and his sons.

Since 1908, Canadian regulations had demanded that steamship companies only sell tickets to new immigrants who arrived directly from a port in their country of origin. Since direct service had been discontinued from Calcutta to Vancouver, Indians, though British subjects, were uniquely disabled by these regulations. Hakim instead bought tickets for his mother and sons to travel to San Francisco, in the hope that there they could buy tickets to Vancouver. However, citing Canadian regulations, U.S. immigration officers held the family at Angel Island, in San Francisco Bay. The family were barred from entry into the United States, refused onward passage to Vancouver, and deported to Hong Kong, where they were stranded for nearly two years. During this time, they were supported by Hakim Singh and by the Sikh *gurudhwara* (temple), where they were allowed to stay while awaiting permission from the Canadian government to reunite with Hakim.

FIGURE 11. The Hundel family at the Mee Chee Leung Studio in Hong Kong, ca. 1911. Left to right: Atma, Iqbal, Bishan Kaur, Teja, Jermeja. Courtesy University of British Columbia Library, Rare Books and Special Collections, Jermeja Singh Hundel Family Fonds BC1953-m.

Finally, after several highly publicized instances in 1912 and 1913 of humanitarian reprieves being granted to Sikh wives and infant children who had accompanied returning Sikh men, been separated from them in Vancouver, and issued deportation orders, the Canadian immigration authorities reluctantly, as an "act of grace," admitted Hakim's mother and sons at Vancouver on July 20, 1913. Reversal of the decision not to admit them, in consideration of Hakim Singh having taken "the peaceable course and left his family in Hong Kong," and thus not obliged the Canadian state to confront the public drama of another family reunification dilemma, was treated as a special case, which would not alter federal policy that disallowed family reunification for Indian male migrants who had established Canadian domicile.[1]

Hakim Singh and his family experienced firsthand how capriciously nation-states interfered with the circulation of migrants, evaluated their kinship and webs of dependency, and blocked their opportunities. In the late nineteenth and early twentieth centuries, the U.S. and British governments coordinated and consolidated their systems to control and police the mobility of workers and travelers by creating a worldwide infrastructure of exit and entry regulations, documentation requirements, and inspection sites and practices, and regulated private passenger steamship companies to monitor and manage human mobility. Racial suspicion guided regulatory scrutiny and influenced the judgments of health inspectors and shipping agents and the policing of smuggling operations.

South Asian migrants confronted and evaded obstacles that the U.S. and British empire-states imposed across multiple jurisdictions in the Pacific and Central America. South Asian migrants mobilized portable and flexible forms of citizenship and identity to navigate barriers and harnessed social, kinship, and institutional networks and forms of intimate dependency to enable their mobility and survival. Like many South Asian and Asian migrants in the early twentieth century, Singh journeyed to find work far from his birthplace village and sent remittances to his family.

Both Canada and the United States created policies toward Asian immigrants to deter permanence and stability by excluding women, and in the process simultaneously pressured South Asian migrants' kinship ties and stretched social networks globally. The exclusion and absence of women among South Asian immigrants made the position of solo male migrants more precarious.

## MIGRATION GEOGRAPHY AND REGULATIONS

The system of labor regulation out of the Indian subcontinent closely monitored the mobility of indentured or contract workers, but left the regulation of merchants, students, and unassisted immigrants free. Controversies over nefarious schemes to dupe South Asians into indentureship contracts and transport them to Caribbean plantations pressured the British Parliament to pass the 1883 Emigration Act, which required government oversight over labor contracts beyond "Ceylon and the Straights Settlements." Since the overwhelming majority of "assisted" emigrants journeyed within that orbit, the regulations also exempted merchants, travelers, soldiers, and military personnel recruited for service in China and Africa and thereby facilitated the migration of "free" service workers, laborers, and merchants.[2] British imperial efforts for the managed containment of indentured workers were matched by the 1885 U.S. Contract Labor Law, which expressly forbade any company or individual to bring foreigners into the United States under contract to perform labor, except for domestic servants. The specter of contract laborers haunted U.S. concerns about the dangers of racialized labor from India and China.[3]

Confronted with several thousand South Asian male laborers migrating to West Coast ports from 1905 to 1912, the U.S. and Canadian governments responded with health inspections intended to identify and deport those suffering from a "loathsome contagious disease" and summarily exclude and deport anyone who inspectors predicted was liable to become destitute. Medical and public charge exclusions were established in 1891 and strengthened in subsequent years. In the first decade of the twentieth century, the United States imposed public health inspection routines in ports across the globe and punished shipping companies that allowed suspect passengers to travel to North America. The intensification of medical exclusion procedures diverted migrants from Hong Kong and Shanghai to U.S. imperial locations such as Manila and the Panama Canal Zone, where after six months' residence, Asian migrants could evade the more strenuous inspections at Seattle or San Francisco. In 1913, when this loophole from U.S. Pacific and Caribbean territories was closed, migrants increasingly used passageways through the Panama Canal Zone, Central America, and Mexico.[4]

The racial scrutiny on migration took a more formal turn in 1917, when the United States restricted the immigration of all laborers from Asia by creating a geographical "barred zone" that extended restrictions on Chinese and Japanese laborers to the broader region. Two years earlier, in 1915, the British government in India had imposed a regulation, implemented in the Defence of India Passport Act, that made it a criminal offense to embark on a journey from any port in British India without a passport.[5]

Under mounting pressure from white settler societies in the British Empire, the British government in India closely followed the attempts made by the Chinese government in 1888 and the Japanese government in 1896 to mandate passports as a defense against the discriminatory and humiliating exclusions of their emigrants to North America.[6] Race became increasingly central to the development of immigration and residency regulations in the British white settler dominions of Australia, Canada, and South Africa. Regulations administered in the British colonial ports of Calcutta, Shanghai, Hong Kong, and Singapore, as well as in the United States and its colonial territories of Hawaii and the Philippines, coordinated the mobility and exclusion of South Asian and Chinese laborers.

Government officials in the United States, Canada, and Britain communicated frequently, sharing information, suspicions, and bureaucratic policies and strategies on how to interpret the value or danger of migrants who arrived from overseas. They traded their assessments of migrant capabilities, theories about geographic and racial predispositions to disease and disability, and the dangers of political and cultural habits to Anglo-American civilization and democracy.

Passage through immigration checkpoints at ports and land borders in Canada and the United States is, as Martha Gardner has explained, "an intimate encounter of the immigrants and the state," guided by legal and administrative procedures. Through "this encounter some immigrants become residents, some aliens become citizens, some non-Americans become Americans, and some do not."[7] The immigrant gateway served as a threshold that converted people into individuals whom the state could test and categorize and then claim or deny. The state's officers filtered the complexity of personal biography and embodiment through a rough mesh that ostensibly measured capacity to labor and prosper. Fearing that migrants would become vagrants and public charges, immigration inspectors and politicians in Canada and the United States particularly scrutinized immigrants from Asia for talents, traits, resources, and networks that would support their livelihood in North America.

The bureaucratic procedures of immigrant entry had contradictory effects. Immigrants were required both to be "autonomous," "independent" individuals and to possess a network of kin, friends, fellow villagers, co-religionists, and compatriots to sustain them. Although the need to find work may have motivated migration decisions, Asian immigrants had to claim to be something other than common "laborers" by documenting their skills, education, and capital. Students, petty merchants and peddlers, skilled tradesmen, religious instructors, and priests, however, required even more precise documentation, thorough interrogation, and government assessment. Immigration inspectors and policy makers required that arriving immigrants provide persuasive documentation to demonstrate their possession of and capacity to organize capital. Immigration officials assessed and judged the resources and liabilities of intimate dependents in their overall assessment of an individual's suitability for entry.

Hakim Singh's experience and that of his family, however, revealed the ironies of dependency when the mother and children he financially supported were denied entry to Canada. As much as the ideology of the self-sufficient individual held sway, the judgment of individual success depended heavily on the evaluation of the social web of dependency. Dependents—spouses, children, parents, siblings, and cousins—could be either a source of concern about immigrants becoming a burden on the state or reassurance of their capacity for self-sufficiency. The dependents of immigrants from Europe served as support for family income, settlement, and potential for assimilation. Those of immigrants from Asia evoked concerns about potential welfare burdens on the state and permanent settlement.

States defined territorial boundaries by means of passports, permits, and visas, monopolizing the sovereign power of channeling human mobility through regulated gateways and transportation systems. Extraterritorial surveillance, documentation, and investigation systems gathered and verified the authority of documentation. The international system of nation-states both acknowledged and overlooked power differentials between states in promoting the ideal of reciprocity between states and universal and equivalent systems of identity and membership, on which mobility and trade between nations depended. The inequality between states emerged both in the crafting of unilateral legislation and in negotiations by Britain and the United States with China and Japan to restrict labor immigration by their subjects. Mobility between different locations in the British Empire and the United States and its imperial territorial possessions became a potent political issue that fractured any assumption of uniform and continuous state authority and power.

The fiction of uniformity and universality was observable in the travel documentation that people were required to carry in the early twentieth century. As the historian Adam McKeown has argued, passports, visas, and permits do not record a "preexisting reality," but create "stable, documentable identities for individuals . . . dividing those individuals across an international system of nation states." The modern passport and visa created a "tangible link" between the individual and the state by specifying "a unique individual within the matrix of standardized physical categories and [guaranteeing] that identification with the marks and seals of a recognized nation-state." The passport was a "tool of global regulation and standardization" that "entrenched the bearer more deeply" in the "machinery of state surveillance." The centralizing of "identities and mobility control" by nation-states usurped the power of local trade and customs institutions, undermined "transnational migrant institutions and networks," and favored large transportation companies and formal charities to manage and facilitate international migration. In the ascendancy of the international system of states, migration became a matter of national controls and international relations.[8]

Systems of state surveillance and regulation produce knowledge through bureaucratic practices that attest to what is true of the individual human body. By subjecting individuals to interrogations, taking standardized photographs of them, fingerprinting them, and describing them, by organizing examinations of the physical body, its fluids and products, these practices produce data for officials to interpret and predict bodily fitness and capacity, creating a racial topography upon which to map individual capacity and destiny. However, racial and gendered assumptions about morality, values, and sexuality exerted a powerful counterweight, and unfavorable assessments and obstacles to individual migration proliferated.

## PUBLIC CHARGES AND JUDGING DEPENDENCY

South Asian migrant men began arriving in Vancouver and Victoria, Canada, by the hundreds in 1904 and by the thousands in 1905 and 1906. Canadian politicians, labor leaders, and newspaper editors railed against the dangers of large-scale migration from India, echoing concerns about the new immigrants' purported uncivilized habits, poverty, and acceptance of low wages as a danger to white Canadians. Victoria Trades and Labor Council Secretary Christian Swartz argued that the South Asians lived in miserable and pitiable conditions because of their "limited funds, in some cases approaching destitution, lack of personal effects, light or unsuitable clothing and difficulty in finding and retaining employment." In the winter of 1906, Canadian newspapers reported on Indian workers' unemployment, destitution, and inability to secure housing.[9]

Labor leaders, politicians, and newspaper editors pressured immigration officials to restrict laborers from India, just as restrictions had previously been imposed on Japanese and Chinese laborers. They advocated enforcing the 1906 Canadian statute that authorized the deportation of any person allowed into Canada who within two years had become a "charge on public funds" as a "pauper, or destitute, or professional beggar." Immigration officials could also bar entry to any person suspected of "vagrancy" and therefore "likely to be a public charge."[10] Government officials presumed that they could assess an individual's physical and moral capacity to be self-sufficient and survive without charity. The diplomatic resistance within the British Empire was on a different order than the exclusion of Chinese and Japanese immigrants. British imperial policy forbade explicit racial restrictions on British subjects, and the British imperial government had to balance and negotiate its purported principles of equality and freedom of mobility of its subjects with the conflicting claims of Canada's sovereign protection of its white residents against the British Indian government's protection of its emigrants.

In 1908, the Canadian government enforced a new immigration regulation that required that all immigrants arrive on a "continuous journey" from their native lands to Canada. The British government had pressured commercial shipping lines to drop direct steamer service from Calcutta to Vancouver. However, passengers could stop at any of the ports of Hong Kong, Singapore, Shanghai, and Yokohama and then cross the Pacific on a ship belonging to another line. Private companies were hindered from facilitating direct travel between India and Canada and severely penalized for issuing tickets to targeted passenger groups. The policy had the predictable impact of sharply curtailing immigration from India. In 1907–8, Canada admitted 2,623 Indians; the following fiscal year, only six were allowed to land.[11] The "continuous journey" regulation disrupted South Asian migration patterns in which male migrants worked for a few months, years, or even a decade in cities in China prior to migration to North America. Male migration from East Asia to North America was halted, and direct chain migration of family members, from brothers, cousins, and uncles to wives, sons, and daughters, became more challenging. Migrants dispersed to Singapore, the Philippines, Hawaii, Panama, Mexico, and Argentina.

Shortly after the large-scale arrival of South Asian immigrants in Vancouver and Victoria, Canadian politicians and newspaper editors reported widespread unemployment, destitution, and homelessness, particularly during the winter months. In December 1906, Blake Robertson, assistant superintendent of Canadian immigration, traveled from Ottawa to Vancouver and led an investigation with local health officials and police. After checking "Hindu" living quarters and reviewing police and charity records, Robertson concluded that the allegations of poverty, vagrancy, and dependency were overblown, and that most of the estimated 6,000 South Asian migrants in Vancouver had steady work and had found housing. Despite the findings, Robertson assured a restive and suspicious white public that immigration authorities would scrutinize new arrivals to make certain that they could endure hard labor and cold winters. He advised Vancouver and Victoria immigration inspectors to pay "particular attention to the general physique of Hindus" and "examine carefully" immigrants who were "anemic, narrow-chested," or appeared to belong to "a class likely to contract or develop tubercular trouble." Scrutinizing immigrant bodies for susceptibility to chronic disease and predicting future disability had developed at the turn of the century as a health-screening technique of border control. Diagnoses of tuberculosis or anemia were punitive predictions that underscored a fear that future disease and disability would make immigrants burdens on local charities, hospitals, and prisons. The health screening for immigrants was reinforced by threats of deportation "[i]f Hindus are public charges" by branding them criminal "vagrants."[12] Health screening of immigrant travelers leapt across the Pacific. The former viceroy of India (1894–99) Lord Elgin, British secretary of state for the colonies (1905–8), had assured Canadian officials that all South Asian migrants to Canada received rigorous health screening in Calcutta and in Hong Kong. The British Empire had regulated transportation companies to assume liability and subjected the companies to steep fines if they brought "destitute persons into Canada."[13]

Over the next few years, Canada and the United States began increasingly to resort to health screening not only to quarantine contagious disease but also to diagnose capacity and fitness to work. The screeners sought to decipher the body's condition to anticipate future disease, disability, and state of mind. This preemptive screening provided an assessment of who was likely to be something else in the future.[14]

The U.S. immigration officer Daniel Keefe, who keenly followed the controversies over South Asian and Chinese migration to white settler societies in the British Empire, viewed the "ordinary Hindu" as an "undesirable acquisition" for the United States. Keefe advocated border control procedures developed by the British Empire's white settler governments of Canada, Australia, New Zealand, and South Africa to curtail South Asian migrants. He recommended first identifying "paupers, criminals or [the] contagiously diseased" and then eliminating the rest by focusing medical scrutiny on "poor physiques" and "physical defects" that would impair potential livelihood and thereby make them "likely to become public charges." The goal was for zero admissions from India, using health inspections to satisfy a political constituency of white working-class residents who expressed "strong prejudice against

Hindus" and were outraged by "their extreme clannishness, their style of dress, [and] methods of living." Even as he acknowledged political prejudice, Keefe predicted that this hostility ensured that South Asian laborers would be "forced into a life of vagrancy," thereby exacerbating the general "dissatisfaction and discontent and often disorder among the [white] laboring classes."[15]

Rudimentary physical inspection, however, gave way to more rigorous and systematic physical screening, including the testing of blood and feces and even x-rays. The bacteriological testing of anemic South Asian immigrants began alongside similar tests administered on Japanese women and Chinese merchant-class men, women, and children, who were all inspected closely at Angel Island in San Francisco Bay. The press reverberated with political accusations that despite South Asian men's "poor physique[s]" and immigration inspectors' initial designation "as likely to be public charges," South Asian men appealed and were allowed to slip into the United States.[16] The Public Health Service administered and interpreted a stool-sample bacteriological test for hookworm. The test would (irrespective of any visible ailment) provide objective proof of a future ailment that could conceivably contribute to listlessness and anemia and diminish the capacity for work. The *San Francisco Bulletin* hailed the procedure and its use to deny entry to hundreds of South Asian immigrants that year as "an effective dam to the torrent of Hindu immigration which has been surging [onto] the shores of the Pacific Coast at a speed of 5,000 of India's riff-raff a year."[17]

Medical officer Dr. M. W. Glover ordered every South Asian immigrant to undergo time-consuming feces and blood tests, which lengthened their time in detention and increased the likelihood of deportation orders.[18] Notwithstanding the lengthening of detention time and the use of laboratory resources, Glover championed the politically expedient result of the bacteriological tests in effectively stopping "the influx of East Indians into this country."[19] Bacteriological investigation fascinated white labor leaders, who believed that it offered objective, nonpartisan support to bolster their partisan agenda of halting the assault of the newest "Asiatic menace" on the white labor market on the West Coast.[20] The use of biopolitical techniques to determine the fitness of the body over subjective calculation marshaled purportedly objective knowledge of the future of the body, as worker, as citizen, and as dependent on the state's resources and public charity. The screening of the body and the diagnosis of its health and capability predicated an immigrant's value and worth on his fitness to work.

The use of diagnostic categories identified future status as the chief problem to assess, rather than a history of behavior, work, or conduct. It also organized new conceptions of the body and new sensibilities regarding the individual body related to and ordered by other notions of bodies. Immigration and public health inspections finessed an interpretation of the individual body organized by its visible signs of capability and deciphered by its wastes and products. This individual body could be prejudged by its racial and ethnic identity, constructed through its linkages with family and kinship systems, and its destiny would have consequences for the national social and political body, metaphorized either in terms of future utility or as a parasite. All of which underscored the state's assertion of sovereign power over human bodies, the ability to administer tests, make predictive judgments, enhance or sever kinship and social ties, and use the body's past and present to determine its future destiny.

The new technology of visualizing and interpreting the body also transformed the conception of the nature of the body under scrutiny. The investigation for hookworm was to identify the body of a parasite within the human body. Rather than directly observing the surface of the human body for signs of the parasite, physicians and lab technicians searched for it in the body's wastes. After demanding that aliens disrobe for a full physical inspection, health inspectors obliged individual immigrants to defecate so that clinicians could obtain a stool sample on a glass slide. Health officers would then interpret the visual cues in the sample smear under the microscope for the parasite worm, which over time was anticipated to reproduce within the intestines and contribute to anemia, diarrhea, and listlessness, characteristic of hookworm's reputation as the "germ of laziness."

This extended the boundaries of the human body beyond its epidermal container to its waste. However, the waste, expelled and manipulated through a series of distancing techniques, rendered visible a residue of the body's inherent truth, invisible to direct physical observation. Suspicions of what was contained within the body could be revealed, interpreted, and authorized by medical expertise. Evidence of other parasites in the intestines, surreptitiously determining the human body's future direction and destiny, also amplified fears of the connections in the invisible social web that tied immigrants to dependent bodies abroad.

The hookworm diagnosis impacted the temporality of the body. The stool smeared on the slide took a snapshot of the body's present condition to offer a prediction of the body's future decay and disability. The measurement was vague, yet it constituted human ability in a certain configuration of the body and the definition of what constituted ability into an expectation that entrants to the United States should have optimal or normative capacity, even when no particular employment was considered a benchmark.

Bacteriological testing effectively sidestepped other strategies of border control and exclusion. In September 1910, Immigration Inspector Frank Ainsworth applauded Medical Examiner Glover's hookworm procedures and insisted that medical examiners had superior authority in ensuring deportation. Unlike other more subjective determinations of being immoral or a public charge that could be challenged and appealed by the immigrant, Ainsworth emphasized the unassailable expertise of the medical examiner's diagnosis that an immigrant suffered from a loathsome, contagious disease that posed a danger to the public. There was "no division of opinion" or appeal that hampered deportation. Identifying a person with hookworm, however, was just as conditional a prediction of future developments as observation of physical strength, financial resources, and work history could be interpreted as a future draw on charity, or belief in the Koran would necessarily result in the practice of polygamy in the United States. Yet the grounds for appeal and lawsuits were far greater in cases of "public charge" and religious belief than exclusion and deportation for hookworm, which was far less successfully contested and overturned in administrative appeal.[21]

Government officials' confidence in hookworm's predictive value was dubious. Its predictive capability was contingent on living conditions and the availability of health care. Even in immigration detention, hookworm was treatable, but the privilege of treatment was not available to all. The course of treatment to expel the parasite took several weeks, and immigration and health inspectors ordered suspected laborers deported, but allowed treatment in detention of persons who could prove that they were students, businessmen, or spouses of already established immigrants, as long as they were able to shoulder the costs. For instance, when Sant Ram, a twenty-one-year-old student, arrived at Angel Island in April 1913, he was diagnosed with hookworm there, even though he had been judged free of disease weeks earlier before departing Hong Kong. He was accompanied by his younger brother Tulsi, and they both intended to travel to Pittsburgh to study engineering. When the Board of Special Inquiry convened, Sant's $90 in gold, certificate of high school graduation, and "general appearance" won him three weeks' treatment on Angel Island and his release once "cured." Sant Ram's student status earned him the privilege of receiving health care and made hookworm a condition that could be overcome. He completed his degree and for decades lived in New York, where he successfully applied for naturalization as a U.S. citizen in 1947.[22]

Although most South Asian immigrants to the United States traveled through Hong Kong, Shanghai, and Yokohama, Manila became a destination for temporary work and a jumping-off port for travel to the United States. In 1911 and 1912, Immigration Commissioner Ellis de Bruler sounded the alarm about the "invasion" of South Asians from the Philippines. He warned that "this back-door entrance" would become a pipeline for "a horde of these East Indians" to invade "our shores creating disturbances" and widespread unrest among the white "laboring classes." In Manila, U.S Customs officers estimated that 6,000 to 7,000 indigent "Hindus" "gambled, peddled" and performed at "fairs giving conjuring exhibitions while awaiting an opportunity to embark for Pacific Coast ports."[23] After the United States vanquished the Philippine rebels and established rule over the archipelago, U.S. and European capital investment and trade increased, and there was a demand for Asian laborers. Former South Asian police officers and soldiers stationed in Shanghai and Hong Kong migrated to Manila at the end of the first decade of the twentieth century. Drawn by reports of higher pay rates and opportunity, some men worked for short periods as night watchmen or peddled clothing and goods on the streets of Manila. U.S. Customs officials administered entry and residency permits. Parsee, Bengali, and Sikh merchants established thriving businesses supplying clothing, tools, and plumbing supplies. The growing Sikh population supported a *gurudhwara* in Manila, following the establishments of similar temples in Hong Kong, Shanghai, Singapore, and Penang. Many South Asian watchmen and guards complained of the oppressive heat, lack of reliable work, and limited business opportunities. At the same time, steamship companies eager to bolster passenger traffic eastbound launched recruitment campaigns promising lucrative, high-wage employment a short distance from the gateway ports of Honolulu, Seattle, and San Francisco. South Asian merchants helped passengers secure loans to pay their passages.[24]

In June 1913, the U.S. Congress closed a loophole that allowed South Asians, Chinese, and Japanese who claimed residency in Puerto Rico, the Philippines, and Hawaii to migrate to the continental United States.[25] After a six-month stay in the Philippines, South Asian migrants could obtain a certificate of residence status there and could bypass rigorous examination in

Seattle and San Francisco.[26] The United States had to balance fostering Philippine trade and economic growth, which needed Chinese and South Asian capital, laborers, and networks, against political pressure to regulate Asian immigration.[27] With the expansion of U.S. empire, the scope for potential Asian migrants widened. Chinese, Japanese, and South Asians labored in plantations across the Pacific and in the Caribbean. Yet even as some migrants were hindered, the U.S. government finessed and reassessed racial taxonomies to facilitate the migration of "indigenous" Puerto Ricans and Filipinos in the 1910s and 1920s to work as farm laborers, in service industries, and in light manufacturing.

Prior to the 1913 shift in regulation, South Asian migrants from Manila gained entry to the United States by documenting financial resources, paternal and fraternal support, ambition for business, trade, or education, and the existence of blood ties and family history of land- and business ownership. The closing of the 1913 loophole was justified as a defense against Asian workers' historical legacy of indenture and contract labor in Hawaii and the Caribbean. Even though promises of jobs and family assistance hardly qualified as abusive corporative contracts, immigration officers collapsed these offers into evidence of "assisted" migration, unilaterally excluded racially suspect immigrants, and branded them as "likely to be a public charge."

The change in government policy swiftly changed passenger ticketing. On June 24, 1913, the steamship *Minnesota* arrived in Seattle from Manila with 201 South Asians on board.[28] Worried about a loss of profits from the passenger trade and the expense of returning rejected migrants, the Great Northern Railroad Company, which owned and operated the *Minnesota*, sought quick clarification of the government's position. After some uncertainty, immigration officials agreed to admit the *Minnesota*'s passengers of South Asian origin, but said they would otherwise strictly enforce regulations. A month later, the immigration authorities made good on their threat and rejected all seventy-seven South Asian passengers on the Great Northern steamer *Persia* as likely to become "public charges," proclaiming that "all Hindus are undesirable."[29] The Great Northern Railroad Company ceased selling tickets to South Asian passengers, switching from this "unprofitable business" to transporting indigenous Filipino laborers from Luzon to the U.S. mainland. The company also stepped up recruitment of European immigrants at Ellis Island, particularly the Dutch, and discounted tickets to white and European immigrant farmers in the Midwest to settle in the Northwest.[30]

South Asian migrants were persistent. In 1914, an immigration officer, Daniel Keefe, reported that more than a thousand Hindus had congregated in Hong Kong and Yokohama scheming about ways to enter the United States from either Mexico or Canada. He described the passengers awaiting passage as a "dirty looking outfit" who were barely cured of "trachoma and hookworm." Keefe continued to share concerns that South Asians in Manila could bypass the more stringent surveillance imposed at ports in China and Japan. Keefe blamed the "lax enforcement" in Manila on the misguided priorities of U.S. Customs Collector Bernard Herstein, "an Austrian Hebrew from New York," who had "no sympathy" for U.S. immigration laws and was, moreover, under pressure to admit laborers from other parts of Asia to work in British and U.S. business in the Philippines.[31]

On September 29, 1914, nearly two hundred South Asian men gathered at O'Brien Hall in Vancouver for a mass meeting to protest new hurdles for entry to the United States. The Seattle detention of seventy-three Hindu men traveling from Manila, only months after the Canadian government had turned back the SS *Komagata Maru* with several hundred would-be Indian immigrants, aroused South Asian men in Canada to rail against the caprice, "immoral" policy, and U.S. claims that the men were likely to be public charges. A Vancouver activist, Rahim, condemned the detention and argued that there was no evidence of South Asian paupers in North America. He successfully urged the assembled crowd to raise $35,000 for bonds for their "brothers detained in Seattle."[32] The protests and fund-raising in both Canada and the United States financed and supported lawyers who defended South Asian men from summary exclusion and deportation. Seattle and San Francisco attorneys consolidated dozens of individual cases into a class action suit and appealed the U.S. federal court's denial of entry to the U.S. Supreme Court.[33] The Immigration Service feared that the Supreme Court might accept the defense of South Asian entrants, since it had already rejected the reasoning for aliens' deportation based strictly on the condition of the overall "labor market" or on their possession of little money and ignorance of the English language. These factors did not achieve the threshold of the "physical disease and infirmity" certification by a physician necessary for the "likely to be a public charge" label. One immigration officer rationalized the evaluation of the labor market in relation to a general unfitness of Hindu men for labor. Rather than a judgment on the robustness of the labor market or the availability of work, the Immigration Service determined the Hindu aliens "personal unsuitability" and "personal unfitness" to compete successfully in any labor market.[34]

Personal unsuitability for labor and "likely to be a public charge" were vague diagnostic categories that meshed judgment about physical capability and capacity to earn an income with assessments of morality and character. After 1908, U.S. immigration officials moved frequently to dismiss the visa applications of South Asian migrants in Vancouver who were planning to move to the United States. Immigration authorities denied applications because of a lack of financial resources, poor physique, or a history of manual labor. Government officials were also pressured to designate whole ethnic and racial groups as unsuitable because of prevailing political tensions, competition, and white worker violence in the Pacific Northwest.[35]

When Harnam Singh, a six-foot-tall twenty-eight-year-old married man, applied in January 1909 for a visa to live and work in Bellingham, Washington, his application did not raise any alarms about his capabilities, resources, or the political climate in the city, which had driven out five hundred South Asian workers sixteen months before. U.S. immigration officers were impressed with his imposing physical stature and experience in the British army in Burma and as police officer in Shanghai prior to his arrival in Canada in 1907. Singh had already spent two weeks in Washington State in May 1908 and returned to work in Vancouver. In a matter of days, the U.S. authorities approved his visa application. Two nights later, Harnam Singh and a Chinese man were arrested after a fight, and Singh was charged with attempted sodomy. Later that week, the Vancouver police department informed the U.S. Immigration Service that Singh had been jailed "on the charge of sodomy, his companion in the offence being a Chinaman." U.S. Immigration authorities immediately withdrew the visa and rejected Singh as "likely to be a public charge."[36]

Harnam Singh's case demonstrates how rapidly the assessment of character and capacity could change, and how sharply moral suspicions could tilt the judgment toward "likely to be a public charge." His application for admission was buffeted by his initial conviction for sodomy, for which he served prison time. Upon appeal, the charge against him was dismissed and he was released, but the lingering shadow of his arrest for sodomy negated an adult history of "honorable conduct." Moreover, the charge of sodomy against him precipitated and heightened suspicions about the moral conduct of South Asian men generally, just as individual charges of polygamy were laid at the door of the entire ethnic group. In his appeal, his attorneys effectively argued that the magistrate who heard his case had no jurisdiction in sentencing him for a criminal offense without a full trial by jury. After his release, his attorneys appealed to the U.S. Immigration Service to restore his visa.[37] In making the case to U.S. immigration authorities, the attorneys emphasized his "honorable" four years' service as a British soldier, his exemplary "conduct" in three years' service as a Shanghai police officer, and his literacy and fluency in English.[38]

However, changes in his appearance and conduct since his visa interview irrevocably altered the U.S. immigration board's assessment of his character and prediction of his future. In jail, Singh was forced to cut his hair, remove his turban, and shave his beard and the immigration board used these changes in appearance to underscore their suspicion of his character, despite his legal success in winning release from imprisonment. Singh was now a suspect person and the sodomy charge preoccupied the board.[39]

Singh claimed that the charge was scurrilous and hid a more mundane history of exchanging insults, fighting, and disputes between the two men, who lived in the same rooming house in Vancouver's Chinatown. The fight escalated from verbal insults to a fistfight and brawl that eventually involved half a dozen Chinese men. After the fight broke out, Singh retreated in the company of a Chinese friend to share a "dram or two of drink." When the chairman of the board inquired whether the Chinese man had been "defending his honor," Singh vigorously disputed the claim and expressed dismay at the damage done to his honor by a spiteful and deceitful adversary.[40]

The immigration board telephoned Vancouver's police chief, who continued to suspect Singh's guilt and blamed a legal "technicality" for his early release after two months' imprisonment. The police accused Singh's attorneys and friends of "secreting him" after his release and of encouraging the disappearance of witnesses that made a full jury trial impossible. The "facts" of disorderly and unsavory conduct, including Singh's participation in brawls and drinking, justified the board's conclusion that he would be "undesirable as a resident of the United States."[41]

For Singh, the brawls, incarceration, and visa rejection had cast a shadow on his personal honor. He insisted that he had been victimized by a Chinese man's vendetta and a miscarriage of justice and wanted to make a fresh start in the United States. Singh did not want to remain in British Columbia because he felt "very much ashamed" and would "rather die than to have such reports about my name." Officer Brundjes expressed no sympathy and argued that shame was the justifiable consequence of Harnam Singh's behavior. Brundjes implicated Singh in a conspiracy of shadowy and unsavory sodomy attempts, suspecting his complicity as the missing witness in Edward Bowen's murder trial a year before: "Was not a friend of yours shot at a downtown hotel just a year ago for exactly the same trouble, one of your old pals who was in business with you? The man the Englishman shot down on Cordova Street."[42] Despite Edward Bowen's conviction of unjustified homicide and the dismissal of his defense of attempted sodomy by the courts, popular suspicions that South Asian men committed sodomy persisted. Singh was haunted by an allegation that he could not shake. Confirming his fear that his reputation had been destroyed, U.S. immigration collaborated with the Canadian police to restrict such potentially immoral men.

As Margot Canaday has demonstrated, in the first decades of the twentieth century, the U.S. immigration bureaucracy was less concerned with assessing an individual's sexual identity than by signs of "moral turpitude" that might predict future criminal conduct and social disorder. It would take several more decades before U.S. immigration would interpret atypical gender behavior, physical features, and reputed sexual behavior as a sign that confirmed homosexuality, necessitating exclusion. However, in the late nineteenth and early twentieth centuries, the government mobilized its suspicions about racial identity and the traits of nations, civilizations, and religions to predict the sexual immorality or criminal behavior to be expected of ethnic groups and justify barriers to their entry. The U.S. and Canadian immigration bureaucracies developed racial taxonomies to predict male predisposition to polygamy, or to procure and traffic women for illicit purposes, and for unmarried or widowed women to serve as prostitutes or concubines.[43] By racializing sexual immorality and predicting moral disorder, immigration officials developed strategies of scrutiny and investigation.

Faced with thousands of South Asian male immigrants living in Vancouver and Victoria, one would have presumed that Canadian officials would have welcomed South Asian residents who sought to bring about the immigration of their wives and children. Instead, the Canadian government pursued a divergent racial policy of immigrant settlement. Although a large, transient male laborer population had been a feature of European settlement in western Canada for a half-century, public discourse had for decades denounced the public disorder, immorality, and sexual degeneracy that the absence of families created for European Canadians in the rapidly growing cities of Vancouver and Victoria. Canadian politicians, social reformers, and journalists encouraged

European Canadians to settle in western Canada with their wives and children in order to build community, cultivate public virtue, and maintain social order. Canadians antagonistic to Chinese, Japanese, and South Asian immigration berated Asian men both for migrating without their families and for lacking these moral virtues, which justified their exclusion from political and social life in Canada.[44] Encouraging the migration of Asian women and children, however, raised the possibility that Asian immigrants would no longer be transients but permanent settlers in Canada.

The debate over reuniting families rallied public opinion in Canada, roused political protests in British India, and aggravated the Canadian state's attempts at racial restriction. In March 1911, immigration officials in Hong Kong and Vancouver relayed rumors of passenger steamers departing Hong Kong with five South Asian women and their children, who planned to reunite with their husbands in British Columbia. Canadian immigration agents feared that the "coming of the women" would "doubtless lead to trouble."[45] An estimated 800 South Asian residents in Vancouver gathered in Orange Hall to enumerate the "disabilities and indignities" of Canada's immigration restrictions and lobby the British government in India to champion the free mobility of South Asians throughout the British Empire. A Canadian immigration service translator and spy named William Hopkinson reported that South Asian men were incensed that even the most "cultivated Hindus who occupy positions of dignity and respect" were not shielded from the "hardship" of being denied the right to bring their wives and children into Canada.[46] These men drew attention to their class standing, educational attainments, and monogamous marriages.

The Canadian government's denial of the immigration of wives and children exploded in legislative and political debates in Canada.[47] Attorneys representing a number of these men argued that marriage was a "matter of religion," and that in denying them the "privilege or benefit of having their wives with them," the Canadian state unjustly abridged their marital rights, and thereby imperiled their "moral condition."[48]

The injustice amplified the disconnection between racial immigration barriers and the nation-state's interest in settled domestic life. The editor of the *Victoria Times*, William Baer, argued that South Asians were even more disadvantaged by government policy than Japanese and Chinese immigrants. As long as he "conform[ed] to our sanitary and social laws," a Japanese immigrant could either import a "picture bride" from Japan or marry in Canada, Baer pointed out. The only financial requirement was a tax, indexed by race;

Japanese wives and children could enter upon payment of a $50 bond, and Chinese merchants paid a $500 head tax apiece for their wives and children. Despite this financial hurdle, Baer argued, Chinese and Japanese men "possess all the privileges of our civilization." Not only could they be naturalized and acquire property, but a Chinese or Japanese man could "bring one, two, three, or four of his wives with him and live in polygamous relations with all these and we do not raise any protest. How do we know? What do we care? It is none of our business." The loudest advocates of sexual fidelity supported regulations that fostered adultery and prostitution, Baer insisted. Unlike the Chinese, he claimed, the "Hindu" was a "monogamist by tradition," similar in this to the "Anglo-Saxon" race.[49]

Baer decried the cruel plight of the South Asian man who was not "permitted to bring his wife in[to] this country and no female child of his may come near enough to smile into his eyes." In Canada, he "hear[d] the happy domestic songs of those for whom he labors," but was denied his own wife and children's proximity. Baer's sentimental portrait of the bereft, alienated immigrant emphasizes the loss of domesticity, depicting the transient "Hindu" laborer as a "family man" nostalgically longing for the "happy domestic songs" heard by other Canadians. The lonely South Asian man's suffering was compounded by public surveillance of his associations with white women that readily converted "an overt look, much less an overt act" into proof that these men were a "menace to our social safety," Baer wrote.[50]

The editor of the *Vancouver News Advertiser* bemoaned that living in barracks "sundered from their women-kind, which the Chinese do not support without grave consequence to morality, is a dangerous experiment in the case of the Sikhs, who have never been herded in cities like the Canton coolies, but are steeped in the domestic traditions of country life." The comparison of "Canton coolies" with Punjabi Sikhs delineated the successive regimes of labor housing, male migration, and exploitation in the capitalist extractive economy on the Pacific edge of the Americas. However, the editor believed that the "grave" yet somehow tolerable "consequences to morality" for Chinese male laborers would have dire and insupportable effects on Sikh men. Sharing a British colonial idealism about the pastoral virtues and values of Punjabi Sikhs, "steeped in the domestic traditions of country life," the editor conveniently sidestepped the history of imperial militarization and the homosocial barrack life of Punjabi Sikh and Muslim men enlisted in the British Army or hired by colonial police forces in Chinese treaty ports. This pastoral nostalgia envisioned all western Canadian settlers as independent rural farmers and Punjabi Sikh men as deserving and capable of sharing the ideals of pastoral self-government, as opposed to the wage-labor dependency anticipated in urban centers. In contrast to Chinese "coolies," who were depicted as subservient, dependent, amoral workers unfit for democratic society, Sikh men were perceived as robust, pastoral, and a "gallant remnant," deserving rescue from the vices of "barrack life" and the "ghastly and unnatural restriction of their rights as citizens, husbands and fathers."[51]

Baer emphasized the shared commitments, feelings, and rights of British imperial subjects. The cruel and dangerous condition of enforced isolation from female company and intimate family life, he argued, defied the reason of "any sane man or domesticated woman in Canada" and outrageously imposed a "condition we do not impose even on our pet animals, and yet we inflict upon a people whose religious traditions [are] older than ours, whose domestic ideas are as pure as our own, and who are men and women of like passions as ourselves. . . . We do not understand what we are doing to these people who, though not of our race, are imperially bone of our bone and flesh of our own flesh." Baer encouraged his fellow Canadians to trust Sikhism's "restraining influences on man's life" because it most resembled the ethical standards of Protestant Christian subjects.[52] The recognition of Sikh men's right to family life sprang from their status as both subjects of the British empire and free, independent men fit to be husbands and fathers. Ironically, by capriciously preventing wives and children from being reunited with their male relatives in Canada, the state undermined the political canard that Asian immigrants lacked interest in family reunification and permanent settlement.

Dr. G.L. Milne, a medical inspector and immigration agent in Victoria, vigorously objected to the "religious and other fancied hardships inflicted on the Hindu race." Instead, he attributed the absence of South Asian women in Canada to South Asian traditions rather than Canadian laws that limited their entry. He railed against the misplaced "sympathy" for the plight of a handful of "wives," since earlier waves of as many as 5,000 South Asian immigrants had arrived with only "two or three Hindu women." The gender disparity, he argued, demonstrated that the South Asian men were sojourners, uninterested in permanent settlement and incapable of assimilation to the "European . . . mode of living."[53]

This political debate, aired in regional newspapers, set the scene for the moral drama of South Asian wives and children seeking passage and being categorically refused steamer tickets and entry permits to join their husbands and fathers in Vancouver and Victoria. Canadian immigration officials detained Hira Singh's wife and child. A Vancouver businessman and persistent activist for the rights of Indians in Canada, Hussain Rahim, rallied Vancouver South Asian and white residents to repeal the unjust policy. Canadian immigration authorities relented after two weeks and released wife and child upon the payment of a $1,000 bond. Rahim claimed that the Canadian authorities had created a new "precedent," while William Hopkinson characterized the release as a humanitarian "act of grace."[54] Yet, as Hopkinson and other Canadian authorities feared, the act was interpreted as a policy change. South Asian men in Vancouver and Victoria began to flood passenger agents with applications to transport their wives and children and wrote their families telling them to proceed to Hong Kong and head for Vancouver. Dr. Sunder Singh, a twenty-nine-year-old physician, hired lawyers to launch a "test case" against transportation companies that refused to sell tickets to South Asian women and children. Superintendent of Immigration W. D. Scott confidentially feared that a court decision favorable to South Asian wives would increase the number of immigrant "Hindus or any other class of the yellow race."[55]

In Canadian newspapers, the debate over spousal immigration circled around sexual morality, monogamy, and the privileges of manhood. "W.C.," a devout Christian and "everyday workingman," expressed dismay that South Asian men experienced "humiliation and deprivation of privileges and rights" of living with their wives and children in Canada. W.C. argued that the Hindu had proven his manhood by his physical and moral characteristics; he was not a "spineless individual," but "physically a fine fellow" who "was sober, industrious and observed the Sabbath." Hindus had demonstrated courage in putting out a local mill fire. W.C. recognized the manhood of the "Hindu," whose moral character, physical prowess, and contributions to the common good compared favorably to those of "his white brother." In "God's country" the South Asian man should be able to "have his wife with him, and Canadian society should take the opportunity to educate wife and children in modern values and civilized living standards." Being recognized as a "man" and as a British subject and yet not able to be able to live with one's wife and children was the height of injustice.[56]

The *Vancouver Sunset* excoriated Inspector J. H. MacGill and the immigration agency as "coarse, corrupt and officious" agents who justified their exclusion of South Asian women and children on false allegations of polygamy. The editor derided MacGill's ignorance of "Oriental manners and customs" and his outrageous claims that the "licentious Hindu invariably kept, not merely one woman, but a seraglio, and that even the poorest native of Hindustan married profusely and possessed a zenana [harem]." Dr. Sunder Singh responded to these allegations, affirming that most South Asian migrants were Sikhs and scrupulously monogamous. Singh estimated that of the 4,000 South Asians in Vancouver, only 150 were Muslims, with the implication that only large numbers of Muslims would justify MacGill's suspicions of widespread polygamy.[57] Sympathetic journalists promoted Sikhism as comparable in domestic relations and values to Christianity.[58]

Racial predictions of polygamy festered in the Canadian government's refusal to accept the immigration of the families of two prominent Sikh men who had already settled in Canada. These men were responsible providers, husbands, and fathers and were astonished that their personal histories had become fodder for Canadian government allegations of fraud and duplicity. Both Bhag Singh, secretary of the Guru Nanak Mining and Trust Company and president of the Khalsa Diwan Society, and Balwant Singh, priest of the Sikh temple in Vancouver, had immigrated to Canada in 1906 and returned to India and brought back their wives and children. The Khalsa Diwan Society was the social organization that administered the *gurudhwara* and the multiple charitable activities that emanated from under its roof. As in India, *gurudhwara*s elsewhere in Asia and in North America served as hostels, where free meals were served to all comers, and places of worship, education, and for discussing politics and employment prospects. All Sikh adult men who had undergone the Sikh baptism ritual were members of the Khalsa (brotherhood), and the organization was therefore both a spiritual center and a home base that provided political representation for the community.

Both men were important leaders, and their struggles to reunite with their families became high-profile issues both within the community and for Canadian society. In 1910, Bhag Singh returned to India to remarry, since his first wife had died while he was in Canada. Bhag married Harnam of Peshawar in November 1910 and shortly afterward left for Calcutta. The Sikh priest Balwant Singh was also a widower but had remarried in 1903. His wife, Katar, had given birth to a daughter, Udum, before he departed for Canada in 1906. On his return visit to India, Balwant's second daughter Narjun was conceived and born. Both families embarked on a tedious and uncertain journey to Canada. Canadian prohibitions on travel stranded the families first in Calcutta and then in Hong Kong for half a year, while the two men tried to purchase steamship passage for their entire families. Bhag Singh's son Jopindra had been born in the Hong Kong *gurudhwara*, where both families lived. Finally, they purchased passage to Seattle, and from there to Vancouver. When they arrived in Vancouver in January 1912, the men were readmitted to Canada, but their wives and children were put in detention awaiting deportation.

Inspector MacGill refused to accept the legitimacy of either marriage, claiming that both were fraudulent and that the men were polygamists.[59] The South Asian community was outraged by the allegations of polygamy and fraud. At a mass meeting at Pender Hall in Vancouver, 400 South Asian men protested the deportation of the two women and their children and vigorously defended all Sikh men as "monogamous by principle."[60] In the *Toronto Globe*, a Reverend Wilkie chastised MacGill for the "prejudic[ing] the [immigration of Hindu wives] unfairly by saying they are polygamists." Wilkie argued that the Canadian policy that created "inhuman" conditions, encouraged immorality, and broke up families was the cause of immorality.[61] Protests and public pressure forced the Canadian government to relent and release the women and children temporarily to the custody of their husbands after two weeks' detention.

Suspicions of other Asian men remained, but journalists and advocates proclaimed the moral and honorable conduct of Sikh married men. One argued for the domesticating role of marriage, believing that "a married Sikh with a wife and baby in his cottage will be a far better Sikh than a glowering, morose and wronged Sikh leading a lonely life and disapproving of all he sees around him." The denial of married life was "barbarous according to our whole theory of civilization, and bound to result in evil one way or another. A man should be married. He is but half a citizen or half a Sikh if he is not."[62] Adult male morality hinged on the restraining influences of marriage and family life, which Sundar Singh, the editor of *The Aryan*, promoted in response to an audience question during a lecture at Vancouver's Empire Club in January 1912. A member of the audience asked, "Are the Sikhs in Canada moral?" to which he replied: "How can you expect a people to be moral without their wives and children?" Singh adeptly sidestepped the issues of race, religion, or civilization and made male morality universally contingent on the presence of wife and children and their restraint on adult men's behavior.[63] Both white Canadian and South Asian leaders emphasized that civilized society required a tightly orchestrated connection between adult male citizenship and marriage in order to maintain spiritual, moral, and social order.

Opponents of South Asian family migration feared that the "humanitarian" issue would explode into an avenue for large-scale immigration and rapid population increases of "Hindus" in Canada. Henry Herbert Stevens, a member of Parliament from Vancouver, disparaged the controversy over spousal immigration for South Asian men as a cynical strategy to "rouse sentimental support from a certain kind of moral busybody," particularly among middle-class and upper-class white Protestant liberals who already gave South Asian leaders an audience. Stevens decried how some ministers absolved Hindu men of "immorality" and even "criminality" (coded language for prostitution, trafficking, rape, and sodomy) on grounds that immigration restrictions fostered "immorality" and "unnatural condition[s]." Stevens stoked sexualized fears to justify immigration restrictions by prophesying the exponential reproductive growth of South Asian families as a consequence of arranged marriages and traditional child-bearing practices that encouraged unrestrained fertility. Stevens argued that opening immigration to South Asian wives and children would within a few years lead up to 3,000 large families, boosting British Columbia's South Asian population to a "colony of 20,000 Hindus" within a decade.[64]

The respite accorded Bhag Singh's family lasted only two short years. The family thrived during this time, and Bhag's wife, Harnam, came to be affectionately called "sister-in-law" in the Khalsa Diwan community. Sikh men at the *gurduwara* played with and brought toys for Bhag and Harnam's toddler son Jopindra. However, shortly before Harnam was to give birth to their second child, the Canadian immigration authorities ordered her to be deported, along with her children. Harnam had a difficult delivery, and nine days after she gave birth to a daughter, she died at home in January 1914.[65] Tragedy continued to dog Bhag Singh. Nine months later, he was killed by a Canadian government spy, Bela Singh, in an outrageous dual murder during a funeral at the Vancouver *gurudhwara*. The couple's infant children were orphaned and stranded in Vancouver.

The Vancouver MP H. H. Stevens saw the campaign to allow South Asian wives to freely immigrate as the opening salvo in full-throated demands for social, legal, and political equality in Canada. Emboldened to claim "rights of travel or settlement in all parts of the empire" as British subjects, South Asians would successfully convert residency claims to political rights of franchise and elected office. Sikh men's investments in British Columbia real estate fed Stevens's alarm that with their wives and children in Canada, the South Asians would claim the country as their home.[66] Their success in organizing capital and investments and their status as British subjects made South Asians' calls for the right of permanent settlement and political and social equality a greater threat than those of Chinese and Japanese immigrants. Ironically, months later, in his official capacity as a member of Parliament, Stevens himself was persuaded by humanitarian sympathy when he requested that the superintendent of immigration waive deportation of the two women—Harnam and Katar—and allow them to remain as an "act of grace."[67]

The alternative to family reunification, however, was interracial marriage. When the Sikh temple was dedicated in Victoria on October 6, 1911, the journalist Walter W. Baer commented on the small presence of "three Hindu women," whom he called "the sole ornament of the domestic memories of a numerous people who have been denied the right to bring their wives into Canada." In addition, there was an Englishwoman accompanying "a swarthy son of India, who was her husband, and though it was a childless marriage, she declares it to be—save for this—a happy one." Baer predicted that this marriage was a "forerunner of what will come to this Western country" because of the inequity of "immigration laws excluding the women-folk of these sturdy sons of the Empire." British Columbia would be populated by "half caste children and no one will venture to predict that this is better than to maintain the integrity and purity of the Hindu and White races separately and distinct."[68]

Denying South Asian wives and their children the right to enter the country, while permitting interracial marriage and the resulting "half-caste" children, underscored the contradictions determining who constituted British subjects in Canada, defining human mobility and the social lives of the nation's people. Even the instances in which the government offered relief to South Asian wives and children constituted exceptional "acts of grace" that demonstrated Canadian sovereign authority. The legal and moral legitimacy and illegitimacy of marriages and children became central concerns of immigration officials seeking to patrol the borders of the Canadian family.

Regulating Chinese and Japanese immigration through special taxes and an outright ban on laborers in the nineteenth and early twentieth centuries became standard Canadian government policy in the 1906 Immigration Act and 1910 amendments that authorized the exclusion of "immigrants belonging to any race deemed unsuited to the climate or the requirements of Canada." The Canadian government enforced racial definitions of "unsuitability" to curtail Asian immigration, but the status of Indians as British subjects challenged the stringency of these barriers.

FIGURE 12. Sikhs aboard the SS *Komagata Maru* in Vancouver Harbor, 1914. Gurdit Singh with white beard and wearing light-coloured suit. Canadian Photo Company. Courtesy Vancouver Public Library, Special Collections, VPL 136.

On October 7, 1913, fifty-six South Asian men arrived in Victoria. The immigration authorities reluctantly permitted seventeen of them to enter the country because they were able to establish that they had previously "established domicile" in Canada and were returning from visits to India but the rest were ordered to be deported. Attorney Edward Bird, who defended the men ordered deported, argued that the regulations were fundamentally unjust, and Chief Justice Hunter agreed that restricting people of Asiatic origin on grounds of their unsuitability to the Canadian climate was "vague." In December 1913, the Canadian cabinet then hastily put up new barriers against immigration, stating that the British Columbia labor market was "overcrowded" and that measures were temporarily necessary to prohibit laborers and artisans from entering British Columbia.[69]

## THE *KOMAGATA MARU* CONFRONTATION

In the spring of 1914, to challenge the immigration restrictions, Gurudit Singh, a wealthy Sikh merchant and labor contractor, brought 376 prospective Punjabi immigrants to Canada on a chartered vessel, SS *Komagata Maru*. The ship arrived in Vancouver harbor on May 23, 1914, and anchored off of Burrard Harbor for a three-month standoff between Canadian authorities, who refused to allow the passengers to land.[70] The Liberal MP Wilfrid Laurier, prime minister from 1896 to 1911, warned ominously that "if these Hindus are allowed to come into British Columbia, there may be riots on the streets of Vancouver and Victoria." Canadian public health and immigration authorities inspected all the passengers and ordered most all of them deported, except for twenty-two who had proven that they had established Canadian domicile and were returning to Canada.

Attorney Bird was again hired to defend the 354 excluded passengers. The Canadian federal government sought a single test case, and Bird selected Munshi Singh, a Sikh farmer from Punjab. Bird argued that the 1906 Canadian Immigration Act discriminated against the rights and protections that South Asians should enjoy as citizens of the British Empire. The 1908 "continuous journey" stipulation was infeasible, since direct steamship service from Calcutta to Vancouver had been discontinued under pressure from the Canadian and British governments. Ignoring the validity of temporary prohibitions on laborers, Bird argued that Munshi Singh was a skilled farmer, not a common laborer. Finally, he disputed the government's racial classification that falsely designated Munshi Singh as a member of the "Asiatic race" and asserted that the Sikhs were rather of the "Aryan, Caucasian race [and] as such were racially cousins of the English." As a British subject and an "Aryan," Munshi Singh was neither legally nor racially an "alien," and he deserved to be admitted to Canada. Chief Justice MacDonald called these contentions "ingenious" but "absurd" and repudiated Bird's arguments in the unanimous decision. MacDonald affirmed Canada's sovereign right to regulate the mobility of British subjects within its borders. Furthermore, because he had been held offshore and therefore had no domicile in British Columbia, Munshi Singh was not entitled to the civil liberties that applied to all British subjects within Canada.[71]

Justice McDonald reinforced the argument for racial incompatibility in the strongest terms. First, he denied that "Hindus" were "of the Caucasian race"; they were accurately of the "Asiatic race," and even as fellow British subjects, Hindus were of different "racial instincts" and in "their family life, rules of society and laws" were "fundamentally different to the Anglo-Saxon, the Celtic races and the European races in general." These differences were fundamentally and violently at odds with Canadian society, he argued, and the government must take seriously its mission to "safeguard" Canadians from migrants who "might annihilate the nation" and be "destructive to the well-being of society and against the maintenance of peace, order and good government."[72] McDonald prioritized the ascendancy of race as critical to Canadian national sovereignty and the exclusive allegiance of the nation to white settlers. By turning back the *Komagata Maru* and forcing its passengers to return to India, the Canadian Navy demonstrated the brute force of white Canada. The court decision affirmed Canadian sovereign power over international mobility to and rights of residence in the country.

Vancouver's South Asian residents mobilized to raise funds for food, legal representation, and landing bonds for the stranded passengers. Immigration authorities and the police cordoned off the ship, anchored in the harbor, and halted any contact with its passengers and their supporters on shore. After three months of public protests, government petitions, legal appeals, and daily newspaper coverage, the Canadian government forced the ship to turn back and return its passengers to India. During the bitter standoff, the Canadian immigration inspector William Hopkinson disguised himself and paid informants in the South Asian community to infiltrate public meetings and report on political conspiracies that British officials alleged fomented anti-British rebellion in India.

The *Komagata Maru's* departure demoralized Vancouver's South Asian residents. With the outbreak of the Great War in August 1914, many South Asian residents rallied to return to Punjab and struggle against British rule. Recriminations and accusations of espionage and betrayal roiled the Vancouver Sikh community. By early September, two known South Asian informants had been murdered. At the funeral of one of the men, on September 6, 1914, another widely known informant, Bela Singh, entered the Sikh Khalsa Diwan Society's *gurudhwara* in Vancouver. During an altercation after the service, Bela Singh pulled out two pistols and murdered both the society's president, Bhai Bhag Singh, and Battan Singh. Many Sikhs blamed the atmosphere that led to the murders on Hopkinson's surveillance and efforts to strictly limit South Asian immigration to Canada. At Bela Singh's murder trial, Hopkinson intended to testify that Bela had acted in self-defense and influence the jury to acquit him, but on October 21, 1914, before Hopkinson took the stand, Mewa Singh, the priest of Khalsa Diwan Society, shot him dead in the court corridor. Hopkinson's assassination stunned Canadians and outraged British officials, but it had the sympathy of South Asian residents in Vancouver and Indian revolutionary nationalists and sympathizers around the globe. Mewa

Singh was tried and convicted without offering a defense and was hanged on January 11, 1915.[73]

A month later, a white Canadian chauffeur named Ralph Pierce met a white-turbaned, forty-five-year-old Sikh named Dalep Singh several times while drinking at the Panama Hotel in Vancouver. Over drinks the first evening, Singh invited Pierce to his lodgings at the Sunset Rooms. Pierce described plainclothes police detectives shadowing their encounters and barging into the room, which "kind of spoilt the whole thing." Later, Pierce conferred with Detectives Ricci and Sinclair and set up an evening encounter at a tram station near the Panama Hotel, where Dalep Singh had agreed to meet again the following day. Their encounters followed the familiar scenario of meeting in saloons, visiting lodging-house rooms, and wandering streets. However, what made these encounters different was how vividly immigration controversies and political assassinations framed the context beneath the male encounters and directly shaped the edges of the action on the streets and in the courts. Over drinks, Dalep spoke about the Komagata Maru controversy, but in court Pierce dismissed the topic as insignificant compared to the sexual transaction that followed. Pierce insisted that within "two minutes," Dalep had invited him "to fuck," to which Pierce had blithely replied, "sure any old thing." After they left the bar at seven in the evening, Pierce walked with Dalep Singh down Pender Street in Chinatown toward the tram station where he introduced Detective Ricci as his friend and they were joined by Nana Singh, a twenty-nine-year-old friend of Dalep's. Nana Singh was wary of Ricci's presence, since they had had hostile encounters at Bela Singh's murder trial. In the witness room, Ricci intimidated and allegedly threatened Nana Singh with a pistol and warned him: "If you tell [false] stories about Bela Singh" on the witness stand "you will get in severe trouble, get seven years in Jail."[74]

When they all appeared in court in 1915, contesting the purpose of money transactions became central to the conflicting versions of the violence that evening. There was little doubt of the bruising fight that left Dalep Singh with a broken jaw. Nana Singh and Ralph Pierce both recalled that after a brief conversation at the tram station, the men had walked together. When they reached the Georgia–Harris Street viaduct on the Canadian Pacific Railway tracks, the men split up; Pierce took Dalep Singh in one direction and Detective Ricci took Nana Singh in another. Ricci asked Nana Singh if he had "any money," and he declared he had none. Meanwhile, Dalep Singh recounted, Pierce had "searched his pockets" for change. When Detective Sinclair arrived,

FIGURE 13. Vancouver Police Detectives Donald Sinclair and Joseph Ricci, Vancouver, ca. 1910s. Courtesy Vancouver Public Library, Special Collections. VPL 997.

both men attacked him, broke his jaw, and left him in the mud. Detectives Ricci and Sinclair dismissed the allegations of robbery and insisted that both South Asian men had made elaborate financial offers to Pierce, involving payment of "seventy-five cents" for each man's participation that evening and "two dollars every Sunday" and tram fare for a recurrent sexual relationship. Pierce obliged, pulled down his pants, and bent over, for which he claimed Dalep Singh paid him 75 cents; Officer Ricci declared that Singh's intentions were clear since he had "had his penis out and everything."[75]

Responding to defense accusations that he was a "stool pigeon for the police" and blackmailer, Pierce contended that Singh's offer and behavior was not a "very just thing he was trying to do." Pierce had purportedly gone along with the entrapment scheme in the service of upholding morality and order, and he believed his masculinity to be immune to aspersions on his character or desire.[76]

Curiously, Dalep Singh explained his interest in Pierce in financial terms as well, describing the dispute as a land deal gone sour. He claimed to have been drinking at the Panama Saloon when Pierce approached him and asked if he had land to sell. Singh had offered to sell his plot for half price to expedite his return to India because of his disgust at the Canadian government's hostility during the *Komagata Maru* standoff and its aftermath. Pierce asked to see a land title, which Singh had showed him at the Sunset Rooms. Singh denied that he had asked Pierce to have sex. [77]

Real estate speculation had percolated in Vancouver since its development by the Canadian Public Railroad in the 1880s. In the latest wave of land speculation from 1909 to 1913, South Asian, Greek, and Italian immigrants participated in a variety of partnerships and owned shares in property-holding corporations to take advantage of rising land values. For South Asian men, investing their savings in land in British Columbia offered favorable returns compared to opportunities in Punjab, Hong Kong, Shanghai, Singapore, or Manila, where retail and petty trade were the chief means of capital accumulation. The steep drop in values and the credit crisis in 1913 had frozen the real estate market and made Dalep Singh's interest in quickly unloading his title plausible.[78]

When the cases against Nana Singh and Dalep Singh were brought to trial, both judge and juries balked at the unsavoriness of the entrapment scheme, Pierce's dubious character, and Detective Ricci's unseemly behavior and refused to convict either man.[79]

## THE THREAT OF IMMORAL IMMIGRANT WOMEN

U.S. immigration authorities also disputed South Asian men's bids for resident status and assumed that the relationships between South Asian women and men were morally suspect and deviant. Both Canada and the United States chipped away at the material basis of male independence and scrutinized men's ties to female dependents and children for hints of immorality, perversion, and corruption. The spotlight on racially suspect immigrants undermined and made unavailable the kinds of intrinsic state support for patriarchal privileges, responsibilities, and capacities that were routinely offered to European immigrants and encouraged their participation in white settler society. Immigrant women's entry to the United States was contingent on immigration inspectors' assessments of their work, their sexual relations, their experiences with reproduction, their roles in the family, and their race. As Martha Gardner writes:

> Marriage provided the linchpin between policies of family reunification and those of immigration restriction. If there was no legal marriage, there could be no legal

family and thus no claims to entry or access. As long as "wife" remained a privileged category under the law, immigration and judicial officials were forced to contend with the question of marriage—what exactly constituted a legal, state solemnized relationship. Religious marriages, common-law marriages, and even polygamous marriages had brought the problem into legal relief. However, picture brides, correspondence marriages, and the marriage of women charged with prostitution brought the problem of marriage into legal crisis.[80]

Immigration inspectors' charges of polygamy, disputes about the legitimacy of religious marriages, and skepticism about the chastity of unmarried women aimed at South Asian women reflected broad suspicion that immigrants'"marriages" could be duplicitous, particularly among Asians and eastern and southern Europeans, who showed patterns of high solo male immigration, followed later by the immigration of spouses, children, and other kin. The reputations and relationships with adult men of South Asian women, whether married, widowed, or unmarried, thus received special scrutiny, and there was skepticism about their moral conduct.[81]

In November 1923, after more than a decade in the United States, thirty-five-year-old Bagh Singh Chotia returned to San Francisco following a six-month trip to India. Chotia was accompanied by his twenty-year-old widowed sister Raj Kaur. They had anticipated interrogation by the Immigration Service, but not that she might be refused entry. Six months later, reporting on the controversy over Raj Kaur's arrival, the Los Angeles Times characterized it as a "factional" quarrel, based on a tip from a South Asian organization that suspected that she had been "brought to the country for immoral purposes."[82]

In January 1923, Chotia had left his wife, Grace, a white woman, and their two sons, Vernon and Noel, behind on a farm near Fresno. In Bagh Singh Chotia's family, the brothers traveled the globe for work and the sisters married Punjabi men and remained in Punjab. The four children were orphaned early in the century. Their mother died shortly after the birth of their youngest sister, Raj Kaur, in 1903, and their father died two years later. Their father's brother, Janta, supported and raised the children who remained at home. The eldest sister had married in 1903, and Bagh's older brother left to find work in Calcutta, Hong Kong, and Manila, where he tragically died in October 1910. Bagh left home next and journeyed to Hong Kong and landed at the port of Seattle in March 1912. In 1915, their uncle Janta arranged for Raj Kaur's engagement and marriage at the age of thirteen. She lived with her husband for a very short time before he died, when she was eighteen.[83]

The San Francisco immigration authorities received a letter from the Malwa Khalsa American Society of Stockton, California, that reported that Bagh Singh Chotia would return to the United States with women of "bad character" and urged immigration authorities to deport the women, because their arrival would be disruptive and cause "much trouble to the Hindoo community." The arrival of a marriageable South Asian woman, the competition among potential suitors, and the operation of a prostitution ring were all disruptive prospects. When informed of the contents of the letter, Chotia speculated about a "grudge against him" and alleged that a climate of jealousy and vindictive behavior pervaded the South Asian community in the United States.[84] When offered the names of the leaders of the Malwa Khalsa American Society, he recognized the president as a man with whom he had had a profit-sharing dispute over a tenancy agreement and the secretary as one whom he had carelessly insulted.[85]

The Immigration Service detained Bagh Singh Chotia and Raj Kaur and dispatched an Inspector Lawler to Stockton and Fresno to investigate the Malwa Khalsa American Society and its allegations.[86] Apparently, a twenty-three-year-old student named Grewal, who worked periodically as farm laborer, had "felt duty bound" to share with authorities an "anonymous letter" he had received from India in May 1922 that alleged that Bagh Singh Chotia would return to Fresno with "two women, one of them his sister and the other a woman of bad character." Grewal was also quick to explain that he received a second letter more recently that claimed that the "Hindu woman of bad character" had not been able to raise the funds to pay her expenses and therefore had not accompanied Bagh Singh Chotia and Raj Kaur.[87] The president of the Malwa Khalsa American Society was a forty-one-year-old immigrant named Rattan Singh, who had lived in the United States for more than a decade. He was dismayed that his "good faith" communication to the immigration authorities had not been kept "confidential" and worried that the revelation would cause "trouble" and "injury" in the community. Rattan Singh boasted that the Malwa Khalsa American Society balanced social and material uplift of the Sikh community with the suppression of criminal activity such as the "manufacture and sale of bootleg whiskey and trafficking in narcotics." The aim was to collaborate with police and immigration and customs officials and improve the public reputation of the South Asian immigrant community. Rattan Singh denied that he had been motivated by personal spite or disputes with Bagh Chotia.[88]

U.S. authorities suspected Raj Kaur of being a trafficked woman for the purposes of prostitution, either as a concubine or to be remarried as a second wife to one of Bagh's cousins in Fresno.[89] These scenarios all participated in the prevailing logic of an Asian woman of dubious virtue who was sexually exploited by Asian men, necessitating the vigilance of U.S. government agents. Raj Kaur modestly responded that she had not come to the United States to find a husband, saying, "God has given me one [husband] and I will not marry again."[90]

Chotia did not exactly fit the profile of a nefarious ethnic procurer of women.[91] He had lived in California for a decade, married Grace Stowe in Yuma, Arizona, in 1917, and farmed on a ranch outside of Fresno. The couple had two sons, Vernon, aged three, and Noel, aged five. Chotia's attorney pled for his release from detention on humanitarian grounds and introduced the imperative of reunifying families with American-born members. The attorney hailed Chotia's "flawless record of character" during the ten years he had lived in the United States and his financial self-sufficiency and property ownership, which demonstrated "an extraordinary badge of zeal and thrift among Indians," but made the strongest moral appeal to the preservation of his marriage and his relationship to his sons.[92] The government's actions would "destroy or impair" his intimate ties to his U.S.-born wife and children and sentence him to an "arbitrary living death" by denying him "his family and flesh and bone." The policy of excluding Asian laborers was a "punishment" that apparently was justifiable in separating men from their families abroad but, the lawyer argued, was never intended to "orphanize children of the tenderest years . . . these [American] children must have their father—it means his existence to them. Nothing appears to becloud their right to be together."[93] The immigration authorities accordingly released Bagh to join his American-born wife and children, affirming the principle of the reunification of parents with children.

The continued detention of Chotia's sister Raj demonstrated the limits of "family reunification" and the anxiety over adult women who were considered neither fully independent nor dependent. Raj faced a long-standing gender bias in immigration law that perceived "immigrant women without husbands and fathers as financial risks and likely drains on the nation's resources."[94] Immigration authorities tested Raj's financial independence, literacy, class background, and interest in remarriage to determine whether the state could offer her a tourist visa. Although Raj confidently outlined her financial resources, including her share of inherited land and a cache of silver, enabling her to afford the expense of visiting her "brother's family and travel," immigration officers skeptically characterized her "peasant . . . appearance, dress and manner" as insufficient to establish her as a member of the "better class" who would more realistically "tour this country for curiosity or pleasure."[95] A literacy exam had been imposed in the 1917 immigration legislation and the vast majority who tested illiterate were women; however, women who were married were exempt.[96] The Immigration Service hired a Christian missionary born in India named Theodore Fieldbrave to administer a test in Gurumukhi script to assess Raj's literacy. She fumbled using his translated Bible verses.[97] Raj offered her own Sikh prayer book instead, which illustrated her abilities with a familiar text, underscored that Gurumukhi was a script developed for Sikh spiritual practice, and rebuked the Christian proselytizing. Fieldbrave observed that she was not reading systematically but rather stumbling over words, repeating phrases, and picking out characters "committed to memory." Raj freely admitted that she lacked formal education, but said that through her home training and attendance of religious ceremonies, she had learned to recite "folk-lore and stories." Fieldbrave concluded that she was "totally illiterate" from his perspective, but conceded that from the "Indian point of view" she was above "the average Indian girl" in intelligence and "not uncultured."[98]

The U.S. secretary of labor approved her application for a six-month tourist visa over the objection of the immigration commissioner. Raj Kaur tried to extend her visa in June 1924 in order to testify in a libel and slander suit against the Malwa Khalsa Society and to continue her high school education. This time, the immigration commissioner, labor secretary, and attorney general denied her extension request. However, a personal bill passed by the House Committee on Immigration and Naturalization awarded her another six-month extension. In December 1924, Raj requested an extension to continue studies she had begun at Kerman High School, outside Fresno. The principal, William Otto, praised her work "under the direction of our Americanization teacher," who reported that Raj was a "good reliable pupil" making "fast progress" in speaking and writing in English.[99] A YWCA board member who lived in Berkeley, Henrietta Thompson, rallied to support Raj's perseverance and marveled that an unlettered woman had come as a "tourist" and assumed the "class of a student" before returning to "India to help her own people." The immigration authorities, however, dismissed the appeal, denied Raj's claim to "special consideration" as a student, and ordered her immediate deportation.[100]

In a strange twist to an already complicated immigration story, Raj's exit from the United States threatened to split Bagh and Grace Chotia's family. As the time drew near for Raj's departure, San Francisco immigration authorities received desperate pleas from Grace Chotia, who was now estranged from her husband. She feared that her sister-in-law's deportation would lead her husband to remove and raise her sons in India. She begged the immigration authorities to prevent her estranged husband from buying passage for "our two small sons," whom he had abducted from their child-care provider while she worked outside the home.[101] In spite of their vigilance in regulating and containing the perceived immorality of incoming immigrants, U.S. immigration officers had no jurisdiction over the mobility of exiting U.S. citizens. They advised Grace to ask the San Francisco Police Department to intervene with steamship agents to determine whether her sons had been kidnapped.[102] In the end, Raj departed alone. Noel and Vernon grew up in the United States and enlisted in the U.S. Army during World War II.[103]

Unlike the married wives and mothers who struggled to land in Canada in the early 1910s, Raj Kaur arrived simultaneously dependent on her brother and potentially independent. The creation of an individual case file and her status as a widow enabled her to speak for herself even under the constraints of an immigration review. She emphasized her financial independence, lack of interest in remarriage, and capacity for and interest in education to overcome the limitations of her background. However, the state never recognized a woman's status as independent and found her indifference to attaching herself to a man worrisome. The conventional expectation in both Canada and the United States was that women immigrants were subordinated to male authority and agency. Women's roles were limited to caring for the household and children; they were restricted to the household economy. When immigration officials questioned relationships and disallowed family migration, the aim was to undermine male prerogatives, honor, and status and reinforced the image of women as silenced and subordinate to men.

Another woman with the same first name Raj arrived on Angel Island in July 1921. She too was widowed, but she had remarried her husband's brother, Dhana Poonian, who ran a thriving orchard for a decade in Loomis, California. Immigration authorities reluctantly released her husband Dhana after a county judge and landowner vouched for his longtime residence and regular employment. The deportation of Raj Poonian and her two sons was narrowly averted after Dhana put up a bond to ensure that the marriage lasted, that the wife and children would not become wards of the state, and that Raj would not seek employment outside the home. After two years on probation, Raj and her sons were released from probation after Dhana continued to prove that he was a "frugal, industrious, intelligent man" and a capable provider, who had proven his financial capacity by acquiring property in California, maintained a "substantial bank account," and had an annual income of $4,000 from his business. Raj had been "occupied solely with her household duties and has undertaken no work or been engaged in any occupation as would serve to defeat the Immigration Act."[104] However, Raj Poonian's work in the family business was disguised in statistics that "enumerated women as wives rather than workers."[105] After Dhana's death in 1934, Raj Poonian ran a thriving nursery business with one of her sons for several decades, becoming well known as an expert grafter and clever businesswoman.[106] Her success story was that of one of the rare South Asian women who raised children in the United States in that era.[107]

## CONCLUSION

Canadian and U.S. immigration regulations categorized male migrants from British India as racially "Asiatic" and targeted them for intensive scrutiny of their bodily fitness and heath and their intimate ties. Immigration regulations simultaneously blocked certain types of mobility and managed the movement of all other people "by requiring extensive state suppression of private and corporate activities that might hinder or exploit certain types of migration."[108] The governments' interest in investigating and regulating the entry of spouses, children, and siblings accompanying resident immigrant adult men revealed an insistence that immigration would shape class order, gender roles, sexual morality, and the structure of the household. The web of intimate dependency that brought people to Canadian and U.S. borders and that shaped their domestic social lives framed both states' immigration bureaucracies and contradictory policies for family settlement and solo male transience.

In the 1910s and 1920s, immigration authorities began to pay attention to forms of sexual and moral behavior, conduct, and belief systems to predict trajectories of immigrant life within national borders. Entry into the two countries was paradoxically contingent both on the fiction of independent male individual autonomy and equally on the judgment and calibration of proper dependency. The capacity of adult males to organize capital and maintain independent households became the criterion for predictive judgments of future capacity, livelihood, and ability to support kin without charitable or government support. While Canada and the United States supported the immigration of European patriarchal families (husband, wife, children, grandparents), immigration from Asia was premised on the model of the solo and temporary male worker who would return to his home country after a career of productive labor. The fear of permanent settlement and reproduction drew heightened scrutiny and deterrence to the migration of Asian immigrants' wives and children. Unmarried adult and widowed women therefore became a particularly vexed and highly scrutinized category for immigrant entry by Asians into the United States and Canada in the early twentieth century. Within the ascendancy of racialization to secure and organize the nation, justified variously by labor competition, health and ability screening, and the politicization of white workers, there was a rise in investigative scrutiny of the sexual morality and character of the racially suspect migrant.

Even when successful appeals were made as acts of grace, states granted permission to make special exceptions to regulation and upheld policies without any necessary revisions. These exceptions bolstered the primacy of the rule of law even as they closed avenues of judicial appeal and enfolded the judicial appeal within the administrative system of inspection and investigation. They reinforced sovereign authority over human mobility and future possibility and enhanced the perception that the state's representatives administered compassionate judgment even when the majority of those excluded experienced caprice, suspicion, and indifference. The system of regulating migration flows focused state scrutiny and sympathy on the individual case.

During the twentieth century, as Martha Gardner has demonstrated on a broader scale, immigration cast a deep "shadow of the law, shading how respectability, domesticity, economic viability and moral character were visualized at the border. Like a prism, morality and immorality, self-sufficiency and dependency, legitimacy and illegitimacy fractured race and gender into individuating hues." Immigrants "flexed the law where they could, broke it when they felt they must, as they carefully constructed stories of work skills, family relationships and moral behavior to prove their admissibility."[109]

Male honor and respectable morality were hinged together. The question of morality was intertwined with a concern for burdens to private charity or state support. The model developed through the Chinese Exclusion Acts and the 1907 Gentleman's Agreement with Japan demanded that immigrants from

Asia prove their economic independence, and particularly their means to support a family, or else be excluded as unskilled laborers.[110] However, the ability of women and children to migrate was strictly circumscribed by racial and sexualized exclusions and by powerful cultural and political hostility, which made the few attempts to immigrate strenuous and exceedingly unwelcome. Most Asian men who did not fit the nuclear family in the United States were suspected of not being morally respectable, in spite of their financial remittances to support transnational families at home. Concerns about male immigrant immorality and moral turpitude became both more vivid and more varied as individual case files accumulated. Suspicions of prostitution, sodomy, polygamy, and violence punctuated the immoral and framed the moral register of "likely to be a public charge."[111] Suspicions about "unattached" persons narrowed the conditions for immigrant entry and exit, as well as the parallel process of political membership. The process of state recognition of membership became increasingly defined by racialization, sexual morality, gender norms, and regularizing households.

## CHAPTER 7

# Strangers to Citizenship

The U.S. and Canadian governments blocked South Asian immigrants' ability to claim national citizenship. In the first decades of the twentieth century, both federal governments addressed the question of the citizenship rights of South Asian immigrants through an emerging division into "white" and "non-white" that reinforced white settlers' subordination of indigenous and "colored" peoples. Serving as the political fusion of privilege and identity, national citizenship became a gateway for the distribution of state resources, access to material benefits, and the privileges of political participation.[1]

The battle over claiming citizenship was contested on the terrain of race. In the United States, where naturalization was limited to "free white persons" by the 1790 Naturalization Act, the interpretation of "white" was slippery. The Fourteenth Amendment and the 1870 Naturalization Act extended citizenship rights and naturalization to "persons of African nativity," but a decade later, the Chinese Exclusion Act prohibited Chinese immigrants from obtaining naturalized citizenship. The subsequent political career of the racialized legal category "alien ineligible for naturalized citizenship" built a wall of exclusion around Asian immigrants in the late nineteenth and early twentieth centuries. Canadian Confederation in 1867 and Dominion status in 1907 created autonomy from the British Empire in domestic self-governance and determining political participation. Following the lead of other British settler colonies such as Natal and the Cape Colony, Canada exercised autonomy by racializing eligibility rules and denying rights of political participation and immigration for British imperial subjects from India. Despite shared British imperial citizenship, South Asians were slotted as undesirable "Asiatics," similar to the Chinese and Japanese immigrants who came to Canada in the nineteenth century. At the dawn of the twentieth century, differentiating immigrants by race and granting naturalization rights to "white" persons became the ascendant strategy of defining and corralling national membership in the English-speaking democracies.[2]

In the United States, fixing the boundary of "white" and "Asiatic," was sharply contested and erupted in federal court cases for immigrants from Syria, Palestine, Persia, Arabia, and Afghanistan seeking naturalized citizenship. In the late nineteenth and early twentieth centuries, Chinese, Japanese, and Korean immigrants were corralled into the racial category of "Asiatic." In western, midwestern, and southern states, white political cartels developed against both "Asiatic" and "black" persons as governing strategies to deny access to the franchise, elective office, jury service, and ability to testify in court, and to severely restrict licensing in professions and the ability to own, use, and lease property. Designating a person as "Asiatic" foreclosed any inquiry into individual character or achievements and converted an applicant into a racial problem who faced blanket prohibitions. In 1917, the U.S. Congress passed the Barred Zone Immigration Act, which extended the geography of laborer exclusion across the Indian subcontinent and the rest of Southeast Asia and provided the geographical template for racial exclusion from naturalization. After World War I, the U.S. Justice Department followed that racial boundary and renewed federal court challenges to Japanese, South Asian, and Middle Eastern men to prove that they were "white."

Roiling beneath the white and Asian racial boundary, there simmered a shadow play of assumptions about conduct, behavior, and allegiance that erupted in government efforts to deny or strip Asian immigrants of the privileges of naturalized citizenship. The caricatures of "conduct and behavior" were critical elements that smoothed over the contradictions of equitable participatory democracy and the production of new status hierarchies and exclusions.[3] By defining membership in the nation-state, immigration and naturalization laws created a "system of belonging and non-belonging," converting people into either "assets or threats to assimilation and nation-building." All female and nonwhite male immigrants were "judged by their work, their sexuality, their moral character, their role in the family and their race."[4] The legal system of naturalized citizenship "endorsed the state's attachment to particular embodiments of [the] desirable citizen" and obscured how the state "reproduced" citizens through either an inheritance system of birthright citizenship or a contractual model of naturalization. Neither birthright inheritance nor contractual naturalization was free of favoritism that created unequal advantages for favored races and classes and for men.[5]

In the early twentieth century, in both Canada and the United States, a hierarchical political system rewarded white adult men exclusively and underlined the possessive investment in both whiteness and masculinity. As economic opportunity was curtailed for different groups of noncitizens, petitioning for naturalized citizenship was necessary to access economic opportunities and enlist state protection. The ability to naturalize was mobilized in state licensing of professions, as well as in the ability to own, lease, and dispose of agricultural property.

National citizenship recognized intimacy and family as the privilege of independent adult men. Naturalization procedures paid attention to the repercussions of acknowledging new male citizens' dependents. Racial exclusion, sometimes justified by the social imperatives for intraracial reproduction, directed increasing attention to the importance and value of the married, heterosexual household to national citizenship.[6]

Naturalization in the United States developed into an ordinary bureaucratic ritual. Yet as the nation-state administratively and judicially created racial barriers for its attainment, the procedure became an index of racial registration and political status. Three different problems arose in Canada and the United States with an individual making a claim for naturalized citizenship. The first involved a process of registering, contesting, and affirming racial identity and establishing the boundaries of white and nonwhite groups. The second problem concerned how people were slotted into group identities and the criteria for judging individuals based on their physical appearance, personal history, and their performance as people who were civilized, educated, and moral. The third involved the proper expression of the sentimental performance of U.S. or Canadian national identity as the vanguard and home of freedom and self-determination. This sentiment for freedom and self-determination could create a maelstrom of tensions, particularly as legislators and bureaucrats demanded singular allegiance to one nation-state. The transition from nation of origin to nation of settlement required careful calibration of individuals' cultural and political interests in their home. Naturalized citizenship emphasized the conversion of political allegiance (which frequently turned a subject of imperial rule into a national constitutional subject). The persistent demand for the nationalization of politics, associations, and alliances confronted the various transnational social and collective strategies that undercut rigid national allegiances. However, when bureaucrats of the nation-state confronted plural national allegiances, they interpreted and handled them as either irreconcilable conflicts or signs of evangelical faith in extending democracy worldwide. An interest in the welfare and political struggles of other nation-states had to be articulated as an expression of international humanitarianism, an affirmation of one's own nation-state's military and strategic alliances, and an affirmation of binational trade and capital investment.

Immigrant claimants often used the courts to contest state power as well as social conventions. Underlying these efforts, claimants demonstrated a respect for social conventions, rather than a desire to change the laws. These were not cases of radical individualism or radical political agendas. Yet the denial of rights to citizenship was an injustice that fitted a frame of liberal individualism that was easier to contest, encompassed within a liberal vision of individual rights. Since the terms of disqualification were expressly racial, the individual claimants mobilized "white" as the sole racial identity gateway to national citizenship.

## THE BUREAUCRATIC CHOREOGRAPHY
## OF PASSING AS WHITE

In the United States, contests over white racial identity structured the acquisition of naturalized citizenship in the early twentieth century. The disqualification of Chinese immigrants from naturalization in 1882 and the rise of immigrants from eastern and southeastern Europe, the eastern Mediterranean, and western and southern Asia made the contests over defining "white" more frequent. In 1907, the U.S. Bureau of Naturalization, under the direction of Attorney General Charles Joseph Bonaparte, lobbied Congress to systematize and consolidate naturalization criteria in the federal courts in consultation with federal attorneys and naturalization examiners.[7] From 1907 to 1925, the Naturalization Bureau and the Department of Justice periodically challenged naturalization certifications of Armenians, Persians, Turks, Sephardic Jews, South Asians, and Japanese, and created test cases to police the cultural and political definition of whiteness. Immigrants from Greece, Syria, Armenia, Persia, India, the Philippines, and Japan made strategic appeals to the category of "free and white." Their appeals were backed by linguistic and physical anthropology, assimilation to Christian belief, the acquisition of the English language, educational attainment, the practice of American social custom, and demonstration of property ownership and regular income in legal challenges to the criteria of naturalization.

The first national-origin barrier to naturalized citizenship against the Chinese in the 1882 Chinese Exclusion Act was converted into the legal status category of "alien ineligible for naturalized citizenship," subsequently analogized to others that could be designated as of "Oriental" or "Asiatic" race. The threat of being considered nonwhite, and labeled "Asiatic" persistently haunted legal contests to naturalize by Syrians, Lebanese, Sephardic Jews, Turks, Persians, Afghans, Arabs, and Hindus.[8]

Soon after their arrival in the United States, immigrants from India tested the definition of "white" and their claims to naturalize as U.S citizens. Taraknath Das, a young student and anti-British revolutionary fled Calcutta, lived in exile in Japan, and arrived in Seattle in July 1906. After working as a railroad laborer in Washington State, he traveled to San Francisco, where he became a hospital janitor. Through the interest of a professor of medicine, he was employed in a laboratory and enrolled as a chemistry student at the University of California in Berkeley. In May 1907, after passing the civil service exam, Das went to work as an interpreter for the U.S. immigration service in Vancouver, British Columbia. Before he left, however, his application for naturalization, filed in Oakland, California, was refused.

His application ignited a flurry of correspondence between naturalization examiners, court clerks, and U.S. federal attorneys to determine whether British Indians racially qualified as "white."[9] Das wrote to Attorney General Bonaparte questioning why "Hindus who belong to the Caucasian stock of the Human Race have no legal right to become citizens of the United States."[10] Bonaparte responded that natives of British India were categorically not "white persons." Das subsequently reapplied in Seattle in February 1908. The following month, a court in New Orleans awarded naturalized citizenship to two Muslim merchants from Calcutta, and courts in Spokane, Washington, accepted a high-caste Hindu man. As dozens more applicants appeared across the country petitioning for naturalization, the U.S. Bureau of Naturalization instructed all federal court clerks to refuse petitions and applications from, and for U.S. attorneys to actively oppose the naturalization of, all "Hindoes or East Indians." The British government, coping with political firestorms over South Asian settlement in South Africa, Australia, and Canada, refused to protest this U.S. policy.[11]

At the same time, Naturalization Bureau examiners aggressively confronted Syrian, Armenian, Jewish, Persian, and Afghan petitioners and challenged their racial eligibility. This policy met with vigorous opposition from established communities of Syrians, Greeks, and Jews. A Syrian businessman in Birmingham, Alabama, H.A. Elkourie, rebuked the Naturalization Bureau's denial of naturalization to "Ottomans regardless of their race whether Syrians, Jews, Greeks or Armenians."[12] Elkourie disentangled Ottoman rule from the Ottoman Empire's multiplicity of ethnic subjects, many of whose Christian and Jewish belief traditions, he argued, affirmed their "white" identity. Simon Wolf, representing the Union of American Hebrew congregations, reinforced biblical heritage by claiming that the exclusion of Syrian Jews from citizenship eligibility would be tantamount to excluding "David and Isaiah and even Jesus of Nazareth himself." In addition to invoking shared heritage, faith, and perhaps bloodlines, Wolf also insisted that Syrian Jews "whose conduct and law-abiding dispositions are irreproachable" had earned the right to naturalize based on individual conduct and character.[13]

On the other side of the policy desk, Richard K. Campbell, commissioner of the Bureau of Naturalization, believed that all immigrants from the eastern Mediterranean were "people wholly different, if not in origin at least in their political and moral ideas," making them divergent from "white people or occidentals" and just as much a "risk" to the political order as "Chinese, Japanese, [or] Malays." Campbell argued that "the Average man in the street" would "find no difficulty in assigning to the yellow race a Turk or Syrian with as much ease as he would bestow that designation to a Chinaman or Korean."[14] For Campbell, the similarity between "Chinamen" and "Turks" rested on their allegedly shared political and moral character, which enabled despotic rule and set them apart from "white people."

This aggressive stance stirred up a political firestorm and created considerable friction between Campbell and his boss, Secretary of Commerce and Labor Charles Nagel, who advocated that naturalization examiners adopt a restrained posture, leaving the interpretation of the law "safely" to the courts. He advised Campbell to "avoid unnecessary agitation and embarrassment to any people who have been admitted into this country" and directed naturalization examiners to pay more attention to "the present reputation" than "the original nativity of the applicant."[15] Despite his anger at Campbell's actions, Nagel defended him strenuously in public, but he pledged that "any aggressive measures" had been discontinued, and that immigrants from the eastern

Mediterranean would be judged on their individual "character," not on their "nativity." Nagel followed the liberal creed of "individual merit," ignoring the fact that it was blanket racial suspicion that caused the controversy, and "white" identity continued to be the racial gateway for naturalization eligibility.[16] F. R. Champion, editor of the *Schenectady Union*, approved judging each Armenian application for naturalization on the "merits of its individual case," inasmuch as "some may not make desirable citizens," and he rebuked as "unjust and unwholesome" the racialization that had summarily denied naturalization to "all Armenians" because they were designated as "Asiatics."[17] The 1909 naturalization examiners' vigorous campaign to ferret out "Asiatics" deterred many who had filed petitions from appearing for court hearings to avoid the humiliation of government objections.[18] By December 1909, naturalization examiners quit raising objections based on "Asiatic" race, and shortly afterward a federal court decision effectively made all Syrians eligible for naturalized citizenship by affirming their racial identity to be "white."[19]

## NOT QUITE BRITISH SUBJECTS: THE PROBLEM OF CANADIAN DOMICILE

Across the border in Canada, the problem of citizenship was directly linked to the struggle for political participation. Despite claims to equal status as British subjects, race prescribed access to citizenship in British settler colonies. At the turn of the century, the white British settler colonies of Natal, Cape Colony, New South Wales, the Transvaal, New Zealand, and Canada thwarted the entry of British subjects from India and circumscribed the exercise of citizenship in participating in domestic politics. As each of the British settler colonies developed democratic elections and legislatures to govern domestic society in the late nineteenth and early twentieth centuries, Indians struggling for self-governance looked to Canada and Australia as models for their political future. This underlined the importance that the ability to exercise the vote had for British adult male imperial subjects from India.

Hussain Rahim, who had championed the cause of Punjabi Sikhs in Vancouver for spousal immigration in 1912, had earlier claimed rights to franchise in British Columbia. Rahim had arrived in Vancouver from Honolulu on January 14, 1910, and entered Canada legally as a "tourist" and "businessman." Within months, he set up residence in Vancouver and became the manager of an import-export trading and real estate investment business, the Canada-India Supply and Trust Company. Hussain Rahim's origins and history were murky. In official immigration records and legal proceedings, he identified himself as a Muslim businessman from Delhi who had worked in Honolulu for several months before traveling to Canada. However, British records from colonial India asserted him to have originally been a Hindu, born Chhagan Khairaj Verma, who hailed from Porbander, a port on the western coast of India between Bombay and Karachi.[20] Rahim had repeatedly and effectively resisted Canadian immigration authorities' attempts to deport him, ultimately winning a court order to stay deportation in October 1911.

The following year, Rahim became an outspoken politician and advocate in Vancouver. In March 1912, he made the exercise of full political participation his crusade, and in the 1912 British Columbia provincial elections, he campaigned for socialist candidates and cast a ballot. The Vancouver police arrested him for voting and charged him with perjury. At his trial a month later, his attorney, George McCrossan, entered a plea of innocent and blamed the registrar of voters for permitting his name to be on the register of voters.

The stakes for the British Columbia provincial government were high. The legislature had successfully restricted Chinese, Japanese, and Native American men from the exercise of the franchise in the nineteenth century. The provincial attorney general, W. J. Browser, actively fought as a member of Parliament to amend the Provincial Elections Act in 1907 to prohibit "any Hindu" from exercising the franchise.[21] Gender restrictions had already begun to give way in municipal elections, and Rahim expected racial restrictions against British subjects to be unenforceable.[22]

British Columbia prosecuted Rahim for racial misrepresentation. The court case was fought over accountability for determining voter qualifications and eligibility. The government argued that it was Rahim's responsibility to know that his "race" disqualified him and charged him with taking a false oath before the registrar of voters and engaging in (racial) identity fraud. Rahim's attorney countered that the election commission was accountable for judging voter eligibility, and that the election commissioner, W. E. Flumerfelt, had personally recognized and approved Rahim's voter registration precisely because Rahim was eligible and politically active in the Socialist Party. An editorial in *The Aryan* newspaper decried the injustice of South Asians' paying taxes and being barred from the polling booth when other marginal "races" such as "Syrians, Bohemians, Galacians, and Negroes" were eligible.[23] In the British Parliament, Joseph King complained that excluding "men of Hindu origin no matter how wealthy, respected and long settled" in British Columbia, while non-British subjects were favored, only fueled "mutual suspicion" and a festering sense of "injustice" among Indian subjects in the British Empire.[24] The jury of twelve white men deliberated for two hours and forty minutes and voted eleven to one to acquit Rahim. Although he was set free, in subsequent elections, commissioners refused to register South Asians on the voting rolls and imposed blanket racial ineligibility on all Asians and Native Americans.

Controversies over the franchise dogged Asian residents in Canada through the 1930s and 1940s. British Columbia and Saskatchewan denied British subjects of Chinese and Indian origin the right to register to vote in municipal and provincial elections. Although the Canadian Parliament in 1919 and 1920 extended federal franchise rights to women as well as a special subset of naturalized Asians and Asian veterans who had served in World War I, attempts by Asian men to vote confronted fierce protests by labor organizations, political parties, and newly enfranchised white women, who refused to share polling places with Chinese, Japanese, and South Asian men. Chinese and Japanese diplomats, British parliamentarians, and local coalitions of politicians, professors, clergy, and businessmen periodically protested against the exclusion of Asian Canadians from political participation. In practice, however, local courts and officials discouraged, hampered, and rejected petitions for naturalization and the franchise from otherwise qualified Asian residents well into the 1930s.[25]

The logic of exclusion that shaped the franchise color line also informed the challenges South Asians faced in claiming Canadian domicile. During and after World War I, South Asians left British Columbia and traveled south to the United States, Mexico, and Panama, or returned across the Pacific and eventually to India. By the 1920s, if they temporarily traveled outside Canada, neither property ownership nor longtime residence protected the fewer than 3,000 remaining South Asians' right to return. After World War I, the Canadian government passed laws to deny rights to return to Canada to British subjects who had left Canada for more than a year. Although Santa Singh had established Canadian domicile and demonstrated his work history and property ownership, the Canadian government halted his reentry into Vancouver in 1920 by applying this new 1919 amendment. Santa Singh had arrived in Canada in December 1907, worked for a sash and door factory and purchased property in Point Grey, outside Vancouver, before leaving Canada in October 1914. Singh left to arrange his son's marriage in India. His return to Canada was delayed by the death of his son's fiancée, the outbreak of World War I, and the need to assist his family. After his son successfully married, Santa Singh returned to Vancouver in 1920.[26]

The attorney general argued that Singh's true home was not Canada, where he worked, but in India, where his children lived. Singh's attorney countered that Canada's policy that vigorously discouraged "admission of [the] wives and children" of South Asian men and enforced "long and unnatural severance of true family conditions" made it impossible for Singh to maintain a true home in either India or Canada.[27] Judge MacDonald sided with Santa Singh and interpreted his seven years' residence in Canada and ownership of property as sufficient to establish Canadian domicile before his departure. However, the ruling was in Singh's favor primarily because the law had been passed after he left Canada. Other similar cases in the future would no longer have that loophole for retention of Canadian domicile status. The Canadian government's designation of domicile made the stakes even more treacherous for South Asian men in Canada who traveled outside the country—leaving for more than a year could close the door to reentry.

## RACE, POLITICAL ALLIANCES, AND THE STRUGGLE FOR U.S. CITIZENSHIP

Taraknath Das continued to juggle the multiplicity of political allegiances and social ties with a desire for national membership in the United States. Das lectured and wrote impassioned editorials advocating self-government and revolution in India, raised funds to defray the legal expenses of student immigrants contesting exclusion orders on Angel Island, and raised funds for Indian students at local universities to finance scholarships and pay for inexpensive room and board. He provided advice and material assistance to his allies in Canada and rallied students and farm laborers to the cause of fighting for freedom from British rule and against discriminatory immigration legislation in Washington and Ottawa.[28]

Das persisted in his quest for citizenship. In 1911, a Seattle court accepted his intent to apply for citizenship while he completed his BA and MA degrees at the University of Washington, and the following year he registered a short-lived business, the Bandon Clay Products Company, in Coos County, Oregon, and began naturalization proceedings there. The assistant district attorney cast aspersions on Das's "moral character" and financial dealings, and the naturalization examiner argued that he was not qualified as a "free white person." However, Das was ultimately disqualified because the name on his landing certificate, "Jogendranath Das," did not correspond to that on his application and had to be corrected by the Seattle Port Authority.[29] Das returned to San Francisco and the University of California at Berkeley in pursuit of a doctoral degree in political science. In 1914, in San Francisco, he again applied for naturalization, and with two professors as character witnesses, he was admitted to citizenship in June 1914, despite vigorous opposition from the British consulate and the spy Hopkinson. As a high-caste educated "Hindu," Das was ruled to be "white." The U.S. attorney objected but did not appeal.

With U.S. citizenship papers and a U.S. passport, Das left the United States for research in Europe and Japan in November 1914. While in Europe in 1916, he informed the British government of his U.S. citizenship and renounced his British citizenship. The British government was alarmed to learn of his naturalization and discovered that nearly a dozen South Asian men had quietly been naturalized throughout the United States since 1909.[30] Despite the objections of naturalization examiners, federal judges recognized South Asians as "white" by virtue of their religion, caste standing, education, complexion, and regional origin, underwritten by a loosely argued theory of Indo-Germanic language similarities and Indo-Aryan racial origins. Making that case, however, was subjective, and not all South Asians were immediately recognized as "white." However, once the precedent affirmed "white" identity for some South Asian immigrants, dozens of South Asians successfully exchanged British imperial citizenship for U.S. citizenship during the mid-1910s in federal courts from Los Angeles to Muskogee, Oklahoma.

Under widespread pressure, the naturalization examiner and Justice Department relented in challenging lower court decisions during World War I. However, wartime alliances and fears of armed revolt and revolution picked up during and after the war. The naturalization examiner played out fears over political allegiances and revolutionary tendencies in the application for naturalization of Bhagat Singh Thind, who arrived in Seattle in 1913, after spending eight months working in Manila. Thind's 1912 diploma from Khalsa College in Amritsar overcame the immigration exclusions for common laborers. Yet, for his first five years in the United States, he had a checkered migrant labor career, joining with other South Asian migrants to find temporary jobs in lumber mills in northwestern Oregon and as a farm laborer in California's

Imperial Valley, with a brief stint studying for a semester at the University of California in Berkeley in 1915.

British consular officers kept tabs on Thind's movements, public speeches, and political associations in 1916, and when he applied for naturalization in 1919, his political associations concerned the naturalization examiner, who enlisted the voluminous British secret service surveillance records. A British intelligence agent in the Pacific Northwest asserted that Singh had "preach[ed] sedition" and been the "soul of the revolutionary movement in Astoria," Oregon, distributing newspapers, raising funds, and making speeches in mill towns on behalf of the Ghadar Party, which aimed during and after World War I at overthrowing British rule in India. Thind's fluency in English and his ability to translate Punjabi and Hindi landed him a position as an interpreter with the Immigration Service in Astoria, but he was dismissed on grounds that he "kept company with a bunch of socialistic I.W.W. [Industrial Workers of the World—the "Wobblies"] anarchistic Finns and finally became so openly sympathetic with the German cause."[31]

During World War I, the British, U.S., and Canadian authorities exchanged information about political subversion, sedition, and conspiracy to destabilize British rule in India.[32] The British Secret Service (MI6) had shared intelligence connecting Ghadar revolutionaries in the United States with a failed German armaments-running mission, which had led to the conviction of eighteen men and women in San Francisco federal court, and British agents were emboldened to share further hints of suspicious behavior with the U.S. authorities. British surveillance documented Thind's associations with convicted Ghadar revolutionaries and insinuated that his sympathies were evidence of the likelihood of future subversion. After Bhagwan Singh, Santokh Singh, and Gopal Singh were convicted in San Francisco in March 1918, Thind visited the men both at the Portland railroad station when they were en route to the McNeil Island Penitentiary in Washington State and subsequently at the prison.

His presumed interest in India's independence did not, however, dissuade Thind from enlisting in the U.S. Army in July 1918. He did not serve in combat, but received training in Oregon. He was honorably discharged in January 1919, and a month later, his first petition for naturalization was made in Camp Lewis in Portland, following the lead of many other immigrant veterans, who were encouraged to naturalize. Immigrant veterans who had served three years in the armed forces were eligible for citizenship, and several Chinese and 184

FIGURE 14. Sikh men in Northern California, ca. 1910s. Courtesy California History Room, California State Library, Sacramento. Neg #9715.

Japanese in Hawaii were granted naturalization, as were nearly 34,000 immigrants nationwide.[33]

Later that year, in October 1919, Thind filed for naturalization again in federal court in Portland. At the hearing, parroting the concerns of the British authorities, who were wary of South Asians receiving military training in the United States, the naturalization examiner evoked the Ghadar arms-running conspiracy with Germany and asserted that Thind's continued visits and correspondence with convicted revolutionaries after his military service were evidence of a seditious agenda. When Gopal Singh was released, Thind secured an attorney to halt deportation proceedings against him, which were strongly favored by the British government, and told local newspapers that Singh's life would be in peril if the United States deported him to India.

Despite the naturalization examiner's concerns about national allegiance and attempt at racial disqualification, a federal judge admitted Thind to citizenship on October 18, 1920, commending his six months' honorable military service and concluding that his "deportment has been that of a good citizen, attached to the Constitution of the United States."[34] Although he acknowledged the seriousness of the U.S. government's allegations about Thind's possible involvement in the Ghadar-German conspiracy, which could have "rendered him an undesirable citizen," the judge expressed dismay at the naturalization examiner's denial of an immigrant's right to express his political beliefs freely and to provide "friendly" comfort and seek legal assistance for men who had served their prison sentences. The judge recognized that Thind had publicly advocated for "the principle of India for Indians and would like to see India rid of the British," particularly after the 1919 massacre of unarmed women, men and children in Amritsar, but noted that "disinterested citizens" had strongly corroborated that he did not "favor armed revolution." Furthermore, the judge said, he could see no harm to public order in Thind's public speeches or participation in the Seattle Labor Union Federation's July Fourth "Pageant of Democracy," where Thind had arranged for Punjabi workers from the Portland neighborhood of Linnton to join the Sinn Féin contingent and display the Indian revolutionary flag, no matter how irksome the alliance of Irish and Indian independence struggles was for the British imperial government. Saying that Thind's "deportment entitles him to become a citizen," the judge praised him for exercising his U.S. constitutional rights to freedom of expression, freedom of association, and legal counsel, which both the naturalization examiner and the British authorities sought to curtail for noncitizens and immigrants during and after the war.[35]

Although the judge recognized the new immigration restrictions imposed in 1917 on Hindus, he separated the question of future labor immigration from that of the citizenship potential of "Hindus lawfully domiciled in this country." He raised an uncomfortable question for the U.S. government in handling legal immigrants: "Shall they remain here as they please, without the privilege of becoming citizens, or shall they be deported whence they came?" The naturalization examiner's analogy to the Chinese Exclusion acts was inadequate, the judge ruled, seeing "no contradiction from new laws barring Hindu entry and permitting their naturalization.[36]

After World War I, petitioning for naturalization appealed to South Asian men across the United States. Appearing at a federal courthouse, registering, signing documentation before a clerk, and swearing the oath of allegiance was a popular ritual of claiming residence, public status, and political membership. In Box Elder County, Utah, half a dozen Punjabi Sikh men petitioned for and received naturalization at the local courthouse. One after the other in 1921, these men registered their legal entry into the United States, their heritage and allegiance, and their claim of residence in Box Elder County. Their claim was a recognized public act that demonstrated their success as farmers who had already availed themselves of local courts to register their land-tenancy partnerships north of Brigham City and their marriages to Mexican American women.[37] By contrast, in the industrial steel town of Lackawanna, New York, eleven miles south of Buffalo, waves of men who worked in the local steel plant and lived as housemates in all-male boardinghouses traveled to the New York State Superior Court in Buffalo and joined Polish Catholics, Russian Jews, and Persian Zoroastrians who were their fellow company workers in submitting their petitions for naturalization. These waves of petitions periodically surged over consecutive weekends in April 1919, January and February 1920, November and December 1922, and January 1924.[38] Although none of these petitions translated into citizenship certificates, dozens of sharply dressed Muslim Bengali migrants appeared before the court clerk, narrating their names, origins, arrival dates and carriers, marital status, and occupations, along with inscribing their marks, in a ritual of registering public presence as members of the community. Sylhetis traversed the oceans in the British merchant marine and jumped ship frequently in Atlantic ports; they would later constitute the overwhelming majority of Bangladeshi settlers in Britain.[39]

Multiple reasons motivated these men to submit naturalization petitions. In the era of the 1919 Red Scare, which targeted the political allegiance and organization of immigrants, immigrant advocates, social welfare charities, and labor unions urged naturalization. The Lackawanna Steel Company also advocated naturalized citizenship. For many of the men, petitioning for naturalization was also perceived as an insurance policy, largely symbolic, against the threat of deportation, or to obtain new "papers" to make job placement and international mobility easier.

In February 1921, the U.S. attorney in Portland filed an appeal against the Thind naturalization with a view to making it a Supreme Court test case. Along with several other appeals of a similar kind, this slowly wound its way to the U.S. Supreme Court docket.

In February 1923, ruling in the Thind case, only three months after the *U.S. v. Ozawa* decision had affirmed the "scientific" use of racial categorization to deny naturalized citizenship to a Japanese man, Associate Supreme Court Justice George Sutherland, a naturalized citizen born in England, distinguished the common usage of "white person" from the "scientific" category of "Caucasian" as employed in the 1790 statute governing naturalization.[40] The term "white persons" had a more limited "popular meaning," Sunderland argued: "It may be true that the blond Scandinavian and the brown Hindu have a common ancestor in the dim reaches of antiquity, but the average man knows perfectly well that there are unmistakable and profound differences between them today." Sutherland emphasized the necessity of welcome by "white" Americans to allow cultural assimilation, which enabled the "children of English, French, German, Italian, Scandinavian and other European parentage" to "quickly merge with the mass of our population and lose the distinctive hallmarks of their European origin." But the reception of white Americans also served as the crucial barrier that made it impossible for "the children born in this country of Hindu parents" to relinquish the "clear evidence of their ancestry." Sutherland denied, as he was obliged to do, that this "familiar observation" was based on "racial superiority or inferiority," bluntly asserting that it was "merely racial difference," so insurmountable that "the great body of our people instinctively recognize it and reject the thought of assimilation."[41] The U.S. Supreme Court decision emphasized how the common sense of race mattered deeply, that it was a physically palpable impediment to social "assimilation," and therefore made "Hindus" undesirable as citizens. Sutherland claimed to speak for the majority of "white Americans" and believed that racial ineligibility should trump any desirable individual qualifications for citizenship.

The U.S. Supreme Court followed the Naturalization Bureau's and U.S. attorney general's legal interpretation that made "white" identity the definitive gateway and barrier to citizenship. If the federal government recognized an applicant as "white," then one's prospects for naturalization could be adjudicated on the basis of individual conduct, character, and allegiance. However, the denial of "white" status made individual attributes and history irrelevant. One's national destiny was irretrievably tied to racial heritage.

### THE PROPERTIES OF PROPER CONDUCT

The 1923 *U.S. v. Bhagat Singh Thind* decision became the landmark case that barred South Asian men from naturalized citizenship. When paired with the *U.S. v. Ozawa* decision in 1922, the cases provided the definitive legal precedent that divided "white" and "Asiatic" races and shaped national membership for half a century. The U.S. Supreme Court in 1923 unequivocally switched the racial designation for persons from the Indian subcontinent from putatively "white persons" to firmly "Asiatic." After federal courts had allowed the naturalization of Taraknath Das in 1914, South Asians had used these precedents to apply successfully for naturalization in jurisdictions from Iowa to Georgia and Utah to New York. Although the Naturalization Bureau questioned whether men from India were racially qualified, the applicants and their attorneys persuasively made the case that their character, educational attainment, complexion, and financial status afforded them status as "white persons" in the communities where they dwelled. From 1908 to 1922, at least sixty-nine South Asians had been naturalized as U.S. citizens.[42]

The Naturalization Service had collected data on racially suspect naturalizations since 1915, when federal attorneys sought to disqualify Sardar Bhagwan Singh's naturalization in a Philadelphia federal court that judged him to be a "Christian and of the Aryan race." In addition to supplying attorneys with the legal briefs of previous racial challenges to naturalization, the Bureau of Naturalization's Commissioner Richard Campbell mobilized its vast bureaucracy to track all individual naturalizations from district-level courts where naturalization examiners had challenged their status as "free white persons." The database required "hundreds of man-hours" to collate thousands of naturalization petitions from "Afghans, Armenians, Filipinos, Hindus, Indians (American), Japanese, Malays, Mongolians, Parsees, Syrians and Turks," and it infuriated examiners who believed that the "white" identity of Armenians, Syrians, and Turks was settled law. However, preparation of a systematic database enabled the Bureau to act when either Congress or the Supreme Court rescinded naturalization of any group based on "race or nationality."[43]

After the 1923 Supreme Court ruling, federal attorneys were directed to cancel the citizenship of more than sixty-nine men who hailed from the subcontinent and had been naturalized in federal and local courts since 1908. The Naturalization Service released the database records to federal attorneys across the country to file equity cases to rescind the naturalization of all men from the Indian subcontinent in federal courts in Georgia, Utah, Louisiana, Nebraska, Oklahoma, Michigan, New Jersey, Pennsylvania, New York, California, Washington, and Oregon.[44]

Prosecutors expanded the racial reach of the category of "alien ineligible for citizenship" to create a white political and economic cartel that exercised exclusive rights to political participation and economic transactions. The unprecedented retroactive blanket denationalization of citizens was justified by a presumption that these individual South Asians had perpetrated racial fraud by allegedly masking their "true" racial identity to obtain undeserved privileges of citizenship. The power of the Supreme Court's definitive racialization not only converted individuals into the bearers of group identity but erased all previous administrative confusion and contradictions. The decision replaced ambiguity with the certainty of universal racial truth and the belligerence of its retroactive and punitive application. In courts across the United States, official calibration of "whiteness," which for seventeen years had weighed South Asian applicants' religion, education, class, caste, military service, political allegiances, and complexion, now judged these men as "non-white" solely because of their geographic origin.[45]

Among the men who were caught in the federal dragnet and denaturalization campaign was Sakharam Ganesh Pandit, a Gujarati Brahmin born into a wealthy land-owning family in Ahmedabad. After receiving his bachelor's degree from Bombay University and his PhD at Benares, he arrived in New York in 1906. He began a career of lecturing in New York and Chicago before moving to Los Angeles. He first applied for naturalization in Chicago in 1911 and did so successfully in Los Angeles in 1914.[46] His naturalization was premised on his unique qualities that set him apart from the majority of immigrants from India. At the time, Pandit was studying law, and the judge supported his naturalization because of his accomplishments and status as a "high-caste educated Hindu," which distinguished him from other "undesirables" from India.

Although Federal Attorney McNabb in Los Angeles called the action to revoke Pandit's citizenship "an inequitable and unconscionable thing," the secretary of labor and commissioner of naturalization were determined to proceed with it, since they had several dozen denaturalization cases pending, and they required and urged the Justice Department to proceed.[47] A decade later, when Judge Paul McCormick presided over denaturalization proceedings, he insisted that Pandit's case presented an instance of the government's interference with "personal individual qualifications." His personal history subsequent to his citizenship underlined the grave consequences of the government's attempt to retroactively rescind citizenship. Three years after his naturalization, the California State Bar had licensed Pandit to practice law. Since 1918, his legal practice and service as a notary public had provided the bulk of his livelihood. In 1920, he had married a white woman, Lillian Stringer, who had served as his personal secretary since his time in Chicago. Judge McCormick argued that Pandit's marriage and license to practice law and serve as a notary were all based on the federal sanctioning of him as a "white person" and a U.S. citizen. His U.S. citizenship, property rights, and marriage were based on the federal sanctioning of him as a "white person." Revoking his naturalized citizenship would put his livelihood, marriage, and residential property in a white-segregated neighborhood in jeopardy.[48] Furthermore, his wife Lillian Pandit, who had purchased 320 acres in Imperial County, would have her rights to property "probably totally defeated, by the revocation of citizenship of her husband," as well as being immediately denationalized if Pandit was deemed ineligible for citizenship.[49]

Judge McCormick observed that Pandit's naturalization had "permitted" him to "change his entire life." McCormick believed it was better for immigrants to "become members of the American national family, to identify themselves with this country in a substantial and patriotic manner and do so by becoming American citizens." He argued for a broader inclusion in the consensual project of political membership in "America" as a durable form of fictive kinship. He argued for a naturalization policy that encouraged "desirable aliens to become citizens rather than ostracizing them from our political family." McCormick recognized Pandit as "a member of our national family" who had passed "the acid test" in judicial hearings in 1914, and he admonished the government for producing not "a scintilla of evidence" or accusation of sedition, immorality, or dishonor. Rather, Pandit had conducted himself properly in the "discharge of his duties of citizenship." The government's efforts to revoke Pandit's citizenship would embroil him in expending money and submitting himself to "humiliation ... if his citizenship is taken from him."[50] In McCormick's eyes, Pandit had already embraced the "American family," and he had demonstrated both individualism and proper intimacies through the propriety of his marriage, his possession of property, and the integrity with which he discharged his profession.

In his case for retaining U.S. citizenship, Pandit strategically disclosed how it had required him to relinquish all archaic dependencies on his caste, family, and custom in India. When he had revealed his plans to seek U.S. citizenship to his mother, she had warned him that he was cutting himself off from the family, his community, and culture. The family would be obliged by custom and religion to sever all social ties with him and ostracize him as "polluted" and unworthy of sharing meals or water with them.[51] Pandit had relinquished his rights to 400 acres of the "best agricultural land in Gujarat" and a home in the "best part" of Ahmedabad. His mother wrote prophetically: "You may not always be in love with America, and if [you] want to return to India, after relinquishing all rights voluntarily to your property, then to the certain ignominy of ostracism would be added the possibility of hunger and exposure."[52] Years later, his marriage to Lillian Pandit solidified his estrangement from his family in India. In addressing his responsibility for his actions, Pandit put forward the consequences of statelessness and ostracism that awaited him if the United States denationalized him, asserting that "renunciation of my family and my property rights" in India demonstrated that his commitment to America outweighed losses of wealth, title, status, and family in his native land.[53] Judge McCormick was further alarmed that denaturalizing an attorney and notary public would wreak havoc on hundreds of legal judgments, since Pandit would effectively lose his license to practice law, and work he did on behalf of his clients could be rendered suspect and void.[54]

McCormick's unusual and exceptional judgment in Pandit's favor emphasized that divesting him of U.S. citizenship would unjustly spread economic and civil harm since Pandit had utilized the privileges of citizenship for himself and his clients. Pandit's victory in the appeals court did nothing to alter the racial barrier that denied South Asians naturalization, since both the attorney general and the Supreme Court allowed the Thind precedent to stand.[55]

In other denaturalization cases, among them cases that Pandit had argued as an attorney, an array of personal qualifications, including property ownership, military service, marriage, and regular employment that required citizenship, such as public school teaching, did not suffice to protect any of the four dozen men involved from being summarily stripped of their naturalization because of a retroactive ruling of racial ineligibility.[56] In the case of Mohan Singh, who had worked as a butler for an elite white family for more than a decade, Pandit argued that that nullifying his citizenship was bad public policy, because it would "unsettle vested rights . . . impair the obligation of contracts [and] upset family relationships."[57] In the case of Tulsa Ram Mandal, Pandit questioned the government's disruptive actions: "Now like Rip Van Winkle, the government wakes from its long slumber and tries to explode a bomb on the peaceful valley where the defendant has made his home. Is it any wonder that the defendant strenuously protests against such procedure by his own government?"[58] However, the arguments that had found a sympathetic audience in Judge McCormick did not prevent the revocation of Mohan Singh's or Tulsa Ram Mandal's citizenship.

## MARRIAGE, RACE, AND EXPATRIATION

The threat to American women citizens such as Lillian Pandit of being deprived of their citizenship continued through the mid twentieth century. Under a 1907 act of Congress, U.S. citizens who married foreign nationals were divested of their citizenship. The law regulating citizenship assumed that a woman's political allegiance would automatically follow her husband's nationality, and that she exercised no independent agency over her citizenship. The 1922 Married Women's Independent Nationality Act, known as the Cable Act, restored citizenship for some U.S. women, as long as they had married men racially eligible for naturalization. These women were made "independent of the husband in both acquisition and loss of American citizenship." However, U.S. citizens who had married Chinese, Japanese, Korean, and later South Asian men were still tied to their husbands' nationalities. Only divorce and remarriage could free such women to exercise agency over their national citizenship. A contemporary legal scholar called this exception to the Cable Law a demonstration of the "piety with which Congress worships the fetish . . . of racial discrimination."[59]

For most women, the loss of this citizenship was only discovered when they approached the federal government for international travel or national entitlements. The scholar and political leader Taraknath Das, who had been granted citizenship in 1914, discovered that not only his own citizenship but also that of his U.S.-born wife was vulnerable. The resulting controversy became a celebrated case of an elite white American-born woman being stripped of her citizenship. The year after the Thind decision revoked naturalized citizenship, Tarakanath Das, at the age of forty married sixty-one-year-old Mary Keating. Their citizenship emerged as a problem when they planned a trip to Europe in 1925 and the U.S. State Department refused to issue Mary Das a passport.[60] Mary Das thus learned firsthand of the collateral damage to women who had married naturalized citizens, only to discover later that that their citizenship had been rescinded.[61]

Mary Das was appalled that an "American-born woman" whose English ancestors predated the nation's founding could be "rendered not only Alien, but [a] stateless person" by a gender "double standard" and racial injustice. Under the Cable Act, an "American man may marry a Japanese, Chinese, Hindu—any woman he pleases" without any loss of his citizenship, but "an

American woman is penalized when she exercises this right granted to the American man. She may marry a Negro from Africa and not lose her American citizenship, but if she marries a Hindu, Chinese or Japanese, however high his reputation as a scholar, she loses her American citizenship."[62] In treating American women's marriages to African, European, and Asian men so differently, Mary Das's attempts to persuade Americans of the injustice of this were steeped in class privileges and racial disparity. In challenging the stigma of marriage across the color line and the void of noncitizenship for "unnaturalizable" Asian men and denationalization for their U.S. citizen wives, she both debunked and affirmed racial stereotypes.

Das invoked the liberty of an American woman to "marry [the] person she loves" and decried paternalistic government policy that " dictated the inner life of an individual" and upheld racial discrimination against women who selected "Asiatic" husbands. Scrupulously avoiding any advocacy of the "right of Asiatics to become American citizens," Mary Das denounced the government's "arbitrary" taking of "American citizenship and protection," which she described as a "violation of a solemn contract" and degradation of "civil rights" far more pernicious than property confiscation by "Soviet Russia or the Mexican Government."[63]

During congressional hearings to amend the Cable Act and to allow American women who had married "aliens ineligible for citizenship" to regain their citizenship, Emma Wold, legislative secretary of the National Woman's Party, testified in support of the restoration of "the dignity of [a] married woman's citizenship." A friend of the Das family emphasized that Mary and Taraknath Das's marriage was a meeting of intellectual interests and devotion that lacked the potential of sexual reproduction, noting that Mary had a grown son and was already a grandmother. Their marriage, a "perfectly beautiful ménage," was denigrated by the State Department's cavalier suggestion that she divorce her husband to retain her American citizenship.[64]

The disenfranchisement of a handful of elite white women garnered the attention of the press, Protestant Church congregations, and legislators.[65] However, there were hundreds more Mexican American, Puerto Rican, and African American women who were disenfranchised through their marriages with South Asian men, whether they had sought U.S. naturalization or not. These women discovered that they had been stripped of citizenship when they traveled outside the United States, when they applied for federal assistance, or when their husbands were threatened with deportation.

Long residence and family ties within the United States did not prevent exclusion. In 1929, Felicita Soto Dhillon, born in Austin, Texas, left the United States and traveled with Harnam Singh Dhillon, her husband of more than ten years, and their children to his family's home in Punjab. However, two years later, when they returned to the United States, immigration officials at Angel Island detained, separated, and threatened to deport members of the family on the basis of a motley array of medical and immigration exclusions.

Harnam and Felicita Dhillon had taken precautions to ensure that the family would be allowed to return. They had made sure that they had proper documentation, birth certificates for the children, proof of his merchant status and business interests, and proper reentry permits. When the family arrived at Angel Island on May 5, 1931, the three American-born children, Besanta, Than, and Ramon, were admitted "as natives of the United States," but their parents' and infant brother's status was suspect. Their mother and their Hong-Kong born brother Jak were diagnosed with hookworm. In a formulaic and rote response by the medical inspector, Jak, as a twenty-two-month-old toddler, was recommended for exclusion because his "affliction" would "affect his ability to earn a living." The disease diagnosis and exclusionary procedures served to wrest him from his siblings and split apart his family. There was a moment in those tense two weeks when his parents agonized over how their varying citizenship statuses would fracture their family. Despite his legal arrival in the United States in the early 1910s and documentation of a restaurant partnership, Harnam Singh was relegated to the status of a "native of barred zone" laborer. Singh's attorneys and Bhola Singh, the priest of the Stockton Sikh temple, pleaded for the family's release. Bhola Singh paid a $200 deposit for the treatment of Felicita and Jak for hookworm. Harnam Singh was released on June 4 to rejoin his older children. Although Felicita Soto was a U.S. citizen, born in Austin, Texas, her marriage to Harnam retroactively annulled her U.S. citizenship. After three days of treatment, Felicita and Jak were cleared of hookworm and able to rejoin their family.[66]

The state continued to underscore male prerogatives of independent movement by judging male capability and making women's citizenship derivative of their husbands' status. The children's national status was distributed by the accidents of their birthplaces. The family returned to their restaurant business in Imperial County, thirty miles from the U.S.–Mexican border. Throughout much of his early life, Jak stayed clear of the border, but once as a young man he was detained and interrogated in Calexico by immigration authorities investigating his status as a legal immigrant. In 1953, he applied for naturalization, three years after his father had become a naturalized citizen.[67]

The twisted racial liabilities of U.S. women marrying Asian men were felt in attempts to secure the distribution of state entitlements. The Great Depression expanded the scope of entitlements to relief, aid, education, and employment programs, but also tied eligibility to benefit from these programs to national citizenship and to the nuclear family. Being ineligible for naturalization or being summarily denationalized prohibited individuals and families in need from accessing employment programs. In April 1937, an African American woman, Ora Barr Singh, filed civil suit in U.S. District court in Southern California to win back her U.S. citizenship. Born in Greenwood, Mississippi, in 1886, Ora had migrated with her family to Southern California. In 1918, at El Centro, California, she had married Billie Singh, a thirty-two-year-old "Hindoo male laborer," who died six years later in a Los Angeles hospital of pulmonary tuberculosis. More than a decade later, she was refused employment and relief, since her previous marriage had revoked her birthright citizenship and her status as a widow did not automatically allow her to reclaim it.[68]

In January 1941, a white woman, Melva Chowdhury of Newark, New Jersey, beseeched Eleanor Roosevelt to intervene in her family's financial plight. Ten years before Melva had married a Bengali sailor who had jumped ship in the 1920s and found regular work at the docks until 1936. Although he had "registered for unemployment" with the government and applied to several employment agencies in Newark, he had been denied jobs because of his ineligibility for naturalized citizenship. Melwa explained that she was an American citizen and raising a large family but that they struggled to "get along on the uncertain income." She found it difficult to understand why a man with strong character references, family responsibilities, and obedience to draft registration and alien registration could not get a job, even if he was unjustly denied naturalization. The response from the U.S. Attorney General's office was swift and unyielding: her husband was ineligible, and there was nothing further the government could to do to aid her and her family.[69]

To deny "Hindus" citizenship, the U.S. and Canadian governments generated, circulated, and applied racist theories. The state saturated persons and blanketed groups with identities, names, labels, and predictions. Migrants' stories reveal how the state interpreted morality, ties of relationship, and fitness in granting mobility and opportunity. Government agents frequently confronted multiracial families that upset tidy racial boundaries.

The Alien Registration Act, or Smith Act, of 1940, which required non-citizens to register with the U.S. government, ensnared a number of undocumented immigrant men and their families. During World War II, the United States suspended deportations by providing relief to aliens of "good moral character" and without violent criminal records. A large proportion of these aliens were sailors and visitors who had overstayed their visas. The registry's purpose was to sustain the loyalty and secure the cooperation of four million foreign-born residents during the war. By formally recognizing and identifying people whose status had been illegitimate, the deportation suspensions provided the "requisite minimum foundation for acquiring citizenship" and also contributed to the broader reformation of racial identity that "reconstructed the 'lower races of Europe' into white ethnic Americans."[70]

With this aim in mind, it comes as little surprise that civic organizations like the National Catholic Welfare Council, which had extensive experience in seeking relief for undocumented southern and eastern European immigrants and their families to regularize their immigration status, should have championed the cause of Catholics from Asia. In 1944, the National Catholic Welfare Council advocated for Salvador Lorenz Fernandez, a baptized Catholic from Goa, India, who had jumped ship in New York in 1925 and lived for nearly two decades in Harlem. He had married a black woman from Virginia and had six children. Bruce Mohler, director of the Bureau of Immigration of the Catholic Welfare Conference, emphasized Fernandez's moral character and described his "blameless life as a good Catholic and a good citizen." He successfully lobbied Congressman Adam Clayton Powell to introduce a private bill to "relieve a Catholic East Indian" from forcible separation from his wife and children and end his scheduled deportation in July 1944.[71]

After the war, in 1947, the Immigration Service resumed proceedings to deport Alsom Ali, who had been born in Sylhet, Bengal, worked as a sailor, and jumped ship in Boston in December 1936. He found work as a dishwasher and cleaner in restaurants in New York City and Hoboken. On June 29, 1940, he married Merminia Pagan, originally of San Lorenzo, Puerto Rico. Merminia had come as a child to New York and applied for permanent residence in 1947. During the 1940s, they had three "American-born" children, Ali, Abid, and Kedsa. Alsom Ali's employment as a dockworker during World War II necessitated that he apply for a Coast Guard security clearance. The Immigration Service investigated and declared his alien status "problematic," but postponed deportation until after World War II.[72]

Ali Alsom rightly claimed that opportunities available to European and Canadian sailors to avail themselves of administrative discretion to grant relief from deportation were denied to him because of race. Alsom decried the injustice that European, Canadian, and Mexican immigrants could seek administrative relief to suspend deportation and legalize entry of immigrants in hardship cases, particularly in instances where deportation would disrupt families and households with children. Immigration authorities had used statutory and administrative measures in the 1930s to avert deportation and keep families reunified in cases of European immigrants, but the same policy was denied to Asians because they were ineligible for naturalization. As Mai Ngai has noted:

> The racism of the policy was profound, for it denied, a priori, that deportation could cause hardship for the families of non-Europeans. . . . the policy recognized only one type of family, the intact nuclear family residing in the United States, and ignored transnational families. It failed to recognize that many undocumented male migrants who came to the United States alone in fact maintained family households in their home country and that migration-remittance was another kind of strategy for family subsistence.[73]

In addressing Alsom's case, the American Committee for the Protection of the Foreign Born urged the government to reclassify "natives of India" as Caucasians and thereby to do away with the racial barrier to deportation relief.[74] Ali Alsom and his attorneys capitalized on the contradictions between the racial identities assigned by different government agencies. "I am of the white race, as appears from the statements of my affidavit for license to marry, which was accepted by the City Clerk," Alsom stated. Like his predecessors in naturalization court hearings in the early twentieth century, he confidently claimed that his "white race" identity was "generally recognized" and affirmed by local authorities. Alsom hoped that the necessity of preserving his "American citizen family" and household would persuade the immigration authorities to extend him relief from deportation, as they had recently done for an undocumented Afghan worker and "his American citizen family."[75]

In the United States, the government's racial purity tests for citizenship were assailed by countervailing imperatives to sustain and keep together married couples and their children. Immigrants facing deportation and their advocates emphasized that whatever antipathy to racial mixture the state wished to enforce, it must recognize and protect the multiracial nuclear conjugal family that existed on the ground.

The right to relief recalibrated race in the overall system of affirming family reunification, recognizing some family forms, mobility practices, and livelihoods as permanent settlement and others as transience. The judgments of bureaucrats weighed some activities and relations as possessing rightful claims to belonging and others as suspect or criminal.

After World War II, South Asian men who had worked, lived and created families in the United States were the most able to summon administrative relief from deportation proceedings and much less likely than men with families overseas to be forcibly returned to independent India or Pakistan. In 1946 the United States Congress removed immigration and naturalization restrictions on "Asian Indians," three years after the Chinese Exclusion law was abolished.[76] In Canada, when racial exclusions were lifted in immigration laws in 1947, the regulations relating to South Asian and Chinese immigrants encouraged entry of married spouses and children of men who had already established domiciles in the country. Independent immigration from Asia only began after the liberalization of Canadian immigration rules in 1967. The registration of a household and family in the United States through the immigration bureaucracy could produce de facto compassionate forbearance of earlier immigration irregularities.

With the decolonization of European and American empires and the emergence of independent nation-states in Asia and Africa in the two decades after World War II, the 1960s Canadian and U.S. governments recalibrated the racial grid of Asiatic, black, and white in immigration visa regulations once again. Even as the United States distributed visas to applicants based on national origin and Canada removed racial obstacles to immigration and citizenship, the government imperative to tabulate race, ethnicity, and national origin proceeded. The tracking of racial origins of migrant diasporas (e.g., Indians in Fiji, Trinidad, Singapore and Kenya) continued to bedevil the assignment of new nation-state identities and the maintenance of erstwhile racial boundaries of continents. Although racial restrictions and the pariah status of East Indians and Chinese eased in Canada and the United States, those designated as "Asiatic" races would continue to carry a liability of suspect foreignness. The appeal to nuclear family normativity, however, provided a select few with the promise of inclusion.

The legacy of a half-century of elaborate racial exclusions and taxonomies haunted Canadian and U.S. policies of granting citizenship and distributing its rewards. Both governments had invoked rationales of skill and property, morality and fitness to justify their exclusions, but all these justifications nevertheless collapsed into the formula of racial hierarchy and division. Immigration rules and regulations varied by designated ethnicity and calculations of poverty potential, but both collapsed into racial hierarchies. Despite pretensions to universal egalitarian status in the British Empire, British colonial subjects were subordinated and disenfranchised both in global migration within the empire and in relation to other countries. The Canadian and U.S. governments both made "Asiatic" or "Oriental" race a particularly vulnerable noncitizen status, which disallowed land rights, suffrage, and naturalization and imposed divestment of national citizenship on native-born female spouses.

The Canadian and U.S. governments acknowledged and assessed kinship dependency and social ties, and immigration and naturalization thus followed an "individualized" course. Even as denial of national membership blanketed a group for exclusion, vigorous contestation was isolated into individual cases. It was far easier to deal with struggles for political status and citizenship on an individual basis, rather than treating them as emerging from a nest of associations and alliances. In this way, the state could offer dispensations and exceptions without altering its fundamental policies. Individual family struggles were also required to exhibit the logic of personal heroism or tragedy. Pandit's ability to retain his citizenship, the Dhillons' ability to return from India and keep their family intact, and Alsom's successful appeal to suspend deportation and stay with his American citizen family underscore how important the signs of individual male rights to property and an intact family in the United States were. The political dissent that these cases produced was sequestered into struggles that sustained respectable families in navigating the perils of everyday life, in which the only solution was legitimate national membership.

Judicial and bureaucratic judgments about citizenship in the United States harnessed racial definitions to challenge the naturalization eligibility of immigrants during the 1910s to the early 1920s. In denaturalization and equity proceedings of the mid 1920s and the contests of several men to save their U.S. citizenship, prosecutors alleged that the defendants had engaged in fraudulent racial masquerades. In the 1940s and 1950s, government officials reconciled racial ineligibility and the illegal entry of male immigrants with their interracial marriages and families in deportation proceedings. Ironically, in an era of continued state prohibitions on mixed interracial marriage, South Asian men's marriages to white, black, Mexican, and Puerto Rican women, along with how some of those marriages also marked a family's Christian faith, and their citizen children produced grounds to avert deportation and the possibility of gaining naturalized citizenship once racial restrictions for immigrants of Indian origin were lifted in 1946.

Migrants eluded barriers to their mobility and opportunity by diverting itineraries, engaging in strategies of racial passing and cultural adaptation, and reorganizing intimacy, kinship, and marriage ties. South Asian migrants were sustained in hostile and bewildering environments by local and global networks of interdependent social ties. Interracial marriages and mixed-ethnic households in rural Mexican-American borderlands and in cities in the Northeast confounded and confused state-determined national and racial taxonomies.

The ties of belonging were frequently uneasy and always under the stress of state surveillance, capitalist dislocation, and the vagaries of racial exclusion in marriage, property, and citizenship. However, no matter how belonging might be expressed by noncitizens and provisional citizens as a variety of mutable interests, needs, and desires that defied easy consolidation, the U.S. nation-state required that people live in ways that could be contained by and tethered to legitimate forms of sociality, domesticity, and livelihood. Even when South Asian migrants engaged in strategies of settlement, marriage, and family formation, their ties continued to be vulnerable to state intervention and repudiation. Little by little, after the 1940s, the explicit racial infrastructure that denied marriage, property ownership, immigration, and naturalization to South Asians began to crumble. But converting foreign migrants into citizens and incorporating them into the broader U.S. nation nevertheless required proof of nationalization, patriotic commitment, and social normalization, including monogamous marriage and a middle-class family life.[77]

# Conclusion

*Estrangement and Belonging*

Migrants participated in communities around the rim of the Pacific Ocean in locations from the British crown colony of Hong Kong and the British Dominion of Canada to the U.S. imperial possessions of the Philippines, Hawaii, and the Panama Canal Zone, through the republic of Mexico and the United States of America. In the first half of the twentieth century, the populations of cities and rural towns boomed around the Pacific Rim and especially in North America, and transient male migrants who worked the fields, canneries, forests, and ships helped transform them physically and materially.

The mobility and survival of transient migrants depended upon how they engaged, collaborated with, and evaded imperial, national, and local agents of government and capitalist employers, traders, retailers, and bankers. The agents of government and capital regarded migrant workers as replaceable and disposable persons. Despite overwhelming barriers and obstacles to participation in legitimate politics and society, transient migrants expressed their beliefs, values, and practices in ways that were not contained by or subservient to the logics of the state and capitalism. In everyday conflicts and collaborations, they shared and tested understandings of status, kinship, spiritual well-being, erotic life, character, friendship, affect, and cultural practices.

Nonetheless, the insistent policing and administration of rule-of-law governance in local, national, and international arenas by the British, Canadian, and U.S. governments aggravated the experience of estrangement for transient migrants in the first half of the twentieth century. This book has charted how states and elites distributed protection and resources in ways that exacerbated the vulnerability of transience for most migrants and enhanced promises of settlement for only a select few. "Estrangement" is an active process of forcible dislocation, removing people from "an accustomed place or set of associations," souring the grounds of shared "membership" by sowing feelings of hostility, distrust, and "unsympathetic and indifferent" regard.[1] Paradoxically, South Asian migrants experienced both affection and scorn in their movements across the North American landscape. Across rapidly shifting legal borderlands, judges, attorneys, juries, newspaper editors, and politicians sorted through the multiplicity of migrants from all over the continent and globe, determining whether the intimate, social, and economic ties they forged were valuable or deplorable. Whose legal standing was assured and whose was vulnerable? Which associations had legal protection and the backing of state enforcement and which were cast as criminal? Who could labor, own land, and dispose of property and wealth with the force of contractual protections, and who was vulnerable to acute systemic exploitation?[2]

By the mid twentieth century, the U.S. and Canadian nation-states pressured national citizenship to contain and tether the ways people lived to legitimate forms of sociality, domesticity, livelihood, and political allegiance. The transformations in the distribution of national citizenship entitlements and resources in the United States and Canada emerged within the context of global transformations and decolonization after World War II. During the war, the recognition of military alliances with the peoples of China, India, and the Philippines drove a reevaluation of racial restrictions in naturalization and immigration. After long and intensive lobbying by immigrant organizations, the restrictions were rescinded for Chinese in 1943 and for Filipinos and Indians in 1946. Intergovernmental negotiating of mobility and national membership was further complicated by the conversion of British imperial subjects in India into citizens of two independent nation-states. In August 1947, decolonization had severed British India into the independent nations of India and Pakistan. However, even with the rescinding of naturalization prohibitions and a symbolic loosening of immigration quotas in the United States and Canada, racial quotas and procedures continued to bedevil immigrants from independent Pakistan and India, as well as the complex citizenship status of persons of South Asian origin from former British colonies in Africa, the Caribbean, and the Pacific. Racial and national immigration quotas were rescinded in the United States in 1965 and in Canada in 1967, resulting in large-scale immigration in the 1970s, 1980s, and 1990s, as well as a redrawing of racial boundaries.

In the two decades after World War II, court battles, grassroots protests, and legislative initiatives began a tumultuous, contradictory, and painfully slow process of eroding the most explicit racial exclusions. First in California and then in other western states, the courts invalidated racial prohibitions in marriage laws and struck down Alien Land Laws. In 1947, British Columbia dropped its barriers to voting and holding elected political office for persons from the South Asian subcontinent.

In the decade following World War II, the U.S. government scrutinized individual immigration histories and intensified deportation proceedings, particularly for those whom the state judged to be politically and socially subversive, non-normative, or perverse. After 1946 in the United States and 1947 in Canada, the opportunity to apply for naturalized citizenship and exercise the rights of national citizenship led South Asian immigrants to appeal to the government to have their political status rationalized, regularized, and upgraded to national citizenship.[3]

Yet the process was beset by the threat of state interrogation of family associations, financial status, and political allegiance. In 1951, Krishna Chandra faced deportation charges forty years after he had landed in San Francisco in 1910 as a five-year-old orphan with his four siblings. During his youth, Chandra had worked as a janitor and elevator boy, cut asparagus and celery, and eventually completed dentistry school and opened a practice in low-income black and Asian neighborhoods in San Francisco's Western Addition district and later in downtown Sacramento during the Great Depression.[4] Chandra's pathway to respectable society involved courting Dolores Moran, his Spanish-language teacher in night school, converting to Catholicism, and overcoming his estrangement from his brothers and sisters, who disapproved more of his religious conversion than of his marriage to an immigrant Mexican woman in 1939. Krishna and Dolores raised three daughters in Sacramento, and in 1945, Dolores Chandra was naturalized as a U.S. citizen. Krishna Chandra immediately applied to become a citizen after 1946 legislation rescinded racial exclusion for immigrants of Indian origin. Chandra's interview with a naturalization examiner in 1947 turned into an interrogation and inquiry about his friends, political beliefs, and participation in formal associations. In the wake of anti-communist suspicions and investigations, the naturalization examiner questioned Chandra about his membership in the International Workers Order (IWO), which he had joined to obtain a life insurance policy, because other fraternal organizations excluded nonwhite applicants. Even after Chandra discontinued membership in the IWO, a federal judge in San Francisco denied him naturalization because of past membership in an alleged communist-front organization, and the Immigration Service initiated deportation proceedings. The Committee for the Protection of the Foreign Born and the American Civil Liberties Union rallied to his cause and developed a persuasive legal case that mobilized his career, his moral and family history, and the specter that the government would forcibly separate him from his U.S. citizen wife and three U.S.-born daughters.[5]

Karm Singh, a fifty-three-year-old resident of Yuba City, not far from Sacramento, discovered that his success as a farmer over twenty years did not outweigh the fact that he had illegally crossed the U.S.–Mexican border in Calexico in January 1933. Despite his demonstration that he was "thrift[y], hardworking and successful," his ownership of a thriving, debt-free "thirty acre orchard of prunes and peaches," accumulated savings, and a record of obedience to the law and paying taxes, he was caught in the crosshairs of the 1952 Immigration and Deportation Act. His desire to bring his children from India to join him had brought his irregular immigration status to the surface, and his lawyers failed to win him a pardon, particularly since his wife and children resided in India and deportation would ironically "reunite" the family.[6]

At mid-century, a U.S.-based family and particularly American-born children could positively shape the government's handling of South Asian immigrants with irregular immigration histories or who were suspected of subversive political sympathies. After the new immigration laws of the late 1960s, the image of socially isolated and maladjusted South Asian and Asian males of the nineteenth and early twentieth centuries gave way in North America to traditional, striving immigrant families in the 1980s and 1990s. Retrospectively, a population predominantly consisting of atypically sexualized, undomesticated bachelor laborers justified the history of Asian racial exclusion and subordination. Inclusion and equality became the just reward of aspiring middle-class nuclear families. This pervasive narrative of racial progress, inclusion, and color-blind meritocracy is premised upon unexamined assumptions of the respectable, propertied, conventionally gendered and sexualized family household as the model for national assimilation.

What had also changed dramatically was the diminishing frequency of any connection of South Asian male laborers with sexual perversity and immorality.

The number of cases of South Asian men in interracial sodomy prosecutions in California, British Columbia, and Washington courts rapidly receded, after spiking in the 1910s and 1920s. Some of the decline can be attributed to South Asian men's returning to India or to other parts of the globe, leading to a drop in their numbers in migrant labor populations. Laborers from the U.S.-colonized Philippines and Puerto Rico took up the slack in the 1920s, along with increased numbers of Chicano and Mexican immigrant laborers, bolstered by guest-worker and bracero programs at mid-century. These migrant laborer waves developed in tandem with the large number of impoverished white and black men from the Midwest and South during the Great Depression.

Police and public scrutiny of interracial male contact, particularly between native-born white and European male youths and South Asian men, circumscribed interracial social association in the early twentieth century. Social isolation was particularly pronounced in the agricultural regions where the vast majority of South Asian men settled in California's Sacramento and Imperial Valleys and the Salt River Valley in Arizona in the 1930s and 1940s. For safety and comfort, men often clung more tightly to their ethnic, kinship, and religious networks. Legal support for men accused of sexual crimes began to diminish as religious and ethnic organizations promoted moral and sexual regulation of their members in order to improve the community's image.

Yet the impact of the earlier court cases had been felt in policing, jurisprudence, and legislation in the mid twentieth century. In the variety of male-victimed sex crime prosecutions, the boundaries of consent, age, and gender became stratified as they were mobilized in the service of greater surveillance and suspicion in the panics concerning the sexual and physical vulnerability of male adolescents and schoolchildren and worries about black, Latino, and white men as sexual predators from the late 1930s through the 1960s. In this era, sex crimes against males, especially male youths, attracted increased scrutiny in urban and suburban areas across the United States.[7]

In both Canada and the United States, even the era of restrictive quota immigration in the late 1940s and 1950s created opportunities for immigrant and enfranchised men to enlist greater numbers of women from India and Pakistan to immigrate as wives. Some Punjabi men divorced Mexican women and acquired young brides from Punjab, others reunited with their wives and more often adult children after a long separation. New immigrant families also began to arrive. All of these trends replaced Mexican-Punjabi families and "bachelor" men whose wives and children lived in India with South Asian married couples and their children living in North America, both in agricultural communities and in cities and suburbs.[8]

## TRANSIENCE AND QUEER SOCIALITY

Transient laborers appear to exist on the margins of society, but their treatment is constitutive of how normative society defines itself. This book calls attention to the occluded forms of queer sociality attendant on transient labor. Patterns of intimacy with strangers challenged the conspicuous barriers of race and class segregation and redefined civic participation beyond the narrow confines of legitimate and official politics. Transient migrant laborers traversed domestic, work, and social spaces, and through their practices, they asserted bodily autonomy and the ability to associate widely, disrupting middle-class married families' exclusive claim to privacy and personal autonomy. Privacy is a class privilege that manages labor and domestic economy and polices public space. Its assertion produces privileged access to mobility, autonomy, and protection. The formation of a heteronormative middle-class zone of privacy required the "support of an elaborate network of state regulations, judicial rulings, and police powers" and defined its survival against the "prejudicial exclusion of others from the rights of association or bodily autonomy."[9]

In both Canada and the United States, the police and laws enforced the middle-class demand for comfort in public space and minimized the unexpected encounter or confrontation. Policing produced the semblance of public safety by targeting transient migrants as pathological dangers and criminalizing their public association.

Government action, ranging from police campaigns to incarcerate vagrants to racial restrictions on immigration, voting, and property ownership, isolated transients from civic association and democratic promises of equality. Vagrancy policing ratcheted up the vulnerability of the poorest and most transient members of society and thwarted their ability to use public space without police harassment and interference. However, the everyday use of public space also became an arena in which to protest harassment and hostility.[10]

This book folds together and analyzes the forms of association and everyday activity that have been too quickly distributed as distinctly public or private. Since "strangerhood" is a crucial ingredient for the public meeting, the unconventional yet widespread sociability of migrants reveals neglected models for democratic livelihood and distributions of ideas, resources, and social well-being. Exchanges between strangers of feelings, beliefs, ideas, and actions have the capacity to create new ethical, political, and social formations of civic living and participation. These alternative models do not give membership priority to the individual subject born into a middle-class normative family. Analytically combining erotics, sociability, and labor in the borderlands of public and private explodes the potential for interpreting the politics and ethics of using commercial and leisure spaces, thoroughfares and public amenities, the spaces of farming, resource extraction, and factory production, and the varieties of sleeping, eating, and bathing by combinations of non-normative and normative groups.

Narrowing civic sociality and politics to the intimacy cultivated within families and with familiars suppresses and marginalizes the alternative frameworks, relationships, and imagination that emerge in meetings between strangers. Queer relations cross boundaries of space, class, race, and gender in ways that make the practice of democratic, egalitarian, and humane relationships both imaginable and viable. The discrepancy between queer relations and a model of subjectivity and sociality learned in the idealized nuclear family hampers our understanding of social movements and social justice.

In the first three decades of the twentieth century, there was an explicit and untrammeled ascendancy of racialization in enforcing exclusion and subordination. The possessive investment and authority of "white privilege as a legitimate and natural baseline" was enlisted to protect property and ensure the privileged autonomy of gender and sexual propriety from the disordered, dangerous, and aberrantly gendered and sexed.[11] In the United States, the conceptualization of "aliens ineligible for naturalization," with the attendant denationalization of their female spouses and the divestment of rights of property and contract, produced a pariah class.

In societies governed by the rule of law, the systemic withdrawal of rights and protections of law sought simultaneously to fracture and make acutely vulnerable all kinds of associations—from informal economic partnerships that organized capital and labor and distributed wages, profits, and resources to mutual assistance, civic, and political associations, to fostering intimate ties of friendship, marriage, and parenthood. By racially differentiating those beneath and outside the umbrella of civic and legal protection, the concept of the "alien ineligible for citizenship" contributed to the unchecked exploitation of laborers and reinforced a cartel of nationalized citizenship against the putatively inassimilable and perpetually foreign Asians. The threat of the morally suspect foreigner continues to haunt how racialization has, across the twentieth century, imperiled and made "impossible" the subjectivity of "illegal aliens," as Mae Ngai has shown, even as the specific populations so targeted have changed. In the early twentieth century, the proliferation of marriage restrictions that ensnared various Asian "races" into a schema of prohibitions against marriage to white partners, as Peggy Pascoe has demonstrated, also served to turn all interracial relationships into immoral, perverse, and eroticized relationships, unworthy of protection. Through these legal restrictions that highlighted racial ineligibility, local and state governments harassed Asians and those associated with them in ways that curtailed the distribution of land and resources, hampered mobility and access, and denied them the benefits of labor and care.[12]

As Margot Canaday has demonstrated, by the mid twentieth century, marriage and the heterosexual family household defined the distributions of resources, entitlements, and the privileges of U.S. national citizenship. In the arenas of immigration, welfare, and military service, the observation by state agents of variable erotic and social ties in the early twentieth century gave way to a more intensive and vociferous standardization of a sexual identity binary into homosexual and heterosexual. During the New Deal and particularly after World War II, the distribution of resources to married couples and to households in support of children consistently, insistently, and inequitably supported white families. Slowly and unevenly, a rationale of universal government support to heterosexual married couples and their children supplanted explicit racialization.[13] Assimilation liberalism promoted the normative family as its subject and goal and prescribed "the forgetting of race and the denial of racial difference," particularly after the civil rights struggles of the 1950s and 1960s. However, in the same period, politicians and bureaucrats absolved the systemic and inequitable distribution of resources and assistance by pointing to a chronic, "pathological" history of sexual non-normativity and gender eccentricity in racialized populations of African Americans, Chicanos, Puerto Ricans, Filipinos, and Native Americans. Against this contrast, members of racialized groups that practiced gender and sexual normativity were championed as those who reinforced a value system of "individualism, personal merit, responsibility, and choice."[14]

Over three decades in the post–World II era, political and social coalitions struggled in the courts, streets, and legislatures to challenge and force the repudiation of explicit racial restrictions on citizenship, marriage, landownership, and immigration. Racialization did not, however, disappear. It persists to buttress the foundational fiction of gender and sexual normativity as the personal and social reform project necessary for social affirmation and state protection. During the twentieth century, the liberal state in the United States and Canada prioritized the civil registration of households to determine the privileged gateway for resources, entitlements, and distributions. In the post–World War II era, the properly gendered and sexualized family household became ascendant as the preeminent point of access for resources and benefits distributed by the state and by employers. Through the family household, the U.S. and Canadian nation-states legitimated institutions that supported health and reproduction, disciplined morality and propriety, organized consumption, and anchored patriotic and nationalist loyalty.[15]

By allowing "worthy" candidates relative privilege, and token admission to model and normative minority subjects, the state facilitated and rationalized the enduring racialized exclusion of the rest of the subordinated group. One of the exceptional and "worthy" men was Dalip Singh Saund, a doctoral student at the University of California at Berkeley and a cannery and casual farmworker during the 1920s, who became a landowner, married Marian, a U.S. citizen of Czechoslovakian immigrant parents, and raised three children in Westmorland township, California. His family prospered financially in a farming and fertilizer distribution business but also experienced racial discrimination in hotels, schools, and social clubs in Imperial County and elsewhere in California. Although the family had business interests in Imperial County, they had effectively moved to Los Angeles for Marian's continuing education and to enroll his three children in unsegregated schools.

Saund's political career developed out of his interest in community welfare, as well as the national campaign for naturalization of people from the Indian subcontinent. Along with South Asian farmers, businessmen, professors, and professionals in California, Arizona, New York, and across the Northeast and Midwest, Saund lobbied for legislation to remove racial exclusions for immigration and naturalization and restore naturalized citizenship in the late 1930s and 1940s. In 1950, less than a year after becoming a naturalized citizen, he was elected justice of the peace in his township but was denied the position because opponents raised the technicality that Saund had been a U.S. citizen for less than the required year. Two years later, he handily defeated his opponent and served as justice of the peace. During his tenure, he famously crusaded against cross-border prostitution in Mexicali and prosecuted prostitutes and pimps in Imperial County. He developed a reputation for fearlessly fighting vice, immorality, and corruption. As his activity and leadership in the Democratic Party increased, he waged a surprisingly successful campaign for Congress over a celebrity Republican opponent and was elected to Congress in 1956, serving three terms and representing Imperial and Riverside Counties until he was incapacitated by a stroke. He was a legendary "pioneer"—the first elected congressional representative who was an Asian immigrant, shortly before Hiram Fong, Daniel Inouye, and Patsy Mink were elected in the newly established state of Hawaii.[16]

Saund's educational, economic, and political achievements illustrate how he and his interracial family were considered "deserving" and "worthy," a testament to the individual success possible in America. Saund overcame both racial barriers and the stigma of the dispossessed racialized group. The "worthy" tokens are encouraged to disidentify with non-normative members of the group. The resulting embrace of the worthy few celebrates the values of individual success and social conformity, rationalizes the organized abandonment and suppression of the rest and holds the state and society blameless for enduring and historical racism and subordination.

Challenging the aspiration that the respectable nuclear family has exclusive purchase on the privileged public life is formidable. The ideal of the respectable nuclear family undergirds the logic of the sacrificing, achievement-oriented, capital-maximizing, marriage-planning, and consolidating, disciplined family unit that undergirds the model-minority mythology of post-1960s South Asian and East Asian Americans. The national media, politicians, and educational institutions promote the image of Asian American traditional patriarchal family values, educational achievement, and middle-class professional and business success as a racial rebuke to the black and brown who are cast as disreputable, disorganized, and deviant. The model-minority racialization of "worthy" Asian Americans also suppresses critiques of the prevailing system of property, privilege, and propriety and obscures the struggles and barriers facing Asian American refugees, immigrants, and generations. It makes alternative social and cultural value systems, the redress of historical inequities, and the redistribution of resources and protections unfathomable.

The valued intimacy of the propertied, normatively gendered, and sexualized family household does offer the tantalizing illusion of tolerance for diversity. Liberal rule-of-law societies provide a capacious embrace for approximating the norm and creating copies of the norm that can receive legitimacy, invite sympathy, address discrimination, and make rights-based demands. We need not look any further than the current debate over gay marriage. In the campaign for the extension of marriage-licensing privileges to gay and lesbian couples, the couples who would benefit and their allies promote the marriage partnership as the crucial mechanism that secures recognizable kinship, care and protection for children and spouses, and the preservation of a home. The argument is that the difference between heterosexuality and homosexuality should not impede one's human rights to marriage partnership, family, and home. The advocates for extending marriage rights reinforce the idea that the capacity to marry represents the measure of full citizenship and access to avenues of human fulfillment in U.S. and Canadian society. Civil unions, domestic partnership, and same-sex marriage as administered by different states, localities, and nations are an attempt to distribute a portion of the privileges and resources of marriage partnership at the price of fixing and naturalizing distinctions between homosexuality and heterosexuality. The opponents denigrate the veracity and longevity of intimate ties between two men or two women, redouble marriage licensing as a powerful form of exclusion, and justify the denial of material resources and protections. They insist that extending marriage will undermine polarized gender roles and threaten heterosexual marriage and child-rearing capacities and privileges. The normative and stable heterosexual family is invoked as the center of state protection and necessary for the flourishing of society and democracy.

In political debates about who benefits from the extension of marriage licensing to gay and lesbian couples in both Canada and the United States, Sikh-Canadian religious leaders and black evangelical preachers condemned homosexuality as a "white disease" and feared that the acceptance of gay and lesbian couples would contaminate their racial and religious minority communities. The urge to make gender and sexual diversity invisible in their own communities is a survival strategy to deflect decades of white suspicion and state persecution that insisted that Asian, black and Latino communities were the source of sexual perversity. Both historically and in the present, presumptions that sexual and gender diversity is restricted to one racial group have been undermined by the life stories of people who struggle for recognition of their intimate ties. In the wake of political and legal battles in extending or denying marriage registration, variations and mixtures of ethnic identities, kinship arrangements, national citizenship status, and households of lesbian and gay marriage applicants have emerged across both the United States and Canada.[17]

In the cosmopolitan spaces where migrants converged in towns, cities, and agrarian communities from the U.S.–Canadian border region of the coastal Northwest to the U.S.–Mexican border, the immense heterogeneity of how persons live in social relations, locales, practices, and cultures confounds the norms of coupled, stable, and racially homogenous households. Yet in liberal assimilation narratives, state regulation and social pressures to conform to stereotypes of the nuclear family, stabilized gender and sexual embodiment, and permanent settlement support a specific model of citizenship and personhood. Simultaneously, both government and society produce an idealized vision of citizens' public and private lives that deserve liberty and autonomy. The possession of a conventional home and standardized family is central to recognition, resources, and state protection. But to be marked as homeless, transient, alien, or disreputable erodes the possibility of privacy and property protections, as well as jeopardizing one's autonomy and dignity.

Despite these pressures to conform to recognizable identities, racialized and non-normatively sexualized and socialized persons have persisted throughout the twentieth century in the United States and Canada. Most frequently sexual non-normativity and racialization have converged in the status of subordinate subjects and noncitizens. Noncitizens' lives are entangled in, proximate to, and enmeshed with the lives of citizens. They share workplaces, social sites, and households in rural, urban, and suburban locations across the North American continent and are refracted in ties across the globe.[18]

The critical analysis strategies developed by scholars engaged in subaltern studies, history from below, and queer-people-of-color-critique diagnose power relations by charting the contradiction, subversion, and excesses of processes of normalization and standardization and their unanticipated consequences. By interrogating the authority of bureaucracies, law, and human sciences to circumscribe dissident sexualities and genders as pathological, dangerous, or deviant, this inquiry may see other human possibilities. Even as it is critical to understand how the nation-state manages and disciplines human mobility, it is important not to limit the horizons of our understanding to presumptions that the nation-state is a natural container of political aspiration or that national citizenship is the superior model of membership. The circulation and meanings of feeling and affect are not reduced to or constrained by national boundaries. Multiple cosmologies, ethics, expressions, and structures of feeling are brought into dialogue through overlapping diasporas and migrations. The cosmologies and structures of feeling may resonate with communities and be expressed in particular languages, but it is important to pay attention to the processes of translation across communities and through different languages.[19]

What conveys and what changes? The multiple moments of encounter of overlapping migrations emerge on a threshold that is both managed on the terrain of the nation-state and exceeds the scope of national containment. This space of encounter that is the meeting ground of overlapping and heterogeneous cultures is often called cosmopolitan. If that is the case, then the cosmopolitan emerges in almost every rural and urban location that cradles convergent migrations. "Cosmopolitan" often signals the extranational, but it can just as often be the localized creation of nations, rendered as opposing the exclusivity and intolerance of difference that national identity can promote. The cosmopolitan may be constrained by race and ethnic identities, class privileges, and national memberships and boundaries.[20]

The paradox of stranger intimacy, however, offers a way of conceptualizing everyday encounters that can either invest in sustaining hierarchy or produce egalitarian social and political arenas, ethics, and associations. In this regard the dynamism of dissident socialities and queer epistemologies can produce fresh ways of seeing, knowing, and organizing social, cultural, and political worlds. These arenas and worlds scale up and down from the local to the global. This perception of world-making does not ignore durable inequalities, but rather dislodges the notion that systems of inequality and the identities that are enlisted to buttress them are perpetual, unchangeable, and without alternative. Queer epistemologies navigate how social and cultural affiliation and political organization are eclipsed, erased, or overwhelmed by seemingly natural and legible identities. Queer ways of life explode constrained understandings of temporality and spatiality, the conceptualization of life course and affiliations, and the use and understanding of affect and social ties. We need not identify sexual and gender dissident subjects to engage in a queer analysis of sociality, capitalist networks and systems, social hierarchies, and political rule.[21]

Queer epistemologies destabilize assumptions that personhood and citizenship emanate from the "domestic private" and conventional coupled intimacy. For those outside such configurations, the "transcendent" possibilities of liberty in intimate conduct, expression, and civic life are all curtailed. In the early twentieth century, "foreign" and racialized migrants, tramps, and hoboes were subject to heightened police surveillance and arrests for vagrancy, disorderly conduct, and suspected sexual violence. In the early twenty-first century, "illegal" migrants, the homeless, "enemy combatants," and refugees awaiting asylum proceedings are the most vulnerable subjects of state power and considered disposable. For those identified as outside the norms and normativity, the freedom to pursue "intimate conduct" remains unfathomable in a liberal ethos that protects intimacy as the "right of privacy" for those whose public status the state respects and recognizes.[22]

The human and social struggle to thrive and to "imagine otherwise" does not flourish without constraints.[23] The principles of rule-of-law governance seek to regularize, replicate, and make transparent the rules to govern and manage social well-being, human conduct, and relationships. Its effectiveness and allure are why many subordinated individuals aspire to normativity as a measure of security in an uncertain and hostile world. However, by understanding the motivations and desires for normativity alongside those severely punished for threatening normal society, we develop deeper insight into the terms of social, political, and erotic belonging and estrangement. In the legal conflicts and bureaucratic registration that have been central to this book's archive, contradictions and confusion made uncertain people's motivations and actions and challenged rules, regulations, and frameworks of evidence. The legal archive unravels with life stories and encounters that reveal meanings, ideas, ethics, and relationships that outflank normative ways of being. It is through the paradox of constraint and possibility that we dwell in a society of strangers.

# NOTES

INTRODUCTION

1. McKeown, *Melancholy Order*; Tinker, *New System of Slavery*; Amrith, "Tamil Diaspora."

2. España-Maram, *Creating Masculinity*; Lowe, "Intimacies on Four Continents"; Ting, "Power of Sexuality"; Ting, "Bachelor Society"; Shah, *Contagious Divides*; Yanagisako, "Transforming Orientalism"; Hsu, *Dreaming of Gold*; Manalansan, *Global Divas*; Ong, *Flexible Citizenship*.

3. Thampi, "Indian Soldiers, Policemen and Watchmen in China."

4. For the North Indian and global context, see Chowdhry, *Veiled Women*; Jakobsh, *Relocating Gender*; Hsu, *Dreaming of Gold*; Gabaccia et al., "Gender and Migration."

5. D'Emilio and Freedman, *Intimate Matters*; Duggan, *Sapphic Slashers*; Chauncey, *Gay New York*; Howard, *Men Like That*; Kunzel, *Criminal Intimacy*.

6. Butler, *Undoing Gender*; Stryker, *Transgender History*; Jagose, *Queer Theory*; Wu, "Asian American History and Racialized Compulsory Deviance"; Katz, *Invention of Heterosexuality*; Canaday, "Thinking Sex"; Meyerowitz, "Transnational Sex and U.S. History"; Grewal and Kaplan, "Global Identities"; Povinelli and Chauncey, "Thinking Sexuality Transnationally."

7. Lowe, "Intimacies." For an examination of the race, gender, class, and imperial exclusions of the conceptualization of the public sphere, see Landes, *Women and the Public Sphere*; Pateman, *Sexual Contract*; Wiegman, "Intimate Publics," 860; Mehta, *Liberalism and Empire*; Habermas, *Structural Transformation of the Public Sphere*, 44–48; Fleming "Women and the Public Use of Reason," 122; Berlant, "Intimacy," 284.

8. Robert Lee, *Orientals*; Ting, "Power of Sexuality"; Ting, "Bachelor Society"; Lowe, *Immigrant Acts*; Takaki, *Strangers from a Different Shore*; Okihiro, *Margins and Mainstreams*; Eng, *Racial Castration*; Lee, *Americas*.

9. Terry, *American Obsession*.

10. U.S. Congress, *Dictionary of Races or Peoples—Reports of the Immigration Commission.*

11. Koshy, *Sexual Naturalization*; Prashad, *Karma of Brown Folk*; Das Gupta, *Unruly Immigrants.*

12. Gross, "'Of Portuguese Origin'"; Molina, "'In a Race All Their Own'"; Gualtieri, *Between Arab and White.*

13. Duggan, *Twilight of Equality*; Halberstam, *In a Queer Time*; Eng, *Feeling of Kinship*; Chuh, *Imagine Otherwise*; Muñoz, *Cruising Utopia.*

## CHAPTER I

1. *San Francisco Chronicle*, April 6, 1899, p. 10; Jensen, *Passage From India*; Bald, "Overlapping Migrations."

2. See Robert Lee, *Orientals*; Lowe, *Immigrant Acts*; Shah, *Contagious Divides*; Okihiro, *Margins and Mainstreams*; Koshy, *Sexual Naturalization*; Lui, *Chinatown Trunk Mystery.*

3. Pascoe, *What Comes Naturally*; Pascoe, "Miscegenation Law"; Volpp, "American Mestizo," 795; Blackhouse, "White Women's Labor Laws."

4. Pfaelzer, *Driven Out.*

5. Canada, Census, 1901, 1911; Ward, *White Canada Forever*, 3rd ed., pp. 170–71; Cheng, *Oriental Immigration to Canada*, p. 271; Hess, "Forgotten Asian Americans"; Mills, "East Indian Immigration."

6. Edward Stevenson, Saskatchewan Executive Committee, Trades and Labor Congress of Canada, Moose Jaw, Canada, letter to colonial secretary, London, November 19, 1906, Canada, Immigration Branch, RG 76, vol. 384, file 536999, pt. 1.

7. Roy, *White Man's Province*; Ward, *White Canada Forever*; Schwantes, *Radical Heritage*; Palmer, *Working-Class Experience*; Saxton, *Rise and Fall of the White Republic.*

8. George Gray, president, Victoria Trade and Labour Congress, letter, October 15, 1906, Canada, Immigration Branch, RG 76, vol. 384, file 536999, pt. 1.

9. Edward Stevenson, Saskatchewan Executive Committee, Trades and Labor Congress of Canada, Moose Jaw, Canada, letter to colonial secretary, London, November 19, 1906; George Gray, president, Victoria Trade and Labour Congress, letter, October 15, 1906, Canada, Immigration Branch, RG 76, vol. 384, file 536999, pt. 1. See Fung, "Burdens of Representation," which references the 1885 Canadian Royal Commission Report on Chinese Immigration. And see also Epprecht, "'Unnatural Vice' in South Africa."

10. Edward Stevenson, Saskatchewan Executive Committee, Trades and Labor Congress of Canada, Moose Jaw, Canada, letter to colonial secretary, London, November 19, 1906, Canada, Immigration Branch, RG 76, vol. 384, file 536999, pt. 1.

11. Pflaelzer, *Driven Out*; Lake and Reynolds, *Drawing the Global Colour Line.*

12. Schwantes, *Pacific Northwest*, pp. 192–193, 251.

13. "Hindus Hounded from the City," *Bellingham Herald*, September 5, 1907, p. 1; "A Public Disgrace" (editorial), ibid., p. 4; "Mob Spirit Subsides," ibid., p. 1; "Dwellings

of Hindus Are Dens of Dirt," ibid., September 6, 1907, p. 3; "Millowners Censured for Importing Hindus," ibid., September 10, 1907, p. 1.

14. Bellingham Municipal Government, City Clerk, City Council Proceedings, NW365–6-7, 3: 483, September 9, 1907, Washington State Archives, Northwest Region.

15. G.C. Hyatt, land agent, letter to H.H. Taylor, president, Bellingham Bay Improvement Co., San Francisco, September 5, 1907, Center for Pacific Northwest Studies, Bellingham Bay Improvement Co. records.

16. Bellingham City Council Proceedings, September 9, 1907.

17. Kay Anderson, *Vancouver's Chinatown*; Jew, "'Chinese Demons'"; Wang, "Race, Gender, and Laundry Work"; Tchen, *New York before Chinatown*; Okihiro, *Common Ground*.

18. "Mob Raids Hindus and Drives Them from City," *Evening American and Morning Reveille*, September 5, 1907, pp. 1, 3; "Bellingham Sees Last of the Hindus" and "Chinese Driven Out of the City in 1885," ibid., September 7, 1907, p. 1; "Mill Owners Are Censured by Council," ibid., September 10, 1907.

19. "Mob in Washington State Attacks British Subjects," *Montreal Daily Herald*, September 9, 1907; "Workingmen Drive Out the Hated Hindoo," *San Francisco Chronicle*, September 6, 1907.

20. Ibid.

21. *The Times* (London), September 8, 1907. See also Bederman, *Manliness*; Giddings, *Ida*.

22. "Races Clash in Indiana City," *Bellingham Herald*, September 6, 1907; "Vancouver Faces Bloody Outbreak and Proclamation of Martial Law" and "Grays Harbor Hindus Attack White Men," ibid., September 10, 1907; "Everett Hindus Ask for Police Protection," ibid., September 9, 1907; "Army of Hindus Spread over British Columbia," p. 1, and "Anacortes Has Big Hindu Scare," p. 2, ibid., September 12, 1907; "Hindus and Whites Clash at Aberdeen," *Morning Reveille and Evening American*, September 12, 1907; "Hindus and Swedes Clash in Seattle," ibid., September 17, 1907, p. 5; "Hindus Are Leaving City," *Everett Herald*, November 4, 1907, p. 1.

23. McDonald, *Making Vancouver*, p. 205.

24. Bender, *Nation among Nations*; Lears, *Rebirth of a Nation*.

25. McDonald, *Making Vancouver*, pp. 58–59; Anderson, *Vancouver's Chinatown*.

26. Bruner and Carr, *Panic of 1907*, pp. 141–42; Sprague, "American Crisis of 1907."

27. Roy, *White Man's Province*, pp. 185–228; Erika Lee, "'Yellow Peril,'" esp. pp. 551–52.

28. Rex v. Bowen, Police Court Transcript, October 28, 1907, p. 49; Attorney General of British Columbia, GR 419, vol. 124, file 1908/2.

29. Ibid.

30. Ibid., pp. 47–48.

31. McDonald, *Making Vancouver*, pp. 224–225.

32. Rex v. Bowen, Police Court Transcript, October 28, 1907, p. 49; Attorney General of British Columbia, GR 419, vol. 124, file 1908/2.

33. Ibid., pp. 7, 12–13, 17–19.

34. Ibid., pp. 22, 25–27, 32–33.

35. Ibid., pp. 40–42.

36. "Bowen's Honor or Hindu's Purse," *Vancouver Daily Province*, May 9, 1908, p. 1.

37. "Convicted of Manslaughter," *Vancouver World*, May 9, 1908, p. 2; "Bowen's Honor or Hindu's Purse," *Vancouver Daily Province*, May 9, 1908, p. 1.

38. "Bowen's Honor or Hindu's Purse," *Vancouver Daily Province*, May 9, 1908, p. 1; McLaren, *Trials of Masculinity*, pp. 125–26.

39. "Says Hindus Are Indecent," *Los Angeles Times*, February 2, 1909.

40. "Raid Hindu Camp, Arrested Next Day" and "Three Young Farmers in Jail on Aliens' Warrant; Section is Stirred Up," *San Francisco Examiner*, December 6, 1911, p. 1.

41. Pettegrew, "Homosociality"; Gonzales-Day, *Lynching*.

42. Hannah Rosen, *Terror*; Ayers, *Vengeance and Justice*; Brundage, *Lynching in the New South*; Tolnay and Beck, *Festival of Violence*; Carrigan, *Making of a Lynching Culture*; Pfeifer, *Rough Justice*.

43. L. T. Paye, "The Anti Hindu Riot in St. Johns, Washington," *The White Man*, I, no. 1 (June 1910), Special Collections of the Knight Library, University of Oregon, Eugene.

44. "The Anti Hindu Riot," *The White Man*, I, no. 1 (June 1910).

45. "Mob Beats Hindus," *Oregonian*, March 22, 1910, p. 1; "State Hurries Hindu Riot Case," ibid., June 14, 1910; "Dickey Poses as Hindus' Friend," ibid., June 15, 1910, p. 4; "Jury Finds Dickey Guilty of Rioting," ibid., June 16, 1910, p. 6.

46. McLeod, "Turban," in *Sikh Identity*, ed. Singh and Barrier, pp. 57–68; Cohn, *Colonialism*; Oberoi, *Construction of Religious Boundaries*.

47. Pettegrew, "Homosociality," p. 318; Nelson, *National Manhood*; both are extending the analysis and insights of Sedgwick, *Between Men*. See also Kimmel, *Manhood in America*, and Rotundo, *American Manhood*.

48. Allan P. Miller, "An Ethnographic Report on the Sikh (East) Indians of the Sacramento Valley" (1950), paper in "Anthropology for David Mandelbaum," p. 38, South Asians in North America collection, Bancroft Library, BANC MSS 2002/78 cz, box 6, folders 19–22.

49. "Hindustani Laborers," Bureau of Labor Statistics, RG 257, box 16, folder "Ethelbert," U.S. National Archives, College Park, MD.

50. Puar, *Terrorist Assemblages*; Axel, *Nation's Tortured Body*.

51. "The 'Filth of Asia,'" *The White Man* I, no. 2 (August 1910).

52. Gerald N. Hallberg, "Bellingham, Washington's Anti-Hindu Riot," *Journal of the West* 12, no. 1(1973): 163–75; see p. 169.

53. "Hindu Women Employed on American Railroads," *The White Man*, I, no. 1 (June 1910).

54. Halberstam, *Female Masculinity*; Sears, "All That Glitters"; Stryker, *Transgender History*.

55. Sears, "All That Glitters," pp. 392–97.

56. Stryker, *Transgender History*; Sears, "All That Glitters."

57. Asiatic Exclusion League, *Proceedings.* See esp. September 1908, pp. 11–12; January 1910, pp. 5–11; March 1910, pp. 7–10; April 1910, pp. 4–8; September 1910, pp. 45–52; October 1910, pp. 59–60; January 1911, pp. 79–80; March 1911, p. 92; Mills, "East Indian Immigration"; Olin "European Immigrant and Oriental Alien."

58. U.S. House of Representatives, Committee on Immigration, 63rd Cong., 2nd sess., *Hindu Immigration: Hearings . . . Relative to Restriction of Immigration of Hindu Laborers* (Washington, DC: GPO, 1914), February 13, 1914, pt. 1, pp. 73–74, 76, 78.

59. Representative Denver S. Church, *Congressional Record*, 63rd Cong., 2nd sess. Appendix, pp. 842–54.

60. San Francisco Labor Council, September 12, 1913; Kern County Labor Council, September 10, 1913; Bakersfield Labor Council, September 11, 1913, U.S. National Archives, Washington, DC, RG 85, file 52903–110A.

61. Stockton Labor Council, letter to U.S. Immigration Service, Sept. 10, 1913, U.S. National Archives, Washington, DC, RG 85, file 52903–110A.

62. "The 'Filth of Asia,'" *The White Man* 1, no. 2 (August 1910).

63. "Stege Girl Killed; Body Sunk in the Bay," *Martinez Daily Gazette*, October 6, 1913, pp. 1, 3.

64. El Cerrito Historical Society, http://elcerritowire.com/history/pages/communityspast1.htm (accessed January 19, 2011).

65. "Stege Girl Killed; Body Sunk in the Bay," *Martinez Daily Gazette*, October 6, 1913, p. 1, 3.

66. Peiss, *Cheap Amusements*; Clement, *Love for Sale*; Meyerowitz, *Women Adrift*; Odem, *Delinquent Daughters*; Ullman, *Sex Seen*; Chauncey, *Gay New York.*

67. D'Emilio, "Capitalism and Gay Identity"; Meyerowitz, *Women Adrift*; Clement, *Love for Sale.*

68. "Asiatic Immigration" (editorial), *The Hindustanee* 1, no. 4 (April 1, 1914): 1.

69. "Canada as the Hindu Saw It," *The Hindustanee* 1, no. 4 (April 1, 1914): 10–11.

70. "Girls Lover Is Still At Large," *Daily Gazette*, October 7, 1913.

71. "Slain Girl's Shoes Are Found," *Oakland Tribune*, October 8, 1913, p. 7.

72. "Police Search Cabin of Missing Suspect," *Oakland Tribune*, October 7, 1913, p. 3.

73. "County Offers Reward for Capture of Hindu," *Martinez Daily Gazette*, October 8, 1913.

74. "Police Search Cabin of Missing Suspect," *Oakland Tribune*, October 7, 1913, p. 3.

75. Lui, *Chinatown Trunk Mystery.*

76. "Hindu Priest Held; May Reveal Secrets," *Martinez Daily Gazette*, October 11, 1913.

77. "Slain Girl's Shoes Are Found," *Oakland Tribune*, October 8, 1913, p. 7.

78. "Police Close on Trail of Murderer; 2 Involved in Murder of Girl," *Oakland Tribune*, October 9, 1913; "Charred Clothes of Murdered Girl Found," *Martinez Daily Gazette*, October 9, 1913, p. 1.

79. "Veale Is on Trail of Hindu," *Martinez Daily Gazette*, October 14, 1913; "Murderer Said Ali Captured," ibid., October 15, 1913; "Said Ali Confesses Brutal Murder of Rosa Domingo," ibid., October 18, 1913.

80. "Veale and Ruiz Coming with Prisoner Friday," *Martinez Daily Gazette*, October 16, 1913.

81. "Accused Slayer of the Girl Denies He Is Murderer," *Martinez Daily Gazette*, October 17, 1913. Curiously, Khan and also witnesses in the San Francisco boarding-house referred to her as "Rosa Domingo Riley," which perhaps indicates a presumed marital relationship with Charles Riley.

82. "Said Ali Confesses Brutal Murder of Rosa Domingo," *Martinez Gazette*, October 18, 1913.

83. Ibid.

84. "Murderer Was a Former Policeman," *Martinez Daily Gazette*, December 17, 1913, p. 1; "Punjabi Murderer Has No Fear of Death," ibid., October 20, 1913.

85. "Defense Fights in Vain to Rule Out Evidence," *Martinez Daily Gazette*, December 11, 1913.

86. "Punjabi Slayer's Fate Lies in the Hands of Jury," *Martinez Daily Gazette*, December 12, 1913, p. 1.

87. "Life in Prison Punishment for Slayer," *Martinez Daily Gazette*, December 15, 1913, p. 1.

88. Gross, "'Of Portuguese Origin.'"


CHAPTER 2

1. Lowe, "Intimacies," pp. 202–3; Cresswell, *Tramp in America*; Chauncey, *Gay New York*; Boag, *Same-Sex Affairs*; Ingram, "Returning to the Scene of the Crime."

2. Chauncey, *Gay New York*; Delany, *Times Square Red, Times Square Blue*, esp. pp. 126–42; Warner, *Trouble with Normal*, pp. 174–79.

3. Butler, *Undoing Gender*, pp. 1–16; 40–43; 48–56; Halberstam, *In a Queer Time and Place*; Scott, *Gender and the Politics of History*; Riley, '*Am I That Name?*'

4. Robin Kelley, *Race Rebels*, p. 9; Hahn, *Nation under Our Feet*; Pandey, "Subaltern Citizens."

5. Warner, *Publics and Counterpublics*, p. 118.

6. Bederman, *Manliness and Civilization*; Hannah, *Governmentality*; Nelson, *National Manhood*; Kimmel, *Manhood in America*.

7. Warner, *Publics and Counterpublics*, pp. 74–75, 199; Gibson-Graham, *End of Capitalism*.

8. McDonald, *Making Vancouver*, p. 214.

9. Kusmer, *Down and Out*; Schneider, "Tramping Workers," in *Walking to Work*, ed. Monkkonen, pp. 212–34, esp. pp. 224–25; Schneider, "Omaha Vagrants," p. 63; Duis, *Saloon*; Duncan, "Men without Property"; Gjorkman, "New Anti-Vagrancy Campaign"; Spence, "Knights of the Tie and Rail."

10. Fifth Census of Canada, 1911, vol. 2, table 16; McDonald, *Making Vancouver*, p. 200–217.

11. Vancouver Report of the Social Survey, in McDonald, *Making Vancouver*, p. 224–25.

12. Nilsen, "Social Evil"; McDonald, *Making Vancouver*, pp. 190–91; Police Court, Prisoners Record Book, 1898–1917, ser. 202, 116-E-1, Prisoners Record Book, 1912–1917, pp. 2–6, City of Vancouver Archives.

13. Rex v. Sam Singh, British Columbia Archives, Attorney General Records, GR 419, box 143, file 1910/49.

14. Ibid.

15. Rex v. Dahl Singh, British Columbia Archives, Attorney General Records, GR 419, box 143, file 1910/53.

16. Rex v. Harri Singh, British Columbia Archives, Attorney General Records, GR 419, box 143, file 1910/48.

17. Chauncey, "The Policed," p. 317; Boag, *Same Sex Affairs*.

18. Rex v. Sam Singh, British Columbia Archives, Attorney General Records, GR 419, box 143, file 1910/49.

19. Ibid.

20. Rex v. Dahl Singh, British Columbia Archives, Attorney General Records, GR 419, box 143, file 1910/53.

21. Rex v. Sam Singh, British Columbia Archives, Attorney General Records, GR 419, box 143, file 1910/49.

22. These figures are drawn from monthly Vancouver Police Court records of criminal charges, arrests, and convictions. Cutler Edwards and I tabulated these monthly reports to develop a data set of crime arrests and convictions from 1906 to 1916. Vancouver Board of Police Commissioners Records, ser. 181, boxes 75-A-5, 75-A-6, 75-A-7 and 75-B-1, 75-B-2, and 75-B-3, City of Vancouver Archives.

23. Rex v. Harri Singh, British Columbia Archives, Attorney General Records, GR 419 Box 143, file 1910/48.

24. Police Court, Prisoners Record Book, 1898–1917, ser. 202; 37-C-2, 1905–1907, pp. 99–100, City of Vancouver Archives.

25. Delany, *Times Square Red, Times Square Blue*, pp. 126–42; 186–92.

26. Foucault, " Friendship as a Way of Life," in *Foucault Live*, ed. Lotringer, p. 204; Berlant and Warner, "Sex in Public," p. 560.

27. Halberstam, *In a Queer Time and Place*; Povinelli, *Empire of Love*; Edelman, *No Future*.

28. These statistics are drawn from the data set compiled from monthly police court reports (see n. 22 above). Vancouver Board of Police Commissioners Records, ser. 181, boxes 75-A-5, 75-A-6, 75-A-7 and 75-B-1, 75-B-2, and 75-B 3, City of Vancouver Archives.

29. Revised Statutes of Canada (1906 ), chap. 146, § 238; Sherry, "Vagrants, Rogues, and Vagabonds," pp. 557–60; "Use of Vagrancy-Type Laws," p. 1351.

30. Monkkonen, *Police in Urban America*, pp. 74–75; McDonald, *Making Vancouver*.

31. Rex v. Nar Singh, British Columbia Archives, Attorney General Records, GR 419, box 134 1909/50, pp. 5, 9.

32. Ibid.

33. Ibid., pp. 6, 7, 8.

34. McDonald, *Making Vancouver*; Schneider, "Tramping Workers," in *Walking to Work*, ed. Monkkonen, pp. 212–34.

35. Rex v. Nar Singh, British Columbia Archives, Attorney General Records, GR 419, box 134, 1909/50, pp. 9–12.

36. Ibid., p. 4. See also W. C. Hopkinson, work history and murder, in U.S. National Archives, College Park, MD, file 52903/110A.

37. Rex v. Nar Singh, British Columbia Archives, Attorney General Records, GR 419, box 134, 1909/50, pp. 1–14.

38. Statutes of Canada, 1892, Criminal Code, chap. 29, § 178; Revised Statutes of Canada 1906, Criminal Code, chap. 146, § 206.

39. British Columbia Archives, Attorney General Records, GR 1883, vol. 1, Provincial Police Court, Victoria. Sidney Richardson pled guilty and was sentenced to six months' hard labor; Harold Emery was arrested in South Vancouver for gross indecency with three men and committed to an asylum in New Westminster; Fred Deousidi was given a suspended sentence on a bond of $500. Boag, *Same-Sex Affairs*, notes a similar ethnic pattern of arrests in Portland and Vancouver in this period.

40. 116-E-1, Prisoners Record Book, 1912–1917, p. 308, City of Vancouver Archives.

41. Chauncey, *Gay New York*; Gilfoyle, *City of Eros*; Clement, *Love for Sale*; Boag, *Same-Sex Affairs*.

42. Moon, "'Gentle Boy'"; Hendler, "Pandering."

43. Rex v. Kehar Singh and Jagat Singh, British Columbia Archives, Attorney General Records, GR 419, box 204, file 1916/35, British Columbia Archives; Prisoners Records Book 116E-1, City of Vancouver Archives. In compliance with the privacy protections of the Youth Criminal Justice Act and § 22 of the Freedom of Protection and Privacy Act of British Columbia, I have created pseudonyms for youths who were witnesses, victims in police courts, or prosecuted in juvenile court in Vancouver and are identified in case files in the British Columbia Archives in Victoria.

44. Wade, *Houses for All*.

45. Rex v. Kehar Singh and Jagat Singh, British Columbia Archives, Attorney General Records, GR 419, box 204, file 1916/35, pp. 7–9.

46. Ibid., p. 18.

47. Confrontations and contact between African American and white passengers on trams, buses, and streetcars in southern U.S. cities in the mid twentieth century can be conceived of as "moving theaters," Robin Kelley argues in "'We Are Not What We Seem'"; see esp. pp. 103–8.

48. Police Court, Police Magistrate C. J. South, Vancouver, BC, July 31, 1916, pp. 1, 5, 7, 14, 23, in Rex v. Jowala Singh, British Columbia Archives, Attorney General Records, GR 419, box 206, 1916/75.

49. In the late nineteenth and early twentieth centuries, as the development of trains, roads, and markets quickened the mobility between Punjabi villages and towns and in regional and transnational migrations, the imagery, themes, and meanings of Ghazal resonated beyond courts and aristocratic circles in performances at fairs and in bazaars and streets. These sensibilities were not limited to Muslim cultures and were expressed and intelligible in peasant and urban cultures, whether the participants were Hindu, Sikh, or Muslim. During the late nineteenth and early twentieth

centuries, religious boundaries were being defined, stratified, and flexed, and distinctions of separate practice, sensibility, and aesthetics were emerging among elite English-educated urban communities, but most communities in urban areas and many rural areas merged cultural expressions and social practices. See Oberoi, "From Ritual to Counter-Ritual."

50. Najmabadi, *Women with Mustaches*; Naim, "Transvetic Words?"

51. George, "Tracking 'Same-Sex' Love"; Naim, "Transvetic Words?" pp. 14–17.

52. Indrani Chatterjee in George, "Tracking 'Same-Sex' Love," p. 19.

53. Ibid.

54. Boag, *Same-Sex Affairs*; DePastino, *Citizen Hobo*; Anderson, "Juvenile and Tramp"; Parker, *Casual Laborer*; Kunzel, *Criminal Intimacy*; Chauncey, *Gay New York*.

55. Rex v. Jowala Singh, Attorney General Correspondence, GR 419, box 206, 1916/75, Police Court, Police Magistrate C.J. South, Vancouver, BC, July 31, 1916, pp. 14–15, British Columbia Archives.

56. Ibid., pp. 9, 20.

57. Ibid., pp. 13, 19–20; 116-E-1, Prisoners Record Book, 1912–1917, p. 328, City of Vancouver Archives.

58. Ibid., pp. 2–3.

59. 116-E-1, Prisoners Record Book, 1912–1917, City of Vancouver Archives, p. 328.

60. People v. Jamil Singh, case #6029 (1918), pp. 2–3, 7–9, Records of the Superior Court, Criminal Division, County of Sacramento, Sacramento Archives and Museum Collection Center (SAMCC).

61. People v. Tara Singh, case #6039 (1918), p. 7, SAMCC.

62. Ibid., pp. 9–10.

63. Ibid., 3. Sacramento Superior Court Criminal Register, 24: 224, 250, 268, 278, 309, 318, and 340, SAMCC.

64. People v. Jamil Singh, p. 2.

65. Ullman, *Sex Seen*; Brunette, "Speech Unseen."

66. People v. Jamil Singh, pp. 2–3.

67. Ibid., p. 4.

68. Ibid., p. 15. Although sentenced to seven years' imprisonment, Jamil Singh was paroled on November 22, 1920, and discharged on parole a year later. Sacramento Superior Court Criminal Register, 24: 218, 222, 256, 258, 263, 265, and 266. City of Sacramento Police Department, Mug Books, Ethnic, 1911–1922, p. 105, SAMCC.

69. People v. Tara Singh, Sacramento County Superior Court Case #6039.

70. Berlant, "Intimacy," pp. 281–86. For an examination of the implications of the U.S. Supreme Court's 2003 *Lawrence v. Texas* ruling and the legal and historical problem of coupled intimacy and public recognition, see Franke, "Commentary," and Shah, "Policing Privacy."

71. Schwantes, *Radical Heritage*; id., *Pacific Northwest*.

72. Don Sing, Washington State Penitentiary Inmate File #6453, pp. 1–5, Department of Corrections, Washington State Archives, Olympia.

73. Ibid., p. 26.

74. Ibid., pp. 25–38.

75. Ibid., pp. 6–22.

76. Ibid., pp. 1–5; 23–26.

77. P.L. Verma, letter to Board of Prisons, August 4, 1912, ibid., pp. 4, 8.

78. Ibid.

79. Halttunen, "Humanitarianism and the Pornography of Pain," p. 307; Rai, *Rule of Sympathy*, p. 162.

80. Elizabeth B. Clark, "'The Sacred Rights of the Weak,'" p. 480.

81. P.L. Verma, letter to Board of Prisons, p. 9

82. Rai, *Rule of Sympathy*, p. xviii; McGowen, "Power and Humanity," in *Reassessing Foucault*, ed. Jones and Porter, pp. 107–10.

83. Letters by John Kim, August 3, 1912; Louis Roberts, August 3, 1912, J.J. Russell, August 2, 1912; C.A. Baxter, August 5, 1912, in Don Sing file cited n. 72 above.

84. Petition from "Hindoos in Portland" to State Prison Board, August 3, 1912, ibid.

85. Stoler, *Along the Archival Grain*, p. 64–65.

86. C.S. Reed, letter to P.L. Verma, August 5, 1912, in Don Sing file cited n. 72 above.

87. Charles Lopez, letter to H.T. Jones, chairman, Washington State Board of Control, September 16, 1913, Washington State Prison Board, October 14, 1913, ibid.

88. Rai, *Rule of Sympathy*, p. 162.

89. Verma's motivation and doggedness in clearing Don Singh's name may have been more personal. Six months before the court case, the immigration authorities at San Francisco had detained Verma in September and October 1911 after his entry into the United States. His appeal for entry into the United States as a student depended on letters from a Berkeley professor and a Los Angeles spiritualist, and his brother-in-law Bishen Das, studying at Washington State University in Pullman, who attested to his character and his ability to support himself financially while continuing his studies. His ability to find temporary work as a laborer depended on his connections with Punjabi workers in Washington and Oregon. U.S. National Archives, Washington, DC, RG 85, file 53319/33.

90. Chauncey, "Christian Brotherhood"; Canaday, *Straight State*.

91. Anzaldúa, *Borderlands*, p. 3.

92. Perez, "Queering the Borderlands," p. 129.

CHAPTER 3

1. U.S. Department of Interior, Bureau of the Census, census reports for 1890, 1900, and 1910; Truesdell, *Farm Population*; Barkan, *From All Points*, pp. 44–48; 463–467.

2. Friday, *Organizing Asian American Labor*; Vaught, *Cultivating California*; Peck, "Reinventing Free Labor"; Lamar, "From Bondage to Contract."

3. Gregory, *American Exodus*.

4. On rural sexualities, see Howard, "Talk of the County"; Kennedy, "'But We Could Never Talk about It.'" On combining rural and urban histories, see Boag,

*Same-Sex Affairs.* And see also Johnson, "Casual Sex"; Bell and Valentine, *Queer Country*; Bell, "Farm Boys and Wild Men."

5. Stanley, *From Bondage to Contract.* Welke, *Law and the Borders of Belonging*

6. Orsi, *Sunset Limited;* Thompson et al., *Pacific Fruit Express;* Yenne, *History of the Southern Pacific;* Lewis, *Iron Horse Imperialism;* Signor and Kirchner, *Southern Pacific.*

7. *Hindustan Ghadr,* ed. Ram Chandra, April 24, 1917, pp. 4, 5, South Asians in North America Collection, 2002/78, Bancroft Library, University of California, Berkeley.

8. Leonard, *Making Ethnic Choices.*

9. Ibid.; La Brack, *Sikhs of Northern California.*

10. People v. Bachin Singh, Imperial Superior Criminal Case #704 (1918), pp. 3–4.

11. Ibid., pp. 8–9.

12. Leonard, *Making Ethnic Choices.*

13. People v. Bachin Singh, pp. 8–9.

14. Ibid., pp. 4–5, 18–22.

15. Ibid., p. 13.

16. Ibid., pp. 32–34.

17. Ibid., p. 6.

18. Ibid., pp. 6, 22–23.

19. Ibid., p. 7.

20. Ibid., pp. 32–34.

21. Ibid.

22. Robertson, "Making Right a Girl's Ruin"; Odem, *Delinquent Daughters;* Haag, *Consent.*

23. For more on nineteenth- and early twentieth-century seduction suits, see Haag, *Consent,* pp. 1–60.

24. People v. Bachin Singh, pp. 31–32, 40.

25. Ibid., p. 40.

26. Ibid., Affidavit of Roy Shepard, May 24, 1918, pp. 23–25.

27. La Brack, *Sikhs of Northern California,* p. 123.

28. Ibid., pp. 91–94, 125.

29. California, Department of Industrial Relations, Division of Immigration and Housing Records, 1912–1939, BANC MS C-A 194, carton 80, Bancroft Library, University of California, Berkeley.

30. People v. Aijmad Khan, Sacramento County Superior Court, Criminal Case #8418 (1924), pp. 2, 13–14.

31. Ibid., pp. 2–14.

32. Ibid., pp. 2, 3, 12.

33. Ibid., pp. 3, 17–23; Sacramento Criminal Court Register, 35: 237; 36: 1, 136.

34. Chan, *This Bittersweet Soil;* McWilliams, *Factories in the Field;* Peck, "Reinventing Free Labor."

35. People v. Hamit Khan, Superior Court for County of Tulare, no. 2463, transcript People v. Hamit Khan, Criminal Case no. 1468, California Second Appellate District, 61, 79–80, California State Archives.

36. "Hindu Deported by Visalia Mob; White Workers Object to Employing of Foreigners during Hard Times," *San Jose Mercury News*, August 25, 1921.

37. Elzy Luna obituary, *Sierra Star*, December 3, 2003; People v. Hamit Khan.

38. "Two Statutory Cases Are Up for Hearings; Probe of One Hindu's Case Results in Another Being Arrested," *Porterville Evening Recorder*, October 9, 1926.

39. People v. Hamit Khan, pp. 46–52, 55.

40. Ibid., pp. 9–10.

41. Ibid., pp. 11–13, 20, 46–52.

42. Ibid., pp. 15–16, 19.

43. Ibid.

44. Ibid., pp. 74–75.

45. Ibid., pp. 69, 74, 77 and 81.

46. Ibid., brief of respondent U.S. Webb, Attorney General, and Lionel B. Browne, filed May 4, 1927, p. 7.

47. Calder, *Financing the American Dream*, pp. 184–199; Rae, *American Automobile Industry*.

48. On the enhanced opportunities for male same-sex relations enabled by automobiles in the rural South and upper Midwest in the post–World War II era, see, respectively, Howard, *Men Like That*, pp. 99–106, and Retzloff, "Cars and Bars."

49. People v. Hamit Khan, pp. 65–66.

50. Ibid., pp. 64–65.

51. Ibid., p. 24.

52. Elzy Luna obituary, *Sierra Star*, December 3, 2003; Virginia Luna obituary, *Sierra Star*, July 3, 2002.

53. People v. Joe Ellis Sing (later changed to Joella Singh) in Justice Court, Exeter Township, Superior Court County of Tulare, no. 1678 (1920).

54. People v. Joe Cabin, 1483, Tulare County Superior Court, March 1918. Joella Singh's wife had died before he left Punjab, and he had two teenage sons in the care of extended family in India.

55. Sutter County General Index Grantees, deed granted from H.W. Butting to Cartah Singh and Mayo Singh, February 11, 1913, 51: 67; deed granted from Mayo Singh to Cartah Singh, March 22, 1915, 55: 38; Cartah Singh from Charles Wilbur, March 30, 1916, 55: 444, in Sutter County Courthouse, Yuba City, California.

56. See "Dehydrated Foods: A List of References to Material in the New York Public Library," *Bulletin of the New York Public Library* 21, no. 10 (October 1917): 645–55; *Proceedings of California Fruit Growers Convention* (Sacramento: State Commissioner of Agriculture, 1916); Cruess, "Rain Damage Insurance."

57. People v. Carter Singh, Sutter County Superior Court, #2495, transcript, pp. 15–16.

58. Ibid., transcript of jury trial, pp. 73–75, California Court of Appeals, #135 (1923), pp. 73–75, California State Archives, Sacramento.

59. Their birthplaces suggest that the Watson family migrated frequently between the Midwest and the Pacific Northwest during the 1910s, following a pattern set by

an earlier generation. Biographical details on the Watson family from the 1920 U.S. Census T625, roll 942, p. 258, Shannon County, Missouri, Montier Township, and the People v. Carter Singh transcript. In the 1920 Census, Manfred C. Watson was stated to be a thirty-five-year-old white man; his wife, Aura, was twenty-eight. Their eldest son, Jessie, aged ten, had been born in Oregon; twin sons named Lloyd C. and Lloyd L. were aged six and had been born in Illinois, as had a daughter aged under five. Manfred's mother had been born in Missouri, and his wife had been born in Washington State.

60. Criminal Complaint in Justice's Court in People v. Carter Singh, Sutter County Superior Court, #2495.

61. People v. Carter Singh, California Court of Appeals, transcript, pp. 21–22, #135 (1923).

62. Ibid., pp. 30–31, #135 (1923).

63. Ibid., pp. 22–24.

64. Ibid., pp. 17–20, 62–63.

65. Ibid., pp. 43–54.

66. Ibid., pp. 73–75, 81–82.

67. Ibid., pp. 84–85.

68. Ibid., pp. 66–67.

69. Subpoena to "Boota, also called Butte, Mark Pease, Sr., C. Gower" and "Kesen Singh, Battan Singh, Hero, John Mohammed, Diwan Singh, Rafael Vasquez, Catalina Vasquez," in People v. Carter Singh, Superior Court, Sutter County, California, issued by Judge K. S. Mahon, February 8, 1923, Superior Court Case #2495.

70. People v. Carter Singh, California Court of Appeals, p. 23.

71. Shasta Lumber Company v. Carter Singh et al., Superior Court of Sutter County, Case #2526, filed March 9, 1923.

72. Shasta Lumber Company v. Carter Singh, Superior Court of Sutter County, Case #2493, January 2, 1923.

73. Kesen Singh v. Cartah Singh, Superior Court of Sutter County, Case #2491, filed December 29, 1922.

74. *Sutter County Farmer*, March 17, 1922; U.S. Census, 1910, Township Yuba T624, roll 111, p. 252.

75. Josephine Conwell v. Cartah Singh et al. Superior Court of Sutter County, Case #2532; Sutter County Deed Records, 79: 404–5 (November 19, 1924).

76. U.S. Naturalization Examiner M. R. Bevington began proceedings in May 1925 to revoke the naturalization of thirty South Asian men in California. "30 Hindus Lose Citizenship Papers," *San Francisco Call*, May 4, 1925.

77. Haney-Lopez, *White by Law*.

78. "Aliens Given New Blow; Fresno County District Attorney Announces No Interest of Any Kind May Be Had in Land." *Los Angeles Times*, January 16, 1924.

79. "Alien Land Law Enforcement Planned," *San Francisco Recorder*, January 15, 1924.

80. "Arizona Anti-Alien Land Law," *New York Times*, February 27, 1921.

81. Letters between the Hindustani Association, Phoenix attorneys, British consulates, and the British Embassy in Washington, DC, September 1934 to April 1935; "Two Suns of Arizona," *Time*, September 3, 1934; *Los Angeles Evening Post*, December 3, 1934, all in India Office, Public and Judicial Department Records, L/P&J/8/321, file 108/37, pp. 312–42, British Library, London; letters from British consul, San Francisco, to British Embassy, Washington, DC, December 7, 12, and 20, 1923, India Office Collection, Economic Department Records L/E/7/1233, file 1819/1921, British Library; August, "Anti-Japanese Crusade."

82. British consul, Los Angeles, letter to Lindsay, September 17, 1934 in India Office, Public and Judicial Department Records, L/P&J/8/321, Collection 108/37, pp. 338–42, British Library, London.

83. Ngai, *Impossible Subjects*; Erika Lee, *At America's Gates*; Fairchild, *Science at the Borders*; Fujita-Rony, *American Workers, Colonial Power.*

84. Pascoe, *What Comes Naturally.*

CHAPTER 4

1. Volpp and Dudziak, "Legal Borderlands."

2. Pascoe, *What Comes Naturally*; Grossberg, *Governing the Hearth*; Hartog, *Man and Wife.*

3. Eskridge, *Dishonorable Passions*; Chauncey, *Gay New York*, p. 140; Chapman, "'An Oscar Wilde Type'"; Robertson, "Shifting the Scene"; Boag, *Same-Sex Affairs.*

4. Chauncey, *Gay New York*; Boyd, *Wide-Open Town.*

5. Eskridge, *Dishonorable Passions*, pp. 55, 388–89.

6. Peiss, *Cheap Amusements*; Langum, *Crossing over the Line*; Keire, "Vice Trust"; Rosen, *Lost Sisterhood*; Haag, *Consent.*

7. See *California Jurisprudence*, ed. McKinney, vol. 22 (1925), esp. pp. 361–65.

8. People v. Dong Pok Yip (1912) is cited in People v. Samuel P. Robbins 171 Cal 466 (1915); People v. Kangiesser 186 Cal 388 (1919); and People v. Carter Singh 62 Cal App 450 (1923). For summaries of the case law, see Hillyer, *Consolidated Supplement*, pt. 2, pp. 6922–33; Kerr, *Codes of California*, vol. 4, *Penal Code 1920*, pp. 277–78, 384–85, 390.

9. Transcript, People v. Dong Pok Yip, California State Archives, pp. 1, 4–7, and People v. Dong Pok Yip 164 Cal 145–46.

10. Transcript, People v. Dong Pok Yip, p. 22.

11. Ibid., pp. 13, 14.

12. People v. Dong Pok Yip 164 Cal 147.

13. Larson, "'Even a Worm Will Turn at Last,'"; Odem, *Delinquent Daughters.*

14. Larson, "'Even a Worm Will Turn at Last,'" pp. 19–20; Odem, *Delinquent Daughters.*

15. People v. Dong Pok Yip; People v. Carter Singh.

16. Moran, *Teaching Sex*; Hall, *Adolescence*; Graff, *Conflicting Paths*; Kett, *Rites of Passage*; Odem, *Delinquent Daughters*; Willrich, *City of Courts*; Knupfer, *Reform and Resistance*; Tanenhaus, *Juvenile Justice.*

17. Merrill, "Summary"; Jones and Janis, "Primary Syphilis"; Freyhan, "Homosexual Prostitution."

18. Rex v. Delip Singh, 26 British Columbia Reports (1918), pp. 390–91, 394.

19. Robertson, *Crimes against Children*, pp. 66–67.

20. Rex v. Delip Singh, 26 British Columbia Reports (1918), pp. 392–93.

21. Ibid., pp. 394–96.

22. People v. Robbins (1916), 171 Cal 145–146.

23. People v. Robbins (1916), 171 Cal 145.

24. Ibid., pp. 145–46.

25. Hopkins, "Signs of Masculinism"; Schlossman, *Love and the American Delinquent*; Tanenhaus, *Juvenile Justice*.

26. Cavallo, *Muscles and Morals*, 15–48; Verbrugge, *Able-Bodied Womanhood*.

27. People v. Robbins (1916), 171 Cal 145–46.

28. People v. Bugga Singh, Imperial County Superior Court (1919), pp. 5–7.

29. People v. Arjan Singh, Tulare County Superior Court, no. 2464; "Two Statutory Cases Are Up for Hearings; Probe of One Hindu's Case Results in Another Being Arrested," *Porterville Evening Recorder*, October 9, 1926.

30. People v. Arjan Singh.

31. People v. Rollo [sic] Singh, Third Court of Appeals, transcript of testimony in District Court of Yuba County, 5, 6, 7, 10, 12, 13, California State Archives, #359 (June 1928).

32. People v. Rollo [sic] Singh, pp. 43–50.

33. People v. Rollo [sic] Singh, appellant's opening brief, p. 7, Third Court of Appeals, California State Archives, #359 (June 1928).

34. Harry J. Carstenbrook Probate Case #3226 in the Superior Court of Yuba City, filed May 18, 1927; Great Register of Yuba County, General Election, 1928; *Marysville Appeal-Democrat*, 1898–1940s, Marysville Public Library.

35. See Larson, " 'Even a Worm Will Turn at Last,'" and Odem, *Delinquent Daughters*.

36. Kerr, *Codes of California*, pp. 277–78.

37. Warner, *Trouble with Normal*; Sears, "All That Glitters."

38. Terry, *American Obsession*.

39. Eskridge, *Dishonorable Passions*, p. 51.

40. The California State Supreme Court overturned the statute because it violated an "anti-Spanish" state constitutional amendment that required laws to be written in English. See Ullman, *Sex Seen*; Brunette, "Speech Unseen."

41. People v. Jack Lynch and Keshn Singh, San Joaquin County Superior Court, Case #4680 (1928).

42. Ibid.

43. Ibid.

44. Robertson, *Crimes Against Children*; Odem, *Delinquent Girls*.

45. Channan Singh, #7342, Washington State Penitentiary Files, Washington State Archives.

46. Ibid., biographical statement of Convict #7342.

47. R. W. McCoy, letter to Superintendent Henry Drum, November 16, 1915; Channan Singh, #7342 Washington State Penitentiary Files, Washington State Archives.

48. Kisken Singh, #11105, Grays Harbor County , Washington State Archives Southwestern Branch, Olympia, Washington.

49. Gilmore, *Golden Gulag;* Lichtenstein, "Good Roads"; Childs, "Angola, Convict Lease"; Miller, *Crime.*

50. Terry, *American Obsession;* Chauncey, *Gay New York;* Heap, *Slumming.*

51. Warner, *Trouble with Normal;* Boag, *Same-Sex Affairs.*

52. Grbich, "Body in Legal Theory," in *At the Boundaries of the Law,* ed. Fineman and Thomadsen, p. 69.

53. Tomlins, "Subordination, Authority, and Law."

54. For a parallel process of tracking sociological knowledge and the racialized sexualization of African Americans, see Ferguson, *Aberrations in Black.*

55. Canaday, *Straight State;* Kunzel, *Prison Intimacy.*


CHAPTER 5

1. The literature on this historical problem is vast. Cott, *Public Vows;* Volpp, "Dependent Citizens and Martial Expatriates"; Grossberg, *Governing the Hearth;* Merry, *Colonizing Hawai'i;* Hartog, *Man and Wife;* and Berry, *Pig Farmer's Daughter* exemplify different interpretive and methodological approaches.

2. Pascoe, *What Comes Naturally;* Gross, *What Blood Won't Tell;* Adelman and Aron, "From Borderlands to Borders"; Gitlin, "On the Boundaries of Empire," pp. 71–89; Deutsch, "Landscapes of Enclaves," in *Power and Place,* ed. White and Findlay, pp. 110–31.

3. Cott, *Public Vows,* p. 4.

4. Brumberg, "Ethnological Mirror," in Harris and McNamara, *Women and the Structure of Society,* pp. 108–10.

5. La Brack, *Sikhs of Northern California;* Dua, "Racialising Imperial Canada."

6. Leonard, *Making Ethnic Choices,* pp. 93–95.

7. Bald, "Overlapping Diasporas"; La Brack, *Sikhs of Northern California;* Leonard, *Making Ethnic Choices.*

8. Leonard, *Making Ethnic Choices,* p. 63.

9. Taylor, "Again the Covered Wagon," p. 348.

10. Leonard, *Making Ethnic Choices,* p. 64.

11. Ibid. Imperial County Recorder's Office, marriage licenses, 5: 164; 5: 388; Albert Joe and Alejandrina, age given as eighteen, 5: 472.

12. Leonard, *Making Ethnic Choices,* p. 95.

13. Pascoe, "Race, Gender and the Privileges of Property," in *Over the Edge,* ed. Matsumoto and Allmendinger, p. 216.

14. Pascoe, *What Comes Naturally,* pp. 6–8.

15. Blackhouse, *Colour Coded.*

16. GR 2962, British Columbia Marriage Registrations, British Columbia Archives; Baboo Singh and Maude Alice Crowley, July 21, 1913, Victoria, roll B 11370; Biaram Singh married Alice Markle November 11, 1913, Victoria, roll B11370; Jagot Singh

married Mamie Freeman, Vancouver, May 27, 1913, Vancouver, roll B11377; Buchan Singh married Margaret Banaloo, March 30, 1914, Victoria, roll B11371; Chinta Singh married Zelda Inez Wattam, December 26, 1916, Vancouver, roll B1139; Banta Singh married Cecila Victa, October 19, 1922, Vancouver, roll B13743; Harry Singh married Matilda Thompson, July 21, 1922, Naksup, roll B13744; Mongal Singh married Ethel Finlay, May 26, 1922, New Westminster, roll B13743; Arjen Singh married Rachel Ollie Minor, June 17, 1924, Vancouver, roll B13747.

17. Kesar Singh, *Canadian Sikhs*, p. 14. GR 2962, British Columbia Marriage Registrations, British Columbia Archives. Joseph Munsha Singh married to Annie Wright, August 17, 1908, Vancouver, Microfilm roll B 11374.

18. Sohoni, "Unsuitable Suitors"; Pascoe, *What Comes Naturally.*

19. Pascoe, *What Comes Naturally*, p. 93.

20. Karthikeyan and Chin "Preserving Racial Identity."

21. Pascoe, *What Comes Naturally.*

22. Sohoni, "Unsuitable Suitors," p. 613.

23. Ibid., pp. 613–14.

24. Pascoe, *What Comes Naturally*, pp. 138–39; Grossberg, *Governing the Hearth*, pp. 77–78, 93; Vernier et al., *American Family Laws* (1931), 1: 59.

25. Pascoe, *What Comes Naturally*, pp. 139, 157.

26. Leonard, *Making Ethnic Choices*; Volpp, "American Mestizo."

27. Raj Kaur and Bagh Singh Chotia, RG 85, file # 22731/3–2 and 3–3, U.S. National Archives, San Bruno, CA.

28. For an early example, see "Hindu Weds White Girl by Stealing Away to Arizona," *El Centro Progress*, April 5, 1918, cited in Leonard, *Making Ethnic Choices*, p. 63. Pascoe, *What Comes Naturally*, p. 118.

29. Felicita Soto Dhillon, RG 85, file 30348/3–2, and Besanta Singh Dhillon, RG 85, file 30348/3–4, box 2989, U.S. National Archives, San Bruno, CA.

30. Leonard, *Making Ethnic Choices*; Luibhéid, *Entry Denied*; Ting, "Bachelor Society"; Lui, *Chinatown Trunk Mystery*. Wu, "Asian American History and Racialized Compulsory Deviance."

31. "Julio Jabala Killed by Train at Mesilla Park Crossing," *Las Cruces Citizen* 31, no. 41 (December 29, 1932): 1; "Killed by Train," *El Paso Times* December 29, 1932.

32. "In the Matter of the Estate of Julio Jubala," Supreme Court of New Mexico, no. 4137, New Mexico Supreme Court Law Library and Archives, Santa Fe, New Mexico.

33. Ibid., pp. 176–77.

34. Ibid., pp. 172.

35. Ibid., pp. 172, 177.

36. Ibid., pp. 100–102, 110–11.

37. Leonard, "Flawed Transmissions?" p. 103. Oberoi, *Construction of Religious Boundaries.*

38. Jakobsh, *Relocating Gender in Sikh History*, p. 189; Chowdhry, *Veiled Women.*

39. "In the Matter of the Estate of Julio Jubala," p. 76.

40. Ibid., pp. 76, 113–16.

41. Ibid., p. 104.

42. Ibid., pp. 100–102.

43. La Brack, *Sikhs of Northern California*, pp. 187–88.

44. "In the Matter of the Estate of Julio Jubala," pp. 100–102, 110–11.

45. Chowdhry, *Veiled Women*.

46. Divorce was possible, however, in Muslim communities. But neither the attorneys nor the judges researched the code of marriage and divorce in British India.

47. "In the Matter of the Estate of Julio Jubala," p. 179.

48. On December 8, 1917, at the age of twenty-seven, he had married twenty-eight-year-old Maria Fierro in her hometown of Guadalupe, New Mexico. Dona Ana County, New Mexico, Marriage Record Book 4, p. 520. According to these records, Julio Jublio was born in "Las Indias."

49. Maria F. Jubala v. Julio Jubala, divorce petition, petitioners' exhibit # 5, Third Judicial Court of Dona Ana County, New Mexico, case # 6697.

50. "In the Matter of the Estate of Julio Jubala," Supreme Court of New Mexico, no. 4137, p. 104.

51. Leonard, *Making Ethnic Choices*, 109–10.

52. Maria F. Jubala v. Julio Jubala.

53. Soba Singh v. Pauline Singh, case # 9371, Clatsop County Circuit Court, Astoria, Oregon (filed October 13, 1920), plaintiff's complaint, pp. 1–3

54. Ibid., answer and cross complaint, pp. 2–3.

55. Nellie P. Khan v. Walayat Khan, Sacramento Superior Court, file # 34040, April 17, 1925, Sacramento Archives and Museum Center Collection.

56. RG 85, 52903/110B52320/1A and 52320/1, U.S. National Archives, College Park, MD. India Office, Public and Judicial Department Records, Ld L/P&J, ser. 12, 202: 4–10, British Library, London.

57. Alice Singh v. Jaggitt Singh or Jaget Singh, San Joaquin Superior Court, # 18690; 1920 Federal Census. Contra Costa, California, Bradford Track, Antioch, supervisor district 3, enumeration district 42, sheet 6-A.

58. Alice Singh v. Jaget Singh, San Joaquin Superior Court, # 18690.

59. Leonard, *Making Ethnic Choices*, pp. 109–10; Hartog, *Man and Wife*.

60. Julio Jubala and Soledad Garcia registered their marriage on March 30, 1929. Dona Ana County, New Mexico, Marriage Record Book 13, p. 310; "Property Settlement Agreement between Julio Jubala and Maria P. Jubala," February 12, 1929, "In the Matter of the Estate of Julio Jubala," pp. 218–19.

61. "In the Matter of the Estate of Julio Jubala," p. 32.

62. Ibid. p. 35

63. Ibid., p. 34

64. Ibid., pp. 54–55

65. Ibid.

66. Ibid., pp. 57, 61–62.

67. New Mexico Supreme Court, "In re Jubala's Estate," 40 N.M. 312.

68. "In the Matter of the Estate of Julio Jubala," pp. 313–4.

69. Ibid, p. 315.

70. Ibid.

71. Ibid., pp. 7–8.

72. "Soledad Jubala Wins Suit," *Las Cruces Daily News*, June 10, 1936.

73. Enrique Tellez and Soledad Garcia registered their marriage on July 27, 1936, in Dona Ana County, New Mexico, Marriage Record Book 25, p. 218.

74. Cott, *Public Vows*, pp. 113–17; Gordon, "' Liberty of Self-Degradation.'"

75. Haag, *Consent*; Cott, *Public Vows*.

76. Cott, *Public Vows*.

77. Mongia, "Always Nationalize."

78. Gabaccia, *From the Other Side*; Hsu, *Dreaming of Gold*; Gilfoyle, "Hearts of Nineteenth-Century Men"; Hartog, *Man and Wife*.

79. People v. Eva McKee Singh alias Eva Marie King, Superior Court, Imperial County, California, Criminal Case #746 (October 1918).

80. British Columbia Divorce Court Orders GR 3255, vol. 12, no. 752, roll B16268. See also GR 3255, Singh Attar Mahil to Hazel Catherine Mahil, vol. 54, record 901, roll B16287; Olive Myrtle Mule (falsely called Olive Myrtle Mall) and Rattan Singh Mall (also known as Attar Singh Mahil), vol. 58, no. 82, roll B16289.

81. In re Estate of Dalip Singh Bir, Harnam Kaur et al., appellants vs. Florence E. Boyes, respondent, 83 California Appellate, 2nd ser. 256 (January 1948); 188 P.2d 499.

82. Yew v. Attorney General, 1 Dominion Law Reports 1166 (1923).

83. Leonard, *Making Ethnic Choices*, p. 180, Probate Case 4427, Office of the County Clerk, Imperial County, California, 1949. Probate Case 11503.

84. Asad, *Formations of the Secular*, p. 199.

85. National Catholic Welfare Council Bureau of Immigration, Annual report on marriage rectification, 1933–34; Cleofas Calleros, Mexican border representative, El Paso, Texas, letter to Rev. Fr. Manuel Moreno, March 23, 1934, Marriage General Correspondence folder, National Catholic Welfare Council Bureau of Immigration Collection, ser. 23, box 53, Center for Migration Studies, Staten Island, New York.

86. Asad, *Formations of the Secular*, pp. 199, 201.

87. Jakobsen, "Sex + Freedom?" p. 286.

88. Ibid., p. 292.

89. Cott, *Public Vows*; Haag, *Consent*.

90. Wiegman, "Intimate Publics," p. 860.

91. Ibid., p. 861.

92. Stanley, "Conjugal Bonds"; id., *From Bondage to Contract*.

93. Plane, *Colonial Intimacies*, p. 12.

94. Constitution of the State of New Mexico 2.22.

95. Haney-Lopez, *White by Law*; Jensen, *Passage from India*.

96. Jensen, "Farm Families Organize"; R. E. Clark, "Management and Control of Community Property in New Mexico."

97. "In the Matter of the Estate of Julio Jubala," pp. 82–84.

98. Ibid., pp. 2–11.

99. Ibid., pp. 59, 61, 62.

100. In 1911, before the development of the Elephant Butte irrigation district, Hispanics had owned 70 percent of the farmland in the Rio Grande Valley, but by 1929, landownership was 60 percent Anglo, with Hispanic and Asian tenants leasing. See Jensen, "Farm Families Organize," in *Essays in Twentieth-Century New Mexico History*, ed. DeMark, pp. 13–28; I. G. Clark, "Elephant Butte Controversy."

101. Perdue, *Cherokee Women*; Hurtado, *Intimate Frontiers*; David Chang, *Color of the Land*.

102. Cott, *Public Vows*; Volpp, "Dependent Citizens." See note 73.

103. Gardner, *Qualities of a Citizen*, p. 147, and documentation there.

104. Stoler, *Carnal Knowledge*, pp. 206–7.

105. Stoler, *Race and the Education of Desire*, p. 129; Stoler, *Carnal Knowledge*, p. 48; Espiritu, *Asian American Women and Men*.

CHAPTER 6

1. Hakim Singh was also referred to as Hakim Singh Hundel or Hakim Singh Jagirdar, both affixed last names referring to the family's status as owners of property. His sons' names were Atma, Iqbal, Teja, and Janmeja. Their cause was not as celebrated in the Canadian and Indian community press as the cases of Sikh men returning with their wives and children. Singh, *Canadian Sikhs and Komagata Maru Massacre*, pp. 4, 6, 7; Canadian immigration agent Malcolm Reid, Vancouver, letter to MP Henry Herbert Stevens, Ottawa, May 29, 1913; Minister of the Interior William James Roche to Stevens, Ottawa, July 9, 1913; Jagpal, *Becoming Canadians*.

2. Mongia, "Historicizing State Sovereignty"; Lake and Reynolds, *Drawing the Global Colour Line*; Amrith, "Tamil Diasporas."

3. Jung, *Coolies and Cane*; Peck, "Reinventing Free Labor."

4. Lee, *At America's Gates*; Fairchild, *Science at the Borders*; Shah, *Contagious Divides*; McKeown, *Melancholy Order*.

5. "Compulsory Passport Regulation," Proceedings A, June 1917, nos. 8–22. Lake and Reynolds, *Drawing the Global Colour Line*.

6. Mongia, "Historicizing State Sovereignty"; Lake and Reynolds, *Drawing the Global Colour Line*.

7. Gardner, *Qualities of a Citizen*, p. 2.

8. McKeown, *Melancholy Order*, pp. 3, 1–2, 90.

9. Christian Schwarz, Victoria, letter to Minister of Interior F. Oliver, Ottawa, December 17, 1906, Library and Archives of Canada, Immigration Branch, RG 76, vol. 384, file 536999, pt. 1; "Vancouver's Black Hole of Calcutta," *Vancouver World*, November 17, 1906; "Nelson Petitions against Hindus," *Vancouver Province*, November 17, 1906; "Col. Whyte Denies Hindoo Story," *Vancouver World*, November 21, 1906; "Hindus Try to Sleep Out of Doors" and "City Officials Move to Assist Hindus," *Vancouver Province*, November 17, 1906; *Daily News Advertiser*, November 21, 1906; *Vancouver*

*Daily Province*, December 6, 1906; U.S. National Archives, Washington, DC, RG 85, file 51388/5, pt. 2.

10. Chapter 93, "An Act Respecting Immigration and Immigrants," in *Revised Statutes of Canada, 1906*, 1: 1709–27.

11. Buchignani and Indra, *Continuous Journey*; Sampat-Mehta, *International Barriers*, pp. 140–50; 217; Kelley and Trebilcock, *Making of the Mosaic*, pp. 146–52; Roy, *White Man's Province*.

12. E. Blake Robertson, letter to Superintendent of Immigration W. D. Scott, Ottawa, December 27, 1906, Library and Archives of Canada, Immigration Branch, RG 76, vol. 384, file 536999, pt. 1.

13. Lord Elgin, telegram to Lord Gray, governor-general of Canada, December 29, 1906, Library and Archives of Canada, Immigration Branch, RG 76, vol. 384, file 536999, pt. 1.

14. Fairchild, *Science at the Borders*; Kraut, *Silent Travelers*.

15. Daniel Keefe Memorandum, April 7, 1913, to the Immigration Service, Washington DC, US National Archives, RG 85, File 53173/40.

16. U.S. Department of Justice, Investigation of the Immigration Service, San Francisco, 1910, U.S. National Archives, Washington, DC, RG 85 General Correspondence, box 184, file 53108/24.

17. "Hookworm Infests Hindu Applicants; Dr. Glover's Discovery Will Raise Barrier Against India's Natives," *San Francisco Bulletin*, September 29, 1910.

18. When SS *Asia* docked on October 1, 1910, with 111 South Asian men in steerage, Glover had the opportunity to order full-scale bacteriological examinations, which took more than a week to complete. "Uncle Sam to Stop Hindu Immigration; Hookworm Discovery at Angel Island Takes Alarming Aspect," *San Francisco Bulletin*, September 30, 1910; M. W. Glover, San Francisco, letters to the surgeon general, October 1 and 14, 1910, all in U.S. National Archives, San Bruno, CA, RG 90, box 666, folder 16090.

19. Dr. M. W. Glover, "Annual Report San Francisco, California, 1910–1911 (Immigration Duty)," U.S. National Archives, Washington, DC, RG 90, box 666, folder 16090.

20. See "The 'Filth of Asia,'" *The White Man* 1, no. 2 (August 1910).

21. "Law is Sufficient to Stop Influx," *San Francisco Chronicle*, September 29, 1910.

22. Sant Ram, U.S. National Archives, San Bruno, CA, RG 85, box 681, file 12650/7–1.

23. Immigration Commissioner Ellis Bruler, Seattle, letter to Immigration Service, Washington, DC, March 29, 1913, U.S. National Archives, Washington, DC, RG 85, file 53173/40.

24. Karam Singh, RG 85, box 731, file 12924/4–9,; Inder Singh, RG 85, box 731, file 12924/4–6; Inder Singh, RG 85, box 736, file 12973/14–1, U.S. National Archives, San Bruno, CA.

25. "Sound Port to Be Strict with Hindus," *Tacoma Ledger*, June 26, 1913. See "In re Rhagat Singh et al." and "In re Sundar Singh et al.," nos. 15479 and 15480, District

Court N.D. California, First Division, 209 F. 700; 1913 U.S. Dist. LEXIS 1142, December 5, 1913.

26. W.C. Hopkinson to Zurbrick, inspector in charge, Vancouver, February 24, 1912, U.S. National Archives, Washington, DC, RG 85, file 52903/110A.

27. Daniel J. Keefe, Kobe, letter to Warner A. Parker, Washington, DC, January 26, 1914, U.S. National Archives, Washington, DC, RG 85, file 52903/110D.

28. "Hindus Arrive in Seattle: There Is No Law to Bar Admission," *Seattle Star*, June 25, 1913, p. 1; L.C. Gilman, Seattle, telegram, to C.R. Gray, St. Paul, June 28, 1913.

29. L.C. Gilman, Seattle, letters to C.R. Gray, St. Paul, June 28 and July 26, 1913; J.H. Carroll, Washington, DC, telegram to C.R. Gray, St. Paul, July 3, 1913. "Hindus from Manila Barred from Country," *Seattle Post-Intelligencer*, July 30, 1913; Commissioner-General Caminetti, Bureau of Immigration, letter to J.H. Carroll, general counsel, Great Northern Railroad Company, Washington, DC, July 31, 1913.

30. Correspondence in Great Northern Railroad Company files, Carroll to Gray, July 31, 1913; W.P. Kenny, letter to R. Budd, January 20, 1921.

31. Daniel J. Keefe, Kobe, letter to Warner A. Parker, Washington, DC, January 26, 1914, U.S. National Archives, Washington, DC, RG 85, file 52903/110D.

32. Hopkinson, letter to Zubrick, September 30, 1913, U.S. National Archives, Washington, DC, RG 85, file 52903/110A.

33. "In re Rhagat Singh et al."; "In re Sundar or Sandhu Singh et al.," 209 F. 700 (1913) Healy v. Backus, Immigration Commissioner 221 F. 358 (1915); "Ex parte Moola Singh et al.," 207 F. 780 (1913).

34. Gegiow v. Uhl, Acting Commissioner of Immigration at the Port of New York, Supreme Court of the United States 239 U.S. 3; 36 S. Ct. 2; 60 L. Ed. 114 (1915).

35. U.S. National Archives, Washington, DC, RG 85, file 51388/5, pt. 1; file 52785/22; file 51807/99; file 51807/42–44; file 51807/68; file 51807/69; file 51807/116.

36. I am grateful to Margot Canaday for sharing the Harnam Singh case file with me. U.S. National Archives, Washington, DC, RG 85, file 52522/15.

37. Memorandum for the acting secretary, July 17, 1909; Brydon-Jack & Ross, Vancouver, BC, letter to inspector of immigration, Vancouver, BC, March 24, 1909, ibid.

38. Brydon-Jack & Ross, Vancouver, BC, letter to secretary of commerce and labor, Washington, DC, July 7, 1909, ibid.

39. Ibid.

40. U.S. Immigration Service board of special inquiry meeting, March 25, 1909, Vancouver, BC, ibid.

41. Correspondence between U.S. commissioner of immigration, Montreal, Canada, and Office of the Inspector in Charge, Vancouver, July 7 and July 17, 1909, ibid.

42. U.S. Immigration Service board of special inquiry meeting, March 25, 1909, ibid.

43. Canaday, *Straight State*; Lubhéid, *Entry Denied*.

44. Anderson, *Vancouver's Chinatown*; Ward, *White Canada Forever*; Roy, *Oriental Question*.

45. Immigration Agent J.H. MacGill, Vancouver, letter to W.D. Scott, Ottawa, March 18, 1911, Library and Archives of Canada, RG 76, vol. 384, file 536999, pt. 1.

46. William Hopkinson, Vancouver, letter to Minister of the Interior Cory, Ottawa, April 17, 1911, and G. D. Kumar, Vancouver, to Immigration Department, May 13, 1911, Library and Archives of Canada, RG 76, vol. 384, file 536999, pt. 4; *Daily News Advertiser* (Vancouver), April 18, 1911.

47. See Dua, "Racialising Imperial Canada."

48. Ellis and Brown, Vancouver, letter to Minister of Interior Frank Oliver, Ottawa, May 30, 1911, Library and Archives of Canada, RG 76, vol. 384, file 536999, pt. 4.

49. Walter W. Baer, "The Problems of Hindu Immigration into Canada," *Victoria Times*, July 8, 1911, Library and Archives of Canada, RG 76, vol. 384, file 536999, pt. 4.

50. Ibid.

51. *Vancouver News Advertiser* editorial excerpted in *The Aryan* 1, no. 3 (October 1911): 3.

52. Baer, "Problems of Hindu Immigration."

53. Medical Inspector and Immigration Agent Dr. G. L. Milne, Victoria, confidential letter to Superintendent of Immigration W. D. Scott, Ottawa, July 8, 1911, Library and Archives of Canada, RG 76, vol. 384, file 536999, pt. 4.

54. H. Rahim letter to *Vancouver News Advertiser*, August 5, 1911; Hopkinson, Library and Archives of Canada, Vancouver, letter to Deputy Minister of the Interior W. W. Cory, Ottawa, August 4, 1911, Library and Archives of Canada, RG 76, vol. 384, file 536999, pt. 4.

55. W. D. Scott, Ottawa, memorandum to Cory, October 11, 1911, Library and Archives of Canada, RG 76, vol. 384, file 536999, pt. 4.

56. *Vancouver Sunset* editorial reprinted in *The Aryan* 1, no. 3 (October 1911): 5; W.C., "A Workingman's View of the Problem," *Victoria Daily Times and Colonist*, July 26, 1911.

57. "Denies Allegations of Polygamy Made by Dominion Immigration Agent," *The Aryan* 2, no. 1 (January 1912): 6; *Vancouver Sunset* report excerpted in *The Aryan* 2, no. 2 (February 1912).

58. "Pleading for Their Wives and Children," *Canadian Courier* report excerpted in *The Aryan* 1, no. 5 (December 1911).

59. J. H. MacGill, Vancouver, telegram and letters to Superintendent of Immigration William Scott, Ottawa, January 18, 1912; Library and Archives of Canada, RG 76, vol. 384, file 536999, pt. 4.

60. Khalsa Diwan Society Sikh missionary priest Garib Singh, Vancouver, telegram, January 31, 1912, to Minister of the Interior R. Rogers, Ottawa; Library and Archives of Canada, RG 76, vol. 384, file 536999, pt. 4.

61. "Admit Hindus' Wives," *The Aryan* 2, no. 2 (February 1912): 4.

62. Ibid.

63. Ibid. See also Sundar Singh, "The Hindu in Canada," *Journal of Race Development* 7, no. 3 (January 1917): 366–68, for his historical assessment.

64. H. H. Stevens "Opposed to Hindu Women and Families Entering Canada," *Manitoba Free Press*, n.d.

65. *The Hindustanee* 1, no. 3 (May 1, 1914): 1. Bancroft Library, South Asians in North America Collection, 2002/78, box 1, folder 13.

66. "Hindu Women Will Make Hindu Colony Permanent," Library and Archives of Canada, RG 76, vol. 384, file 536999, pt. 4.

67. Fortier, for superintendent of immigration, letter to J.A. Cote, September 23, 1912; Library and Archives of Canada, RG 76, vol. 384, file 536999, pt. 5.

68. "The Sikh Temple at Victoria BC," *Canadian Courier*, cited in *The Aryan* 2, no. 9 (November 1912): 5–6.

69. Walker, "*Race*." In re Narain Singh (1913) 18 British Columbia Reports, 506.

70. Morse, "Status of British East Indians," pp. 71–80; id., "Some Aspects of the *Komagata Maru* Affair, 1914," p. 102; Canada Indian Committee, *Hindu Case*, p. 11; Ward, *White Canada Forever*, pp. 87–88; *News Advertiser*, May 28 and June 24, 1914; Canada, *House of Commons Debates*, 1914, pp. 4556–57.

71. "In re Munshi," *British Columbia Law Reports*, 20: 243–92 (1914).

72. Ibid., pp. 290–91.

73. "Hindu Feudists Kill Canadian Official," *New York Times*, October 22, 1914.

74. Rex v Nana Singh and Dalep Singh (1915), GR 419, box 197, file 1915/31, British Columbia Archives, Vancouver.

75. Ibid.

76. Ibid.

77. Ibid.

78. British Columbia probate cases reveal the sophisticated financing managed by real estate corporations, such as the Guru Nanak Mining and Trust Company and the Sikh Realty Company, to administer fractional interest shares, promissory notes, and mortgages. GR-1415 British Columbia Supreme Court (Vancouver) Probate Records. See B02554 Singh, Jawala; B02557 Singh, Dhalip; B02557 Singh, Bhagat; B02558 Singh, Nihal; B02558 Singh, Inder; B07260 Singh, Bhag; B08422 Singh, Isher.

79. Police Court, Prisoners Record Book, 1898–1917, ser. 202, 116-E-1, Prisoners Record Book, 1912–1917, p. 248, City of Vancouver Archives.

80. Gardner, *Qualities of a Citizen*, pp. 48–49.

81. Ibid.

82. "Deporting Indian Woman Postponed: House Committee Grants Stay of Order after Long Legal Fray," *Los Angeles Times*, June 16, 1924.

83. "In the Matter of Bagh Singh Chotia and Raj Kaur," U.S. National Archives, San Bruno, CA, RG 85, file nos. 22731/3–2 and 3–3, p. 2.

84. Ibid., p. 4

85. Ibid., pp. 10–11

86. Immigrant Inspector J.P. Lawler, letter to the commissioner of immigration, San Francisco, November 10, 1923, ibid.

87. Interview of B.S. Grewal by Inspector George W. Moore in Fresno, California, November 13, 1923, ibid.

88. Ibid., pp. 3–4.

89. Luibhéid, *Entry Denied*.

90. "In the Matter of Bagh Singh Chotia and Raj Kaur," pp. 3–4.

91. Luibhéid, *Entry Denied*; Langum, *Crossing over the Line*; Beckman, "White Slave Traffic Act"; Haag, *Consent*.

92. Appeal before the Secretary of Labor, Immigration Department, Washington, DC. "In the Matter of Bagh Singh Chotia and Raj Kaur," U.S. National Archives, San Bruno, CA, RG 85, file nos. 22731/3–2 and 3–3.

93. Ibid., p. 4.

94. Gardner, *Qualities of a Citizen*, p. 100.

95. "In the Matter of Bagh Singh Chotia and Raj Kaur," U.S. National Archives, San Bruno, CA, RG 85, file nos. 22731/3–2 and 3–3, pp. 6- 12.

96. Gardner, *Qualities of a Citizen*, p. 29.

97. Fieldbrave, "East Indians in the United States." Fieldbrave was born in Lucknow, India, and was the grandson of a Methodist minister and the son of a Presbyterian minister. After studying at Colby College in Maine and Crozer Seminary in Chester, Pennsylvania, he became a Baptist missionary on the West Coast. In 1921, he married Alice Mable Bux in India, and the couple subsequently returned to the United States and had two children. His U.S. citizenship was rescinded as a result of the Thind decision, however, and he was forced to seek the return of British citizenship. Theodore Fieldbrave, "A Short Sketch of Life," Survey of Race Relations, box 26, file 122, Stanford University.

98. "In the Matter of Bagh Singh Chotia and Raj Kaur," pp. 12–13.

99. "Deporting Indian Woman Postponed: House Committee Grants Stay of Order After Long Legal Fray," *Los Angeles Times*, June 16, 1924; Attorneys White and White, San Francisco to commissioner of immigration, Angel Island, December 4, 1924; William A. Otto, Kerman, California, to commissioner of immigration, October 25, 1924, "In the Matter of Bagh Singh Chotia and Raj Kaur."

100. Henrietta Thompson, Committee for Friendly Relations with Foreign Students, YWCA, San Francisco, letter to commissioner of immigration, Angel Island, December 6, 1924; John Nagle, Angel Island, letter to commissioner-general, DC, December 10, 1924. Ibid.

101. Grace Chotia, San Jose, California, undated letter to immigration officer. Ibid.

102. Edward L. Haff, commissioner, Angel Island Station, letter to Grace Chotia, May 17, 1924. Ibid.

103. The older son, Noel, died in combat. The younger son, Vernon, survived the war. Vernon married Doris while stationed at a training camp in Oklahoma. They raised a family in the San Joaquin Valley and lived on for nearly sixty years. Vernon Chotia died at the age of eighty-four on September 19, 2001, in Manteca Park, California, a year after his wife passed away. Doris Chotia obituary, *Shawnee News-Star*, Oklahoma, October 10, 2000.

104. Attorneys Thomas B. Dozier and Edward G. White, letter to Secretary of Labor James J. Davis, Washington, DC, June 8, 1923. U.S. National Archives, San Bruno, CA, RG 85, Paritem S. Poonian, file 54988/50.

105. Gardner, *Qualities of a Citizen*, p. 101.

106. Rasmussen, *Yesteryear*, p. 58; "In the Matter of the Estate of Dhana Singh," Superior Court, Placer County # 4557, Placer County Archives and Research Center.

107. U.S. National Archives, San Bruno, CA, RG 85, Paritem S. Poonian, file 54988/50.

108. McKeown, *Melancholy Order*, p. 3.

109. Gardner, *Qualities of a Citizen*, pp. 9, 245.

110. Ibid., p. 23; Luibhéid, *Entry Denied*.

111. Ibid.; Canaday, *Straight State*; Luibhéid, "Queer/Migration"

CHAPTER 7

1. Menzies et al., "Rethinking the Citizen," in *Contesting Canadian Citizenship*, p. 37; Gardner, *Qualities of a Citizen*, p. 4.

2. Policy models, political and administrative techniques, and inequities of citizenship and political subjecthood informed the treatment of people under different jurisdictions of the British empire-state and the emergent U.S. empire-state in the late nineteenth and twentieth centuries. Scholars have examined the circulation of policies between the jurisdictions of the British Empire from colonial states such as India to dominions such as Canada and Australia. See, e.g., Gorman, *Imperial Citizenship*. New research has also examined the ties between the British empire-state and the United States, which has also exhibited varied and hierarchically organized regimes of political subjects for the inhabitants of the various locations of U.S. sovereign rule in the continental nation-state and "domestic" and overseas territories across the Caribbean and the Pacific Ocean.

For the specificity of British imperial citizenship and its application and contradiction in the Dominion of Canada, see Pal, *Interests of the State*, pp. 61–77; Brodie, "Three Stories," in *Contesting Canadian Citizenship*, pp. 43–66; Knowles, *Forging Our Legacy*, pp. 31–40.

For examples of the U.S. hierarchical system and reflections on the linkages within the U.S. empire-state and the formation of the idea of imperial citizenship, see Rogers M. Smith, *Civic Ideals*; Kazanjian, *Colonizing Trick*; Erman, "Meanings of Citizenship"; Gerstle, *American Crucible*; Gutierrez, "Politics of the Interstices"; Glenn, *Unequal Freedom*.

For the circulation of citizenship exclusion policies in the British Empire, its settler colonies, and the United States and the pivotal political and policy interest in denying political status to "Asiatic" labor and settler migrants, principally Indian, Chinese, and Japanese people in South Africa, Australia, Canada, and the United States, see Jensen, *Passage from India*; Price, *Great White Walls*; Huttenback, *Gandhi in South Africa*, pp. 139–44; Lake, "From Mississippi to Melbourne via Natal"; Lake and Reynolds, *Drawing the Global Colour Line*; Chang, "Enforcing Transnational White Solidarity"; Martens, "Transnational History of Immigration Restriction."

3. Volpp, "Divesting Citizenship."

4. Gardner, *Qualities of a Citizen*, pp. 3–4.

5. Somerville, "Notes," pp. 661–62; Novak, "Legal Transformation of Citizenship."

6. Lowe, "Intimacies."

7. Bishop, *Charles Joseph Bonaparte;* Goldman, *Charles J. Bonaparte.*

8. Haney-Lopez, *White by Law;* Jensen, *Passage from India.* The contentious struggle over being recognized as white contributed to the persistent political and cultural separation of Middle Eastern Americans and Asian Americans. For the complexity of relational racialization for Mexicans, see Molina, "'In a Race All Their Own.'"

9. Attorney General Charles Joseph Bonaparte to U.S. Attorney Robert Devlin, San Francisco, U.S. National Archives, Washington, DC, RG 85, file 19783; Mukherjee, *Taraknath Das.*

10. Taraknath Das, Leavenworth, Kansas, letter to U.S. Attorney General Mitchell Palmer, May 19, 1919, U.S. National Archives, Washington, DC, RG 60, Department of Justice, Central Files, file 38–927; Mukherjee, *Tarakhath Das.*

11. Jensen, *Passage from India,* pp. 248–50; U.S. National Archives, Washington, DC, RG 118, file 97415.

12. H. A. Elkourie, Birmingham, AL, letter to U.S. attorney general, November 1, 1909, U.S. National Archives, Washington, DC, RG 85, file 19783/43.

13. Simon Wolf, letter to secretary of commerce and labor, Washington, DC, November 5, 1909, U.S. National Archives, Washington, DC, RG 85, file 19783/43.

14. Justin Kirreh, New York, letter to secretary of commerce and labor, Washington, DC, November 1, 1909, U.S. National Archives, Washington, DC, RG 85, file 19783/43.

15. Charles Nagel, Washington, DC, letter to Richard Campbell, November 11, 1909, ibid.

16. Charles Nagel, letter to Justin Kirreh, November 13, 1909, ibid.

17. F. R. Champion, letter to Charles Nagel, Washington, DC, November 30, 1909, ibid.

18. Correspondence with commissioner of the Bureau of Naturalization, Washington, DC, January 6, 1916, U.S. National Archives, Washington, DC, RG 85, file 10674/82.

19. In correspondence dated December 8, 1909, to field examiners cited in letter from W. M. Ragsdale, Pittsburgh, to commissioner of the Bureau of Naturalization, Washington, DC, January 28, 1916, U.S. National Archives, Washington, DC, RG 85, file 10674/82.

20. Singh, *Canadian Sikhs and the* Komagata Maru *Massacre,* pp. 83–85. Porbander was also the birthplace of Mohandas Gandhi, who as a London-trained lawyer was organizing South Asians in South Africa during the same period.

21. See details of the loss of Japanese franchise in British Columbia and legislation to remove South Asians in Walker, "Race," p. 254.

22. British Columbia and Victoria extended municipal suffrage to propertied widows and spinsters in 1873 and to propertied single women and wives for the election of school trustees in 1884. However, the 1885 Franchise Act denied white women the vote in federal and provincial elections until federal legislative amendments accorded white women voting rights in 1919. Pal, *Interests of the State,* pp. 61–77.

23. "The Colour Bar in Canada" and "No Votes No Taxes," *The Aryan*, March–April 1912.

24. "Hindu Question in British Parliament," ibid.

25. H. F. Angus, "Legal Status," p. 10; *Victoria Times*, September 19, 1935, cited in Roy, *Oriental Question*, pp. 154–57

26. In re Immigration Act and Santa Singh, British Columbia Reports, vol. 28 (1920), 357–363; *Statute Act of 1919*, c. 1, s. 2 (1)(D)(iii).

27. In re Immigration Act and Santa Singh, British Columbia Reports, 28: 361 (1920).

28. See Mukerjee, *Taraknath Das*.

29. Ibid., pp. 34–39.

30. Declaration of Taraknath Das, Zurich, March 29, 1916; U.S. State Department, letter to Cecil Arthur Spring Rice, British Embassy, Washington, DC, July 21, 1916, India Office Records, L/E/7/1331 File 544/1924, British Library.

31. Bhagat Singh, confidential file, India Office, L/P&J/12/289, British Library, London.

32. Jensen, *Passage from India*.

33. Jensen, *Passage from India*, p. 256; Salyer, "Baptism by Fire"; Cole, "Determining Citizenship."

34. Bhagat Singh, confidential file, India Office, L/P&J/12/289, British Library, London.

35. Ibid. In re Bhagat Singh Thind, 268 Fed 683, 684.

36. In re Bhagat Singh Thind, 268 Fed 685.

37. United States v. Didar Singh, no. 7602; United States v. Puna Singh, no. 7603; United States v. Amer Singh, no. 7604; United States v. Bhan Singh, no. 7605, U.S. Federal District Court, Northern California, RG 21, U.S. National Archives, San Bruno and San Francisco, Equity Case Files; United States v. Channon Singh (alias C. S. Tom), no. 7606, U.S. Federal District Court, Utah, RG 21, U.S. National Archives, Denver, Equity Case Files; "Asks Cancellation of Hindus' Naturalization," *Deseret Evening News*, Salt Lake City, Utah, May 14, 1923.

38. For instance, during January 12–19, 1924, the following declarations of intention were recorded in U.S. District Court, Western District of New York: Argan Allie, no. 15731; Ashod Ali, no. 15742; Dawin Miha, no. 15743; Mohar Ali, no. 15744; Tahir Ali, no. 15745; Baijed Ali, no. 15746; Rashid Ulla, no. 15747; Dada Meah, no. 15926; Jamshed Ali, no. 15927; Wasir Meah, no. 15928; U.S. Naturalization Service, Record of Declaration of Intention, vol. 34, Western District of New York, U.S. National Archives, New York City.

39. Sylhet is a city and region adjacent to the tea plantations in the hills of Assam in northeastern Bangladesh (then northeastern Bengal), which a web of waterways to the Bay of Bengal had made commercially important since the eighteenth century. In the mid nineteenth century, the British dredged and connected the waterways and introduced steamers, creating a new inland system of water transportation and communication from Calcutta to upper Assam, through the central lowlands of Sylhet.

Many Sylhetis later moved to Calcutta, finding employment on British merchant ships. See Balachandran, "Conflicts in the International Maritime Labour Market"; id. "South Asian Seafarers"; Tabili, *We Ask for British Justice*; Bald, "Overlapping Diasporas."

40. United States v. Ozawa, 1922; Haney-Lopez, *White by Law*.

41. United States v. Bhagat Singh Thind 261 US 204 (1923).

42. Carbado, "Yellow by Law," p. 691; George A. Crutchfield, chief examiner, San Francisco, to commissioner of naturalization, Washington, DC, December 29, 1915, U.S. National Archives, Washington, DC, RG 85, file 10674/82; Jensen, *Passage From India*.

43. Ibid.; Robert Campbell, Office of Commissioner of Naturalization, Washington, DC, letters to chief examiner, Philadelphia, December 27, 1915, and January 11, 1916; Robert K. Campbell, letter to all chief examiners, December 22, 1915, U.S. National Archives, Washington, DC, RG 85, file 10674/82.

44. "30 Hindus Lose Citizenship Papers," *San Francisco Call*, May 4, 1925.

45. See Haney-Lopez, *White by Law*; Jensen, *Passage From India*.

46. United States v. Sakharam Ganesh Pandit, transcript of record, filed August 13, 1926, U.S. Circuit Court of Appeals for the Ninth Circuit, RG 276, no. 4938, pp. 21, 24, 27, 28, U.S. National Archives, Riverside, CA.

47. U.S. National Archives, RG 60, file 38–927; file 38–524.

48. United States v. Pandit, RG 276, no. 4938, pp. 36–39; 144–45.

49. Ibid., p. 152; Volpp, "Dependent Citizens and Marital Expatriates"; id., "Divesting Citizenship."

50. United States v. Pandit, RG 276, no. 4938, pp. 153–54.

51. Ibid., pp. 28, 29.

52. When Pandit's sister died in 1920, his mother redistributed the inheritance from their father to other siblings and nephews. Ibid., p. 30–31.

53. Ibid., p. 35.

54. Ibid., p. 156.

55. "Alienation of Hindu Asked," *Los Angeles Times*, June 3, 1923; "Attorney May Be Deprived of His Citizenship," ibid., June 5, 1923; "Citizenship Revocation Attempted," ibid., June 24, 1923; "Plea Made for Hindu's Citizenship," ibid., September 25, 1923; "Fight Begun to Maintain Citizenship," ibid., December 16, 1925; "Judge Lets Hindu Keep Citizenship," ibid., December 17, 1925; "Hindus Again Raise Citizenship Question," *New York Times*, November 15, 1925.

56. "Alienation of Hindu Asked," *Los Angeles Times*, June 3, 1923,

57. S. G. Pandit, "Memorandum of Points and Authorities in Support of the Defendant's Motion to Dismiss," pp. 18–19, 21, United States v. Mohan Singh, U.S. District Court for the Southern District of California, RG 21, G-104, U.S. National Archives, Riverside, CA.

58. Pandit represented Mandal in his denaturalization hearing. United States v. Tulsa Ram Mandal, B 90-T, District Court of the United States, Southern District of California Northern Division, U.S. District Court, Fresno. National Archives, Riverside, RG 21, box 80.

59. McGovney, "Race Discrimination in Naturalization," pp. 143–44. See also Bredbenner, *A Nationality of Her Own*; Cott, "Marriage and Justice for All"; Volpp, "Dependent Citizens and Marital Expatriates."

60. Charlton, British Embassy, Washington, DC, to London, November 6, 1925; notarized statement from Taraknath Das, April 30, 1925; Frank Kellogg, State Department, letter to Mary K. Das, June 25, 1925; British consul, Berlin, letter to secretary of foreign affairs, London, November 6, 1925, British Library, India Office Collection, London, L/E/7/1331, file 544/1924.

61. Das, "Woman without a Country." Extensive correspondence in British Library, India Office Collection, London, L/E/7/1331, file 544/1924.

62. Das, "Woman without a Country."

63. Ibid.

64. U.S. House of Representatives, Committee on Immigration and Naturalization, *Immigration and Citizenship of American-Born Women Married to Aliens*, pp. 23–27.

65. "Petitions from Miss Ida Trask, Los Angeles, and Mrs. C. Loomis, Brookline, Massachusetts, to President Coolidge," December 3 and 17, 1926, U.S. National Archives Washington, DC, RG 85, file 20–59.

66. "Dhillon, Felicita Soto," U.S. National Archives, San Bruno, CA, RG 85, box 2989, file 30348/3–2; "Dhillon, Besanta Singh," ibid., 3–4; "Dhillon, Tanh [*sic*] (John)," ibid., 3–5; "Dhillon, Ramon," ibid., 3–6.

67. "Dhillon, Jak Singh," U.S. National Archives, San Bruno, CA, RG 85, box 2989, file 30348/3–3, Western Union telegram dated March 13, 1950.

68. Application of Ora Singh (oath of allegiance to the United States under the Act of June 25, 1936), U.S. National Archives, Riverside, CA, RG 21, file 246-R-62; Volpp, "Divesting Citizenship."

69. Melva Chowdhury, U.S. National Archives, Washington, DC, RG 85, file 29/1512.

70. Ngai, *Impossible Subjects*, p. 89.

71. National Catholic Welfare Conference, Washington, DC, press release in American Committee for the Protection of the Foreign Born, Labadie Collection, University of Michigan, box 26 and 27, Krishna Chandra file.

72. American Committee for the Protection of the Foreign Born, Labadie Collection, University of Michigan, box 21, Ali Alsom file.

73. Ngai, *Impossible Subjects*, pp. 84–87.

74. Abner Green, executive secretary, American Committee for the Protection of the Foreign Born, letter to George S. German, chief, Alien Appeal Section, Immigration and Naturalization Service.

75. American Committee for the Protection of the Foreign Born, Labadie Collection, University of Michigan, box 21, Ali Alsom file.

76. Wayne M. Collins Papers, Bancroft Library, MSS 78/177 c, carton 1, various files. Gould, *Sikhs*.

77. Canaday, *Straight State*; Somerville "Sexual Aliens and the Racialized State"; Reddy, "Asian Diasporas, Neoliberalism, and Family."

## CONCLUSION

1. Merriam-Webster's Dictionary OnLine, www.merriam-webster.com/dictionary/estrange (accessed March 21, 2011).

2. For an eloquent synthesis of three decades of legal history scholarship that has reframed the historical problem of belonging, systemic dispossession, and U.S. legal and political institutions, see Welke, *Law and the Borders of Belonging*.

3. Ngai, *Impossible Subjects*; Kanstroom, *Deportation Nation*; Somerville, "Sexual Aliens and the Racialized State"; Menzies et al., "Rethinking the Citizen."

4. In the Matter of Krishna Chandra, Deportation Proceedings, San Francisco, CA, January 10, 1951, pp. 18–21, U.S. Department of Justice, INS A-4894489. U.S. National Archives, Washington DC.

5. Chandra Defense Committee, San Francisco, "The Case of Dr. Krishna Chandra," American Committee for the Protection of the Foreign Born, Labadie Collection, University of Michigan, Krishna Chandra file.

6. Wayne Collins Papers, Bancroft Library, carton 1, folder 45, Karm Singh file.

7. Chauncey, "Postwar Sex Crime Panic"; Freedman, "Uncontrolled Desires"; Robertson, *Crimes against Children*; Fejes, "Murder, Perversion and Moral Panic"; Denno, "Before the Modern Sex Offender Statutes"; Maynard, "'Horrible Temptations'"; Simon Cole, "From the Sexual Psychopath Statute to 'Megan's Law'"; Iacovetta, "Sexual Politics of Moral Citizenship."

8. Leonard, *Making Ethnic Choices*.

9. Warner, *Trouble with Normal*, pp. 174–75.

10. Gilmore, *Golden Gulag*; Duggan, *Twilight of Equality*; Wild, *Street Meeting*; Delany, *Times Square Red, Times Square Blue*.

11. Harris, "Whiteness as Property"; Eng, *Feeling of Kinship*; Lipsitz, *Possessive Investment*.

12. Ngai, *Impossible Subjects*; Pascoe, *What Comes Naturally*.

13. There is a rich debate on the racial inequalities, gender roles, and maternalist politics in the historical formation of the U.S. and Canadian welfare states. Mink, *Wages of Motherhood*; Nancy Christie, *Engendering the State*; Canaday, *Straight State*.

14. Eng, *Feeling of Kinship*, pp. 4–5; Ferguson, *Aberrations*.

15. Cohen, *Consumer's Republic*; May, *Homeward Bound*; Stern, *Eugenic Nation*.

16. Saund, *Congressman from India*.

17. Smith, "Framing"; Warner, "Normal and Normaller"; Cahill, "Disproportionate"; and Reidel, "Religious."

18. De Genova, "Migrant 'Illegality' and Deportability"; Coutin, *Legalizing Moves*.

19. Ferguson, *Aberrations*; Gopinath, *Impossible Desires*; Muñoz, *Disidentifications*; Reddy, "Asian Diasporas"; Eng, *Feeling of Kinship*; Pandey, "Subaltern Citizens"; Terry, *American Obsession*.

20. There is a rich critical debate regarding political theories of cosmopolitanism, state, rule-of-law societies, and norms. See Benhabib, *Another Cosmopolitanism*; Waldron, "Cosmopolitan Norms."

21. Halberstam, *In a Queer Time*; Freeman, *Time Binds*; Povinelli, *Empire of Love*; Butler, *Undoing Gender*.

22. Shah, "Policing Privacy"; Eng, *Feeling of Kinship*; and Franke, "Commentary" are all engaged with the critical meaning, implications, and consequences of the U.S. Supreme Court decision in *Lawrence v. Texas* (2003), which decriminalized adult consensual sodomy in the United States.

23. Chuh, *Imagine Otherwise*.

# SELECT BIBLIOGRAPHY

PRIMARY SOURCES

*Manuscript Collections*

✦ Bancroft Library, University of California, Berkeley

South Asians in North America Collection, 2002/78.
Wayne M. Collins Papers, MSS 78/177 c.
California Department of Industrial Relations, Division of Immigration and Housing
    Records, 1912–1939 BANC MS C-A 194.
Agricultural Laborers in California, ca. 1906–1911.

✦ British Columbia Archives, Victoria, British Columbia

Attorney General of British Columbia Records GR 419.
British Columbia Marriage Registrations GR 2962.
British Columbia Divorce Court Orders GR 3255.

✦ British Library, India Office Collection, London

L/E: India Office: Economic Department Records ca. 1876–1950.
L/P&J: India Office: Public and Judicial Department Records 1795–1950.

✦ California State Archives, Sacramento, California

Department of Justice, Attorney General—San Francisco Records F3632.
Department of Justice. Criminal Identification and Investigation Records F3672.
Supreme Court of California Records. Criminal Case Files, 1850–1965.

✦ Center for Migration Studies, Staten Island, New York
National Catholic Welfare Council, Immigration Bureau Records.

✦ Center for Pacific Northwest Studies, Western Washington University
Bellingham Bay Improvement Co. records.

✦ Library and Archives of Canada, Ottawa, Canada
RG 76 Immigration.

✦ New Mexico Supreme Court Library and Archives, Santa Fe, New Mexico
Supreme Court of New Mexico, Case Files.

✦ University of British Columbia Archives, Vancouver, Canada
Jemreja Singh Hundel Collection.

✦ University of California, San Diego, Special Collections, La Jolla.
Joan Jensen Collection.

✦ University of Michigan, Ann Arbor.
American Committee for the Protection of the Foreign Born, Labadie Collection.

✦ Bentley Library, University of Michigan, Ann Arbor.
Royal Samuel Copeland, Papers, 1892–1938.
Angela Morgan Papers, 1893–1957.

✦ University of Oregon, Special Collections, Eugene.
William C. Smith Collection.

✦ U.S. National Archives II (College Park, Maryland)
RG 10 National Commission on Law Observance and Enforcement.
RG 59 State Department.
RG 60 Department of Justice Central Files.
RG 65 Records of the Federal Bureau of Investigation.
RG 118 Records of U.S. Attorneys and Marshals.
RG 165 Military Intelligence Division.
RG 257 Bureau of Labor Statistics.

✦ U.S. National Archives (Washington DC)
RG 85 Immigration and Naturalization Service.

+ U.S. National Archives (Denver, Colorado)
RG 21 U.S. District Court Records.

+ U.S. National Archives (New York City)
RG 85 Immigration and Naturalization Service.

+ U.S. National Archives (Riverside, California)
RG 21 U.S. District Court Records.

+ U.S. National Archives (San Bruno, California)
RG 21 U.S. District Court, Records.
RG 85 Immigration Service.
RG 276 9th Circuit Court of Appeals.

+ City of Vancouver Archives
Prisoners Record Book, 1898–1917, Series 202.
Vancouver Board of Police Commissioners, Series 181.
Vancouver Police Department Scrapbook, Series 204.

+ Washington State Archives, Olympia
Washington State Department of Corrections, Penitentiary Case Files.
Washington State Supreme Court Case Files.

+ Washington State Archives, Northwest Region, Bellingham
Series NW365–6-7. Bellingham City Council Proceedings.
Series NW 337–3-18. Whatcom County Criminal Court Docket.

*Local Court Records (criminal, civil, probate records, marriage registers, title and
tenancy agreements, and naturalization petitions)*
Clatsop County Superior Court, Astoria, Oregon
Colusa County Superior Court, Colusa, California
Doña Ana County Superior Court, Las Cruces, New Mexico
Imperial County Superior Court, El Centro, California
Sacramento County Archives and Museum
San Joaquin County Superior Court, Stockton, California
Sutter County Superior Court, Yuba City, California
Tulare County Superior Court, Visalia, California
Whatcom County Superior Court, Olympia, Washington
Yuba County Superior Court, Marysville, California

*Local Public Library Collections and Historical Societies*

Clatsop County Historical Society and Museum, Astoria, Oregon
Contra Costa County Historical Society, Martinez, California
Doña Ana County Public Library, Las Cruces, New Mexico
Imperial County Historical Society, El Centro, California
Imperial County Public Library, Brawley, California
Placer County Historical Society, Auburn, California
Porterville Public Library, Porterville, California
San Joaquin County Historical Society, Stockton, California
Sutter County Public Library, Yuba City, California
Thurston County Public Library, Olympia, Washington
Vancouver Public Library, History Room, Vancouver, British Columbia
Yuba County Public Library, Marysville, California


*Newspapers and Periodicals*

*The Aryan*
*Bellingham Herald* (Bellingham, Washington)
*Canadian Courier*
*Deseret Evening News*
*The Hindustanee* (Vancouver)
*Hindustan Ghadr* (San Francisco)
*India West*
*Manitoba Free Press*
*Martinez Daily Gazette*
*Montreal Daily Herald*
*Morning Reveille* and *Evening American* (Bellingham, Washington)
*Oakland Tribune*
*Oregonian*
*Porterville Evening Recorder*
*San Francisco Bulletin*
*San Francisco Call*
*San Francisco Examiner*
*San Francisco Chronicle*
*San Jose Mercury News*
*Seattle Star*
*Seattle Post-Intelligencer*
*Sierra Star*
*Sutter County Farmer*
*Tacoma Ledger*
*The Times* (London)
*Valley Indian Times* (Chandler, Arizona)
*Vancouver Daily Province*

*Vancouver Sunset*
*Vancouver World*
*Victoria Daily Times and Colonist*
*The White Man*


SECONDARY SOURCES

Adelman, Jeremy, and Stephen Aron. "From Borderlands to Borders: Empires, Nation-States, and the Peoples in between in North American History." *American Historical Review* 104, no. 3 (1999): 814–41.

Ahuja, Ravi. "Mobility and Containment: The Voyages of South Asian Seamen c. 1900–1960." *International Review of Social History* 51, no. S 14 (2006): 111–41.

Alexander, M. Jacqui. "Erotic Autonomy as a Politics of Decolonization: An Anatomy of Feminist and State Practice in the Bahamas Tourist Economy." In *Feminist Genealogies, Colonial Legacies, Democratic Futures*, ed. M. Jacqui Alexander and Chandra Talpade Mohanty (New York: Routledge, 1997), 63–100.

Amrith, Sunil S. "Tamil Diaspora across the Bay of Bengal." *American Historical Review* 114, no. 3 (June 2009): 547–72.

Anderson, Kay. *Vancouver's Chinatown: Racial Discourse in Canada, 1875–1980*. Montreal: McGill-Queen's University Press, 1991.

Anderson, Nels. "The Juvenile and the Tramp." *Journal of the American Institute of Criminal Law and Criminology* 14, no. 2 (1923): 290–312.

Angus, Henry F. "The Legal Status in British Columbia of Residents of Oriental Race and Their Descendants." *Canadian Bar Review* 9 (January 1931): 1–13.

Anzaldúa, Gloria. *Borderlands / La Frontera: The New Mestiza*. San Francisco: Spinsters/Aunt Lute, 1987.

Arondekar, Anjali. *For the Record: On Sexuality and the Colonial Archive in India*. Durham, NC: Duke University Press, 2009.

Asad, Talal. *Formations of the Secular: Christianity, Islam, and Modernity*. Stanford, CA: Stanford University Press, 2003.

Asiatic Exclusion League. *Proceedings of the Asiatic Exclusion League*. New York: Arno Press, 1977. Reprint from original publication by the Asiatic Exclusion League in San Francisco, 1907–13.

August, Jack. "The Anti-Japanese Crusade in Arizona's Salt River Valley, 1934–35." *Arizona and the West* 21, no. 2 (1979): 113–36.

Axel, Brian. *The Nation's Tortured Body: Violence, Representation, and the Formation of a Sikh "Diaspora."* Durham, NC: Duke University Press, 2001.

Ayers, Edward L. *Vengeance and Justice: Crime and Punishment in the Nineteenth-Century American South*. New York: Oxford University Press, 1984.

Backhouse, Constance. "The White Women's Labor Laws: Anti-Chinese Racism in Early Twentieth-Century Canada." *Law and History Review* 14, no. 2 (1996): 315–68.

Balachandran, Gopalan. "Conflicts in the International Maritime Labour Market: British and Indian Seamen, Employers and the State, 1890–1930." *Indian Economic and Social History Review* 39, 1 (2002): 71–100.

———. "South Asian Seafarers and Their Worlds: c. 1870–1930s." Paper presented at Seascapes, Littoral Cultures and Trans-Oceanic Exchanges conference, Library of Congress, Washington, DC, February 12–15, 2003. www.historycooperative.org/proceedings/seascapes/balachandran.html (accessed January 19, 2011).

Bald, Vivek Renjen. "Overlapping Diasporas, Multiracial Lives: South Asian Muslims in U.S. Communities of Color, 1880–1950." *Souls: A Critical Journal of Black Politics, Culture, and Society* 8, no. 4 (2006): 3–18.

———. "Hands across the Water: Indian Sailors, Peddlers and Radicals in the U.S. 1890–1965." PhD diss., New York University, 2009.

Barkan, Elliott Robert. *From All Points: America's Immigrant West, 1870s–1952.* Bloomington: Indiana University Press, 2007.

Baynton, Douglas. "Defectives in the Land: Disability and American Immigration Policy, 1882–1924." *Journal of American Ethnic History* 24 (Spring 2005): 31–44.

Beckman, Marlene D. "The White Slave Traffic Act: Historical Impact of a Criminal Law Policy on Women." In *Gender and American Law: The Impact of the Law on the Lives of Women*, ed. Karen Maschke, 33–49. New York: Garland, 1997.

Bederman, Gail. *Manliness & Civilization: A Cultural History of Gender and Race in the United States, 1880–1917.* Chicago: University of Chicago Press, 1995.

Bell, David. "Farm Boys and Wild Men: Rurality, Masculinity, and Homosexuality." *Rural Sociology* 65, no. 4 (2000): 547–61.

Bell, David, and Gill Valentine. "Queer Country: Rural Lesbian and Gay Lives." *Journal of Rural Studies* 11, no. 2 (1995): 113–22.

Bender, Thomas. *A Nation among Nations: America's Place in World History.* New York: Hill & Wang, 2006.

Benhabib, Seyla. *Another Cosmopolitanism.* New York: Oxford University Press, 2008.

Berlant, Lauren. "Intimacy: A Special Issue." *Critical Inquiry* 24, no. 2 (1998): 281–88.

Berlant, Lauren, and Michael Warner. "Sex in Public." *Critical Inquiry* 24, no. 2 (Winter 1998): 547–66.

Berry, Mary Frances. *The Pig Farmer's Daughter and Other Tales of American Justice: Episodes of Racism and Sexism in the Courts from 1865 to the Present.* New York: Vintage Books, 2000.

Bishop, Joseph Bucklin. *Charles Joseph Bonaparte: His Life and Public Service.* New York: Charles Scribner's Sons, 1922.

Bjorkman, Frances Maule. "The New Anti-Vagrancy Campaign." *American Review of Reviews*, February 1908.

Blackhouse, Constance. "The White Women's Labor Laws: Anti-Chinese Racism in Early Twentieth Century Canada." *Law and History Review* 14, no. 2 (Fall 1996): 315–68.

———. *Colour Coded: A Legal History of Racism in Canada, 1900–1950.* Toronto: University of Toronto Press, 1999.

Boag, Peter. *Same-Sex Affairs: Constructing and Controlling Homosexuality in the Pacific Northwest.* Berkeley: University of California Press, 2003.

Boyd, Nan Alamilla. *Wide-Open Town: A History of Queer San Francisco to 1965.* Berkeley: University of California Press, 2003.

Bredbenner, Candace Lewis. *A Nationality of Her Own: Women, Marriage and the Law of Citizenship.* Berkeley: University of California Press, 1998.

Brodie, Janine. "Three Stories of Canadian Citizenship." In *Contesting Canadian Citizenship: Historical Readings,* ed. Robert Adamoski, Dorothy Chunn, and Robert Menzies, 43–66. Peterborough, Ontario: Broadview Press, 2002.

Brumberg, Joan Jacobs. "The Ethnological Mirror: American Evangelical Women and Their Heathen Sisters, 1870–1910." In *Women and the Structure of Society,* ed. Barbara J. Harris and JoAnn McNamara. Durham, NC: Duke University Press, 1984.

Brundage, W. Fitzhugh. *Lynching in the New South: Georgia and Virginia, 1880–1930.* Urbana: University of Illinois Press, 1993.

Bruner, Robert F., and Sean D. Carr. *The Panic of 1907: Lessons Learned from the Market's Perfect Storm.* Hoboken, NJ: John Wiley & Sons, 2007.

Brunette, Christopher H. "Speech Unseen: Social Vagrancy Investigations in Long Beach 1914." Critical Gender Studies Honors Thesis, University of California San Diego, 2002. Copy in the author's possession.

Buchignani, Norman. "A Review of the Historical and Sociological Literature of East Indians in Canada." *Canadian Ethnic Studies / Etudes ethniques de Canada* 9, no. 1 (1977): 86–107.

Buchignani, Norman, and Doreen M. Indra. *Continuous Journey: A Social History of South Asians in Canada.* Generations: A History of Canada's Peoples. Toronto: McClelland & Stewart, 1985.

Butler, Judith. *Undoing Gender.* New York: Routledge, 2004.

Cahill, Sean. "The Disproportionate Impact of Antigay Family Policies on Black and Latino Same-sex Couple Households." *Journal of African American Studies* 13, no. 3 (2009): 219–50.

Calder, Lendol Glen. *Financing the American Dream: A Cultural History of Consumer Credit.* Princeton, NJ: Princeton University Press, 1999.

*California Jurisprudence: A Complete Statement of the Law and Practice of the State of California.* Edited by William M. McKinney. San Francisco: Bancroft-Whitney Co., 1921–26.

Campbell, David. *Writing Security: United States Foreign Policy and the Politics of Identity.* Minneapolis: University of Minnesota Press, 1992, rev. ed., 1998.

Canada Indian Committee. *The Hindu Case.* Toronto: The Committee, 1915.

Canada. Census of Canada, 1901. Library and Archives of Canada. www.collections canada.gc.ca/databases/census-1901/001013–100.01-e.php (accessed March 30, 2011).

———. Census of Canada, 1911. Library and Archives of Canada. www.collections canada.gc.ca/databases/census-1911/001003–100.01-e.php (accessed March 30, 2011).

———. Parliament. House of Commons. *House of Commons Debates: Official Report.* Ottawa, 1914.

Canaday, Margot. *The Straight State: Sexuality and Citizenship in Twentieth Century America.* Princeton, NJ: Princeton University Press, 2009.

————. "Thinking Sex in the Transnational Turn: An Introduction." *American Historical Review* 114, no. 5 (December 2009): 1250–57.

Carbado, Devon. "Yellow by Law." *California Law Review* 97, no. 3 (June 2009): 633–92.

Carrigan, William D. *The Making of a Lynching Culture: Violence and Vigilantism in Central Texas, 1836–1916*. Urbana: University of Illinois Press, 2004.

Cavallo, Dominick. *Muscles and Morals: Organized Playgrounds and Urban Reform, 1880–1920*. Philadelphia: University of Pennsylvania Press, 1981.

Chadha, Ena. "'Mentally Defectives' Not Welcome: Mental Disability in Canadian Immigration Law, 1859–1927." *Disability Studies Quarterly* 28 (Winter 2008), www.dsq-sds.org/article/view/67/67 (accessed March 16, 2011).

Chan, Sucheng. *This Bittersweet Soil : The Chinese in California Agriculture, 1860–1910*. Berkeley: University of California Press, 1986.

Chang, David. *Color of the Land: Race, Nation, and the Politics of Landownership in Oklahoma, 1832–1929*. Chapel Hill: University of North Carolina Press, 2010.

Chang, Kornel. "Enforcing Transnational White Solidarity: Asian Migration and the Formation of the U.S.–Canadian Boundary." *American Quarterly* 60, no. 3 (September 2008): 671–96.

Chapman, Terry. "'An Oscar Wilde Type': The Abominable Crime of Buggery in Western Canada, 1890–1920." *Criminal Justice History* 4 (1983): 97–118.

Chauncey, George, Jr. "Christian Brotherhood or Sexual Perversion? Homosexual Identities and the Construction of Sexual Boundaries in the World War One Era." *Journal of Social History* 19, no. 2 (1985): 189–211.

————. *Gay New York: Gender, Urban Culture, and the Making of the Gay Male World, 1890–1940*. New York: Basic Books, 1994.

————. "The Policed: Gay Men's Strategies of Everyday Resistance." In *Inventing Times Square: Commerce and Culture at the Crossroads of the World*, ed. William R. Taylor, 315–55. New York: Russell Sage Foundation, 1991.

————. "The Postwar Sex Crime Panic." In *True Stories from the American Past*, ed. William Graebner, 160–178. New York: McGraw-Hill, 1993.

Cheng, Tien-fang. *Oriental Immigration to Canada*. Shanghai: Commercial Press, 1931.

Childs, Dennis. "Angola, Convict Lease, and the Annulment of Freedom: The Vectors of Architectural and Discursive Violence in the U.S. 'Slavery of Prison.'" In *Violence and the Body: Race, Gender and the State*, ed. Arturo Aldama, 189–208. Bloomington: University of Indiana Press, 2003.

Chowdhry, Prem. *The Veiled Women: Shifting Gender Equations in Rural Haryana, 1880–1990*. Delhi: Oxford University Press, 1994.

Christie, Nancy. *Engendering the State: Family, Work, and Welfare in Canada*. Toronto: University of Toronto Press, 2000.

Chuh, Kandice. *Imagine Otherwise: On Asian Americanist Critique*. Durham, NC: Duke University Press, 2003.

Clark, Elizabeth B. "'The Sacred Rights of the Weak': Pain, Sympathy, and the Culture of Individual Rights in Antebellum America." *Journal of American History* 82, no. 2 (1995): 463–93.

Clark, Ira G. "The Elephant Butte Controversy: A Chapter in the Emergence of Federal Water Law." *Journal of American History* 61, no. 4 (1975): 1006–33.

Clark, Robert Emmet. "Management and Control of Community Property in New Mexico." *Tulane Law Journal* 26 (1952): 324–43.

Clement, Elizabeth Alice. *Love for Sale: Courting, Treating, and Prostitution in New York City, 1900–1945.* Chapel Hill: University of North Carolina Press, 2006.

Cohen, Lawrence. "Holi in Banaras and the Muhulan of Modernity." *GLQ: A Journal of Lesbian and Gay Studies* 2 (1995): 399–424.

Cohen, Lizabeth. *A Consumers' Republic: The Politics of Mass Consumption in Postwar America.* New York: Knopf, 2003.

Cohn, Bernard S. *Colonialism and Its Forms of Knowledge: The British in India.* Princeton, NJ : Princeton University Press, 1996.

Cole, Lauren. "Determining Citizenship: Race, Military Service, and Naturalization in Hawaii, 1898–1939." Phd diss. in progress, University of California, San Diego. Manuscript chapters in the possession of the author.

Cole, Simon. "From the Sexual Psychopath Statute to 'Megan's Law': Psychiatric Knowledge in the Diagnosis, Treatment, and Adjudication of Sex Criminals in New Jersey, 1949–1999." *Journal of the History of Medical and Allied Sciences* 55, no. 3 (2000): 292–314.

Cott, Nancy F. "Marriage and Justice for All." In *Justice and Injustice in Law and Legal Theory,* ed. Thomas R. Kearns and Austin Sarat, 77–99. Ann Arbor: University of Michigan Press, 1996.

———. *Public Vows: A History of Marriage and the Nation.* Cambridge, MA: Harvard University Press, 2000.

Coutin, Susan Bibler. *Legalizing Moves: Salvadoran Immigrants' Struggle for U.S. Residency.* Ann Arbor: University of Michigan Press, 2000.

Cresswell, Tim. *The Tramp in America.* London: Reaktion Books, 2001.

Cruess, W. V. "Rain Damage Insurance." *Bulletin of the California Department of Agriculture* 10, no. 2 (February 1921): 58–66.

Dahmi, Sadhu Singh. *The Sikhs and Their Religion: A Struggle for Democracy.* Vancouver: Khalsa Diwan Society, 1943.

Das, Mary K. "A Woman without a Country." *The Nation* (New York), August 4, 1926; *Calcutta Forward,* September 9, 1926.

Das Gupta, Monisha. *Unruly Immigrants: Rights, Activism, and Transnational South Asian Politics in the United States.* Durham, NC: Duke University Press, 2006.

D'Emilio, John. "Capitalism and Gay Identity." In *Powers of Desire: The Politics of Sexuality,* ed. Ann Snitow, Christine Stansell, and Sharon Thompson, 100–113. New York: Monthly Review Press, 1983.

D'Emilio, John, and Estelle Freedman. *Intimate Matters: A History of Sexuality in America.* New York: Harper & Row, 1988.

Delany, Samuel R. *Times Square Red, Times Square Blue.* New York: New York University Press, 1999.

De Genova, Nicholas P. "Migrant 'Illegality' and Deportability in Everyday Life." *Annual Review of Anthropology* 31 (October 2002): 419–47.

Denno, Deborah W. "Before the Modern Sex Offender Statutes." *Northwestern University Law Review* 92, no. 4 (1998): 1317–1414.

DePastino, Todd. *Citizen Hobo: How a Century of Homelessness Shaped America.* Chicago: University of Chicago Press, 2003.

Deutsch, Sarah. "Landscapes and Enclaves: Race Relations in the West, 1895–1990." In *Power and Place in the North American West*, ed. Richard White and John M. Findlay, 110–31. Seattle: University of Washington Press, 1999.

Dua, Enakshi. "Racialising Imperial Canada: Indian Women and the Making of Ethnic Communities." In *Gender, Sexuality and Colonial Modernities*, ed. Antoinette Burton, 119–33. London: Routledge, 1999.

Dudziak, Mary L., and Leti Volpp. "Legal Borderlands: Law and the Construction of American Borders." *American Quarterly* 57, no 3 (September 2005): 593–610.

Duggan, Lisa. *Sapphic Slashers: Sex, Violence, and American Modernity.* Durham, NC: Duke University Press, 1999.

———. *Twilight of Equality: Neoliberalism, Cultural Politics and the Attack on Democracy.* Boston: Beacon Press, 2004.

Duis, Perry. *The Saloon: Public Drinking in Chicago and Boston, 1880–1920.* Urbana: University of Illinois Press, 1983.

Duncan, James. "Men without Property: The Tramp's Classification and Use of Urban Space." *Antipode* 10, no. 1 (1978): 24–34.

Edelman, Lee. *No Future: Queer Theory and the Death Drive.* Durham, NC: Duke University Press, 2004.

Eng, David L. *Racial Castration: Managing Masculinity in Asian America.* Durham, NC: Duke University Press, 2001.

———. *The Feeling of Kinship: Queer Liberalism and the Racialization of Intimacy.* Durham, NC: Duke University Press, 2010.

Epprecht, Marc. "'Unnatural Vice' in South Africa: The 1907 Commission of Enquiry." *International Journal of African Historical Studies* 34, no. 1 (2001): 121–40.

Erman, Sam. "Meanings of Citizenship in the U.S. Empire: Puerto Rico, Isabel Gonzalez, and the Supreme Court, 1898 to 1905." *Journal of American Ethnic History* 27, no. 4 (Summer 2008): 5–33.

Eskridge, William J., Jr. *Dishonorable Passions: Sodomy Laws in America, 1861–2003.* New York: Viking Press, 2008.

España-Maram, Linda. *Creating Masculinity in Los Angeles's Little Manila: Working-Class Filipinos and Popular Culture, 1920s–1950s.* New York: Columbia University Press, 2006.

Espiritu, Yen Le. *Asian American Women and Men: Labor, Laws and Love.* Thousand Oaks, CA: Sage Publications, 1997.

Fairchild, Amy L. *Science at the Borders: Immigrant Medical Inspection and the Shaping of the Modern Industrial Labor Force.* Baltimore: Johns Hopkins University Press, 2003.

Fejes, Fred. "Murder, Perversion, and Moral Panic: The 1954 Media Campaign against Miami's Homosexuals and the Discourse of Civic Betterment." *Journal of the History of Sexuality* 9, no. 3 (2000): 305–47.

Ferguson, Roderick A. *Aberrations in Black: Toward a Queer of Color Critique.* Minneapolis: University of Minnesota Press, 2004.

Fieldbrave, Theodore. "East Indians in the United States." *Missionary Review* 57 (June 1934): 291–93.

Fleming, Marie. "Women and the Public Use of Reason." In *Feminists Read Habermas: Gendering the Subject of Discourse,* ed. Johanna Meehan, 117–38. New York: Routledge, 1995.

Foucault, Michel. "Friendship as a Way of Life." In *Foucault Live: Collected Interviews, 1961–1984,* trans. John Johnston, ed. Sylvère Lotringer. New York: Semiotext(e), 1996.

Franke, Katherine M. "Commentary: The Domesticated Liberty of *Lawrence v. Texas.*" *Columbia Law Review* 104, no. 5 (2004): 1399–1426.

Freedman, Estelle. "Uncontrolled Desires: The Response to the Sexual Psychopath, 1920–1960." *Journal of American History* 74, no. 1 (June 1987): 83–106.

Freeman, Elizabeth. *Time Binds: Queer Temporalities, Queer Histories.* Durham, NC: Duke University Press, 2010.

Freyhan, F. A. "Homosexual Prostitution: A Case Report." *Delaware State Medical Journal* 19 (May 1947): 92–94.

Friday, Chris. *Organizing Asian American Labor: The Pacific Coast Canned-Salmon Industry, 1870–1942.* Philadelphia: Temple University Press, 1994.

Fujita-Rony, Dorothy B. *American Workers, Colonial Power: Philippine Seattle and the Transpacific West, 1919–1941.* Berkeley: University of California Press, 2003.

Fung, Richard. "Burdens of Representation, Burdens of Responsibility." In *Constructing Masculinity,* ed. Maurice Berger, Brian Wallis, and Simon Watson, 291–298. New York: Routledge, 1995.

Gabaccia, Donna R. *From the Other Side: Women, Gender, and Immigrant Life in the U.S., 1820–1990.* Bloomington: University of Indiana Press, 1994.

———. "Is Everywhere Nowhere? Nomads, Nations, and the Immigrant Paradigm of United States History." *Journal of American History* 86, no. 3 (June 1996): 1115–35.

Gabaccia, Donna R., Katharine Donato, Jennifer Holdaway, Martin Manalansan, and Patricia Pessar. "A Glass Half Full: Gender in Migration Studies." *International Migration Review* 40, no 1 (2006): 3–26.

Gardner, Martha. *The Qualities of a Citizen: Women, Immigration, and Citizenship, 1870–1965.* Princeton, NJ: Princeton University Press, 2005.

George, Rosemary Marangoly. "Tracking 'Same –Sex' Love from Antiquity to the Present in South Asia." *Gender & History* 14, no. 1 (2002): 7–30.

Gerstle, Gary. *American Crucible: Race and Nation in the Twentieth Century.* Princeton, NJ: Princeton University Press, 2001.

Gibson-Graham, J. K. *The End of Capitalism (as We Knew It): A Feminist Critique of Political Economy.* Minneapolis: University of Minnesota Press, 2006.

Giddings, Paula. *Ida: A Sword among Lions: Ida B. Wells and the Campaign against Lynching.* New York: Amistad, 2008.

Gilfoyle, Timothy J. *City of Eros: New York City, Prostitution, and the Commercialization of Sex, 1820–1920.* New York: Norton, 1992.

———. "The Hearts of Nineteenth-Century Men: Bigamy and Working-Class Marriages in New York City, 1800–1890." *Prospects: An Annual of American Cultural Studies* 19 (1994): 135–58.

Gilmore, Ruth Wilson. *Golden Gulag: Prisons, Surplus, Crisis, and Opposition in Globalizing California.* Berkeley: University of California Press, 2007.

Gitlin, Jay. "On the Boundaries of Empire: Connecting the West to Its Imperial Past." In *Under an Open Sky: Rethinking America's Western Past,* ed. William Cronon, George Miles, and Jay Gitlin, 71–89. New York: Norton, 1992.

Gjorkman, F. M. "The New Anti-Vagrancy Campaign." *Review of Reviews* 37 (February 1908): 208–9.

Glenn, Evelyn Nakano. *Unequal Freedom: How Race and Gender Shaped American Citizenship and Labor.* Cambridge, MA: Harvard University Press, 2004.

Goldman, Eric F. *Charles J. Bonaparte, Patrician Reformer: His Early Career.* Baltimore: Johns Hopkins University Press, 1943.

Gonzales-Day, Ken. *Lynching in the West, 1850–1935.* Durham, NC: Duke University Press, 2006.

Gopinath, Gayatri. *Impossible Desires: Queer Diasporas and South Asian Public Cultures.* Durham, NC: Duke University Press, 2005.

Gordon, Sarah Barringer. "The Liberty of Self-Degradation: Polygamy, Woman Suffrage, and Consent in Nineteenth-Century America." *Journal of American History* 83, no. 3 (1996): 815–47.

Gorman, Daniel. *Imperial Citizenship: Empire and the Question of Belonging.* Manchester: Manchester University Press, 2006.

Gould, Harold. *Sikhs, Swamis, Students and Spies: The India Lobby in the United States, 1900–1946.* Thousand Oaks, CA: Sage Publications, 2006.

Graff, Harvey J. *Conflicting Paths: Growing up in America.* Cambridge, MA: Harvard University Press, 1995.

Grbich, Judith E. "The Body in Legal Theory." In *At the Boundaries of the Law: Feminism and Legal Theory,* ed. Martha A. Fineman and Nancy Thomadsen. New York: Routledge, 1991.

Gregory, James N. *American Exodus: The Dust Bowl Migration and Okie Culture in California.* New York: Oxford University Press, 1989.

Grewal, Inderpal. "The Postcolonial, Ethnic Studies and the Diaspora: Contexts of Ethnic Immigrant/Migrant Cultural Studies in the U.S." *Socialist Review* 24, no 4 (1994): 45–74.

Grewal, Inderpal, and Caren Kaplan. "Global Identities: Theorizing Transnational Studies of Sexuality." *GLQ: A Journal of Lesbian and Gay Studies* 7, no. 4 (2001): 663–679.

———. "Introduction: Transnational Feminist Practices and Questions of Postmodernity." In *Scattered Hegemonies: Postmodernity and Transnational Feminist Practices*, ed. Inderpal Grewal and Caren Kaplan, 1–33. Minneapolis: University of Minnesota Press, 1994.

Gross, Ariela Julie. "'Of Portuguese Origin': Litigating Identity and Citizenship among the 'Little Races' in Nineteenth-Century America." *Law and History Review* 25, no 3 (Fall 2007): 467–512.

———. *What Blood Won't Tell: A History of Race on Trial in America*. Cambridge, MA: Harvard University Press, 2008.

Grossberg, Michael. *Governing the Hearth: Law and the Family in Nineteenth-Century America*. Chapel Hill: University of North Carolina Press, 1985.

Gualtieri, Sarah. M. *Between Arab and White: Race and Ethnicity in the Early Syrian American Diaspora*. Berkeley: University of California Press, 2009.

Gutiérrez, David. "The Politics of the Interstices: Reflections on Citizenship and Non-Citizenship at the Turn of the Twentieth Century." *Race/Ethnicity: Multidisciplinary Global Contexts* 1, no. 1 (Autumn 2007): 89–120.

Haag, Pamela. *Consent: Sexual Rights and the Transformation of American Liberalism*. Ithaca, NY: Cornell University Press, 1999.

Habermas, Jürgen. *The Structural Transformation of the Public Sphere: An Inquiry into a Category of Bourgeois Society*. Translated by Thomas Burger. Cambridge, MA: MIT Press, 1991. Originally published in German in 1962.

Hahn, Steven. *A Nation under Our Feet: Black Political Struggles in the Rural South, from Slavery to the Great Migration*. Cambridge, MA: Harvard University Press, 2003.

Halberstam, Judith. *Female Masculinity*. Durham, NC: Duke University Press, 1998.

———. *In a Queer Time and Place: Transgender Bodies, Subcultural Lives*. New York: New York University Press, 2005.

Hall, G. Stanley. *Adolescence: Its Psychology and Its Relations to Physiology, Anthropology, Sociology, Sex, Crime, Religion and Education*. New York : D. Appleton, 1904.

Hallberg, Gerald N. "Bellingham, Washington's Anti-Hindu Riot." *Journal of the West* 12, no. 1 (January 1973): 163–75.

Halperin, David M. *How to Do the History of Homosexuality*. Chicago: University of Chicago Press, 2002.

Halttunen, Karen. "Humanitarianism and the Pornography of Pain in Anglo-American Culture." *American Historical Review* 100, no. 2 (1995): 303–34.

Haney-Lopez, Ian. *White by Law: The Legal Construction of Race*. New York: New York University Press, 1996.

Hannah, Matthew G. *Governmentality and the Mastery of Territory in Nineteenth-Century America*. New York: Cambridge University Press, 2000.

Harris, Cheryl. "Whiteness as Property." *Harvard Law Review* 106, no. 8 (1993): 1709–1795.

Hartog, Hendrick. *Man and Wife in America: A History*. Cambridge, MA: Harvard University Press, 2000.

Heap, Chad C. *Slumming: Sexual and Racial Encounters in American Nightlife, 1885–1940*. Chicago: University of Chicago Press, 2009.

Helweg, Arthur Wesley, and Usha M. Helweg. *An Immigrant Success Story: East Indians in America*. Philadelphia: University of Pennsylvania Press, 1990.

Hendler, Glenn. "Pandering in the Public Sphere: Masculinity and the Market in Horatio Alger." *American Quarterly* 48, no. 3 (1996): 415–38.

Hess, Gary R. "The Forgotten Asian Americans: The East Indian Community in the United States." *Pacific Historical Review* 43, no. 4 (1974): 576–96.

Hillyer, Curtis. *Consolidated Supplement to the Codes of the State of California: Showing All the Changes Affecting the Codes Passed by the Forty-Seventh, Forty-Eighth and Forty-Ninth Sessions of the Legislature (1927–1931)*. San Francisco: Bender-Moss, 1932.

Hopkins, Jeff. "Signs of Masculinism in an 'Uneasy' Place: Advertising for 'Big Brothers.'" *Gender, Place & Culture: A Journal of Feminist Geography* 7, no. 1 (2000): 31–55.

Howard, John. *Men Like That: A Southern Queer History*. Chicago: University of Chicago Press, 1999.

———. "The Talk of the Country: Revisiting Accusation, Murder and Mississippi, 1895." In *Where These Memories Grow: History, Memory, and Southern Identity*, ed. W. Fitzhugh Brundage, 191–218. Chapel Hill: University of North Carolina Press, 2000.

Hsu, Madeline Y. *Dreaming of Gold, Dreaming of Home: Transnationalism and Migration between the United States and South China, 1882–1943*. Stanford, CA: Stanford University Press, 2000.

Hurtado, Albert L. *Intimate Frontiers: Sex, Gender, and Culture in Old California*. Albuquerque: University of New Mexico Press, 1999.

Huttenback, Robert A. *Gandhi in South Africa: British Imperialism and the Indian Question, 1860–1914*. Ithaca, NY: Cornell University Press, 1971.

Iacovetta, Franca. "The Sexual Politics of Moral Citizenship and Containing 'Dangerous' Foreign Men in Cold War Canada, 1950s–1960s." *Social History / Histoire sociale* 33 (November 2000): 361–89.

Ingram, Gordon Brent. "Returning to the Scene of the Crime: Uses of Trial Dossiers on Consensual Male Homosexuality for Urban Research, with Examples from Twentieth Century British Columbia." *GLQ: A Journal of Lesbian and Gay Studies* 10, no. 1 (2003): 77–110.

Jagose, Annamarie. *Queer Theory: An Introduction*. New York: New York University Press, 1996.

Jagpal, Sarjeet Singh. *Becoming Canadians: Pioneer Sikhs in Their Own Words*. Vancouver: Harbour Publishing, 1994.

Jakobsen, Janet. "Sex + Freedom = Regulation: Why?" *Social Text* 23, no. 84–85 (Fall 2005): 285–308.

Jakobsh, Doris R. *Relocating Gender in Sikh History: Transformation, Meaning and Identity*. New Delhi: Oxford University Press, 2003.

Jensen, Joan M. *Passage from India: Asian Indian Immigrants in North America*. New Haven, CT: Yale University Press, 1988.

———. "Farm Families Organize Their Work, 1900–1940." In *Essays in Twentieth-Century New Mexico History*, ed. Judith Boyce DeMark, 13–28. Albuquerque: University of New Mexico Press, 1994.

Jew, Victor. "'Chinese Demons': The Violent Articulation of Chinese Otherness and Interracial Sexuality in the U.S. Midwest, 1885–1889." *Journal of Social History* 37, no. 2 (2003): 389–410.

Johnson, Colin R. "Casual Sex: Towards a 'Prehistory' of Gay Life in Bohemian America." *Interventions* 10, no. 3 (November 2008): 303–20.

Johnson, David K. *The Lavender Scare: The Cold War Persecution of Gays and Lesbians in the Federal Government*. Chicago: University of Chicago Press, 2004.

Johnson, Susan Lee. "The Gold She Gathered: Difference, Domination and California's Southern Mines, 1848–1853. PhD diss., Yale University, 1993.

———. *Roaring Camp: The Social World of the California Gold Rush*. New York: Norton, 2000.

Johnston, Hugh. "The Surveillance of Indian Nationalists in North America, 1908–1918." *British Columbia Studies*, no. 78 (Summer 1988): 3–28.

Jones, A.J., and Lee Janis. "Primary Syphilis of the Rectum and the Gonorrhea of the Anus in a Male Homosexual Playing the Role of the Female Prostitute." *American Journal of Syphilis, Gonorrhea, and Venereal Disease* 28 (July 1944): 453–57.

Jung, Moon-Ho. *Coolies and Cane: Race, Labor, and Sugar in the Age of Emancipation*. Baltimore: Johns Hopkins University Press, 2006.

Kanstroom, Dan. *Deportation Nation: Outsiders in American History*. Cambridge, MA: Harvard University Press, 2009.

Karthikeyan, Hrishi, and Gabriel J. Chin. "Preserving Racial Identity: Population Patterns and the Application of Anti-Miscegenation Statutes to Asian Americans, 1910–1950." *Asian Law Journal* 9 (2002): 1–39.

Kazanjian, David. *Colonizing Trick: National Culture and Imperial Citizenship in Early America*. Minneapolis: University of Minnesota Press, 2003.

Keire, Mara L. "The Vice Trust: A Reinterpretation of the White Slavery Scare in the United States, 1907–1917." *Journal of Social History* 35, no. 1 (2001): 5–41.

Kelley, Ninette, and Michael Trebilcock. *The Making of the Mosaic : A History of Canadian Immigration Policy*. Toronto: University of Toronto Press, 1998.

Kelley, Robin D.G. "'We Are Not What We Seem': Rethinking Black Working-Class Opposition in the Jim Crow South." *Journal of American History* 80, no. 1 (1993): 75–112.

———. *Race Rebels: Culture, Politics, and the Black Working Class*. New York: Free Press, 1994.

Kennedy, Elizabeth Lapovsky. "'But We Could Never Talk about It': The Structures of Lesbian Discretion in South Dakota, 1928–1933." In *Inventing Lesbian Cultures in America*, ed. Ellen Lewin, 15–39. Boston: Beacon Press, 1996.

Kerr, James M. *The Codes of California. Vol. 4: Penal Code*. San Francisco: Bender-Moss, 1921.

Kett, Joseph F. *Rites of Passage: Adolescence in America, 1790 to the Present*. New York: Basic Books, 1977.

Kimmel, Michael S. *Manhood in America: A Cultural History*. New York: Free Press, 1996.

Knowles, Valerie. *Forging Our Legacy: Canadian Citizenship and Immigration, 1900–1977*. Ottawa: Public Works and Government Services Canada, 2000.

Knupfer, Anne Meis. *Reform and Resistance: Gender, Delinquency, and America's First Juvenile Court*. New York: Routledge, 2001.

Koshy, Susan. *Sexual Naturalization: Asian Americans and Miscegenation*. Stanford, CA: Stanford University Press, 2004.

Kraut, Alan M. *Silent Travelers: Germs, Genes, and the "Immigrant Menace."* New York: Basic Books, 1994.

Kunzel, Regina G. *Criminal Intimacy: Prison and the Uneven History of Modern American Sexuality*. Chicago: University of Chicago Press, 2008.

Kusmer, Kenneth L. *Down and Out, on the Road: The Homeless in American History*. New York: Oxford University Press, 2002.

La Brack, Bruce. *The Sikhs of Northern California, 1904–1975*. New York: AMS Press, 1988.

———. "Early South Asian (India) Immigrants in California." Paper read at "Reclaiming the Legacy: Asian Americans and Pacific Islanders in U.S. History" conference, University of San Francisco, May 4, 2002.

Lake, Marilyn. "From Mississippi to Melbourne via Natal: The Invention of the Literacy Test as a Technology of Racial Exclusion." In *Connected Worlds: History in a Transnational Perspective*, ed. Ann Curthoys and Marilyn Lake, 215–22. Canberra: Australian National University Press, 2005.

Lake, Marilyn, and Henry Reynolds. *Drawing the Global Colour Line: White Men's Countries and the International Challenge of Racial Equality*. Cambridge: Cambridge University Press, 2008.

Lamar, Howard. "From Bondage to Contact: Ethnic Labor in the American West, 1600–1890." In *The Countryside in the Age of Capitalist Transformation: Essays in Social History of Rural America*, ed. Steven Hahn and Jonathan Prude, 293–324. Chapel Hill: University of North Carolina Press, 1985.

Landes, Joan B. *Women and the Public Sphere in the Age of the French Revolution*. Ithaca, NY: Cornell University Press, 1988.

Langum, David J. *Crossing over the Line: Legislating Morality and the Mann Act*. Chicago: University of Chicago Press, 1994.

Larson, Jane E. " 'Even a Worm Will Turn at Last': Rape Reform in Late Nineteenth-Century America." *Yale Journal of Law and the Humanities* 9, no. 1 (1997): 1–71.

Lears, T.J. Jackson. *Rebirth of a Nation: The Making of Modern America, 1877–1920*. New York: HarperCollins, 2009.

Lee, Erika. *At America's Gates: Chinese Immigration during the Exclusion Era, 1882–1943*. Chapel Hill: University of North Carolina Press, 2003.

———. "Hemispheric Orientalism and the 1907 Pacific Coast Race Riots." *Amerasia Journal* 33, no. 2 (2007): 19–47.

———. "The 'Yellow Peril' and Asian Exclusion in the Americas." *Pacific Historical Review* 76, no. 4 (2007): 537–62.

Lee, Rachel C. *The Americas of Asian American Literature: Gendered Fictions of Nation and Transnation*. Princeton, NJ: Princeton University Press, 2001.

Lee, Robert G. *Orientals: Asian Americans in Popular Culture*. Philadelphia: Temple University Press, 1999.

Leonard, Karen. *Making Ethnic Choices: California's Punjabi Mexican Americans*. Philadelphia: Temple University Press, 1992.

———. "Flawed Transmissions? Punjabi Pioneers in California." In *Transmission of Punjabi Heritage to the Diaspora*, ed. Pashaura Singh, 97–111. Ann Arbor: University of Michigan Press, 1996.

Lewis, Daniel. *Iron Horse Imperialism: The Southern Pacific of Mexico, 1880–1951*. Tucson: University of Arizona Press, 2007.

Lewis, Earl. "To Turn As on a Pivot: Writing African Americans into a History of Overlapping Diasporas." *American Historical Review* 100 (June 1995): 765–87.

Lichtenstein, Alex. "Good Roads and Chain Gangs in the Progressive South: 'The Negro Convict Is a Slave.'" *Journal of Southern History* 59, no. 1 (February 1993): 85–110.

Lipsitz, George. *The Possessive Investment in Whiteness: How White People Profit from Identity Politics*. Philadelphia: Temple University Press, 1998.

Lowe, Lisa. *Immigrant Acts: On Asian American Cultural Politics*. Durham, NC: Duke University Press, 1996.

———. "Intimacies on Four Continents." In *Haunted by Empire: Geographies of Intimacy in North American History*, ed. Ann Stoler, 191–211. Durham, NC: Duke University Press, 2006.

Luibhéid, Eithne. *Entry Denied: Controlling Sexuality at the Border*. Minneapolis: University of Minnesota Press, 2002.

———. "Queer/Migration: An Unruly Body of Scholarship." *GLQ: A Journal of Lesbian and Gay Studies* 14, nos. 2–3 (2008): 169–90.

Lui, Mary Ting Yi. *The Chinatown Trunk Mystery: Murder, Miscegenation, and Other Dangerous Encounters in Turn-of-the-Century New York City*. Princeton, NJ: Princeton University Press, 2005.

Manalansan, Martin F. *Global Divas: Filipino Gay Men in the Diaspora*. Durham, NC: Duke University Press, 2003.

Markovits, Claude. *The Global World of Indian Merchants, 1750–1947: Traders of Sind from Bukhara to Panama*. Cambridge: Cambridge University Press, 2000.

Martens, Jeremy. "A Transnational History of Immigration Restriction: Natal and New South Wales, 1896–1897." *Journal of Imperial and Commonwealth History* 34, no. 3 (September 2006): 323–44.

May, Elaine Tyler. *Homeward Bound: American Families in the Cold War Era*. New York: Basic Books, 1990.

Maynard, Steven. "Through a Hole in the Lavatory Wall: Homosexual Subcultures, Police Surveillance, and the Dialectics of Discovery, Toronto, 1890–1930." *Journal of the History of Sexuality* 5, no. 2 (October 1994): 207–42.

———. "'Horrible Temptations': Sex, Men, and Working-Class Male Youth in Urban Ontario, 1890–1935." *Canadian Historical Review* 78, no. 2 (1997): 191–235.

McDonald, Robert A. J. *Making Vancouver: Class, Status, and Social Boundaries, 1863–1913*. Vancouver: University of British Columbia Press, 1996.

McGovney, Dudley O. "Race Discrimination in Naturalization." *Iowa Law Bulletin* 8, no. 3 (March 1923): 129–61.

McGowen, Randall. "Power and Humanity, or, Foucault among Historians." In *Reassessing Foucault: Power, Medicine and the Body*, ed. Colin Jones and Roy Porter. New York: Routledge, 1994.

McKeown, Adam. *Melancholy Order: Asian Migration and the Globalization of Borders*. New York: Columbia University Press, 2008.

McLaren, Angus. *The Trials of Masculinity: Policing Sexual Boundaries, 1870–1930*. Chicago: University of Chicago Press, 1997.

McLeod, W. H. "The Turban: Symbol of Sikh Identity." In *Sikh Identity: Continuity and Change*, ed. Pashaura Singh and N. Gerald Barrier. Delhi: Manohar Publishers, 1999.

McWilliams, Carey. *Factories in the Field*. Boston, Little, Brown, 1939.

Mehta, Uday Singh. *Liberalism and Empire: A Study in Nineteenth-Century British Liberal Thought*. Chicago: University of Chicago Press, 1999.

Menzies, Robert, Robert Adamoski, and Dorothy E. Chunn. "Rethinking the Citizen in Canadian Social History." In *Contesting Canadian Citizenship: Historical Readings*, ed. Robert Adamoski, Dorothy Chunn, and Robert Menzies. Peterborough, Ontario: Broadview Press, 2002.

Merrill, Lilburn. "A Summary of Findings in a Study of Sexualisms among a Group of One Hundred Delinquent Boys." *American Journal of Urology and Sexology* 15 (1919): 259–60.

Merry, Sally Engle. *Colonizing Hawai'i: The Cultural Power of Law*. Princeton, NJ: Princeton University Press, 2000.

Meyerowitz, Joanne J. *Women Adrift: Independent Wage Earners in Chicago, 1880–1930*. Chicago: University of Chicago Press, 1988.

———. "Transnational Sex and U.S. History." *American Historical Review* 114, no. 5 (December 2009): 1273–86.

Miller, Vivien M. *Crime, Sexual Violence, and Clemency: Florida's Pardon Board and Penal System in the Progressive Era*. Gainesville: University Press of Florida, 2000.

Mills, H. A. "East Indian Immigration to British Columbia and the Pacific Coast States." *American Economic Review* 1, no. 1 (March 1911): 72–76.

Mink, Gwendolyn. *The Wages of Motherhood: Inequality in the Welfare State, 1917–1942*. Ithaca, NY: Cornell University Press, 1995.

Molina, Natalia. "'In a Race All Their Own': The Quest to Make Mexicans Ineligible for U.S. Citizenship." *Pacific Historical Review* 79, no. 2 (May 2010): 167–201.

Mongia, Radhika. "Always Nationalize: Gender, Migration and the Nation-State in the British Empire (2004) paper in the possession of author.

———. "Historicizing State Sovereignty: Inequality and the Form of Equivalence." *Comparative Studies in Society and History* 49 (2007): 384–411.

Monkkonen, Eric H. *Police in Urban America, 1860–1920*. New York: Cambridge University Press, 1981.

Moon, Michael. "'The Gentle Boy from the Dangerous Classes': Pederasty, Domesticity, and Capitalism in Horatio Alger." *Representations* 19 (1987): 87–110.

Moran, Jeffrey P. *Teaching Sex: The Shaping of Adolescence in the Twentieth Century.* Cambridge, MA: Harvard University Press, 2000.

Morse, Eric W. "Some Aspects of the *Komagata Maru* Affair, 1914." Canadian Historical Association Report of the Annual Meeting, 1936. pp. 100–108.

———. "Status of British East Indians." MA thesis. Queen's University, 1936.

Mukherjee, Tapan K. *Taraknath Das: Life and Letters of a Revolutionary in Exile.* Calcutta: National Council of Education, 1998.

Muñoz, José Esteban. *Disidentifications.* Minneapolis: University of Minnesota Press, 1999.

———. *Cruising Utopia: The Then and There of Queer Futurity.* New York: New York University Press, 2009.

Naim, C.M. "Transvestic Words? The Retki in Urdu." *Annual of Urdu Studies* 16 (2001): 3–26.

Najmabadi, Afsaneh. *Women with Mustaches and Men without Beards: Gender and Sexual Anxieties of Iranian Modernity.* Berkeley: University of California Press, 2005.

Nelson, Dana D. *National Manhood: Capitalist Citizenship and the Imagined Fraternity of White Men.* Durham, NC: Duke University Press, 1998.

Ngai, Mae M. *Impossible Subjects: Illegal Aliens and the Making of Modern America.* Princeton, NJ: Princeton University Press, 2004.

Nilsen, Deborah. "The Social Evil: Prostitution in Vancouver, 1900–1920." In *In Her Own Right: Selected Essays on Women's History in British Columbia,* ed. Kathy Kess and Barbara Latham, 205–28. Victoria: Camosun College, 1980.

Novak, William J. "The Legal Transformation of Citizenship in Nineteenth Century America." In *The Democratic Experiment: New Directions in American Political History,* ed. Meg Jacobs, William Novak, and Julian E. Zelizer, 85–119. Princeton, NJ: Princeton University Press, 2003.

Oberoi, Harjot S. *The Construction of Religious Boundaries: Culture, Identity, and Diversity in the Sikh Tradition.* Chicago: University of Chicago Press, 1994.

———. "From Ritual to Counter-Ritual: Rethinking the Hindu-Sikh Question, 1884–1915." In *Sikh History and Religion in the Twentieth Century,* ed. Joseph T. O'Connell et al., 136–58. Toronto: University of Toronto, Centre for South Asian Studies, 1988.

Odem, Mary E. *Delinquent Daughters: Protecting and Policing Adolescent Female Sexuality in the United States, 1885–1920.* Chapel Hill: University of North Carolina Press, 1995.

Okihiro, Gary Y. *Margins and Mainstreams: Asians in American History and Culture.* Seattle: University of Washington Press, 1994.

———. *Common Ground: Reimagining American History.* Princeton, NJ: Princeton University Press, 2001.

Olin, Spencer. "European Immigrant and Oriental Alien: Acceptance and Rejection by the California Legislature of 1913." *Pacific Historical Review* 35 (1966): 303–15.

Ong, Aihwa. *Flexible Citizenship: The Cultural Logics of Transnationality.* Durham, NC: Duke University Press, 1999.

Orsi, Richard J. *Sunset Limited: The Southern Pacific Railroad and the Development of the American West, 1850–1930.* Berkeley: University of California Press, 2005.

Pal, Leslie A. *Interests of the State: The Politics of Language, Multiculturalism, and Feminism in Canada.* Montreal: McGill-Queen's University Press, 1993.

Palmer, Bryan D. *Working-Class Experience: Rethinking the History of Canadian Labour, 1800–1991.* 2nd ed. Toronto: McClelland & Stewart, 1992.

Pandey, Gyanendra. "Subaltern Citizens and Their Histories." *Interventions: International Journal of Postcolonial Studies* 10, no. 3 (2008): 271–84.

Parker, Carleton H. *The Casual Laborer, and Other Essays.* New York: Harcourt, Brace & Howe, 1920.

Pascoe, Peggy. "Miscegenation Law, Court Cases, and Ideologies of Race in Twentieth Century America." *Journal of American History* 83, no. 1 (June 1996): 44–69.

———. "Race, Gender and the Privileges of Property: On the Significance of Miscegenation Law in the U.S. West." In *Over the Edge: Remapping the American West,* ed. Valerie Matsumoto and Blake Allmendinger. Berkeley: University of California Press, 1999.

———. *What Comes Naturally: Miscegenation Law and the Making of Race in America.* New York: Oxford University Press, 2008.

Pateman, Carole. *The Sexual Contract.* Stanford, CA: Stanford University Press, 1988.

Peck, Gunther. "Reinventing Free Labor: Immigrant Padrones and Contract Laborers in North America, 1885–1925." *Journal of American History* 83, no 3 (December 1996): 84–87.

Peiss, Kathy Lee. *Cheap Amusements: Working Women and Leisure in Turn-of-the-Century New York.* Philadelphia: Temple University Press, 1986.

Perdue, Theda. *Cherokee Women: Gender and Culture Change, 1700–1835.* Lincoln: University of Nebraska Press, 1998.

Perez, Emma. "Queering the Borderlands: The Challenges of Excavating the Invisible and Unheard." *Frontiers: A Journal of Women Studies* 24, no. 2–3 (2003): 122–31.

Pettegrew, John C. "Homosociality and the Legal Sanction of Male Heterosexual Aggression in the Early Twentieth Century." In *Legal Imagination: Violence and Brutality in American History,* ed. Michael A. Bellesiles, 317–325. New York: New York University Press, 1999.

Pfaelzer, Jean. *Driven Out: The Forgotten War against Chinese Americans.* New York: Random House, 2007.

Pfeifer, Michael J. *Rough Justice: Lynching and American Society, 1874–1947.* Urbana: University of Illinois Press, 2004.

Plane, Ann Marie. *Colonial Intimacies: Indian Marriage in Early New England.* Ithaca, NY: Cornell University Press, 2002.

Povinelli, Elizabeth. *The Empire of Love: Toward a Theory of Intimacy, Genealogy, and Carnality.* Durham, NC: Duke University Press, 2006.

Povinelli, Elizabeth A., and George Chauncey. "Thinking Sexuality Transnationally." *GLQ: A Journal of Lesbian and Gay Studies* 5, no. 4 (1999): 439–50.

Prashad, Vijay. *The Karma of Brown Folk.* Minneapolis: University of Minnesota Press, 2000.

———. *Everybody Was Kung Fu Fighting: Afro-Asia Connectons and the Myth of Cultural Purity.* Boston: Beacon Press, 2002.

Price, Charles Archibald. *The Great White Walls Are Built: Restrictive Immigration to North America and Australasia, 1836–1888.* Canberra: Australian National University Press, 1974.

Puar, Jasbir. *Terrorist Assemblages: Homonationalism in Queer Times.* Durham, NC: Duke University Press, 2007.

Rae, John Bell. *The American Automobile Industry.* Boston: Twayne, 1984.

Rai, Amit S. *Rule of Sympathy: Sentiment, Race, and Power, 1750–1850.* New York: Palgrave, 2002.

Rasmussen, Vivian. *Yesteryear: Loomis and the Surrounding Area.* Loomis, CA: V. Rasmussen, 1994.

Reddy, Chandan. "Asian Diasporas, Neoliberalism, and Family: Reviewing the Case for Homosexual Asylum in the Context of Family Rights." *Social Text* 23, nos. 3 and 4 (2005): 101–19.

Reidel, Laura. "Religious Opposition to Same-Sex Marriage in Canada: Limits to Multiculturalism." *Human Rights Review* 10, no. 2 (2009): 261–81.

Retzloff, Tim. "Cars and Bars: Assembling Gay Men in Postwar Flint, Michigan." In *Creating a Place for Ourselves: Lesbian, Gay, and Bisexual Community Histories,* ed. Brett Beemyn, 227–52. New York: Routledge, 1997.

*The Revised Statutes of Canada, 1906.* Ottawa: S. E. Dawson, 1906–7.

Richards, Penny L. "Points of Entry: Disability and the Historical Geography of Immigration." *Disability Studies Quarterly* 24, no. 3 (Summer 2004), www.dsq-sds.org/article/view/505/682 (accessed March 16, 2011).

Riley, Denise. *'Am I That Name?': Feminism and the Category of 'Women' in History.* Basingstoke, Hants, UK: Macmillan, 1988.

Robertson, Stephen. "Making Right a Girl's Ruin: Working-Class Legal Cultures and Forced Marriage in New York City, 1890–1950." *Journal of American Studies* 36, no. 2 (2002): 199–230.

———. *Crimes against Children: Sexual Violence and Legal Culture in New York City, 1880–1960.* Chapel Hill: University of North Carolina Press, 2005.

———. "Shifting the Scene of the Crime: Sodomy and the History of Sexual Violence." *Journal of the History of Sexuality* 19, no. 2 (May 2010): 223–42.

Rosen, Hannah. *Terror in the Heart of Freedom: Citizenship, Sexual Violence, and the Meaning of Race in the Postemancipation South.* Chapel Hill: University of North Carolina Press, 2009.

Rosen, Ruth. *The Lost Sisterhood: Prostitution in America, 1900–1918*. Baltimore: Johns Hopkins University Press, 1982.

Rotundo, E. Anthony. *American Manhood: Transformations in Masculinity from the Revolution to the Modern Era*. New York: Basic Books, 1993.

Roy, Patricia. *A White Man's Province: British Columbia Politicians and Chinese and Japanese Immigrants, 1858–1914*. Vancouver: University of British Columbia Press, 1989.

———. *The Oriental Question: Consolidating a White Man's Province, 1914–1941*. Vancouver: University of British Columbia Press, 2003.

Salyer, Lucy E. "Baptism by Fire: Race, Military Service, and U.S. Citizenship Policy, 1918–1935." *Journal of American History* 91, no. 3 (December 2004): 847–76.

Sampat-Mehta, Ramdeo. *International Barriers*. Ottowa: Harpell's, 1973.

Saund, Dalip Singh. *Congressman from India*. New York: Dutton, 1960.

Saxton, Alexander. *The Rise and Fall of the White Republic: Class Politics and Mass Culture in Nineteenth-Century America*. New York: Verso, 1990, 2003.

Schlossman, Steven L. *Love & the American Delinquent: The Theory and Practice of "Progressive" Juvenile Justice, 1825–1920*. Chicago: University of Chicago Press, 1977.

Schneider, John C. "Omaha Vagrants and the Character of Western Hobo Labor, 1887–1913." *Nebraska History* 63 (Summer 1982): 255–72.

———. "Tramping Workers, 1890–1920: A Subcultural View." In *Walking to Work: Tramps in America, 1790–1935*, ed. Eric Monkkonen, 212–34. Lincoln: University of Nebraska Press, 1984.

Schwantes, Carlos. *Radical Heritage: Labor, Socialism, and Reform in Washington and British Columbia, 1885–1917*. Seattle: University of Washington Press, 1979.

———. *The Pacific Northwest: An Interpretive History*. Lincoln: University of Nebraska Press, 1996.

Scott, Joan Wallach. *Gender and the Politics of History*. New York: Columbia University Press, 1988.

Sears, Clare. "All That Glitters: Trans-ing California's Gold Rush Migrations." *GLQ: A Journal of Lesbian and Gay Studies* 14, no. 2 (2008): 383–402.

Sedgwick, Eve Kosofsky. *Between Men: English Literature and Male Homosocial Desire, Gender and Culture*. New York: Columbia University Press, 1985.

———. *Epistemology of the Closet*. Berkeley: University of California Press, 1990.

Shah, Nayan. *Contagious Divides: Epidemics and Race in San Francisco's Chinatown*. Berkeley: University of California Press, 2001.

———. "Between 'Oriental Depravity' and 'Natural Degenerates': Spatial Borderlands and the Making of Ordinary Americans." *American Quarterly* 57, no. 3 (2005): 703–25.

———. "Policing Privacy, Migrants, and the Limits of Freedom." *Social Text* 23, nos. 3–4 (2005): 275–84.

———. "Contested Intimacies: Adjudicating 'Hindu Marriage' in U.S. Frontiers." In *Haunted by Empire: Geographies of Intimacy in North American History*, ed. Ann Laura Stoler, 116–39. Durham, NC: Duke University Press, 2006.

Sherry, Arthur H. "Vagrants, Rogues and Vagabonds: Old Concepts in Need of Revision." *California Law Review* 48, no. 4 (1960): 557–73.

Signor, John R., and John A. Kirchner. *The Southern Pacific of Mexico and the West Coast Route.* San Marino, CA: Golden West Books, 1987.

Simmel, Georg. "The Stranger" (1908). In *The Sociology of Georg Simmel*, trans. Kurt H. Wolff, 402–8. Glencoe, IL: Free Press, 1950.

Singh, Kesar. *Canadian Sikhs and* Komagata Maru *Massacre.* Vancouver: A-I Graphics, 1989.

Singh, Sundar. "The Hindu in Canada." *Journal of Race Development* 7, no. 3 (January 1917): 361–82.

Smith, Marian. "Framing Same-Sex Marriage in Canada and the United States: Goodridge, Halpern, and the National Boundaries of Political Discourse." *Social Legal Studies* 16, no. 1 (March 2007): 5–26.

———. "Race, Nationality, and Reality: INS Administration of Racial Provisions in U.S. Immigration and Nationality Law since 1898." *Prologue* 34, no. 2 (Summer 2002), www.archives.gov/publications/prologue/2002/summer/immigration-law-1.html also -2.html-3.html (accessed February 28, 2011).

Smith, Rogers M. *Civic Ideals: Conflicting Visions of Citizenship in U.S. History.* New Haven, CT: Yale University Press, 1997.

Sohi, Seema. "Echoes of Mutiny: Race, Empire and Indian Revolutionaries on the Pacific Coast." PhD diss., University of Washington, 2007.

Sohoni, D. "Unsuitable Suitors: Anti-Miscegenation Laws, Naturalization Laws, and the Construction of Asian Identities." *Law and Society Review* 41, no. 3 (2007): 587–618.

Somerville, Siobhan B. "Notes toward a Queer History of Naturalization." *American Quarterly* 57, no. 3 (2005): 659–75.

———. "Sexual Aliens and the Racialized State: A Queer Reading of the 1952 U.S. Immigration and Nationality Act." In *Queer Migrations: Sexuality, U.S. Citizenship, and Border Crossings,* ed. Eithne Luibhéid and Lionel Cantú. Minneapolis: University of Minnesota Press, 2005.

Spence, Clarke C. "Knights of the Tie and Rail: Tramps and Hoboes in the West." *Western Historical Quarterly* 2, no. 1 (January 1971): 5–19.

Sprague, Oliver M. W. "The American Crisis of 1907." *Economic Journal* 18, no. 71 (1908): 353–72.

Stanley, Amy Dru. "Conjugal Bonds and Wage Labor: Rights of Contract in the Age of Emancipation." *Journal of American History* 75, no. 2 (1988): 471–500.

———. *From Bondage to Contract: Wage Labor, Marriage, and the Market in the Age of Slave Emancipation.* New York: Cambridge University Press, 1998.

Stern, Alexandra Minna. *Eugenic Nation: Faults and Frontiers of Better Breeding in the United States.* Berkeley: University of California Press, 2005.

Stoler, Ann Laura. *Race and the Education of Desire: Foucault's History of Sexuality and the Colonial Order of Things.* Durham, NC: Duke University Press, 1995.

———. *Carnal Knowledge and Imperial Power: Race and the Intimate in Colonial Rule.* Berkeley: University of California Press, 2002.

———. *Along the Archival Grain: Epistemic Anxieties and Colonial Commonsense.* Princeton, NJ: Princeton University Press, 2008.

Stryker, Susan. *Transgender History.* Berkeley, CA: Seal Press, 2008.

Tabili, Laura. *"We Ask for British Justice": Workers and Racial Difference in Late Imperial Britain.* Ithaca, NY: Cornell University Press, 1994.

Takaki, Ronald T. *Strangers from a Different Shore: A History of Asian Americans.* Boston: Little, Brown, 1989.

Tanenhaus, David Spinoza. *Juvenile Justice in the Making: Studies in Crime and Public Policy.* New York: Oxford University Press, 2004.

Taylor, Paul S. "Again the Covered Wagon." *Survey Graphic* 24, no. 7 (July 1935).

Tchen, John Kuo Wei. *New York before Chinatown: Orientalism and the Shaping of American Culture, 1776–1882.* Baltimore: Johns Hopkins University Press, 1999.

Terry, Jennifer. *An American Obsession: Science, Medicine, and Homosexuality in Modern Society.* Chicago: University of Chicago Press, 1999.

Thampi, Madhavi. "Indian Soldiers, Policemen and Watchmen in China in the Nineteenth and Early Twentieth Centuries." *China Report: A Journal of East Asian Studies* (Delhi) 35, no. 4 (October–December 1999): 403–37.

Thompson, Anthony W., Robert J. Church, and Bruce H. Jones. *Pacific Fruit Express.* Berkeley, CA: Signature Press, 1992.

Ting, Jennifer. "Bachelor Society: Deviant Historiography and Asian American Heterosexuality." In *Privileging Positions: The Site of Asian American Studies,* ed. Gary Okihiro, 271–80. Seattle: University of Washington Press, 1995.

———. "The Power of Sexuality." *Journal of Asian American Studies,* 1, no. 1 (1998): 65–82.

Tinker, Hugh. *A New System of Slavery: The Export of Indian Labour Overseas, 1830–1920.* New York: Oxford University Press, 1974.

Tolnay, Stewart E., and E.M. Beck. *A Festival of Violence: An Analysis of Southern Lynchings, 1882–1930.* Urbana: University of Illinois Press, 1995.

Tomlins, Christopher. "Subordination, Authority, Law: Subjects in Labor History." *International Labor and Working-Class History,* no. 47 (1995): 56–90.

Torpey, John. *The Invention of the Passport: Surveillance, Citizenship, and the State.* New York : Cambridge University Press, 2000.

Truesdell, Leon E. *Farm Population of the United States.* Washington, DC: GPO, 1926.

Ullman, Sharon R. *Sex Seen: The Emergence of Modern Sexuality in America.* Berkeley: University of California Press, 1997.

United States. Congress. House of Representatives. Committee on Immigration and Naturalization. *Immigration and Citizenship of American-Born Women Married to Aliens.* Hearings. 69th Cong., 1st sess., March 23, 1926. Washington, DC: GPO, 1926.

———. Congress. Senate. *The Dictionary of Races or Peoples—Reports of the Immigration Commission.* 1907–1910. 61st Cong., 3rd sess. Senate document 662. Washington, DC: GPO, 1911. Reprint. Detroit: Gale Research, 1969.

———. Department of Interior. Bureau of the Census. *Compendium of the Eleventh Census, 1890. Part 1. Population.* Washington, DC: GPO, 1895.

———. *Twelfth Census of the United States Taken in the Year 1900*. Vol. 2. *Population.* Washington, DC: GPO, 1902.

———. *Thirteenth Census of the United States Taken in the Year 1910*. Vols. 2 and 3. *Population 1910*. Washington, DC: GPO, 1913.

"Use of Vagrancy-Type Laws for Arrest and Detention of Suspicious Persons." *Yale Law Journal* 59, no. 7 (1950): 1351–64.

van der Veer, Peter. "Religion in South Asia." *Annual Review of Anthropology* 31, no. 1 (2002): 173–187.

Vaught, David. *Cultivating California: Growers, Specialty Crops, and Labor, 1875–1920*. Baltimore: Johns Hopkins University Press, 1999.

Verbrugge, Martha H. *Able-Bodied Womanhood: Personal Health and Social Change in Nineteenth-Century Boston*. New York: Oxford University Press, 1988.

Vernier, Chester Garfield, et al. *American Family Laws: A Comparative Study of the Family Law of the Forty-Eight American States, Alaska, the District of Columbia, and Hawaii (to Jan 1, 1931)*. Stanford, CA: Stanford University Press, 1931. Reprinted Westport, CT: Greenwood Press, 1971.

Volpp, Leti. "American Mestizo: Filipinos and Anti-Miscegenation Laws." *UC Davis Law Review* 33, no. 4 (Summer 2000): 795–835.

———. "Dependent Citizens and Marital Expatriates." Paper read at "Rethinking Asian American History" Conference, Los Angeles, May 2002.

———. "Divesting Citizenship: On Asian American History and the Loss of Citizenship through Marriage." *UCLA Law Review* 53, no. 2 (December 2005): 405–83.

Wade, Jill. *Houses for All: The Struggle for Social Housing in Vancouver, 1919–50*. Vancouver: University of British Columbia Press, 1994.

Waldron, Jeremy. "Minority Cultures and Cosmopolitan Alternative." In *The Rights of Minority Cultures*, ed. Will Kymlicka. Oxford: Oxford University Press, 1995.

———. "Cosmopolitan Norms." In Seyla Benhabib, *Another Cosmopolitanism*, ed. Robert Post. New York: Oxford University Press, 2006. 83–101.

Walker, James W. St. G. *"Race," Rights and the Law in the Supreme Court of Canada: Historical Case Studies*. Ottawa: Wilfrid Laurier University Press, 1998.

Wang, Joan. "Race, Gender, and Laundry Work: The Roles of Chinese Laundrymen and American Women in the United States, 1850–1950." *Journal of American Ethnic History* 24, no. 5. (Fall 2004): 58–99.

Ward, W. Peter. *White Canada Forever: Popular Attitudes and Public Policy toward Orientals in British Columbia*. Montreal: McGill-Queen's University Press, 1990. 3rd ed., 2003.

Warner, Michael. *The Trouble with Normal: Sex, Politics and the Ethics of Queer Life*. New York: Free Press, 1999.

———. "Normal and Normaller: Beyond Gay Marriage." *GLQ: A Journal of Lesbian and Gay Studies* 5, no. 2 (1999): 119–71.

———. *Publics and Counterpublics*. New York: Zone Books, 2002.

Welke, Barbara Young. *Law and the Borders of Belonging in the Long Nineteenth Century United States*. New York: Cambridge University Press, 2010.

Wiegman, Robyn. "Intimate Publics: Race, Property, and Personhood." *American Literature* 74, no. 4 (2002): 859–85.

Wild, Mark. *Street Meeting: Multiethnic Neighborhoods in Early Twentieth-Century Los Angeles.* Berkeley: University of California Press, 2005.

Willrich, Michael. *City of Courts: Socializing Justice in Progressive Era Chicago.* Cambridge: Cambridge University Press, 2003.

Wolf, Christopher Preston. "Casting the 'Hindu' in the Crucible of Nationhood: Racial Formation and the Imagined Nation in the Early Twentieth Century." MA thesis, University of Oregon, 2001.

Wu, Judy. "Asian American History and Racialized Compulsory Deviance." *Journal of Women's History* 15, no. 3 (Fall 2003): 58–62.

Wunder, John R. "South Asians, Civil Rights, and the Pacific Northwest: The 1907 Bellingham Anti-Indian Riot and Subsequent Citizenship and Deportation Struggles." *Western Legal History* 4, no. 1 (1991): 59–68.

Yanagisako, Sylvia. "Transforming Orientalism: Gender, Nationality and Class in Asian American Studies." In *Naturalizing Power: Essays in Feminist Cultural Analysis,* ed. Sylvia Yanagisako and Carol Delaney, 275–98. New York: Routledge, 1995.

Yenne, Bill. *The History of the Southern Pacific.* New York: Bonanza Press, 1995.

# INDEX

A note on names: Sikh traditions of egalitarianism prescribe the use of *Singh*, meaning "lion," as a last name for male Sikhs and *Kaur*, meaning "princess," as a last name for female Sikhs. However, some Sikhs retained their family names, which indicated caste, and used *Singh* and *Kaur* as middle names.

living patterns of young unmarried women and, 44; male migration and extractive economy of, 210; marriage and, 153; mobile populations created by, 64; political tensions and, 9; queer sociality and, 273; sexual regulation and, 181; survival of transient migrants and, 261; work-parole system and, 148

Carstenbrook, Harvey, 142–43, 147

Carter, Virginia, 112

Catholic Church, 180–81

Caucasian. *See* white racial identity (whiteness)

Cayley, Judge, 137–38

Central America, 194

Ceylon, 193

Chamberlain, Clif, 80, 81

Champion, F. R., 237

Chandra, Krishna, 263–64

Chandra, Ram, 95. *See also* Ghadar Party (India)

Chauncey, George, 59, 86

Chicanos, 36, 93, 265, 268

children, 35, 44, 93; child ("infant") marriage, 165, 175, 176, 185; child-protection associations, 131; divorce cases and, 171–72, 183; as farm laborers, 92, 107; gender differences in sexual assault cases, 138; "half-caste," 216; harassment of, 20; heterosexual marriage and, 50; idealized domestic household and, 92; "illegitimacy" (bastardization) of, 174, 177; immigration restrictions on, 209, 210–16, 230; male honor and defense of, 52; panics over sexual predators and, 265; South Asian men as sexualized menace to, 28, 37; statutory protection of, 132, 147

Chin, Gabriel, 162

Chinatown, in Vancouver (B.C.), 30, 31, 56–58, 62, 63, 207; map of, 57; men in public space, 70; police surveillance in, 65

Chinese, 1, 3, 27, 88; Alien Land Laws and, 125; in "Asiatic" racial category, 232; in British Columbia, 22–23, 24, 25, 29; "Canton coolies," 210, 211; farm workers, 90; feminization of Chinese men, 40; gross-indecency arrests in Canada, 67; health screening of, 200; labor contractors, 102, 106; miscegenation laws and, 161; mob violence against, 30; plural marriage and, 16; racialization of, 14, 15; sexual fear of Chinese men, 20; tax on immigration to Canada, 126, 209–10; veterans of World War I, 242; in work gangs, 102, 103

Chinese, immigration restrictions on, 42, 123, 196, 197, 203, 294n2; "Asiatic Barred Zone" and, 43, 194; Chinese Exclusion Acts, 229, 231, 235, 244; lifting of, 262

Chotia, Bagh Singh, 164, 223–25, 227

Chotia, Grace Stowe, 223, 225, 228

Chotia, Noel, 223, 227, 299n103

Chotia, Vernon, 223, 227, 299n103

Chowdhury, Melva, 254

Chowdry, Prem, 167, 168

Christianity, 104, 226; evangelical Christians, 58, 155, 165; "free and white" status and, 234, 236; interracial marriages and, 258; monogamous marriage and, 153, 155, 156, 177, 188; Sikhism compared to, 213. *See also* Protestantism

Church, Denver S., 42–43

citizenship, British imperial, 25, 184, 215–16, 218, 231–32; Canadian domicile and, 237–40; exchanged for U.S. citizenship, 241

citizenship, naturalized, 3, 5, 153, 185; after World War II, 263; "alien ineligible for," 119, 123, 182, 231, 235, 247, 267; Alien Land Laws and, 121; capitalist interests and, 29; crumbling of racial barriers to, 255, 259; loss of (denaturalization), 249–50, 251–54, 299n97; marriage and, 154, 176, 186, 214, 233, 271; passing as white and, 234–37; racial restrictions on, 13, 123, 124, 231–33; rescinded for South Asians, 119; struggles for dignity and, 4; white men as standard of, 9, 231

civilization, 155, 185, 214

civil rights struggles (1950s and 1960s), 268

civil unions, 271

Clark, Ernest, 120

Clark, Frank, 62

class distinctions, 42, 54, 62, 94, 266; dress and, 100; interethnic relations and, 93; "rule of sympathy" and, 83

Coats, Arthur, 115

*Codes of California*, 144

cohabitation, 6, 50, 93, 124, 155; dispute resolution outside courts, 154; married couples and divorce, 171; men and boys, 107–13

Cold War, 14

colonialism, 154, 186

communism, 122, 264

community, 2, 3, 50

concubinage, 153, 155, 174, 177, 185; anxieties about moral/social dangers of, 185; "frontier" tolerance of, 186; immigration restrictions and, 208

"legal borderlands" and, 12; legal standardization of proper intimacy, 130; male-to-
male intimacy delegitimized, 124; property
in public life and, 181–88; public norms
of, 10; state processing of, 11, 188; trust in
financial exchanges and, 96. *See also* border
intimacies; stranger intimacy
Irish independence movement, 244
Italians, 23, 56, 72, 222

Jakobsen, Janet, 181
Jakobsh, Doris, 167
Japanese, 1, 27, 81, 90, 156; Alien Land Laws and,
119, 120, 121, 122, 125; arrests of, 88; in "Asiatic"
racial category, 232; in British Columbia,
22–23, 24, 25, 29; health screening of, 200;
immigration restrictions and, 123, 196, 197,
203, 294n2; labor contractors, 102, 106, 107;
miscegenation laws and, 161; mob violence
against, 30; "picture brides," 42, 176, 209;
racialization of, 14, 15; tax on immigration
to Canada, 126, 209–10; veterans of World
War I, 243; "white" status and, 182, 234, 247;
in work gangs, 103
Jewitt (police detective), 61, 62
Jews: Russian/Eastern European, 176, 245;
Sephardic, 182, 234, 235; "white" status and,
235, 236
Jubala, Julio (Jawala Singh), 155, 165–70, 173–78,
181, 187; Alien Land Law and, 183; contractual economic relations and, 182; estate value
of, 183–84
Jubala, Soledad Garcia, 155, 165, 166, 168, 169,
174–77; administration of Jubala estate
and, 183; citizenship status, 184; "concubine"
status of, 185
judges, 3, 67, 152, 262; consent in sexual relations
and, 130, 137, 144; entrapment schemes and,
222; juvenile justice system, 73; legitimacy
of relationships and, 153, 154, 156; marriages
in British India and, 167; prejudices of, 76;
racial taxonomies and, 185; statutory protection laws and, 132, 133, 135, 147; surveillance
of homosocial spaces and, 88
juries, 132, 147, 222, 262
juvenile justice system, 73, 136, 148

*karewa* (remarriage), 168–69
Karthikeyan, Hrishi, 162
Kaur, Harnam, 178, 213, 215–16
Kaur, Jiwi, 178

Kaur, Katar, 213, 216
Kaur, Raj, 223–27
Keefe, Daniel, 199–200, 205
Kelley, Robin, 54
Kerr, James, 144–45
Khalsa Diwan Society, 160, 213, 215, 219. *See also*
Sikhism
Khan, Aijmad, 103–5
Khan, Hamit, 107–13, 119
Khan, Musa, 47, 48, 49
Khan, Nellie, 171–72
Khan, Said Ali, 21, 43–52, 280n81
Khan, Walayat, 171–72
Khan, Zemair, 47
King, Joseph, 238–39
kinship networks, 6, 9, 55, 166, 258; of Asian
Americans, 7; in British colonial India, 187;
conquest and, 153; interracial marriage and,
164; legal reasoning about, 131; male honor
and protection of women in, 34; marriage
and, 153; between private life and state rec-
ognition, 181; secular state authority over,
180; state-sanctioned, 11, 123; technologies
and, 13; in work gangs, 102
*Komagata Maru* confrontation, 217, 217–22
Koreans, 14, 42; Alien Land Laws and, 125;
in "Asiatic" racial category, 232; miscegenation laws and, 161; in work gangs, 102,
103
Kurnick, Stanley, 74, 77, 78

labor competition, white fears of, 20, 23, 27–29,
107, 161; defense of male honor and, 36–38;
racialization justified by, 229
labor contractors, 10, 11, 92, 102, 106–7, 111
laborers. *See* workers (laborers)
labor unions, 23, 27, 245
landlords, 35, 36, 52, 83–84, 93
Lattice, Judge, 49
Laurier, Wilfrid, 218
law, rule of, 4, 9, 11, 153, 261; marriage and, 153,
174; rights-based demands, 270; withdrawal
of rights and, 267
law and legal records, 2, 14, 63, 272, 274; agriculture and legal contracts, 95; as archival
repository, 9–13; borderlands histories and,
87; divorce petitions, 170; as instrument of
intimidation, 123; liberalism and, 151; murder
trials and, 51; normalization of legal subjects,
151. *See also* miscegenation laws
*Lawrence v. Texas*, 306n21

TEXT
10.5/14 Adobe Jenson Pro Open Type

DISPLAY
Adobe Jenson Pro Open Type

COMPOSITOR
BookComp, Inc.

CARTOGRAPHER
Bill Nelson

INDEXER
Alexander Trotter